electronic marketing

PEARSON
Education

We work with leading authors to develop the
strongest educational materials in marketing,
bringing cutting-edge thinking and best
learning practice to a global market.

Under a range of well-known imprints, including
Financial Times Prentice Hall, we craft high quality
print and electronic publications which help readers
to understand and apply their content, whether
studying or at work.

To find out more about the complete range of our
publishing, please visit us on the World Wide Web at:
www.pearsoned.co.uk

electronic
marketing

Theory and Practice for the Twenty-First Century

John O'Connor,
Eamonn Galvin and
Martin Evans

FT Prentice Hall
FINANCIAL TIMES

An imprint of **Pearson Education**
Harlow, England • London • New York • Boston • San Francisco • Toronto
Sydney • Tokyo • Singapore • Hong Kong • Seoul • Taipei • New Delhi
Cape Town • Madrid • Mexico City • Amsterdam • Munich • Paris • Milan

Pearson Education Limited
Edinburgh Gate
Harlow
Essex CM20 2JE
England

and Associated Companies throughout the world

Visit us on the World Wide Web at:
www.pearsoned.co.uk

First published 2004

© Pearson Education Limited 2004

The rights of John O'Connor, Eamonn Galvin and Martin Evans to be identified as authors of this work have been asserted by them in accordance with the Copyright, Designs and Patents Act 1988.

ISBN 0 273 68476 0

British Library Cataloguing-in-Publication Data
A catalogue record for this book is available from the British Library

10 9 8 7 6 5 4 3 2 1
09 08 07 06 05 04

Typeset in 9/12pt Stone Serif by 35
Printed and bound by Ashford Colour Press Ltd, Gosport

The publisher's policy is to use paper manufactured from sustainable forests.

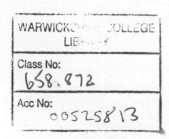

Contents

Part II: Getting to know the customer

Part III: Managing the customer relationship

Part IV: Developing the customer offering

Part V: Delivering the offering to the customer

Preface

The rapid advance of new technology and its applications demands that the student and practitioner of electronic marketing keep up to date with all its new developments – this discipline has undergone a major transformation in a matter of years. For instance, SMS marketing has moved into the mainstream and its multimedia counterpart MMS, radio frequency identification (RFID) tags and other new applications have begun to emerge. On the other hand, the exuberance that once surrounded internet companies and dot-com business models has given way to scepticism. Data privacy concerns have increased to new levels as junk e-mail, or spam, has reached epidemic proportions. And one event that could not have been predicted was the terrorist attacks of 11 September 2001. This day not only had huge political implications; its reverberations have been felt throughout the marketing world too.

Electronic Marketing addresses these issues, preparing the student and practitioner for the challenges that confront them. Its roots emanate from an earlier textbook called *Marketing in the Digital Age* by John O'Connor and Eamonn Galvin, both marketing practitioners. This is a new text, designed specifically to meet the needs of a new age in electronic marketing and the added involvement of Martin Evans provides extra academic rigour to the practitioner views provided by O'Connor and Galvin.

Additional learning resources, for both the lecturer and student, can be found on at www.booksites.net/oconnor.

We would like to thank all the lecturers, students and marketing executives who contributed their views and opinions towards this book. We are much indebted to them for their time and effort, helping to make *Electronic Marketing* the relevant text book it is for the twenty-first century. We would also like to thank everyone at Pearson Education who worked on this text. In particular, we would like to acknowledge Thomas Sigel, Karen McLaren and Peter Hooper for all their support, encouragement and advice.

Finally, we hope that you enjoy this textbook and you find it to be both useful and informative, whether you are a lecturer, student or practitioner. To make sure we continue to provide up-to-date and relevant future editions of this book, we welcome your feedback. Please feel free to send your comments to us at:

john.oconnor@hotorigin.com
eamonng@indigo.ie
evansm7@cardiff.ac.uk

John O'Connor
Eamonn Galvin
Martin Evans

Acknowledgements

We are grateful to the following for permission to reproduce copyright material:

The Nasdaq Stock Market Inc. for Figure 1.2 from www.nasdaq.com; The Procter & Gamble Company for Figure 1.3 from www.sunnyd.com; Sainsbury's Supermarkets Ltd for Figure 1.5 from www.j-sainsbury.co.uk/sid; e-centre for Figure 2.2 from www.e-centre.org.uk; Exostar, LLC for Figure 2.7 from www.exostar.com; Alexander Osterwalder for Figure 3.1 from *Modelling Customer Relationships in E-Business, Illustrated through the Mobile Industry*, http://inforge.unil.ch/aosterwa/ Documents/eBusinessModels/Publications/SM03.pdf (Osterwalder, A. and Pigneur, Y. 2003); (Osterwalder, A. & Pigneur, Y. 2002); Egg for Figure 3.2 from http://new.egg.com, © Egg, 2003. All rights reserved. Egg and the Egg logo are either registered trade marks or trade marks of the members of the Egg group of companies in the United Kingdom and/or other countries; Banco Popular for Figure 3.3 from www.bancopopular-e.com; The Cartoon Bank for Figure 3.4 from *New Yorker* (5 July 1993); Ryanair.com for Figure 3.7 from www.ryanair.com; National Statistics for Figure 4.2 from www.statistics.gov.uk, Crown copyright material is reproduced with the permission of the Controller of Her Majesty's Stationery Office and the Queen's Printer for Scotland; Dialog for Figure 4.3 from www.dialog.com, a Thomson business; ACNielsen for Figure 4.7 from www.acnielsenbases.com; AGB Media Services S.A. for Figure 4.8 from www.agbgroup.com; World Advertising Research Center for Figure 4.9 from Extending the communications process: the significance of personal influencers in the UK motor market, *International Journal of Advertising*, Vol. 19, No. 2 (Evans, M. & Fill, C. 2000); Centaur Communications Ltd for Figure 4.10 from *Big Issues for the Next Five Years: Data Fusion, Reach the Parts Others Don't* (Cowling, A.B. 1996); CACI Ltd for Figure 4.11 from www.insite.info/retail3.htm; SmartFOCUS Ltd for Figure 4.12 from SmartFOCUS VIPER software, leading providers of intelligent marketing solutions worldwide; Starbucks Coffee International for Figure 4.13 from www.starbucks.co.jp; Butterworth-Heinneman for Figure 5.1 from *Market-led Strategic Change: Transforming the Process of Going to Market* (Piercy, N. 2002); Experian Limited for Figure 5.2 from www.experian.com; IBM Corporation for Figure 5.5 from http://www.lotus.com/products/product4.nsf/wdocs/ noteshomepage, Lotus Notes web page screen capture (lotus.com) Copyright 2003, IBM Corporation. Used with permission of IBM Corporation. Lotus Notes is a trademark of IBM Corporation, in the United States, other countries, or both; Chivas Brothers Ltd for Figure 6.2 from www. aberlour.com; Marks & Spencer Money, Marks & Spencer Financial Services plc, for Figure 6.4 from www6.marksandspencer.com; Thomson Intermedia plc for Figure 7.1 from www.thomson-intermedia.com; Getty Images and Vodafone for Figure 7.4 from www.vodafone.com; Consumers Against Supermarket Privacy Invasion and Numbering (CASPIAN) for Figure 7.5 from www. boycottbenetton.org; Benetton Group SpA for Figure 7.6 from www.benetton.com; Tesco Stores Limited for Figure 8.2 from www.tesco.com/clubcard; CRMGuru.com for Figure 8.4 from www.crmguru.com; SAP AG for Figure 8.5 from www.sap.com; Galileo International Limited for Figure 8.6 from www.travelport.com; VTech for Figure 9.1 from www.vtech.com; BMW AG for

Figures 9.2, 9.9 and 9.10 from www.bmw.com; 3M United Kingdom plc for Figure 9.3 from www.3m.com; IntraLinks, Inc. for Figure 9.4 from www.intralinks.com; ACNielsen BASES for Figure 9.7 from www.acnielsenbases.com; The McGraw-Hill Companies, Inc. for Figure 9.8 from *Business Week*, (30 April 1990); Yahoo! Inc. for Table 10.1 from http://dir.yahoo.com; CNET Networks, Inc. for Figure 10.1 from www.mysimon.com, CNET Networks, Inc. disclaims any responsibility for products described on this site. All product information, including prices, features and availability, is subject to change without notice. Copyright © 1995–2003 CNET Networks, Inc. All rights reserved; Priceline.com for Figure 10.2 from www.priceline.com; eBay International A.G. for Figure 10.4 from www.ebay.co.uk, these materials have been reproduced with the permission of eBay Inc. Copyright © eBay Inc. All rights reserved; Lands' End and My Virtual Model for Figure 11.1 from www.landsend.com by permission of both Lands' End and My Virtual Model Inc., © Lands' End, Inc., 2003 and © My Virtual Model Inc., 2003; DoubleClick for Figure 11.2 from *MultiChannel Holiday Shopping Study* (2002), www.doubleclick.com; Vollmer Public Relations for Travelocity.com LP for Figure 11.3 from www.travelocity.com; European Group of Television Advertising for Figure 12.1 from www.egta.com; easyJet for Figure 12.4 from www.easyjet.com; Freeview for Figure 12.6 from www.freeview.co.uk, © Freeview 2003; Henry Stewart Publications for Figure 13.2 from Customer relationship management: a capabilities portfolio perspective, *Journal of Database Marketing*, Vol. 9, No. 3 (Plakoyiannaki, E. & Tzokas, N. 2002); Salesforce.com for Figure 13.3 from www.salesforce.com; J2 Global Communications, Inc. for Figure 14.3 from http://home.efax.com, eFax is a registered trade mark of J2 Global Communications, Inc.; Performix Technologies Ltd for Figure 14.5 from www.performix.com, all rights reserved; Hewlett-Packard for Figure 14.8 from www.hp.com; The Future Foundation, Bristol, for Figure 15.1 from *The Challenges of E-Commerce: Creating Workable Models to Predict Consumer Needs in the Network Society* (Howard, M. 2000).

Case Study Chapter 1 from www.competition-commission.org.uk/fulltext/446a11.4.pdf, Competition Commission; Exhibits 5.4 and 5.7 from Better targeted briefs, *Financial Times*, 28 May 2002, © Alex Benady; Exhibit 6.3 from Catching up with its glitzier cousin, *Financial Times*, 24 July 2002, © Claire Murphy.

Exhibit 2.1 Big savings in time and money, © *Financial Times*, 19 June 2002; Table 2.1 Italians urged to learn to love IT, © *Financial Times*, 20 July 1999; Exhibit 2.2 Internet is no substitute for EDL, © *Financial Times*, 3 June 1998; Exhibit 2.3 At last, a low-cost solution, © *Financial Times*, 2 September 1998; Exhibit 3.3 An urgent rethink on internet strategies, © *Financial Times*, 5 June 2002; Case Study Chapter 3 A challenge from online agencies, © *Financial Times*, 11 March 2002; Exhibit 4.7 Key role for IT in the marketing mix, © *Financial Times*, 2 September 1998; Exhibit 5.1 Halifax launches exclusive plastic, © *Financial Times*, 14 September 2002; Exhibits 6.1 and 6.2 Let's get personal again, © *Financial Times*, 28 May 2002; Exhibit 6.7 Dead men's blues, © *Financial Times*, 28 May 2002; Exhibit 7.5 The full picture, © *Financial Times*, 28 May 2002; Exhibit 7.6 Wal-Mart doubles size of its data warehouse, © *Financial Times*, 15 June 2002; Exhibit 7.7 EU deal agreed on internet privacy, © *Financial Times*, 31 May 2002; Exhibit 8.2 Some optimism amid the gloom, © *Financial Times*, 17 October 2001; Exhibit 8.3 Battle to woo customers to loyalty cards hots up, © *Financial Times*, 12 September 2002; Exhibit 8.9 Support for the frontline, © *Financial Times*, 28 May 2002; Exhibit 11.3 Operators pin hopes on Japanese success story, © *Financial Times*, 20 November 2002; Exhibit 11.4 Persuading viewers to pay for services could be tough, © *Financial Times*, 5 September 2001; Exhibit 11.10 Buzzword – or the way of the future? © *Financial Times*, 1 December 1998; Exhibit 12.5 Putting Yahoo back in the picture, © *Financial Times*, 17 February 2003; Exhibit 12.6 Old economy stakes a claim on the web, © *Financial Times*, 15 January 2003; Exhibit 13.4 Cutting the wires of the workplace, © *Financial Times*, 16 October 2002; Exhibit 14.1 Message may soon be: don't call us, we'll call you, © *Financial Times*, 5 February 2003; Exhibit 14.2 Queue busting, © *Financial Times*, 18 September 2002; Exhibit 15.3 Why BPO is the next big thing, © *Financial Times*, 5 February 2003; Exhibit 15.5 Sales teams need convincing too, © *Financial Times*, 2 September 1998.

Every effort has been made by the publisher to obtain permission from the appropriate source to reproduce material which appears in this book. In some instances we have been unable to trace the owners of copyright material, and we would appreciate any information that would enable us to do so.

Part I

THE ELECTRONIC MARKETING REVOLUTION

Part I of this book deals with the changing nature of marketing. Although the marketing function has been successful up to now, a number of changes within industry and society are challenging the way that marketing should be conducted today. The greatest change of all is the impact of the information age and it is in this electronic revolution that marketing managers must find their future.

Part I contains three chapters: the first examines how traditional marketing has recently been transformed into electronic marketing; the second examines the rise of electronic commerce in the past 10 or 15 years; the final chapter takes a closer look at some of the e-commerce business models to have emerged recently.

1 THE EMERGENCE OF ELECTRONIC MARKETING
2 THE RAPID RISE OF ELECTRONIC COMMERCE
3 E-COMMERCE BUSINESS MODELS

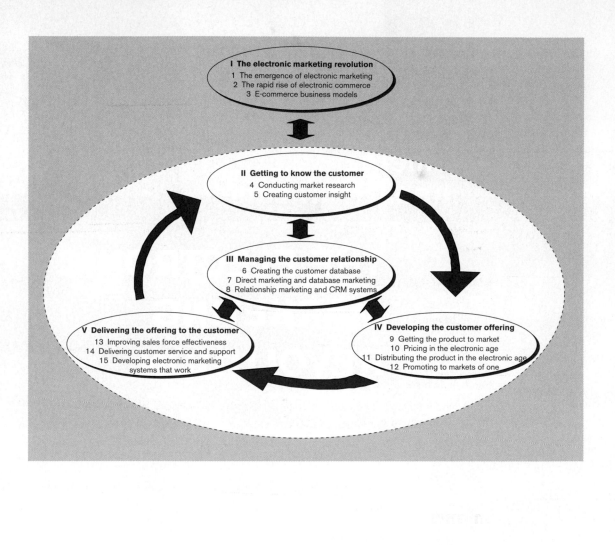

I The electronic marketing revolution

1 The emergence of electronic marketing
2 The rapid rise of electronic commerce
3 E-commerce business models

II Getting to know the customer

4 Conducting market research
5 Creating customer insight

III Managing the customer relationship

6 Creating the customer database
7 Direct marketing and database marketing
8 Relationship marketing and CRM systems

V Delivering the offering to the customer

13 Improving sales force effectiveness
14 Delivering customer service and support
15 Developing electronic marketing
      systems that work

IV Developing the customer offering

9 Getting the product to market
10 Pricing in the electronic age
11 Distributing the product in the electronic age
12 Promoting to markets of one

1

The emergence of electronic marketing

Learning objectives

Once you have read this chapter you will:

- appreciate how the three ages of computerisation have driven electronic marketing;
- understand how changes in the marketing environment have led to the use of new electronic marketing tools;
- understand how the virtualisation of distribution channels, services and payments has changed the way we conduct business;
- appreciate how electronic data interchange (EDI) provided a foundation for internet-based e-commerce.

Contents

MARKETING IN A VIRTUAL WORLD

■ The virtualisation of distribution channels and services

■ The virtualisation of payments

SUMMARY

CASE STUDY

Introduction

For some marketing managers, the twenty-first century may appear a very strange place indeed. Much of that strangeness comes from the 'electronification' of traditional marketing practices. Direct and database marketing may be fairly well understood, but what about concepts such as SMS and e-mail marketing, interactive digital television, electronic marketplaces, customer relationship management (CRM) applications and contact management software? These are just some of the new tools and capabilities available to today's marketing managers. In truth, the migration from traditional marketing to 'electronic marketing' or 'e-marketing' is part of a process that has taken place over the past 50 years. But what exactly is electronic marketing and how is it different from ordinary marketing?

In this opening chapter we examine the recent emergence of electronic marketing. We start by looking at how the three ages of computerisation have provided a backdrop for the changes that have taken place in marketing. We then explore some of wider societal changes that have accompanied computerisation – increasing customer sophistication and individualism, the pressures on product development and brand management and the increasing globalisation of markets. Finally, we see how commerce itself has changed and how distribution channels, services and even payments have been 'virtualised'. In particular, we look at the way in which electronic data interchange (EDI) networks – the forerunners of electronic commerce networks – have become a standard feature of commercial transactions between large organisations. Let us begin with a brief history of computerisation.

Marketing during the three ages of computerisation

Three ages of computerisation

The natural starting point for any discussion on electronic marketing is a brief examination of the 'electronic' component of the term. Many commentators have tried to categorise the timelines of the electronification, or computerisation, of business but typically from a technical perspective – mainframe, personal computer (PC) systems, client-server systems and so on. From a marketing perspective, the categorisation is easier. We believe that marketers have lived and worked through three distinct stages of development of computerisation since the 1960s (*see* Figure 1.1):

- the PC age (1960–90)
- the internet age (1990–2000)
- the wireless age – or the post-dot-com age (2000–present).

The PC age

Since the 1960s there has been an explosion of computing power, fuelled mainly by developments in the microchip. In 1965 Gordon Moore made his now-famous

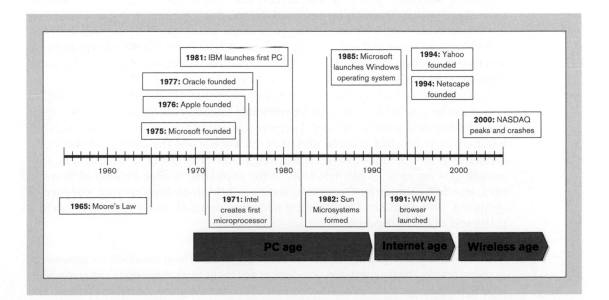

Figure 1.1 Three ages of computerisation

observation that the number of components that could be crammed into a single chip would double every 18 months. The corollary is also true – the cost of computing power halves every year and a half. Moore's Law has almost become a self-fulfilling prophecy that still drives the computer industry today. To put this into perspective, the processing power of a PC in the mid-1990s was greater than that of Mission Control in 1969 when a man first walked on the moon. Today, the same computing power can be found in a mobile phone.

Intel developed its first microprocessor in 1971 in an era when computers came in one size – mainframe. The development of these microprocessors led to IBM's launch of the first personal computer (PC) a decade later. The operating system for these PCs was licensed from a small, unknown company called Microsoft. Although the first PCs more closely resembled suitcases than today's laptops, they heralded the beginning of a wave that would transfer computing power from information technology (IT) departments to the hands of marketers. Today's marketing managers make use of customer databases, data mining technology and the internet as part of their daily work. It is sometimes difficult to believe that none of these capabilities were available a few decades ago.

And yet the true impact on marketing has been somewhat less dramatic. Marketing costs have not halved every 18 months. Nor has marketing effectiveness increased correspondingly. The truth is that applying technology to business and marketing is a slower process than many people would like to believe.

The internet age

In the early 1980s the US government was working on networking technologies that, by the end of the decade, began to move into the universities. In 1991 an obscure programming language written by Tim Berners-Lee at the CERN research laboratory in Switzerland became the basis for a networking technology that soon became known as the World Wide Web. However, it was only in the mid-1990s that the web, or internet, became accepted and widely used. Netscape's Navigator and Microsoft's Explorer fought out the 'Battle of the Browsers' that determined which software would become the dominant product on PCs to access the internet.

Towards the end of the 1990s the explosion of internet usage combined with a long-running bull market spawned an economic bubble. This 'dot.com bubble' was a fantastic breeding ground for new business models and novel marketing concepts. Internet companies like Amazon and eBay quickly became the darlings of the stockmarket. Pop-up and 'mouse-over' advertising, interactive digital television and viral marketing were some of the new tools in the marketing manager's arsenal. It was a wild, wonderful time where marketers found it difficult to keep up with the pace of change. A 1998 article in *The Economist* magazine summed up the state of marketing at the end of the millennium:

> Marketing has become a complex art. Technology and trade have increased the potential for global brands. The fragmentation of audiences and rising costs of television and print advertising are making other media attractive. And direct marketing and the internet are rewriting all the marketing rules.[1]

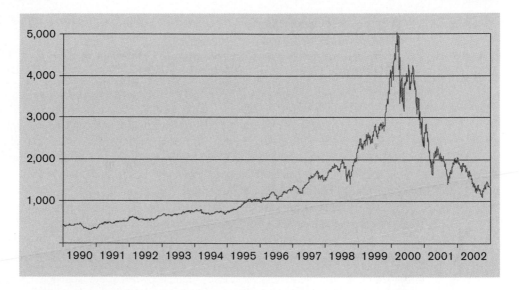

Figure 1.2 The rise and fall of NASDAQ (1990–2002)

Source: Nasdaq website (www.nasdaq.com, 2003), © copyright 2003 The Nasdaq Stock Market, Inc. Reprinted with permission.

The wireless age (post-dot-com age)

The dot-com bubble finally burst in early 2000. As with all good parties, the subsequent hangover left business people and marketers in a somewhat reflective and sombre mood. Spending on technology and new marketing gimmicks was reined in as the stockmarkets moved into freefall. The bellwether of technology stocks, the Nasdaq Composite index, fell from a peak of more than 5,000 in March 2000 to less than 1,500 in the wake of the terrorist attacks on the USA on 11 September 2001. In the following 12 months it continued to fall back to levels not seen since 1995 (*see* Figure 1.2).

Other stockmarkets suffered the same fate as many internet-based companies floundered. Amazon and eBay had reached sufficient size and had enough cash reserves to survive, but companies such as Boo.com, First-e, Webvan, Pets.com, eToys and others went into liquidation (*see* Exhibit 1.1).

However as the dust settles on the crash we can see that marketing has undergone significant changes. While most of the smaller dot-com ventures have disappeared, some survivors have become success stories. Perhaps more important than the success of online companies like Amazon (www.amazon.com) is the way that traditional businesses have adopted e-commerce and electronic marketing models. Nearly every business now has a website to provide customers with information. The more successful are taking orders online and transacting large volumes over the internet. As we will see in Chapter 2, there have been huge opportunities in using online procurement. Almost every aspect of how a business markets itself and transacts has been impacted.

From a technology viewpoint, the tools available to marketers have also evolved in leaps and bounds. The first decade of the new millennium will not simply be confined

EXHIBIT 1.1

DOT-BOMB

In recent weeks, a logo-emblazoned cord that eToys employees wore around their necks to display company IDs sold online for $21.50. A single business card from Webvan fetched $3.02 plus shipping, and a copy of its first annual report, sent to every shareholder for free, went for $26.26. The peak price paid so far for a bright orange Kozmo.com messenger bag? $187.50. Since the internet bubble burst last spring, day-trading may be out, but buying and selling the artefacts of the dot-com companies that soared and then crashed are suddenly in. Collectors are paying rapidly rising prices for a wide range of items bearing the names of high-profile internet failures like Kozmo.com, Webvan, Pets.com, eToys, and others. The buyers apparently believe the stuff may be worth big money one day, the same kind of sunny speculation that fuelled the dot-com craze.

'It's a bubble on the bubble', said Rudy Franchi, owner of the Nostalgia Factory in the North End and a collectibles consultant for *Antiques Roadshow*, the PBS programme. And this one will burst too, he predicted, because few dot-com companies ever established highly recognizable names. 'In five years, people won't even know what Kozmo was,' Franchi said.

Source: *The Globe* (6 August 2001).[2]

EXHIBIT 1.2

COMING TO A MCDONALD'S NEAR YOU: WIRELESS ACCESS TO THE INTERNET

Being wired is old hat. It's time to get unwired. So says Intel, the world's largest chip-maker, which has launched a new family of chips under the name 'Centrino'. Its aim is to turn 'Wi-Fi', a way to gain access to the internet wirelessly, into a standard feature of portable computers. The launch was accompanied by a barrage of announcements from firms planning to charge for Wi-Fi access via 'hotspots' in public places. Take your laptop to a hotspot and you can surf the net unplugged. Toshiba and Accenture have announced plans to set up 10,000 hotspots in America. Cometa, a joint venture between Intel, IBM, AT&T and others, has already said it will build 20,000. A consortium of five Asian telecoms firms plans to build 20,000 hotspots across Asia by the end of the year, and similar moves are afoot in Europe. An hour's free Wi-Fi access is being thrown in with every meal at a handful of McDonald's hamburger restaurants.

Source: *The Economist* (27 March 2003).[3]

to history as an extended post-dot-com hangover. It will also be remembered as the decade that spawned a variety of new technologies based on a wireless, or mobile, revolution. E-commerce has become m-commerce (mobile commerce) with the proliferation of short messaging service (SMS) and multimedia messaging service (MMS) software, third generation (3G) applications and wireless devices that make the internet available to consumers and business people on the move (*see* Exhibit 1.2).

While many of the changes to the marketing function been driven by technology, it is also important to understand they have taken place in parallel with changes in the marketplace. Now is a good time to reflect on these changes.

The changing marketplace for electronic marketing

Half a century of change

Over the last 50 years marketing has developed into a well-defined discipline with accepted frameworks and models. In the 1950s, before the PC age started, marketing embraced the new technology of television and developed mass marketing techniques that have built many of today's well-known brands such as Coca Cola, McDonald's and Sony. It developed models of consumer behaviour and we have seen the development of the role of the brand manager as the cornerstone of the marketing concept. By and large, marketing's role in identifying and meeting customers needs has served companies well. However, changes in the way people go about their daily lives have caused a major redefinition of the role and concept of marketing. The most important of these are changes in the way that:

■ customers have become more sophisticated and individually focused;

■ the management of products and brands has become more complex;

■ markets have become increasingly global.

Although technology has helped to drive and shape these changes, it is interesting to note that the changes themselves are societal rather than technological. To understand the context for electronic marketing today, we need to examine these changes in a little more detail.

Increasing customer sophistication and individualism

According to Ogilvy & Mather Direct (1990),[4] the main impetus behind the growth of marketing based on data and direct interaction approaches has been the 'demassification' of markets. It attributes this to demographic and lifestyle changes producing more, smaller households and greater individualism among consumers. Linked to these trends there have also been 'profound social changes in terms of people's life-styles'.[5] This has resulted in more fragmented households, with individuals not only having different interests but having different brand choices. One implication has been consumers' increasingly specialised requirements for the products and services they use, and the subsequent necessity to communicate with household members as individuals rather than as homogenous family groups.

This market fragmentation also manifests itself in greater pluralism within society, evident in the high street through greater diversity in styling. One dramatic illustration of increasing individualism and self-expression is provided by a Levi's advertising campaign. As a result of focus groups that revealed that personal music tastes were oriented towards different specific music styles of the time, Levi ran a poster campaign that showed 12 head shots of different young people who clearly had different fashion tastes, many of them music based.

This is not to say that people are wholly 'inner-directed'. After all, they are apparently identifying with style groups, which is outer-directed behaviour, but what is being suggested is that there is a shift along the inner-outer-directedness continuum, toward greater individualism and inner direction. This has been identified by the Henley Centre for Forecasting (1978, 1992),[6,7] Shay (1978),[8] MINTEL (1981)[9] and Evans (1981, 1989).[10,11] Research reported by Publicis[12] suggests that from 1973 to 1989 there was a shift in 'motivators' from functional/rational factors (down from 40 per cent to 27 per cent of the population) and outer-directedness (static at 35 per cent) to more inner-directedness (up from 25 per cent to 38 per cent).

Today, customers are more individualistic, demanding, less loyal and less willing to forgive companies whose products and services do not meet their high standards. Customer loyalty programmes and relationship marketing are responses to customers who have become progressively more disloyal and more likely to switch. The main trends in customers' lifestyles and attitudes include the following:

- *Cash rich, time poor*. Many people have more disposable income today but find themselves with less time to do the things they can now afford. Such people are looking for convenience and speed and are comfortable doing business over the phone and the internet. There are interesting variations to this theme in different countries. Online auctions, for example, are a big hit in Germany where consumers are prepared to spend free time searching for online bargains. High personal taxation means it is more attractive for consumers to spend time seeking out bargains on the internet than to work overtime and get taxed heavily on their additional earnings.

- *Increased leisure time*. While many consumers are moving to a cash-rich, time-poor lifestyle, others are moving to a 35-hour week while maintaining their levels of disposable income. These changes are reflected in the growing popularity of eating out, use of health and fitness clubs, and other leisure and gaming activities.

- *Increased technology ownership*. Consumers are eagerly adopting new technologies such as mobile phones, personal digital assistants (PDAs), digital video disk (DVD) players, digital televisions and, of course, home computers. Older age groups, the so-called 'grey panthers' or 'silver surfers', have also eagerly embraced the internet. There are even personal video recorders (PVRs) that allow consumers to fast-forward exactly 30 seconds (the typical length of a commercial) at the press of a button. This puts extra pressure on traditional mass media advertisers because their audiences will fragment even more. It reinforces the 'direct' and more interactive approach we are exploring in this text.

The other changes, which we will examine in the following pages, are a response to this fundamental change in customer sophistication. Customers are demanding better products and quicker introduction of new features – hence the proliferation of products and the shortening of product life cycles. The demand for greater flexibility in the purchase of goods and services is leading to a proliferation of distribution channels. One of the drivers for global brands is the fact that customers seek out similar goods, values and standards of service as they travel abroad.

Challenges to product and brand management

The PC age (1970–90) coincided with the golden age of product and brand management. Unilever and Procter & Gamble turned product management from an art form into a more precise science and pushed their marketing managers through well-developed training programmes that turned them into effective and successful brand managers. As marketing entered the internet age, the value of manufacturers' traditional brands came under pressure from retailers and 'own label' products.

Marketing's mid-life crisis

One specific event worth recalling is 'Marlboro Friday'. On 2 April 1993 Philip Morris slashed the price of Marlboro cigarettes in the face of an onslaught from cheaper rivals whose share of the USA's cigarette market had jumped from 28 per cent to 36 per cent in less than a year. It appeared as if traditional brand management had failed to deliver and commentators talked about 'marketing's mid-life crisis'. Marketing's issues were summed up in a seminal 1994 article in *The Economist* magazine (*see* Exhibit 1.3).

The Economist spotted the trends of buying on price and the switch of power from manufacturers to retailers. It also highlighted the power of information technology as a key driver in the growing power of the retailers. As we will see later in this book, some of the world's most successful retailers such as Wal-Mart and Tesco have invested heavily in information technology for marketing purposes. More recently, Drawbaugh (2001)[13] has examined the issues that brands are facing in the internet age. There are other, wider changes that also threaten to change radically the way product and brand management are conducted. These include:

- shortened product life cycles
- product proliferation and brand extensions
- the impact of 'disruptive' technologies.

EXHIBIT 1.3

MARKETING'S MID-LIFE CRISIS

Ever since the 1950s, when they were developed by American manufacturers of fast-moving consumer goods (FMCG), marketing departments have revolved round brand managers. Yet the pains of the FMCG manufacturers are also linked to two more permanent changes in the pattern of shopping. The first trend is that people increasingly buy goods on price, not because they carry a famous name. The second trend is the shift in power from manufacturers to retailers. Investment in new shops and information technology, and the weakening power of brands, have helped retailers to exploit their proximity to the consumer and dictate terms to their suppliers. Sales of own-label goods continue to rise, pushing branded goods from the shelves, especially if they are not leaders in their category.

Don Leemon of the Boston Consulting Group points out that some FMCG have created geographical teams that include people from marketing, sales, finance and production. Their job is to keep retailers happy. It would be better, Mr Leemon says, if they revamped arguably the most important marketing function of all: developing new products that consumers want. That means yet more expensive research and even quicker ways to rush new products to market in the hope of inventing a new Coca-Cola. The odds against that speak for themselves. Marketing's mid-life crisis is far from over.

Source: *The Economist* (9 April 1994).[14]

Shortened product life cycles

Over the past decade many companies have both cut the average time to bring a product to market and shortened the life cycle of the product. All major pharmaceutical companies are attempting to slash the time it takes to test a new drug and get it to market. These trends are not confined to products in the high-technology or pharmaceutical industries. The same can be seen in the automobile industry, the consumer goods industry – in fact, in almost every industry. The impact on the marketing function has been dramatic, with demand for more and more revenues in shorter and shorter timescales. The success in the UK of the citrus drink Sunny Delight (*see* Exhibit 1.4) shows how good marketing and the appropriate use of technology are required to refresh brands in the notoriously fickle world of fast-moving consumer goods (FMCG).

Product proliferation and brand extensions

While marketing departments were pressurised into bringing newer products to market more quickly, they were also exposed to higher launch costs and greater risks of failure. In response, many FMCG companies chose to extend existing brands. The result has been an explosion of brand extensions and new variations on existing brands. As Figure 1.3 shows, Sunny Delight can now be enjoyed in Caribbean, California and Florida styles.

EXHIBIT 1.4

SUNNY DELIGHT

Procter & Gamble planned the UK launch of Sunny Delight for April 1998. It tested the product extensively during the previous 12 months, and it involved the retailers in early promotional campaigns, by employing data from loyalty card schemes to select young, low-income families. It sent out mails to these families offering discounts on the product. The combination of sophisticated test marketing and targeted direct mail helped the drink to jump straight into the UK's league table of top brands within 16 months of its launch, with annual sales of almost £160 million.

Unfortunately for Procter & Gamble, the initial success was difficult to maintain. Sales fell by more than a third in 2001 as the brand was hit by perceptions that the product was less healthy than more natural brands. The product dropped to 42nd in the league table in 2001 from 16th position the previous year. The brand was relaunched in 2002 with a revised formula (15 per cent fruit – three times the previous amount) and a £12 million marketing campaign including a £2 million SMS (short messaging service) marketing campaign in a bid to halt the slide.

Source: Authors' research (2003); Sunny Delight website (www.sunnyd.com, 2003).

Figure 1.3 Sunny Delight brand extensions
Source: Sunny Delight website (www.sunnyd.com, 2003), The Procter & Gamble Company.

EXHIBIT 1.5

COFFEE BARS IN INDIA

Drinking coffee while hanging out with friends might soon become the hippest thing to do, with coffee major Nestlé gearing up to launch its globally popular coffee bars, 'Cafe Nescafé', all over India. The Nescafé brand of coffee has a presence in over a hundred countries. A couple of years ago, the company launched its coffee bar concept in markets across the world, including Japan and the UK, as a novel method of communication about the brand. Cafe Nescafé will introduce Indian palates, used to the taste of traditional filter coffee, to a variety of ways the drink is enjoyed the world over. The coffee bar will have on offer a range of speciality Italian coffee, like the Cappuccino, Moccacino, decaffeinated black and white and Nesquik hot chocolate and Nestea among hot beverages. The coffee bar will also have a range of cold beverages, including cold coffee, iced teas and coffee in lemon and strawberry flavours, to begin with.

Source: *Kodagu Front* (19 October 2002).[15]

Nestlé's brands in the UK instant-coffee market include Nescafé, Gold Blend, Blend 37, Alta Rica, Cap Colombie, Nescafé Decaffeinated, Gold Blend Decaffeinated, Alta Rica Decaffeinated, Fine Blend, Nescafé Cappuccino, Unsweetened Cappuccino and Espresso – a fine combination of product proliferation and brand extension. Although it may seem a bewildering array of products, it is one of the reasons why Nestlé holds more than 50 per cent of the UK's £500 million instant-coffee market. Nestlé has taken the concept of brand extension even further by launching its own retail sites in the UK to capture a share of the growing take-away coffee market. These Café Nescafé sites are located in internet cafés, motorway service stations, shopping centre food outlets and hotel lobbies. By 2002, more than 40 Café Nescafé sites had been opened in the UK as part of a global brand extension throughout Europe, Japan and even India (*see* Exhibit 1.5).

However, there is growing evidence that consumers no longer want an ever-increasing number of products when the level of differentiation is minimal. Cristol and Sealey (2002)[16] wonder how we managed to become a world of:

- 40,000 products in a supermarket
- hundreds of long-distance and cellular calling plans
- 52 versions of Crest toothpaste
- 37 available configurations of a Dodge caravan
- more than 200 brands of conference room chairs
- 225 models of mobile phone handsets
- 100-plus brands of desktop and laptop computers.

The challenge for marketing managers becomes how to add useful line extensions without confusing or annoying customers. To do this successfully requires accurate market research on what the market really values and wants.

'Disruptive' technologies

Perhaps more important than the reduction in product life cycles is what Christensen (1997)[17] refers to as 'disruptive' technologies – new products that quickly cannibalise sales of existing products and render those products obsolete. Some products no longer mature and decline gracefully – their sales simply fall off the face of a cliff and disappear almost overnight. Exhibit 1.6 examines one company that failed to manage the commercialisation of a disruptive technology in the computer industry – the disk drive in a PC.

These technologies cause great difficulties for traditional marketing organisations, as they require significant resources to develop at a time when the market for the product is still immature or even non-existent. They also force marketers to make hard decisions about when to stop investing in existing products, even if such products are very profitable. What is interesting about the disk drive example in Exhibit 1.6 is that the computer industry has undergone at least one additional disruptive cycle since Christensen's book. Today's PC has migrated completely from disk drives to CD drives, and many PCs (and Apple Macintoshes) are now shipped without any drive at all.

EXHIBIT 1.6

HARD DRIVE AT SEAGATE

Seagate Technology used to be a world leader in disk drive technology in the PC industry. When engineers at Seagate showed prototypes of new 3.5-inch disk drives to the marketing personnel, they asked whether a market for the smaller, less expensive drives existed. The marketing organisation, using its habitual procedure for testing the market appeal for new drives, showed the prototypes to leading customers, asking them for an evaluation. One customer, IBM, showed no interest in Seagate's disruptive technology because they were looking for higher-capacity drives. In any case, they had already had a slot for the larger drives designed into their computers. Seagate's marketers drew up pessimistic sales forecasts and senior managers shelved the project, just as the 3.5-inch drive was becoming firmly established in the laptop market. In this case, Seagate made a conscious decision not to pursue the disruptive technology. In other cases, engineers and marketers starved the disruptive technology of the resources necessary for a successful launch.

Source: Christensen (1997).[18]

Increasing globalisation of markets

As the world becomes a global village, companies are looking to extend their geographic boundaries. They achieve this either through organic growth or through acquisition. Despite a slowdown in mergers and acquisitions (M&A) activity since 2000, M&A activity continues to be a driving force in the globalisation of markets. Consider the following recent 'mega-mergers':

- *Hewlett-Packard* (www.hp.com) concluded the largest technology merger in history in 2002 with its $19 billion acquisition of Compaq.

- *Vodafone* (www.vodafone.com) followed up its $69 billion acquisition of AirTouch Communications in the US with a takeover of Germany's Mannesmann to consolidate its position as the world's largest mobile telecommunications company.

- *GlaxoSmithKline* (www.gsk.com) became the world's largest pharmaceutical company and the largest company in the UK in 2000 following the merger of Glaxo Wellcome and SmithKline Beecham (an earlier merger of Glaxo and Wellcome in 1995 was, in its day, the largest ever merger in the UK).

- *Nordea* (www.nordea.com), the pan-Nordic financial services group with more than 10 million customers, was created in 2000 following a series of cross-border mergers that brought together Merita (Finland), Nordbanken (Sweden), Christiania (Norway) and Unidanmark (Denmark).

In addition, other global alliances are forming. Some of the more interesting alliances of recent years have occurred in the airline industry. As airlines improved their abilities to share computer data and integrate their reservation systems, they started to build 'code-sharing' agreements that enabled them to offer customers a wider choice of destinations. (The fact that air travellers still had to change flights, or terminals, in order to make the appropriate connections seemed irrelevant to the airline marketing managers.) Today, most of the major and many of the minor airlines have allied themselves into one of four major alliances that account for the majority of the total world traffic market:

- *Star Alliance* (www.star-alliance.com) comprises the 14 airlines of Air Canada, Air New Zealand, ANA, Austrian Airlines, BMI, Lauda, Lufthansa, Mexicana, SAS, Singapore, Thai Airways, Tyrolean, United and Varig (*see* Exhibit 1.7).

- *Oneworld Alliance* (www.oneworldalliance.com) comprises the eight airlines of Aer Lingus, American Airlines, British Airways, Cathay Pacific, Finnair, Iberia, Lan Chile and Qantas.

- *SkyTeam* (www.skyteam.com) is an alliance of six member airlines – Aeromexico, Air France, Alitalia, Czech Airlines, Delta and Korean Air.

- *Wings Alliance* is still in its early stages of development but includes Continental, KLM and Northwest Airlines.

And yet there is still considerable room for further globalisation of brands. Of the top 100 brands in the FMCG market in Europe, the USA and Japan, only seven are

EXHIBIT 1.7

STAR PERFORMER

If you look at comparisons between the world's top airline alliances, Star Alliance still ranks first with more flights and more airports than any other alliance. It currently offers more than 10,700 daily flights to over 720 destinations and more than 7,000 daily flights carry a flight number of at least one other member carrier. Furthermore, IATA statistics reveal that Star Alliance airlines share 24 per cent of the world's passengers but account for 28 per cent of the total available revenue, which means they are targeting and attracting high-yield business. But maintaining a lead is hard work and the competition is heated. SkyTeam didn't exist two years ago but now is aggressively expanding its network. Delta Airlines and Air France, two key players at SkyTeam, were recently granted anti-trust immunity. Without a doubt they will challenge Star in many important international air traffic markets, specifically on the North Atlantic. Although SkyTeam is growing, Oneworld is still the main competitor. Its key assets are strong hubs in London, Chicago and Miami, as well as global network coverage. In addition, Oneworld enjoys exclusivity rights on routes between London and the USA, one of the most important international air traffic markets.

Source: Air Canada, *Online Horizons* (October 2002).[19]

common to all three markets. In most European countries, many of the top ten FMCG products are still relatively unknown outside their own national boundaries, suggesting that there is still significant potential for the creation of global brands. A good example in Europe is the diversity of pasta brands in different countries. The Barilla pasta brand is the leading FMCG brand in Italy, while Lyon-headquartered Panzani dominates the French market with a 35 per cent market share. In contrast, Marshalls is the leading pasta brand in Scotland, Nestlé's Buitoni brand is the market leader in England and Roma is the leader in the Irish market.

Marketing in a virtual world

The virtualisation of distribution channels and services

Having looked at some key marketing trends such as product proliferation and globalisation, it is useful to understand how commerce has become virtualised. Today, sales and service are increasingly conducted through a variety of different channels and, in some instances, through virtual channels only. Virtual channels include:

- telephone

- internet

- mobile internet

- interactive digital television (iDTV or iTV)

- automated teller machines (ATMs) and kiosks

These channels are examined more closely as part of a wider discussion on distribution channels in Chapter 11.

The virtualisation of payments

The virtualisation of products and services and the swift acceptance of electronic commerce are recurring themes throughout this book. In this section, we briefly review the following virtual payment mechanisms:

- plastic cards

- smart cards

- electronic cash

- electronic data interchange (EDI).

Plastic cards

Regardless of where the sale takes place – in the virtual or the real world – another form of virtualisation has taken off, namely the virtualisation of the payment process. Plastic cards, typically with a magnetic stripe that holds a limited amount of data, have become commonplace and allow cardholders to perform a variety of different functions, including:

- withdrawing money from an automated teller machine (ATM card);

- paying for goods in a store or supermarket (credit or debit card);

- acting as a means of identification for gaining entry into secure buildings (identity card);

- accumulating points on a loyalty scheme (loyalty card).

It should be recognised that payment methods vary hugely from country to country. The paper cheque is still a hugely popular payment mechanism in the USA. In the UK the cheque has been overtaken in popularity by the plastic card (both credit and debit varieties). In Sweden and Finland, paper cheques are simply not a feature in consumer payments.

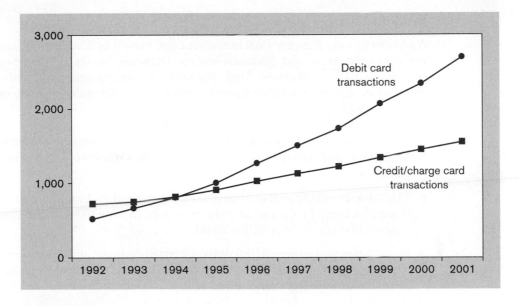

Figure 1.4 UK debit and credit/charge card transactions (millions, 1992–2001)
Source: Association for Payment Clearing Services (www.apacs.org.uk, 2001).

Despite the variations, the trend in most countries is a decline of paper in favour of electronic payments by credit card or debit card. In the 1980s the most common type of virtual payment in the UK was the credit card transaction. By the end of the 1990s the debit card had overtaken the credit card as the most popular form of plastic card payment (*see* Figure 1.4).

Smart cards

A variant of the plastic card is the smart card, which is one of the latest applications of chip miniaturisation. A microprocessor is embedded into a piece of plastic that gives it an astonishing increase in functionality over the capabilities of traditional magnetic-stripe cards. Smart cards have been in use for many years. For example, French Visa cards have carried microchips since the 1980s. A variation of the smart card is already used in many countries in the form of public telephone cards.

Despite the technological advantages of smart cards, the commercial reality is that so much investment has been made in traditional magnetic stripe cards (for example, upgrading ATMs and in-store card readers to accept smart cards) that the introduction of smart cards has been painfully slow. In the UK, the oil company Shell has had a smart card initiative in operation for a number of years. Customers use their Shell SMART card to collect electronic points when they purchase petrol. For every £6 spent on petrol or services, the customer receives one SMART Point. The points are stored in the smart card's memory and can be redeemed for free cinema tickets, air miles, tapes and CDs. Alternatively, the points can be donated to charity.

Electronic cash

A wide variety of electronic cash initiatives exist, known by a variety of names including electronic purses and electronic wallets. Electronic purses are stored-value cards that hold cash in an electronic form. The card is typically a smart card and more than one billion had been issued worldwide by the end of 1998 under a variety of different brands, including:

- *Mondex* (www.mondex.com), a smart card technology company owned by MasterCard International and a consortium of 28 major companies across the globe.

- *Visa Cash*, the card-based electronic wallet sponsored by Visa International (www.visa.com). By the end of 1998 there were 25 million Visa Cash cards in issue in 18 countries around the world.

- *Proton* (www.protonworld.com), the only 'small country' electronic wallet scheme left. Originally launched by the Belgian bank Banksys, it is now supported by American Express and Visa International.

- *GeldKarte* (www.geldkarte.de), the nationwide stored-value system operated by a German central banking agency.

Despite the less-than-enthusiastic take-up of electronic purses initially (*see* Exhibit 1.8), many electronic money initiatives are in operation across the world.

EXHIBIT 1.8

THE FUTURE OF 'GRUBBY NOTES AND COINS'

Visions of a cashless society were dented in November 1998 when Visa and MasterCard, which stand to gain most from the end of what they call 'grubby notes and coins', abandoned their high-profile New York trial of electronic money. The finish of the year-long test in Manhattan's glitzy upper west side followed the ending of a similar experiment in which digital cash was carried on a card in buses and telephone boxes in Swindon, west of London.

Electronic money is here, but hardly anybody is eager to use it. Even the people of Hong Kong and Singapore – notorious technophiles and shoppers – seem unenthusiastic, despite the fact that smart or 'stored-value' cards are already in use for everything from parking meters in Hong Kong to road-pricing in Singapore. In Hong Kong, Mondex claims 8,000 merchants accept its cards. That still seems too few, too many of whom are selling things like clothes, for which standard-issue credit or debit cards are just as good. Groceries offer better prospects, but the total volume of cashless transactions in Hong Kong is still estimated at less than $10 million a year – just $30 for each user.

Sources: *Financial Times* (21/22 November 1998); *The Economist* (21 November 1998).

There are also different variations on the electronic cash theme – software products that assist in the transmission of payments over the internet. These are sometimes referred to as peer-to-peer or person-to-person (P2P) payment mechanisms. This category of payments has seen a large numbers of entrants but most have failed to make any significant impact. Two notable failures are:

- *DigiCash.* A Dutch firm founded in 1990, DigiCash was one of the earliest companies to create a software-based payments system called eCash that allows users to 'withdraw' digital coins from their bank accounts, store them in a 'purse' on their PC, and use them to buy low-cost items over the internet. Despite licensing its technology to a number of European banks, it filed for bankruptcy in late 1998 after failing to make headway in the USA.

- *CyberCash.* CyberCash launched its CyberCoin micropayment service in 1996 for transactions between 25 cents and $10. In the UK, Barclays Bank licensed the software for its BarclayCoin application. However, CyberCash had accumulated losses of more than $60 million on sales of less than $5 million in 1998. It went bankrupt in 2001 and the technology was sold to Verisign.

Few of these alternative payment mechanisms have achieved critical mass. One practical hindrance to the success of electronic cash systems is their inherent lack of anonymity. Cash carries no electronic audit trail, which explains its popularity in the so-called black and grey economies. Goodhart and Krueger (2001)[20] argue that this informal economy will continue to maintain its demand for physical cash. Yet some products have attained some degree of acceptance. The most successful to date is PayPal (*see* Exhibit 1.9), but only time will tell whether it be a ubiquitous payment mechanism.

Interestingly, the internet auction giant eBay (www.ebay.com) purchased PayPal (www.paypal.com) for $1.5 billion in 2002, after trying for three years to build its own payment system called Billpoint.[21] About 40 per cent of all eBay purchases are made online and the company wanted to tap a potentially lucrative revenue stream. But eBay's efforts were unsuccessful when small businesses using the auction site overwhelmingly rejected Billpoint, concerned that eBay would use the system to create even greater leverage over them. The company has a curious relationship with its 46 million customers, many of whom could not operate without it, but nonetheless resent its power. Instead, they mostly adopted PayPal. The acquisition neatly sidestepped this problem. PayPal had 10 million users, of which 2 million were small businesses and 8 million retail customers. About 60 per cent of PayPal's business is on eBay.

The future of electronic cash is difficult to predict. Stand-alone payment mechanisms may never take off. PayPal and similar systems such as Paybox do not really bypass the banking system, since most payments are ultimately routed through a bank account. Exceptions to this are telephone-billing systems of mobile phone companies. Vodafone (www.vodafone.com) and T-Mobile (www.t-mobile.com), the biggest operators in Europe, announced plans in 2002 to develop a common platform for mobile payments. However, mobile phone operators have been coy about using the full potential of their monthly or pre-paid accounts.[22] In general, the explosive adoption of pre-pay mobile phones suggests another way in which these electronic payment systems might achieve take-off. These payment mechanisms have proved very attractive to those who do not have access to credit cards or the banking system in general. This

EXHIBIT 1.9

NEW WAYS TO BILL CUSTOMERS

Around the time he immigrated to Chicago from Ukraine, Max Levchin became obsessed with cryptography. Living under the old Soviet regime convinced him of the need to carry out communications undetectable by authorities. He moved to Silicon Valley after graduation in 1998 to found PayPal (www.paypal.com), the company that has suddenly become the leading processor of person-to-person, or P2P, payments over the internet. Just as Napster allowed people to share music directly online, PayPal enables people to exchange money instantly without having to open expensive merchant accounts to accept credit cards. PayPal's success rested on two technological feats: simplicity and fraud prevention. Yet to Levchin's surprise, advanced cryptography has had little to do with PayPal's success. Rather, the company's rapid adoption by millions of small businesses and individuals operating chiefly on internet auction site eBay is largely credited to Levchin's more recent obsession: developing financial surveillance software that closely monitors PayPal's customers and almost instantly alerts both the company and law enforcement officials to any suspicious account activity. 'We mine millions and millions of transactions in real time', Levchin says.

Sources: MIT Technology Review (9 July 2002);[23] *Financial Times* (9 July 2002).[24]

reduces the danger of social exclusion and allows a large expansion of the network.[25] These pre-pay systems are also attractive because they carry limited liability: the maximum loss is restricted to the amount programmed into the card.

Electronic data interchange (EDI)

The virtual payment mechanisms outlined above are primarily used by the consumer market. What about the business market and inter-company payments? Even though the term 'e-commerce' was coined during the 1990s, companies were trading with each other long before the internet, using a technology called electronic data interchange (EDI). EDI is primarily used in the 'billing cycle' where invoices and purchase orders are generated and sent electronically between buying and selling organisations. EDI offers significantly lower transaction costs and higher levels of accuracy than other methods such as phone and fax. Large retailers such as Tesco (www.tesco.com) and Wal-Mart (www.walmart.com) were some of the first to embrace EDI as they were operating large and expensive 'paper factories' to process thousands of paper orders to suppliers. As the forerunner of modern e-commerce transactions, the topic of EDI deserves a more in-depth discussion. We will return to it again in the next two chapters, but in the meantime the case study at the end of this chapter demonstrates how important EDI has been as a virtual payment mechanism between businesses.

Summary

Marketing as a discipline has been with us for over 50 years. During that time it has provided us with many useful concepts and frameworks. Putting the customer first, the brand manager, mass advertising and market research are just a few of the innovations that businesses have used successfully. During the 1980s and 1990s marketing was faced with challenges such as to how to globalise brands and how to personalise product and service offerings for customers. By and large, marketing has responded well to these challenges with new frameworks. However, the mid-1990s saw a huge increase in the adoption of the internet and other electronic tools. By the beginning of the twenty-first century marketing managers were faced with a seemingly bewildering array of new challenges and opportunities. This was when traditional marketing truly started to become 'electronic marketing' or 'e-marketing'.

Electronic marketing is a very logical extension of traditional marketing. The standard frameworks are still relevant but we now have many more tools and ways in which to apply them. We will see for example in Chapter 4 how many new electronic tools can be used to conduct marketing research. However, the basic frameworks for conducting market research, such as defining the research problem and calculating a valid sample size, are still very relevant. So we must not throw away our traditional marketing texts but seek to understand how these new technologies and tools can be applied in today's marketing environment.

Case study

UK retailers go online with suppliers

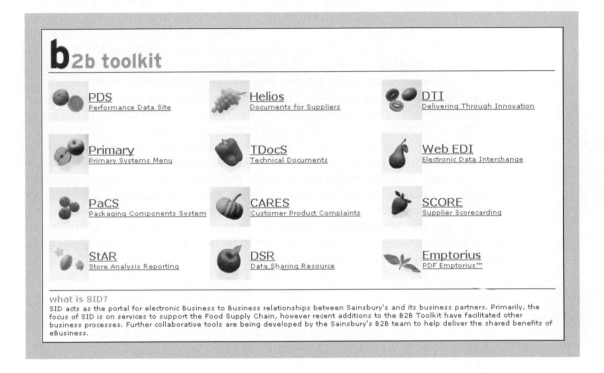

Figure 1.5

J. Sainsbury

J. Sainsbury operates a supply chain process that requires the management of over 2,000 suppliers at one end of the supply chain and 12 million stocking points in its stores at the other end of the chain. Sainsbury is using the internet to provide its suppliers with direct access to its data warehouse. Sainsbury's Information Direct (SID) system includes a supplier's guide to terms and conditions, information on promotional planning, stock movements, and supplier performance data including service levels, depot stock data and range distribution. The application incorporates a 'collaborative planning system' as a tool for improving supply chain responsiveness and speeding information flows. Monitoring promotions is a key capability of the system, allowing Sainsbury's suppliers to tap into the system, via the internet, to obtain an instant update on the progress of any promotional campaign to help with demand forecasting and assessing profitability. It also means that trading partners have a single information source for information about each campaign, so ending confusion about start and stop dates.

An additional use of Sainsbury's SID is that it allows smaller suppliers to link to Xtra-Trade, an internet-based EDI-style operation. Sainsbury has bought subscriptions to the service for its small and medium enterprise (SME) suppliers. It hopes eventually to roll out the system to all its smaller suppliers, replacing an existing fax order mechanism and so improving lead-times and reducing errors. Although initially Xtra-Trade is being used for orders, invoices, and forecasts, eventually it will also include a wider assortment of message types such as export/import data, stock availability, dispatch notifications, remittance advice and price file exchange. Sainsbury has also joined GlobalNetxchange, an online system that should allow it and other companies to purchase supplies via the internet.

Sainsbury's trading partners appear to like SID, judging by some of their comments:

- 'SID is a very powerful B2B [business-to-business] tool that can benefit suppliers greatly by providing the latest information from Sainsbury and its various departments.' *Bev Jones, Nestlé Cuddington (Edenvale)*

- 'Here at Kellogg's, retailer extranet sites are primarily used by the sales and supply chain to monitor performance, proactively respond to shortages, review effectiveness of promotions and identify distribution issues further than the customer depot. SID is really the cutting edge in the area of retailer extranets, both for its content and structure. Sainsbury publishes a lot of internal information providing suppliers with transparency on their business. The site is user-friendly and well structured. Especially now with the new functionality piloted (e.g. alerts, etc.), it really provides the supplier with a handy tool.' *Dimitri Vlouchakis, Kellogg*

- 'We have integrated the EPOS [electronic point-of-sale] data into our sales forecasting system and now can see what is happening with promotions and launches directly, without having to wait several months for Nielsen data. It is so popular that the demand managers chase us up if the data doesn't come through on time.' *Cathy Driscoll, Unilever*

- 'Over the last few years we have continuously refined the way we use SID data in our day-to-day operations: it is used regularly by customer service and by our demand planners to maximise in store availability; the customer complaints system CARES is used by our quality team to support the information gathered by our customer careline; we have used the scorecard in all our categories to identify opportunities for making our supply chain more efficient and effective. SID is an integral part of the way we work with Sainsbury's.' *Lorna Fleck, Scottish Courage Brands*

Safeway

In 1997 Safeway was one of the first UK retailers to launch its Supplier Information Service (SIS). With SIS, suppliers reach the Safeway home page using a standard internet browser, then they click on icons to obtain details of Safeway staff contacts, trading terms, news items and a report section that allows them to search the data warehouse for details of relevant product sales broken down by delivery depot and store. Safeway's SIS started with Bird's Eye Walls and Walkers Snack Foods, but during 1998 rapidly rolled out to several dozen suppliers. Each is able to access Safeway's central data warehouse for information on product sales and demand forecasts, down to store level in real time. The result is not so much 'co-managed inventory' but 'collaborative inventory', with buying and selling teams working closely together to streamline lead-times, maximise the customer offer and generally improve performance.

Tesco

The Tesco Information Exchange (TIE) system offers suppliers a stores directory, online access to Tesco's manuals, and information about products and sales. TIE encourages collaborative working by breaking up the business process into a series of tasks and elements. There is a promotions tracking module, for example, which provides manu-facturers with up-to-date information, such as how a three-for-two customer offer has been received. Early benefits included better co-management of forecasts with suppliers and more rapid feedback on consumer preferences and dislikes.

Sources: Competition Commission;[26] J. Sainsbury website (www.j-sainsbury.co.uk/sid, 2003).

Case study questions

1 Outline three advantages of a retailer operating close electronic links with a supplier.

2 'The internet offers a flexible way of sharing information with partners.' Discuss.

3 Outline three advantages of placing orders using the internet instead of faxes.

4 Why is it important for suppliers to have timely information on the progress of promotions?

5 'Investment in information technology is a key differentiator for retailers.' Discuss.

Questions and exercises

Questions

1 Outline why 'electronic marketing is a very logical extension of marketing'.

2 What are the biggest marketing opportunities in the wireless age?

3 Discuss the advantages and disadvantages of product proliferation from both a manufacturer's and a consumer's perspective.

4 'Electronic marketing is being driven as much by societal changes as it is by technology changes.' Discuss.

5 How will e-commerce accelerate the globalisation of business?

6 Why is the virtualisation of payments important to the development of e-commerce?

Online exercises

1 Access the sites of Ryanair (www.ryanair.com) and BA (www.britishairways.com). Compare their approaches to using the web and key differences in the way the sites are organised.

2 Access the sites of www.ebay.com and www.paypal.com. Write a short note to the CEO of eBay outlining why it would make sense to buy a business like PayPal.

References

1 *The Economist* (1998). 'Battle of the brand', 13 June.

2 Kirsner, S. (2001). 'Pieces of the bubble', *The Globe*, 6 August.

3 *The Economist* (2003). 'Hotspots and fries', 27 March.

4 Ogilvy & Mather Direct (1990). *Identifying and Keeping Customers in the Single Market: The Strategic Role of Direct Marketing in Europe*, London: Ogilvy & Mather Direct.

5 Henley Centre (1991). *Positive Response: The Prospects for Direct Mail in the 1990s*, report prepared in conjunction with Ogilvy & Mather Direct, London: Henley Centre.

6 Henley Centre (1978). *Commercial Report: Planning Consumer Markets*, London: Henley Centre.

7 Henley Centre (1992). Presentation to Market Research Society, Bristol, 5 March.

8 Shay, P. (1978). 'The consumer revolution is coming', *Marketing*, September.

9 MINTEL (1981). *Market Intelligence Special Report on the Teenage Market*.

10 Evans, M.J. (1981). 'Dedicated follower of fashion', SSRC, MEG Research Seminar, University of Strathclyde.

11 Evans, M.J. (1989). 'Consumer behaviour toward fashion', *European Journal of Marketing*, Vol. 23, No. 7.

12 Block, R. (1992). 'Sales talk', Transcribed from BBC Radio 4, January.

13 Drawbaugh, K. (2001). *Brands in the Balance: Meeting the Challenges to Commercial Identity*, London: Financial Times Prentice Hall.

14 *The Economist* (1994). 'Death of the brand manager', 9 April.

15 www.kodava.org/KF/Oct2000/kf102000.htm, 19 October 2000.

16 Cristol, S.M. and Sealey, M. (2002). *Simplicity Marketing: End Brand Complexity, Clutter and Confusion*, New York: The Free Press.

17 Christensen, C.M. (1997). *The Innovator's Dilemma: When New Technologies Cause Great Firms To Fail*, Boston: Harvard Business School Press.

18 Christensen, *The Innovator's Dilemma*.

- The response of industry consortia
- The effectiveness of private marketplaces

BUSINESS-TO-CONSUMER (B2C) E-COMMERCE

- B2C phases of development
- First blood to the early movers
- The return of the dinosaurs
- The post-dot-com era

GOVERNMENT-TO-CITIZEN (G2C) AND CONSUMER-TO-CONSUMER (C2C) DEVELOPMENTS

- The role of government in the internet age
- Cooperative consumer buying groups

SUMMARY

CASE STUDY

Introduction

Although companies have transacted with each other electronically for decades, the term electronic commerce, or e-commerce for short, is synonymous with the internet age (1990–2000) and with internet-based mechanisms for transacting business. There are significant differences in the way industrial companies like Siemens or GE market and sell large power plants to industrial customers, and the way in which fast-moving consumer goods (FMCG) companies market to large consumer audiences. During the internet age these differences were reflected in the different ways in which business-to-business (B2B) and business-to-consumer (B2C) e-commerce developed.

In this chapter we begin with a discussion of B2B e-commerce, since it represents a much larger market than its B2C counterpart. We then examine the extraordinary developments in B2B marketplaces – the electronic exchanges through which major procurement deals are conducted – during the late 1990s. From there, we move to an exploration of B2C e-commerce and, finally, we examine other categories of electronic business such as government-to-citizen (G2C) and consumer-to-consumer (C2C) e-commerce.

Business-to-business (B2B) e-commerce

From EDI to B2B e-commerce

As the volume of transactions on the internet has grown, much of the attention has focused on sales to consumers of products like books and CDs. However in the background the real revolution has taken place in business-to-business (B2B) transactions. The volume and value of B2B e-commerce transactions has increased significantly each year (*see* Figure 2.1). In value terms, B2B e-commerce equates to approximately 90 per cent of total e-commerce payments.

We will now look at some of the reasons why the B2B market has grown so fast:

■ businesses want to trade electronically to reduce costs;

■ the internet provides a cheaper, more flexible way of trading;

■ electronic trading works for small companies;

■ the trend towards increased electronic links between organisations is continuing.

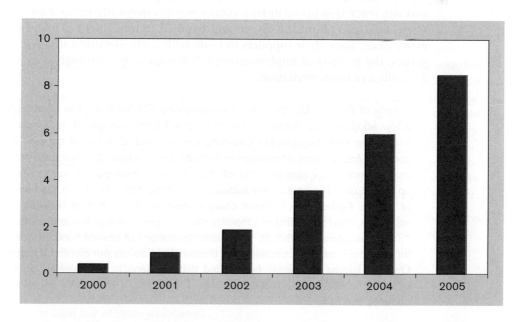

Figure 2.1 Worldwide B2B market (US$ trillion, 2000–5)
Source: Gartner website (www.gartner.com, 2002).

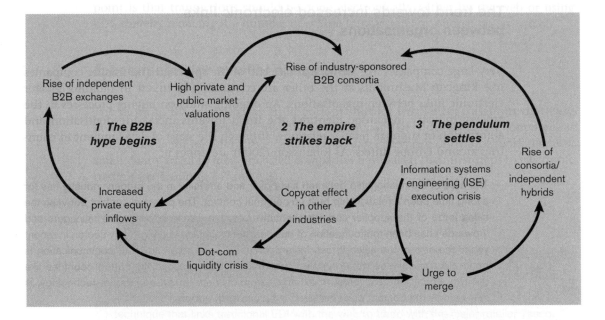

Figure 2.3 The battle of the marketplaces – independent exchanges versus industry consortia
Source: Sawhney and Acer (2000).[6]

- the rapid proliferation of independent marketplaces
- the response of industry consortia
- the effectiveness of private marketplaces.

The rapid proliferation of independent marketplaces

Sawhney and Acer (2000)[7] provided a timely reminder about the realities of small organisations attempting to muscle in on large industrial conglomerates. Independent B2B exchanges became hugely popular in the late 1990s, a phenomenon that was reinforced by the general rise in value of internet stocks. Organisations like Chemdex and PlasticsNet (global chemicals and plastics exchanges) and VerticalNet (various industry vertical marketplaces) sprang up and achieved phenomenal valuations within a short number of years. By early 2000, literally thousands of such marketplaces had emerged and were attempting to grab market share (*see* Figure 2.4).

The response of industry consortia

It did not take long for the industrial giants to work out what was happening. They did not want the new upstarts taking a cut of their procurement business and responded with their own announcements of industry-sponsored B2B exchanges. Some of the larger exchanges were:

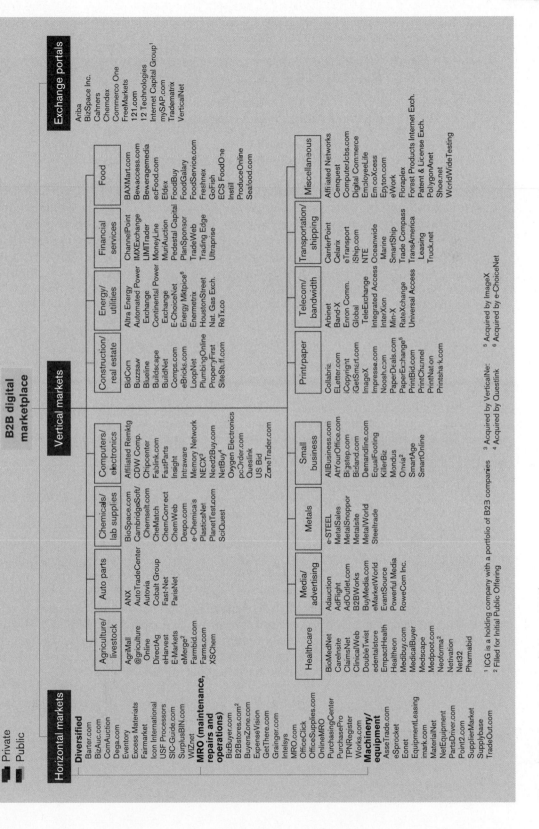

Figure 2.4 B2B marketplaces (February 2000)
Source: Horner (2000).[8]

- *Automotive industry*. February 2000: 'Covisint' consortium led by Daimler Chrysler, General Motors and Ford ($240 billion market).

- *Food industry*. March 2000: 'Transora' consortium led by Coca-Cola, Kraft and Proctor & Gamble ($200 billion market).

- *Aerospace industry*. March 2000: 'Exostar' consortium led by BAE Systems, Boeing, Lockheed Martin and Raytheon ($71 billion market).

- *Airline industry*. April 2000: consortium led by British Airways, Air Canada, Continental, Delta and United Airlines ($32 billion market).

Most, but not all, of these exchanges were American. In the UK, National Power, Powergen, Anglian Water and SouthWest Water announced the creation of the Achilles marketplace for the utilities industry. Few of these consortia were more than press releases when they were announced, but the very fact of the announcement was sufficient to upset the applecart for the independent marketplaces. By mid-2000, most of the independents were in serious trouble. As the major players in each industry came together to commit their e-procurement spending to their own consortia, the independents ran into financial difficulties, resulting in the subsequent demise of the vast majority of such exchanges.

The effectiveness of private marketplaces

Some of these industry consortia gained traction in the marketplace and were successful. However, many were not, often because of squabbling between the various industry partners. When the dust finally settled on the B2B marketplace battle, two types of e-commerce business model survived:

- B2B consortia – but only in some industries

- private B2B exchanges – similar to the EDI networks of old.

The real winners were the private exchanges. By 2002, 15 per cent of Fortune 500 companies in the USA had established these invitation-only exchanges, with an additional 28 per cent planning to have one by the end of 2003. These private exchanges combined the functions of internet-based platforms with the security of EDI systems. Unlike independent B2B marketplaces and industry consortia, private exchanges keep control in the hands of an active participant (*see* Exhibit 2.4) – an arrangement that helps focus activity on process rather than price. Because suppliers in a private exchange are either invited guests or hosts, buyers have already chosen to do business with them and may even have negotiated prices offline.

EXHIBIT 2.4

DOW CHEMICAL GOES PRIVATE

Dow Chemical launched a private exchange called MyAccount@Dow. Initially a pilot serving 200 customers, primarily in Latin America, it now has more than 8,000 registered users in 35 countries, captures 40 per cent of the company's total sales volume in Latin America and, as of late 2001, reportedly generated about $100 million in revenues a month. The exchange allows customers to review their account histories, to check the availability of products, and to manage their order-delivery schedules. Such capabilities give the supplier, in turn, a clearer picture of its customers' inventory levels and buying patterns – information that permits it to manage its own inventory more efficiently and to book its customers' orders with greater certainty. The exchange, which is linked to Dow's internal systems, tracks all interactions with customers, by telephone, fax, or computer, cutting the company's cost per transaction to about $1, from $50 to $100. Overall, the company claims to have wrested more than $30 million a year in productivity improvements from its self-service system. These processes could not have been automated through less flexible EDI networks or less closely controlled open e-markets.

Source: Hoffman et al. (2002).[9]

Business-to-consumer (B2C) e-commerce

B2C phases of development

While B2B drives most of the internet growth, much of the glitz and glamour is in the business-to-consumer (B2C) sector, where millions of advertising dollars have been spent to create brands. This is where there have been spectacular successes like Amazon, Yahoo and eBay, and spectacular failures like Webvan and Boo.com. The B2C market is significantly smaller than its B2B equivalent; in value terms, B2C e-commerce equates to approximately 10 per cent of total e-commerce payments. The B2C market has gone through a very similar development path to its B2B counterpart:

- first blood to the early movers
- the return of the dinosaurs
- the post-dot-com era.

3

E-commerce business models

Learning objectives

Once you have read this chapter you will:

- understand different internet-based business models;
- understand the importance of brand, revenues and profit in the world of e-commerce;
- be able to assess some e-commerce 'myths' and 'realities';
- understand the fundamentals of electronic marketing.

Contents

- Electronic marketing is technology-enabled marketing
- Electronic marketing is more than internet marketing
- A framework for electronic marketing in the twenty-first century

SUMMARY

CASE STUDY

Introduction

The rise of internet commerce, or e-commerce, has been phenomenally swift (as we have seen in Chapter 2) and, despite the double blow of falling internet stock prices and some failed companies, e-commerce is here to stay. The conundrum is that a wide variety of different business models emerged during the internet age, some of which were successful but most of which failed – so which are the best business models to embrace? As marketers, it is critical that we understand which models are likely to succeed and which are destined to struggle. If we cannot understand e-commerce business models, how can we become successful at electronic marketing?

In this chapter we begin by taking a closer look at the different business models that have emerged, going more deeply than the B2B and B2C classifications that we introduced in the last chapter. We then make a critical examination of conventional wisdom in e-commerce to try to separate myth from reality. Finally, we propose a framework for electronic marketing built around the principles of a buyer-driven world and a more holistic approach to conducting electronic and mobile commerce.

Business models in the internet age

Categorising e-commerce business models

Classifications such as B2B, B2C and G2C are helpful in setting out the broad scope of e-commerce activities but do little to explain the underlying business models. In the late 1990s commentators were struggling to construct frameworks that defined clearly how these new business models worked in the internet age. Rappa's online categorisation of internet-based business models is an excellent starting point for understanding e-commerce – we show some of the main categories in Table 3.1. Other

The importance of profit

In 1999 and 2000 internet companies were valued on the basis of revenues. With many internet companies in 'land-grab' mode, spending vast amounts of money on advertising and marketing, revenues were considered key and profitability was an issue for the future. The focus for companies like Lastminute (www.lastminute.com) in the UK and Amazon (www.amazon.com) in the USA was to generate revenue and market share. Profitability was assumed to be a natural consequence of the 'land-grab' but rarely examined critically. In 2000 and 2001 dot-com became dot-bomb as profits failed to materialise and sources of funding dried up. Companies attempted to adjust their business models to slash costs and hasten the move to profitability, but in many cases the change came too late.

A framework for assessing e-commerce business models

Some observers, such as Osterwalder and Pigneur (2002),[3] have managed to address the issue of financial success in their framework for assessing internet business models (*see* Figure 3.1). Their model identifies four pillars to any successful business model:

- product innovation
- customer relationship
- infrastructure management
- financials.

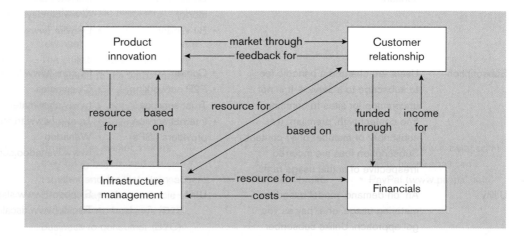

Figure 3.1 Business model framework
Source: Osterwalder and Pigneur (2002).[4]

Product innovation

Osterwalder and Pigneur start with the assumption that an internet company (or any company) must create a series of products or services that meet real customer needs. Amazon sold books at attractive prices. It also created new services (book reviews, alerts, its affiliate programmes) that met customer needs. Many other internet businesses failed to do this. These businesses included a very large number of 'content' companies that provided information free of charge to their customers on the basis that a 'no-cost' offering would attract sufficient numbers of cyber-visitors to make the company attractive to drive up the valuation of the company. This strategy worked initially when internet users were not particularly discriminating. As competition increased, many of these sites were forced to charge for their content in order to generate revenues. Only when it became clear that customers were unwilling to pay did these companies realise they were in serious trouble. Similarly, the reason that the thousands of B2B marketplaces failed (*see* Chapter 2) was because they did not provide a sufficiently compelling offering to attract customers.

It is sobering to see how many e-commerce business models fail at the first hurdle – creating products that customers want. There is a major linkage between this pillar and the second pillar of customer relationship.

Customer relationship

If the product innovation pillar is in place, the next critical capability is the establishment of a strong relationship with the customer. This is a key theme in this book. Understanding why and how customers buy becomes critical when interactions with customers are not always conducted face-to-face. Customer relationship management (CRM) must be capable of being supported in an internet environment and must be adapted to handle electronic transactions and customer interactions. One of the reasons that companies like Dell (www.dell.com), Egg (www.egg.com) and Ryanair (www.ryanair.com) manage to conduct the majority of their business over the internet is because they have learned how to make it easy for the customer to interact with them electronically. This is another theme that will run throughout this book.

Infrastructure management

Osterwalder and Pigneur define infrastructure as including people as well as the technology and underlying processes. While it may seem unusual to think of staff as infrastructure, there is an important truth in this categorisation. Not all interactions can be conducted electronically. Most people are happy to conduct certain banking transactions by telephone, internet or mobile phone but few would purchase a pension product or mortgage without dealing personally with a qualified advisor. Most large B2B electronic marketplace transactions are still negotiated in person, even if the actual payment is conducted and settled electronically.

Under Osterwalder and Pigneur's definition, the internet is relegated to the role of channel rather than the core of the business. This is not so say that technology and processes are unimportant. There are still too many incidences of poor website design, inefficient processes and technology failures (particularly when transaction volumes become too large). Poor technology is enough to destroy the credibility of any internet offering before it gets off the ground.

Financials

Osterwalder and Pigneur correctly identify the financial component as one of the key pillars in any business model – unfortunately it was the missing pillar in many recent business models. Adding the suffix '.com' to a company name did not automatically generate additional revenues, even if it did result in a doubling of some company's share price, albeit briefly. One example of this is provided by the consulting company McKinsey.[5] According to its analysis of 159 online media companies, the business models behind most internet companies were deeply flawed from the beginning. First, the vast majority of advertising-based revenue models simply could not work. Seven US television networks and 214 cable stations competed for $16 billion and $13 billion in advertising during 2001. More than 9,000 US websites fought for $6 billion in advertising. More important, this revenue was concentrated in just a handful of properties: 76 per cent of the advertising went to the ten biggest sites.

As discussed above, charging for digital content was another source of revenue that failed to materialise. In 2002 American consumers paid just over $1 billion for various internet content (excluding gambling and pornography) – a fraction of the revenues achieved from internet advertising. However, this source of revenue is doubling each year, as more and more sites are charging for content that previously was free (*see* Exhibit 3.1).

Despite the move away from free content and the greater migration towards business models that generate revenues at lower cost, there are still only a handful of websites that are truly financially successful. According to the Online Publishers Association (OPA), a mere fifty sites collect 85 per cent of all internet revenues. The internet sites that have achieved significant brand presence and revenues, spend such large amounts of cash building their brands that few are profitable yet. Even Amazon achieved profitability in only a single three-month period in its first seven years of operation.

EXHIBIT 3.1

FAREWELL TO THE FREE

As people find less free stuff available on the internet, they will become more comfortable with the notion of buying online content. It is already hard to find such former staples as a good free e-mail service or free online data storage, as firms like Yahoo nudge customers towards new 'premium' services by making the free services less useful. Theendoffree.com, a website that tracks the shift towards paid-for content and services, posts daily evidence. The latest news? Visitors to filathlos.gr should no longer expect their Greek sports news free.

Source: *The Economist* (21 December 2002).[6]

E-commerce myths and realities

Promises of destruction of the old order

These new models promised to revolutionise the way in which business and marketing would be carried out in the twenty-first century. Indeed, in a previous edition of this book, we stated that the digital revolution was likely to result in the destruction of the old order of doing business. Companies like Amazon (www.amazon.com), eBay (www.ebay.com) and others were rewriting the business rules. The implications that we and others then saw for businesses included the following:

■ *'Old' businesses and business supply chains will be destroyed.* Traditionally businesses have been organised into industries and industries into 'supply chains' – a division of labour between different organisations, which turns raw materials into products. As technologies enable organisations and individuals to connect with each other in new ways, old supply-chain relationships will be destroyed.

■ *New, knowledge-based goods and services will be created.* Firms will supplement physical outputs with new electronic 'knowledge products'. For pharmaceutical companies, this means offering online medical advice as well as drugs. Pharmaceutical companies are evaluating how to deliver the right information effectively from their vast knowledge of drugs to medical staff when a treatment is being made.

■ *Some organisations will die.* Businesses that fail to embrace the information age will die and be replaced by nimbler, information-rich competitors. Successful organisations will develop approaches to gathering, storing and disseminating knowledge, both between and within organisations.

■ *New global networks will be created.* Global networks will be created which consist of people and organisations who can communicate but who do not know each other. In this environment, buyers will look to brand names they can trust, and a strong brand will be increasingly important in a crowded advertising marketplace.

With the benefit of hindsight, it is interesting to look at how these predictions have fared. While some old businesses and business models were indeed destroyed, most proved surprisingly resilient. New knowledge-based services were certainly created, but for the most part they were extensions or enhancements to existing products or services. Only a few 'pure-play' companies or products managed to gain a real foothold in the marketplace. In the UK one of the most successful was Egg (www.egg.com), which captured the imagination of consumers with its innovative brand, bold images and low pricing (*see* Figure 3.2). Or was it the fact that it was backed by the Prudential, one of the safest and trusted brands in financial services in the UK?

Even if the old order was not destroyed, many of the internet-only companies that managed to survive the initial post-dot-com period went on to thrive. The struggle against the old order may have been somewhat Darwinian at times, but the result was

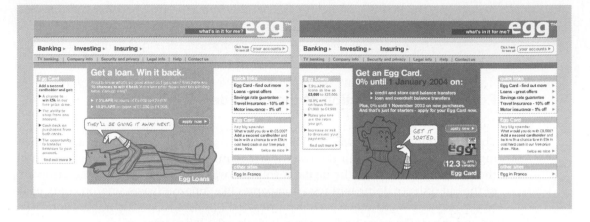

Figure 3.2 Strong branding and imagery at Egg

EXHIBIT 3.2

WEIRD – PROFITABLE NET COMPANIES!

For once, the ever-tart website F**kedcompany.com, which keeps track of the death struggles of troubled companies, didn't have something nasty to say about a dot-com in its crosshairs. 'Hey look', the site's proprietor, Philip Kaplan, noted in a posting on Jan. 28. 'FC favourite Looksmart.com posted a profit. Weird.' Indeed, LookSmart, a search engine company, bagged its first quarterly profit, $3.4 million on $31 million in sales. In spite of the wretched economy and molasses-slow corporate spending on technology, profitable web companies are no longer weird or even unusual. The tally of profitable internet companies in the fourth quarter reached 84 – more than 40 per cent of the 208 publicly traded Net companies. That's up from 49 profitable dot-coms for the first quarter of 2002, the last time *BusinessWeek* conducted such a survey. In key areas such as e-tailing and online finance, profitability has become the rule rather than the exception.

Source: *Business Week* (7 March 2003).[7]

---

an increasing number of profitable and fast-growing companies that were truly 'born on the web' (*see* Exhibit 3.2). The result of the struggle is a richer combination of traditional and modern companies that, between them, have evolved a slightly different set of business processes and rules for competing in today's electronic age.

The internet is a channel (not a business model)

Osterwalder and Pigneur hinted in their framework that the internet is not a business model in itself. For most companies it simply provides an additional channel that has the potential to improve customer service and reduce costs. In some cases it genuinely does enhance the product, but in the majority of cases it is a 'clicks and mortar' extension to the existing product, service or business. The reason why the so-called dinosaurs survived is that their business models were robust and, once they had grafted on an internet channel to the existing business model (often at great expense), they were more than a match for the internet-only upstarts.

And it was expensive to build these internet channels. For example, the leading European banks invested huge sums on their online offerings during the dot-com boom. Spain's SCH spent more than €500 million to acquire the Latin American financial website Patagon in 2000. Spanish rival BBVA linked up with French bank to create an online financial empire covering Spain, UK and Germany. (The UK and German arms closed a year later and only BBVA's Spanish internet bank, uno-e.com, survives.) SCH has similarly had to scale back Patagon's operations: after a major cost-cutting exercise, its losses were reduced to €600,000 in the first quarter of 2002 compared with €5.1 million a year earlier. It is also instructive to learn that European banks invested €13 billion on internet and call centre technologies between 1999 and 2001. To what end? According to the research company Forrester, the five biggest internet banks in Spain lost more than €15 million in the first quarter of 2002, a rise of 9 per cent on the previous year. Banco Popular's bancopopular-e.com (*see* Figure 3.3) was the only online bank to be trading profitably in Spain during 2002.

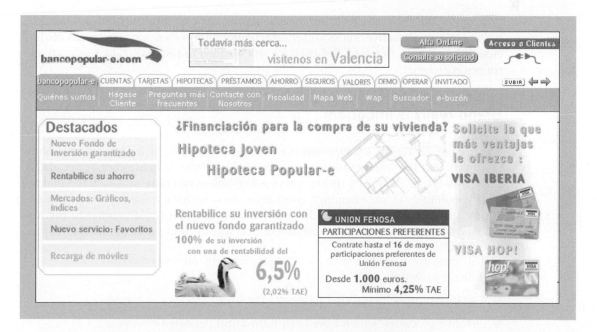

Figure 3.3 Banco Popular's profitable online banking offering
Source: Banco Popular-e website (www.bancopopular-e.com, 2003).

EXHIBIT 3.3

RETHINKING INTERNET BANKING IN SPAIN

The land-grab is over in Europe's internet banking market and many banks are reining in their ambitions, to counter mounting losses. Once, it was claimed that the internet would make bank branches obsolete. But internet banking is supplementing rather than replacing branches and so banks are having to rethink their strategies. When Forrester Research asked European banks what impact the internet has had on branch distribution, three quarters said little or none and 61 per cent believe the branch will remain the primary retail banking interface in 2007.

'The branch continues to be the most important channel', says Gerardo Babio, director of technology services at Grupo Popular, Spain's third largest banking group. Spain has the biggest branch network in Europe relative to its population. Grupo Popular, which includes flagship Banco Popular and five other banks, has more than 2,400 branches. 'Spanish customers use branches a lot and the branch network is growing', says Babio. In northern Europe, the picture looks different. Anticipating the demise of the physical distribution network, banks in the UK, France and Germany closed 11 per cent of their branches between 1995 and 2000, according to the study by Forrester. In Sweden, 39 per cent of consumers bank online, while in Germany penetration is 22 per cent. But for Europe as a whole, internet banking is used by less than 20 per cent.

Source: Financial Times (5 June 2002).[8]

It may have taken them longer, and at significant cost, but most European banks today have an attractive 'clicks and mortar' combination that suits the needs of their customers who, as Exhibit 3.3 shows, are still wedded to the branch as a primary distribution channel.

Brand really is important

The cartoon in Figure 3.4 appeared the *New Yorker* in 1993. It reflected a commonly held view that the internet hid a company's failings from the customer. A decade on, the reality is that everybody thinks you're a dog, unless you have managed to build the same capabilities as 'old-economy' companies. So what have these so-called dinosaurs got that the new-age companies do not? The answer is not too dissimilar to the four pillars of Osterwalder and Pigneur's model that was introduced earlier in the chapter:

- a strong customer base, with many customers who are extremely loyal and difficult to switch;

- a well-positioned brand that reinforces the loyalty factor;

- effective processes, which have been honed and perfected over years;

- a proven financial model that consistently generates not just revenues but profits as well.

"On the Internet, nobody knows you're a dog."

Figure 3.4 'On the internet, nobody knows you're a dog'
Source: *New Yorker* (5 July 1993).

A new model for electronic marketing

B2B = 'back to basics'

This leads us to one of the most important conclusions of all, with significant implications for electronic marketing. Technology allows us to different things, but more often than not its real benefit is to allow us to do the same things better, or more efficiently. Successful marketers are not blinded by technology or the internet. Rather, they use it wisely to get the basic things right – create good products, focus on the customer, generate a profit. In the rest of this book we will concentrate on these basics of marketing.

All this suggests that we require a modified (as opposed to radically different) marketing model. In the following section, we present such a model as the basis for the discussions in the rest of this book. It builds on four themes:

- marketing must be driven by an acceptance that we now live in a buyer-driven world;

- traditional marketing must become technology-enabled – in other words, electronic marketing;

- electronic marketing is more than internet marketing;

- a new electronic marketing framework is required to integrate all these new components.

Figure 3.5 Patient and doctor information at WebMD
Source: WebMD website (www.healtheon.com, 2003).

Electronic marketing in a buyer-driven world

As we discussed in the previous chapter, control over the customer interaction can shift as the electronic age puts more power into the hands of the buyer than the seller (for example C2C or C2B models). The shift empowers the buyer with information and allows consumers to decide for themselves what, where and when they should buy. Car insurance is routinely purchased over the telephone, after ringing around to find the best price. Car buyers can check and compare car prices over the internet before they enter the showroom. With internet auctions, buyers set the price, not the sellers. In the USA many patients will search for advice on their symptoms on websites such as WebMD (*see* Figure 3.5) before they go to see their family doctor – a feature that shifts the balance of power significantly away from the GP into the hands of the patient.

This is a lesson that marketers must learn. The world has changed – and the marketing function needs to adapt as well.

Electronic marketing is technology-enabled marketing

Throughout this book we will explore the impact that technology and the internet will have on the marketing function. Customer segmentation is moving into a new information-rich era based on behaviour rather than the traditional demographic

Table 3.2 Traditional versus electronic marketing

Marketing area	Traditional marketing	Electronic marketing	Marketing methods
Pricing	Seller-driven	Buyer-driven	Internet/digital TV
Segmentation	Demographic	Biographic	Customer database
Advertising	Broadcast	Interactive	Internet/digital TV
Promotions	Mass	Tailored	Customer database
Sales management	Data with sales department	Shared data	Marketing information systems
Distribution channels	Intermediaries	Direct	Multi-channel
Customer ownership	Company	Network	Alliances
Product	Constrained	Buyer-driven	Marketing information systems

methods. Promotional and marketing communications activities are becoming more targeted as a result of more, and better, information. Distribution channels are multiplying and intermediaries are coming under increasing threat as manufacturers market their products directly to the customer. Companies will be forced to adapt their marketing models in order to create an effective response to these changes. Technology and the greater availability of data are increasingly driving changes in the organisation–customer interaction. Some of the responses required, and the implications for marketing, are summarised in Table 3.2.

Electronic marketing is more than internet marketing

Much of Part I of this book refers to the role of the internet and the realities of e-commerce and e-commerce business models. While e-commerce is indeed about the internet, it also encompasses much more. Electronic marketing is not just marketing carried out over the internet. It involves the effective use of technology in all its forms, but in a manner in which the technology plays a supporting role, driven by the business and by marketing's needs. In fact, the most important piece of technology in electronic marketing is probably not the internet at all. It is more likely to be the database that holds valuable data about the most critical resource that a marketer needs – the customer. We will explore the role of the customer database later in this book, but we will also expand our discussion of electronic marketing into other areas of technology. We will cover customer relationship management (CRM) systems, applications of technology in market research, call centre technology and sales force automation tools, among others. By the end of this book, we hope to have convinced you that internet marketing is only one small component of a much broader subject area known as electronic marketing.

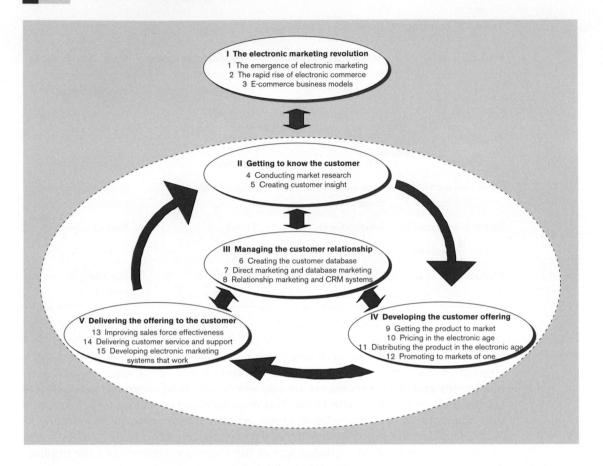

Figure 3.6 Framework for electronic marketing in the twenty-first century

A framework for electronic marketing in the twenty-first century

In the remainder of this book, we examine some of the specific ways in which marketing must change in the twenty-first century. We will use a framework (*see* Figure 3.6) for:

■ getting to know the customer more intimately than we have in the past, and creating new insights into the customer base;

■ managing the relationship with the customer through more effective use of customer information and customer database technology;

■ developing the customer offering, using technology and the internet to enhance the product, price, place and promotion elements of the offering;

■ delivering the offering to the customer, again using technology and the internet to support effective sales and service delivery.

Part II

GETTING TO KNOW THE CUSTOMER

Part II of this book deals with getting to know and understand your customers: who they are, what they want, and how they wish to be served. This customer insight is created by analysing and mining the information that has been gathered from both external market research and internal customer information from the company's own systems.

Part II contains two chapters:

4 CONDUCTING MARKET RESEARCH
5 CREATING CUSTOMER INSIGHT

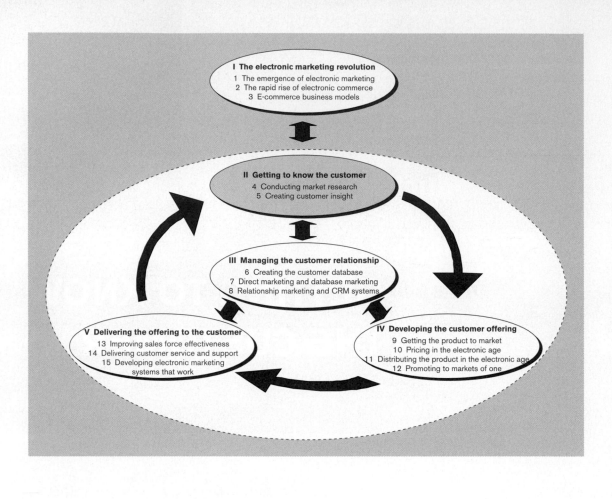

We have deliberately built the book around this framework, which we repeat at the beginning of each of the five sections into which the chapters of this book have been organised.

Summary

While classifications such as B2B, B2C and G2C are useful in setting the broad scope of e-commerce activities, we require other frameworks to show how new business models work. Rappa's online categorisation is an excellent starting point, with categories such as affiliates, communities, infomediaries and merchants. Osterwalder and Pigneur (2002) shed further light with their four pillars of product innovation, customer relationship, infrastructure management and financials. While many internet start-ups had the first three pillars in place, only a few have a strong financial model and underlying profitability. While some old businesses have been destroyed in the face of internet-based competition, many have proved remarkably resilient. With hindsight, marketers must conclude that the internet is a new channel rather than a new business model, and that brand is still very important. We propose a new model for electronic marketing based around acceptance that we live in a buyer-driven world, that marketing must become technology-enabled, that electronic marketing is more than internet marketing and, finally, that a new electronic marketing framework is required to integrate these new components.

Case study

European air travel

Figure 3.7

The rise of the low-cost airlines

The big airlines may rule the skies, but on the internet they face tough competition from upstart online agencies and 'no-frills' airlines that only sell via the web. Type in the words 'low cost European flights' into a search engine and Ryanair, a 'no-frills' European carrier, should appear high in the list of sites found. The airline uses a search engine optimisation service to stand out in the crowded online travel market. This is just one example of how low-cost carriers and online agencies such as Expedia are challenging the traditional airlines with clever online strategies and products designed specifically for the internet age. The websites of travel suppliers – airlines, hotels and car rental firms – retain a slender lead over the independent agencies in online bookings in the USA. But the gap is closing fast. In 2001 agencies captured 45 per cent of online bookings, a 22 per cent increase over the previous year. The suppliers' share, meanwhile, fell by 25 per cent. Despite depressed economies and the collapse in air travel after September 11, the online travel market has proved surprisingly robust. US leisure travellers spent $14.2 billion online in 2001, a drop of only 15 per cent on a forecast made before the terrorist attacks. In 2003 more than 10 per cent of the US travel market will be booked online. 'There is no question that more and more tickets will be bought on the internet,' says Trevor Heley, marketing director at SITA, the airline-owned travel technology provider.

Industry consolidation

The online travel industry is rapidly consolidating. The five largest online agencies account for two thirds of the market and are using their muscle to get better deals from suppliers. They are also diversifying beyond air travel – Priceline.com now sells more hotel and car rentals than airline tickets. This diversity allowed the online agencies to weather the recent slump in air travel better than the airline websites. The web agencies have finally shaken off the dot-com stigma to become sizable and profitable businesses. Travelocity handled $3.1 billion of gross bookings in 2001 and its revenues rose 50 per cent to more than $300 million. Compared to the aggressive growth strategies of the web agencies, the airlines' enthusiasm for e-commerce often seems half-hearted. 'Their attitude of mind varies a lot', says Heley of SITA. 'Some are willing to commit a great amount of money to their website. Others, however, are still trying to find their way.'

Traditional airlines spend about 15 per cent of their revenues on selling their tickets through travel agents. They have long sought to cut these distribution costs by getting more customers to buy tickets direct from them. However, many people prefer to buy via an agent because they get a better deal – agencies can compare rival carriers and may offer special fares. 'There really is no incentive to use the airline's website when you can get a better deal through an agent', says Mark Raskino, research director at Gartner G2. The result is that around 80 or 90 per cent of a traditional airline's inventory of seats is still sold through travel agents. The remaining share is typically split equally between online agencies and the airline's own website. But every ticket sold online means less commission for the travel agents and, because of their importance, the airlines have had to tread carefully on the internet. 'In the early days, many airlines did not want to upset their agents and were nervous about the channel mix', says Heley. Despite the agents' opposition, the trend to buy travel online seems unstoppable. In January, US carrier Delta Air Lines sold more than half a million tickets via its website, double the figure of January 2001. Around 10 per cent of Delta's ticket sales are made online compared with the two to six per cent achieved by other carriers.

The move to the internet

Another carrier taking the lead on the internet is British Airways. Along with other cost-cutting measures, the troubled airline plans to cut agents' booking fees and encourage customers to book on its website. BA wants to emulate the success of the low-cost airlines in selling online. It accepts agents are important but has targeted £100 million in annual savings from getting more customers to book online. To encourage travellers to buy direct, BA will make its cheapest fares available only on its website. This move is likely to further irritate travel agents, but BA believes tough measures are essential to turn around its business. 'BA's announcement has served as a wake-up call for other airlines'. says Heley. The low-cost carriers have no worries about upsetting travel agents. From the outset, most have chosen to only sell direct, first via call centres and more recently via their websites. EasyJet, a UK-based low-cost carrier, has seen the percentage of online sales soar from 50 per cent in 1999 to 89 per cent in December 2001.

Sources: *Financial Times* (March 11 2002);[9] Ryanair website (www.ryanair.com, 2003).

Case study questions

1 Why is the travel industry consolidating rapidly?

2 Why have some online agencies diversified beyond air travel?

3 Why do some travellers still prefer to buy through travel agents?

4 Many airlines are moving very tentatively into direct online booking. Why do you think this is so?

5 'The trend to buy travel online is unstoppable.' Discuss.

Questions and exercises

Questions

1 Why is profitability so important in assessing business models?

2 Why should we consider the internet as a channel rather than a business model?

3 What do you understand by the term 'electronic marketing'?

4 Why is brand still so important in the age of electronic marketing?

Online exercises

1 Name ten websites that you have accessed recently and categorise them in terms of Rappa's framework in Table 3.1.

2 Visit Priceline.com's website (www.priceline.com). What services is it offering in addition to online travel?

References

1 www.netmarketseurope.com/insider/basics2.shtml

2 Rappa, M. (2002). *Managing the Digital Enterprise*, www.digitalenterprise.org/models/models.html

3 Osterwalder, A. and Pigneur, Y. (2002). 'An e-business model ontology for modelling e-business', paper presented at the 15th Bled Electronic Commerce Conference, 17–19 June.

4 Osterwalder and Pigneur, 'An e-business model ontology for modelling e-business'.

5 Bughin, J.R., Hasker, S.J., Segel, E.S.H. and Zeisser, M.P. (2001). 'What went wrong for online media?', *McKinsey Quarterly*, No. 4.

6 *The Economist* (2002). 'Profits at last', 21 December.

7 Mullaney, T. (2003). 'The web is finally catching profits', *Business Week*, 7 March.

8 Nairn, G. (2002). 'An urgent rethink on internet strategies', *Financial Times*, 5 June.

9 Nairn, G. (2002). 'A challenge from online agencies', *Financial Times*, 11 March.

4

Conducting market research

Learning objectives

Once you have read this chapter you will:

- appreciate the market research process;
- understand how electronic marketing and the internet has changed the way secondary market research is conducted;
- understand the impact of electronic marketing and the internet on primary data collection;
- understand the use of technology in analysing market research data.

Contents

DATA COLLECTION – PRIMARY RESEARCH

■ Three methods of primary data collection

■ Technology-enabled observation

■ Technology-enabled surveying

■ Technology-enabled experimentation

■ Continuous market research

OTHER PRIMARY RESEARCH APPLICATIONS

■ Advertising research

■ Public relations research

■ Linking research databases: T-groups

USING TECHNOLOGY TO ANALYSE INFORMATION

■ Providing faster statistical analysis

■ Analytical tools

SUMMARY

CASE STUDY

Introduction

Market research is the cornerstone of any successful marketing plan. The success of the big names in consumer branding, such as Proctor & Gamble and Unilever, is built upon extensive market research. Market research is the principle that before you can meet your customers needs, you first have to understand who your customers are and what needs they have. The market research industry has grown to the extent that in the USA alone it is a $6-billion-a-year industry.

Market research used to be dominated by companies that employed large teams of field researchers equipped with clipboards and pens, set loose on the general public to conduct face-to-face interviews. Not any more. Information technology, the internet and software applications have revolutionised the process by which modern marketing research is conducted. It used to be project-based where a marketing director would commission research for a specific purpose such as a new product launch. The advent of new technology and the internet now means that market research can be conducted on a continuous and dynamic basis. We also see market research principles applied in many of the approaches to quality. One of the first steps, for example, in the 'six sigma' quality programme is to get 'the voice of the customer'. The foundation of any quality programme is understanding what your customer wants. We will now look in more detail at how electronic marketing and technology have changed the way we conduct market research.

The market research process

The overall market research process

There are many different reasons for conducting market research. These can range from developing a new product to testing the effectiveness of a new advertising campaign. Typically, a key driver of the scope and extent of research will be the size of the overall investment. New product introductions requiring significant investment tend to have a significant budget for market research.

The five steps in market research

There are typically five steps in the market research process:

- *Define research objectives*. The first step in the process is to define clearly the research objectives. These should be specific and measurable. An example of a poorly defined research objective for the launch of a new car would be 'to identify the potential market for a new family saloon in Europe'. A more effective objective would be 'to identify the market size for a 2000cc saloon amongst 25–35-year-old young professionals in France'. This revised objective provides the market researcher with a more well-defined research problem and the result is likely to be a much more meaningful piece of research.

- *Develop research plan*. The next step is to develop the research plan. After the list of specific informational requirements (the data list) has been built up in problem definition, it is necessary to determine the sources from which the data can be found. These sources can be either primary (where we conduct the research directly) or secondary (where we rely on existing research). The size of the budget is often a key determinant of whether to choose primary or secondary sources, since primary research is typically more expensive.

- *Collect data*. There is often a misconception that market research involves little more than an interviewer in the street with a questionnaire and clipboard. While this is appropriate for some research programmes, there are others where the interviewing is conducted in someone's home, others that require no interviewer at all (for example, postal surveys), some that involve no questioning (such as observation studies), and yet others that rely exclusively on existing reports or other documentation (that is, secondary data sources).

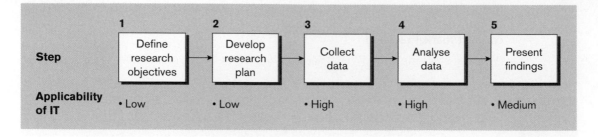

Figure 4.1 Applicability of IT in the five steps of market research

■ *Analyse data.* Once the research data has been collected it must be analysed. Depending on the size and complexity of the research, it may be necessary to use statistical tools to analyse the data. The statistical tools will also give measures of how confident the researchers can be that the results are representative of the total market, based on a given sample size.

■ *Present findings.* The final step in the process is to present the findings to management. It is at this stage that the importance of having a very well-defined market research process becomes clear. The results can be inconclusive unless the market researcher has used the correct sample size and there has been no bias in the data collection.

As can be seen from Figure 4.1, electronic marketing and IT have different roles to play in different stages of the process.

In this chapter, we will focus primarily on steps three and four. We begin with an analysis of the applicability of IT and other forms of technology in data collection, starting with secondary research before moving to primary research.

Data collection – secondary research

Start with secondary data collection

Secondary sources involve information that already exists, such as company records, company reports, government statistics, newspaper and journal articles and commercial market research agency reports. It is always worth exploring using secondary sources – as a first resort – before commissioning more expensive and time-consuming programme of collecting 'new' information using 'primary' research methods.[1] In fact, the major search activity that precedes the purchase of agency research or starting an in-company research project involves secondary data and, because of the heavy use of such sources, there is a need to adopt a critical perspective in using them. Researchers need to satisfy four conditions:

■ the secondary sources must be impartial to be reasonably sure that there is no slant or bias in the information resulting from the provider or compiler attempting to make a case for or against something;

■ the sources must be valid – that is, whether the information is what the researcher wants to know;

■ the sources must be reliable – that is, whether the information is representative of the group it purports to describe (for instance, a sample of 12 consumers is unlikely to reflect all consumers in a national population);

■ the sources must provide information with internal homogeneity, or consistency of, for example, a set of figures.

We will now look at some of the key sources of secondary data as well as some of the recent changes that have been driven by the internet. The key areas we are going to look at are:

■ internal data sources

■ general external data sources

■ specialised external data sources

■ the trend towards internet-based market research

■ the globalisation of information services companies.

Internal data sources

Internal company data can be an invaluable source of customer information. This information can include things like price lists, inventory levels, receivables and payables. Internal sales figures are routinely analysed by both sales and marketing managers to provide a perspective on trends in product sales, distribution channels and customers. Internal data sources are also becoming more information-rich as the cost of holding information decreases, providing marketing managers with perhaps the most valuable source of information for market research purposes. A quote from Mitchell (1996)[2] gives some idea of the amount of customer and product data that is held by today's large retailers, and how this data is being used for marketing purposes:

> An inspection of a resulting retail loyalty scheme database revealed, for a certain 'Mrs Brown', her address and a variety of behavioural information including: she shops once per week, usually on a Friday, has a baby (because she buys nappies), spends £90 per week on average and usually buys two bottles of gin every week. This information can often be overlaid with data from external data sources such as geo-demographics, lifestyle and financial profiles.

We will see shortly how internal versions of the internet, known as intranets, have also become commonplace in the collation and dissemination of internally-generated market research around organisations. Financial research, in particular, is routinely shared across divisions in large banks and insurance companies, using intranet technology.

External data sources

While internal sources provide the richest source of customer information, external data can also yield valuable information on consumer markets and trends. Many of these are free (either because they are to be found in most public libraries or because they are available free from government departments). As many of these sources are now available online they are even easier to access. Even some of the expensive commercial reports can be found in some libraries. Typical sources of external market research in the UK include:

■ *National press*, such as the *Financial Times*, *The Economist* and *The Times*.

■ *Government sources*, especially the Office of National Statistics (ONS) which records UK official statistics, including data on the economy, population and society at national and local level (*see* Figure 4.2). Other sources include the Business Statistics Office (BSO) and Her Majesty's Stationery Office (HMSO), which publishes a wide range of market reports. The electoral register can also be used to help define the catchment areas of retail outlets and the number of potential customers.

■ *Trade associations*, such as the British Toy and Hobby Association (BTHA).

■ *Local chambers of commerce*, which have statistics on companies in their trading area and information on trading conditions.

■ *Trade magazines*, including *The Grocer*, *Motor Trader*, *The Publican*, *Marketing Week* and *Campaign*.

Yearbooks and trade directories can also provide a surprising amount of good research data, providing names and addresses of companies by country and by product category. Some of the more popular in the UK include:

■ *Kelly's Guide* – lists industrial, commercial and professional organisations in UK, giving a description of their main activities and providing their addresses. Listings are alphabetical according to trade description and also according to company name.

■ *Key British Enterprises* – a register of 25,000 top UK companies that provides the company name and address and also some basic financial data such sales, number of employees, and the Standard Industrial Code (SIC).

■ *UK Trade Names* – lists trade names and the parent company.

■ *Who Owns Whom* – lists firms and their parent organisation.

Specialised external data sources

Having exhausted the general external sources, the next step can be to consult some of the many specialised research companies that provide a variety of off-the-shelf and customised market research reports. These include the following UK companies:

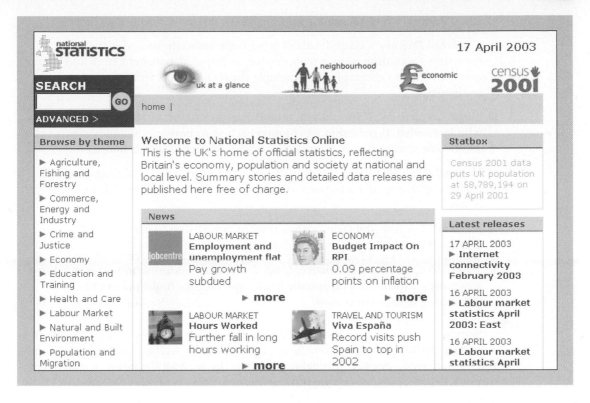

Figure 4.2 UK Office of National Statistics online service

Source: Office of National Statistics website (www.statistics.gov.uk, 2003), Crown copyright is reproduced with the permission of the controller of HMSO.

- *Business Monitor* – gives statistics for different products, for example, numbers of manufacturers, industry sales and import levels.

- *Family Expenditure Survey* – gives average weekly expenditure on many products and services according to different regions, size of household, age of head of household and household income levels (this is particularly useful for estimating market size and potential sales levels).

- *Regional Trends* – plots population size and structure trends through the regions, together with more on regional income and expenditure.

- *ICC Business Ratio Reports.*

- *Economist Intelligence Unit, Euromonitor,* and *Datamonitor.*

- *Henley Centre* – projects future social attitudes, lifestyles, income and expenditure.

- *Market Intelligence (MINTEL)* – monthly reports on profile of different markets.

- *Market Assessment* – reports on profile of different markets.

- *KeyNote* – reports on profile of different markets.

- *Retail Business* – monthly reports on profiles of different retailing markets.

- *The Retail Directory* – gives details of retail trade associations and lists retail companies according to type (cooperative, multiple, department store and so on) and according to geography (for example the retail outlets within many towns are listed).

- *Target Group Index (TGI)* – annual profile of most product markets in terms of who buys what. It publishes 34 volumes each year, based on samples of around 26,000 consumers, and is compiled by British Market Research Bureau.

- *National Readership Survey* – profile of readers of newspapers and magazines (for advertising media selection); that is, when matched with profile of target market.

- *BRAD (British Rate And Data)* – gives costs of advertising in press, radio, poster, cinema, TV and all other mass media.

- *MEAL (Media Expenditure Analysis Limited)* – provides information on competitors' advertising expenditure on specific brands per month. It also names the advertising agency concerned.

Similar sources are available in other countries. For example, the Central Bureau voor de Statistiek provides government statistics in the Netherlands, while Kompass and Euromonitor operate throughout Europe. Increasingly, market research companies are providing their information in online format, both on CD-Rom and via the internet.

The trend towards internet-based market research

Last but not least, the internet continues to offer ever-expanding quantities of data about markets. Search engines such as Yahoo (www.yahoo.com) and Google (www.google.com) will return literally millions of results for the most simple of internet searches, though the sources and criteria for evaluating the data must be uppermost in the researcher's mind when trawling through some websites. It is a free research service and can provide researchers with an abundance of good market information.

For most serious marketing research situations, a commercial online service is likely to provide more comprehensive information. Already, the internet has become the medium of choice for accessing the many commercial online services that are currently available. For example, marketers can access DataStar's databases on the internet (*see* Figure 4.3). Similarly, Questel•Orbit's QWEB internet service makes all of its 100 databases (covering patents, trademarks, technical and scientific information, and chemistry) available through the web. Most large companies will use at least one of these commercial online services for accessing general news information or research on more specialised subjects. Today, there are tens of thousands of commercial databases available worldwide, covering information on business, technical and scientific information, company reports, broker reports, newspaper and journal articles and patent documents. The advantages of these commercial online information services include:

Figure 4.3 DataStar service from Dialog

Source: Dialog website (www.dialog.com, 2003), a Thomson business.

- *Variety*. Many online services provide a 'supermarket' service whereby many different services can be accessed by subscribing to a single supplier.

- *Up-to-date information*. Many databases are updated on at least a daily basis and a large number even more frequently.

- *Cost efficiency*. Although commercial online services charge either an up-front or monthly/quarterly charge, or charge on an actual usage basis, they can provide an extremely cost-efficient means of accessing a wide variety of information.

- *Accessibility of information*. Using the internet, databases can be accessed 24 hours a day, 7 days a week from any part of the globe.

More of the market research companies operating in this space can be termed content aggregators, in other words companies that gather and aggregate information from a variety of different sources and market them in an online format to their own customer base. Some of the major online content aggregators are included in Table 4.1.

Table 4.1 Selected commercial online information services

Service	URL	Description
Dialog	www.dialog.com	One of the pioneers of online information. Encompasses three product lines: DataStar, Dialog, and Profound. Purchased by the Thomson Corporation in 2000.
Dun & Bradstreet	www.dnb.com	Provider of business information for credit, marketing, purchasing and receivables management decisions.
Hoover's	www.hoovers.com	All-round provider of business information services. Products include Hoover's Online and The Business Network. Hoover's now lists more than 2,800 company names and addresses. It lists all US public companies, large US private companies and the largest non-US companies. In addition, a UK site mirrors the services found for UK company searches.
LexisNexis	www.lexis-nexis.com	A subsidiary of Reed Elsevier, the Anglo-Dutch world-leading publisher and information provider. Provides 10,000 databases of legal, business, government and academic information.
Questel•Orbit	www.questel.orbit.com	Scientific, technical and intellectual property service formerly owned by France Telecom. Specialises in patent, trademark, scientific, technical and chemical information. Serves 12,000 clients worldwide.

Globalisation of information services companies

The increasing use of technology in market research has led to a need for significant capital expenditure. This has driven the market research industry, which was traditionally a fragmented and nationally-based industry, into a more professional, highly capitalised, multinational industry. The extent to which the online information services industry has changed and consolidated is hinted at in Table 4.1. Most of the online service providers are owned by a small number of multinational information companies. A typical example is Dialog, whose history shows how information services companies grew and consolidated through the three ages of computerisation that we introduced in Chapter 1 (*see* Exhibit 4.1).

EXHIBIT 4.1

CREATING A GLOBAL DIALOG

1964 The Space Race is in full swing. Apollo is on the drawing board and the USA has made a dramatic entrance into the Space Age. In a small office in Palo Alto, Roger Summit is assigned to manage an obscure programme for Lockheed. One year later, the laboratory demonstrates its first interactive retrieval service.

1968 Though they're still a year away from putting a man on the moon, NASA is focused on even more distant goals. They've asked Lockheed to study methods for managing large data files and the Recon Project is underway. Summit responds with an innovation in the way data is handled. He calls this new language 'Dialog'.

1972 Dialog offers the first publicly available online research service. A company is born. Our world continues to change at a dizzying pace. Though the internet is still 15 years away, technologists have seen the vision of worldwide instantaneous data communication. More and more content is added to the Dialog databases.

1981 The PC is born and Dialog is there, now a subsidiary of Lockheed. Others are now entering the fray. The Swiss Government participates in the formation of Radio Suisse to provide information services to industry. The service initially focuses on a niche market: biomedical and pharmaceutical information. Its name: DataStar. DataStar quickly grows to become a major player in European news and professional information. At the same time, a young London market researcher decides there must be a better way. Founded on a shoestring, his Market Analysis and Information Database (MAID) quickly became invaluable to market research professionals.

1988 The game is on! Knight-Ridder purchases Dialog from Lockheed. A few years later, DataStar is also acquired. MAID joins the internet revolution with the launch of Profound. DataStar introduces its web interface, too.

1997 Three of the most powerful brands in online information are united for the first time, providing unprecedented researching power.

2000 As people around the world celebrate the new millennium, there is yet another convergence as Thomson acquires Dialog. The cycle is complete. New possibilities arise as the most powerful information company in the world joins with the company that started it all.

2001 NewsEdge, a leading provider of innovative global real-time news solutions, and Intelligence Data, a business unit of Thomson responsible for developing, marketing and providing support for financial products and services, become part of Dialog.

Source: Dialog website (www.dialog.com, 2003).

Data collection – primary research

Three methods of primary data collection

Primary research, or field research, is of critical importance when developing a new product or service, and in determining if that product or service will be accepted and bought by particular categories of consumer. Because of its complexity, primary data collection is typically managed as a discrete project and usually outsourced to special-ist market research companies, most of which have invested large sums of money in automating the data collection process. Primary data is collected through:

- observation techniques
- surveying techniques
- experimentation.

Figure 4.4 shows that the techniques of observation, interview and experiment are more than mere categories and actually fit a continuum in terms of the degree of con-trol the researcher can exert over the variables being researched.

Technology-enabled observation

Observation is regarded as the classical method of research and can be carried out in one of three main ways:[3]

- *Audits and consumer panels*, including manual shop audits as practised by market research companies such as ACNielsen and Taylor Nelson Sofres, as well as research of traffic patterns and volumes at shopping centres, stores or poster sites.

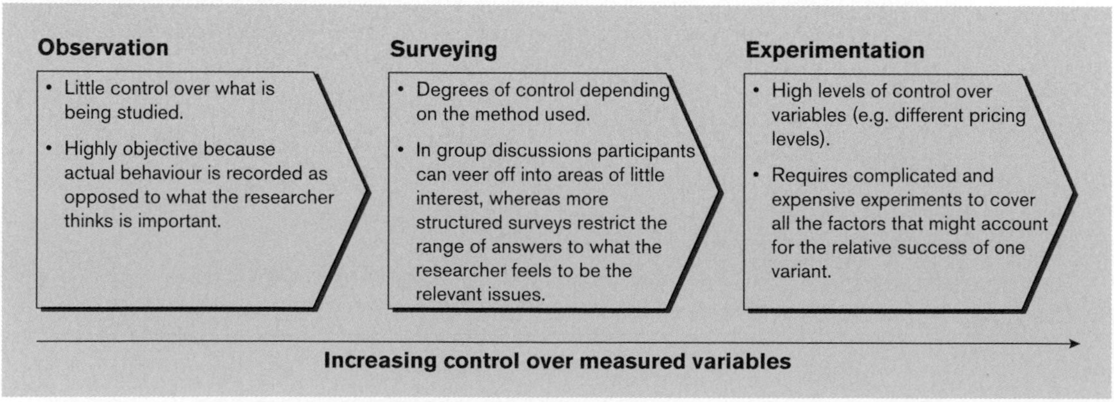

Figure 4.4 The primary data continuum

■ *Recording devices*, including a wide variety of counting meters as well as devices that identify reactions to different types of advertisements (such as psycho-galvanometers, for tracking minute changes in perspiration rates, and the tachistoscope for measuring pupil dilation).

■ *Watching buyer behaviour*, including a number of observation techniques from hidden video cameras to 'mystery shoppers'.

Traditionally, technology played little or no role in observation techniques. This was particularly true of audits and watching buyer behaviour, where research was typically conducted by the ubiquitous researcher with clipboard and pen. Nowadays, auditing has become more sophisticated and technology plays a much greater role in this type of research.

Different types of recording devices

Various electronic devices offer alternatives to a human observer watching an event. Recording devices come in many different varieties, including:

■ *Psycho-galvanometer*, or *lie detector* – records changes in perspiration rates as a result of emotional reaction to stimuli such as test advertisements.

■ *Tachistoscope* – allows an object such an advertisement or a product package to be illuminated for a fraction of a second to test the advertisement or package for initial impact, legibility and recognition. The marketer can use such techniques to pre-test alternative colour combinations or positions for their brand name and copy headline.

■ *Eye camera* – traces the path the eye takes over a space. For example, a photograph of a street scene with a billboard can be shown to respondents, whose eye-paths over the picture can be tracked. Whether the eye goes to the billboard or not, and if it does, whether it goes to the main copy headline or brand name can be recorded with some objectivity.

■ *Videotaping* – pioneered by companies like SAS Airlines and now common practice in market research (*see* Exhibit 4.2).

■ *Checkout EPOS* (electronic point-of-sale) and *EFTPOS* (electronic funds transfer at point of sale) – used in supermarkets for scanning information linked with loyalty cards to record customer purchase behaviour. This is observation as no questions are asked of the customer. Companies like Brickstream (www.brickstream.com) sell software that allows marketers to build a more complete understanding of the customer experience in the shopping environment.

■ *Set meters* – used for monitoring the television viewing habits of respondents in consumer panels. Response levels to advertisements can be matched with time (and TV channel) of viewing such commercials. The set meter records whether the set is on or off at regular intervals and, if it is on, which channel has been selected. As we will see later in this chapter, these electronic devices have become more sophisticated and are typically now referred to as *peoplemeters*.

EXHIBIT 4.2

UNDERSTANDING WHAT HAPPENS IN THE SHOWER

Determined to figure out what people really wanted in a showerhead, Moen Inc. began to look for ways to videotape people in the shower. It engaged QualiData Research, one of the pioneers of a growing field called 'observational research' or 'ethnography'. The immediate challenge was how to install a small moisture-proof camera next to a shower-head without it fogging up or electrocuting someone. Getting volunteers was simpler. The company contacted nudists and others, offering money for the chance to videotape them lathering up in their own homes. 'Most people thought it was fun to be a part of', recalls Hy Mariampolski, managing director of QualiData. 'It's the kind of thing you do on a dare.' So in 2001, QualiData taped several dozen people of all shapes and sizes while a camera crew monitored the event from just outside the bathroom. 'We found the spray was too restricted to be really comfortable', says Dr Mariampolski. On tape, the subjects used the water to relax or energise themselves. They lost track of time. One man prayed. For many people, 'it's more than a cleaning experience', Mariampolski explains. 'They're looking for some psychic outcome.' Based on Moen's research, its *Revolution* showerhead was born. Priced at the upper end of showerheads, the *Revolution* offers users a dial that can be easily adjusted with one hand. The shower-head spins the droplets, which hit all points of the body with more force. The observational research has 'given us a much better understanding about what occurs in people's showers', says Jack Suvak, director of market research for Ohio-based Moen.

Source: Christian Science Monitor (28 May 2002).[4]

Marketing via the internet provides related examples of non-human observation of behaviour – in terms of the digital recording of which websites are visited and by whom. In an internet environment, market research companies like DoubleClick (www.doubleclick.com) observe and track consumers' web-surfing habits on a routine basis. In fact, the widespread use of the internet for research purposes has also spawned a number of companies that focus specifically and solely on internet research. These include Jupiter Media Metrix (www.jmm.com), Harris Interactive (www.harrisinteractive.com) and Nielsen NetRatings (www.nielsennetratings.com).

Benefits of observation

The advantage of observation is its objectivity, because what actually happens is recorded, compared with the subjectivity of questioning approaches, which, by the very nature of question wording and interviewing, can introduce some bias. However, such objectivity is lost if subjects are aware of the observation and modify their behaviour. In practice, the researcher may be unable even to approach the ideal of effective data collection through observation. But does the fact that the researcher does not have to gain respondent cooperation pose an ethical problem? The shower example in Exhibit 4.2 might not fall foul of this because cooperation was sought, but what if respondents are observed in similarly intimate situations without their permission? Crawford (1970)[5] discusses the use of (unknown to those being observed) one-way mirrors in ladies changing rooms in American department stores to observe how bras were put on and taken off. This was part of a new product development programme by an American women's underwear manufacturer and was employed because it was thought less provocative than asking women direct questions about this sort of intimate product. It was, of course, a totally unethical research approach but it does beg the question of where the line should be drawn for what to observe – and also it raises the ethical issue of whether respondents' cooperation should be initially gained. If it is, then we return to the problem of modified behaviour.

Technology-enabled surveying

Surveying is the most widely used means of collecting primary market research data. Personal interviewing has traditionally been the dominant means of conducting interviews and has typically accounted for the majority of interviewing expenditure. Traditional face-to-face interviewing is now sometimes referred to as PAPI (paper and pencil interviewing) but this interviewing technique has been declining in popularity for some years with the increasing greater use of technology-enabled surveying techniques. In Germany, PAPI has decreased from 65 per cent of all quantitative interviews to 24 per cent between 1990 and 2002 (*see* Figure 4.5).

More commonly used acronyms refer to the three other computer-assisted techniques that have made major inroads into observation and interviewing in recent years:

- computer-assisted personal interviewing (CAPI)
- computer-assisted telephone interviewing (CATI)
- computer-assisted web interviewing (CAWI).

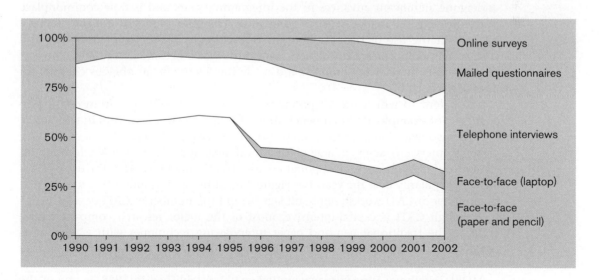

Figure 4.5 Quantitative interviewing techniques in Germany (1990–2002)
Source: ADM website (www.adm-ve.de, 2003).

Computer-assisted personal interviewing (CAPI)

Face-to-face interviewing is becoming increasingly technology-enabled. CAPI is a computer-aided interviewing technique that allows the interviewer to follow an interview script where the sequence of questions is determined by the answers that the interviewee gives (and which are entered into the computer in real time). As each response is given and entered into the PC by the interviewer, the interviewer's next question is determined by the previous response and is immediately flashed on to the interviewer's PC screen. CAPI is, in effect, an electronic hand-held clipboard.

CAPI can be employed in the field or at central market research stations. In some instances, interviewees will complete self-assessment questionnaires without the aid of any interviewers, cutting the cost per response dramatically. The benefit is clear. Consider the situation in which an interviewer is equipped with as many hard copies of the questionnaires needed for that day's interviewing. Each respondent requires a fresh questionnaire and the interviewer has to complete each. Not only will the physical size of the resulting stack of paper create potential problems but the electronic hand-held clipboard helps to avoid errors of routing through the questionnaire. Even the most experienced and highly trained interviewers can easily slip up. For example, if the answer to Question 3 is 'No' then perhaps Question 4 is not relevant and the next question to ask might be, say, Question 22. In the rush of recording answers, watching which should be the next question to ask, an interviewer might go to Question 23 instead. The hand-held clipboard automatically presents the next relevant question to ask, depending on the last answer given.

Computer-assisted telephone interviewing (CATI)

Although the telephone has always been used as an interviewing tool, it is only in recent years that it has become fully technology-enabled through the use of CATI, the telephone-based equivalent to CAPI. CATI originated in the USA in the 1960s but has undergone significant advances in the intervening years and is now commonplace in telephone-based market research companies. The primary reasons for the dramatic increase in the use of the telephone in market research are speed, flexibility and cost. As telecommunications markets around the world became deregulated, the cost of telephone interviewing dropped and made the telephone an obvious channel for interviewing.

The extent to which the telephone is used differs significantly from country to country. For example, the high penetration of telephone-based surveys in the Nordic countries is a reflection of cultural acceptance of the telephone, difficulties of conducting personal interviews across a large geographical area, and relatively low telecommunications costs. As Europe's most populous country, Germany has seen the use of CATI grow in popularity over the years (*see* Figure 4.6), although it is interesting to note that the number of CATI workstations still lags behind the number of CAPI devices.

Although CATI is capital-intensive, most of the major research companies have replaced the traditional pen and paper interviewing techniques with a telephone-based system of data collection. This is true not only in Europe but in other countries as well (*see* Exhibit 4.3).

MORI Telephone Surveys (www.moritel.co.uk), established in 1988, is one of the UK's largest CATI specialists with 80 interviewer stations. In Sweden, which boasts the highest proportion of telephone-based surveying in Europe, research firms like

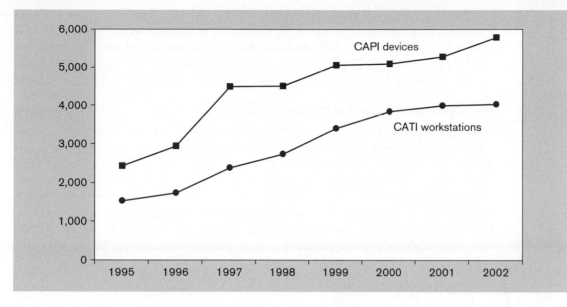

Figure 4.6 CAPI and CATI growth in Germany (1995–2002)
Source: ADM website (www.adm-ve.de, 2003).

EXHIBIT 4.3

HIGH-TECH RESEARCH IN HONG KONG

Taylor Nelson Sofres in Hong Kong no longer uses pen and paper for fieldwork. Instead we have adopted the very latest technologies for our research including CATI (computer-assisted telephone interviewing), CAPI (computer-assisted personal interviewing) and CAWI (computer-assisted web interviewing).

CATI Centre

Our international CATI Centre (CATI Central) is unrivalled in Asia Pacific. Our investment in computer-assisted interviewing technology has resulted in clients selecting us for the speed and accuracy of our data turnaround. If you need to conduct an international study by telephone, then CATI Central is your best option. Our centralised management of projects means that we will take care of coordinating research across different countries so that you need only deal with one point of contact. CATI Central features:

- 55 stations
- calling into 16 Asia Pacific countries
- more than 200 trained interviewers
- native speakers of 8 different Asian languages
- monitoring by multilingual supervisors.

Source: Taylor Nelson Sofres website (www.tnsofres.com, 2003).

SKOP (www.skop.se), Gallup (www.gallup.com) and SIFO (www.sifo.se) can conduct telephone-based surveys and report the findings in a matter of hours. SIFO's 700 part-time interviewers and 200 CATI stations make it the largest and most sophisticated CATI specialist in Sweden.

Computer-assisted web interviewing (CAWI)

CAWI is a self-service version of CAPI conducted over the internet. It usually involves e-mailing respondents with a hyperlink, directing them to a self-completion question-naire hosted by the research agency. The Hong Kong arm of market research firm Taylor Nelson Sofres profiled in Exhibit 4.3 uses CAWI but states that its use in the Asia-Pacific region is still limited. However, a new breed of marketing company has taken up the CAWI challenge. Companies like Deep-insight claim positive feedback from international clients on the speed with which survey results can be delivered by merging traditional research methods with an internet interface (*see* Exhibit 4.4).

EXHIBIT 4.4

DEEP-INSIGHT AT SONOPRESS

Sonopress Ireland is a subsidiary of Sonopress GmbH in Germany, an international company that offers manufacturing services for CD/CD-Rom replication, DVD-Rom and DVD video replication, CD-R/DVD-R sample service, music cassette production and floppy disk replication. The company has a number of significant international clients but was concerned about the quality of its relationships with those clients.

According to Alan Crean, director of sales and marketing: 'We decided to analyse the quality of our customer relationships in a new way. The methodology was recommended to us in view of its depth of analysis, ease of use and flexibility.' The Deep-insight methodology, developed by founder and CEO Dr Pierre Chenet, is based on extensive research in some 700 firms in Scandinavia and Ireland, and measures the quality of relationships between companies and their customers and employees. This novel ele-ment is the delivery mechanism – the assessments are online – delivered via e-mail and the internet. Crean added: 'The relationship quality assessment was targeted at our most strategic customers and confirmed our fears: that we were in a very precarious position where we might rapidly lose a significant number of our most strategic clients.' Deep-insight's analysis of the return on investment (ROI) on customer relationships showed that seven of Sonopress's most strategic clients had a negative ROI. The assessment revealed the reasons why, and in particular that Sonopress suffered from important quality and reliability problems. More importantly, the assessment was able to accurately pinpoint issues relevant to each client. Sonopress's clients perceived the company as being far more 'product' than 'customer' orientated.

Today, Sonopress uses Deep-insight's internet-based assessment tools to monitor customer relationship quality on an ongoing basis.

Source: Deep-insight website (www.deep-insight.com, 2003).

While the use of CAWI is clearly on the increase, there are some drawbacks to its use. Loscher (2001)[6] outlines some of these drawbacks:

> With the exceptions of simplicity and speed, it is hard to identify other significant benefits from using CAWI to access public opinion. Some people are not online – let's call them Joes – so online surveys will not include any Joes. Marys only log on every two weeks, so if you close off the survey after a few days, no Marys. Do not forget about the Berties. They are too busy dealing with the punters to ever log on. Sorry, no Berties. Missing out on the Joes, Marys and Berties would matter less if you were trying to flog holidays or books, but market research is founded on the principles of sampling theory. A fundamental principle of sampling theory is that everyone in the population has an equal chance of selection for interview. Omitting certain segments from the sample raises serious doubts about the integrity of the findings.

This is certainly true of consumer surveys, where sampling techniques are important. However, companies like Deep-insight point to higher response rates, faster responses and lower costs that make the technology particularly attractive in business environments. In business-to-business surveying where most respondents have e-mail addresses and access to the internet at work, it is our experience that response rates in excess of 50 per cent can be achieved due to the ease-of-use of the surveying technique.

Technology-enabled experimentation

Experimentation is the third generic method of collecting primary market research data. It is commonly used in new product development in the form of test marketing. Given the high failure rates among new product launches, it is important to test out new products in a rigorous fashion. Test marketing is standard practice among consumer product manufacturers, but has not reached the same level of sophistication in industrial markets or financial services. Many banks and insurance companies still fail to carry out adequate test marketing before they launch new financial products. There are typically three forms of test marketing:[7]

- standard test marketing
- controlled test marketing
- simulated test marketing.

Standard test marketing

Standard test marketing involves an actual product launch, typically in a small market, to test out consumer reaction to a product. It includes sell-in to the trade and involves complete marketing support. As a means of experimentation in a limited geographical market, standard test marketing provides the best possible insight into potential market acceptance, but it does suffer from some drawbacks. It is regarded by some companies as slow and expensive and, more important, it can provide competitors with advance warning of new product launches. Although standard test marketing has become accepted and sophisticated, newer technology-enabled approaches such as controlled test marketing and simulated test marketing attempt to address its deficiencies.

Controlled test marketing

Controlled test marketing will typically involve a panel of stores with good geographic dispersion to test out new products as well as merchandising for displays, promotions and pricing. It provides an accurate barometer of trade reception and is effective in evaluating issues like unusual shelving requirements. It is more affordable than standard test marketing and minimises exposure if a product fails. A key element of controlled test marketing is scanner-based test marketing, which utilises barcode scanning as a means of providing instantaneous feedback. The growth of EPOS (electronic point of sale) and barcoding in retail stores allows new products to be evaluated very quickly – an important consideration when the success or failure of new fast-moving consumer goods (FMCG) products in a controlled test marketing environment must be determined in a matter of weeks rather than months.

Simulated test marketing (STM)

Simulated test marketing (STM) is also seen as an attractive alternative to standard test marketing. It involves product testing in a simulated environment that does not alert competitors to a new product launch. Consumers are either recruited to buy new items in a 'laboratory store' or are recruited at shopping malls to provide feedback on product and promotional concepts. More high-technology versions involve the use of electronic panellists who sample products at home, review concepts and promotions online, and then provide feedback. STM involves the lowest execution costs of all test marketing and provides the quickest feedback. Market research giant ACNielsen claims that its STM system, known as BASES, has been applied successfully to more than 38,000 new product concepts and holds a 60-per-cent global share of all simulated test marketing for consumer packaged goods (*see* Figure 4.7).

Experimentation in direct marketing

In direct marketing, 'experimentation' is usually referred to as 'testing' and there are two general types that can be distinguished:

- comparing the results from different mailing lists or creative campaigns;
- testing a direct marketing approach on a small scale in order to predict how it works in full.

The former type is a comparative test and the latter is a predictive test. Direct marketers test response rates to, for example:

- different lists, such as lifestyle lists from research companies Experian and Claritas;

Figure 4.7 ACNielsen's STM offering – BASES

Source: ACNielsen BASES website (www.acnielsenbases.com, 2003).

■ timing of campaigns: whether business customers are more likely to spend their budgets at the beginning or end of a financial year.

Marketing experiments can use data from consumer panels or retail audits, and have the advantage that they can demonstrate changes over time more effectively than ad hoc research. The test market is the largest marketing experiment because the whole mix is tested, rather than just one variable. Panel data is particularly useful in test markets because not just sales, but customer profiles, new and repeat buying levels, attitudes, retail preferences, and so on are analysed over a period of time. Such data can be collected using handheld barcode readers. Households in relevant panels are asked to scan all their groceries, key in prices of every item, and scan a barcode on a card to indicate from which store it was purchased and whether a special offer was involved. They may also be asked to scan barcodes that indicate the newspapers and magazines that were read that day and to which radio stations the household had listened. However, it is perhaps doubtful whether those willing and able to perform all these tasks on a daily basis are really representative of the population! Similar experimentation can also be carried out on television audience panels (*see* Exhibit 4.5).

Exhibit 4.5 is an example of how technology facilitates experimentation because it demonstrates a practical way of sending out alternative direct response TV (DRTV) commercials to different, but matched, audiences. Indeed the consumer panel has introduced all three forms of primary data collection method: observation, interview and experimentation. The key element is that the research is continuous. That is, the same respondents are monitored or questioned over time, rather than merely asking people with similar characteristics the same questions at different time intervals.

EXHIBIT 4.5

EXPERIMENTING WITH THE WELSH

A panel in which one of the authors was a participant provides a good example of the uses of this technique. The ITV region of concern was HTV which is a 'split' region consisting of HTV Wales and HTV West. The panel was set up in South Wales where many households tune in to one or other transmitter. The panel was funded in association with retailers and split-run experiments were possible, with different versions of the same direct response TV (DRTV) advertisement being broadcast via the different transmitters. The results could be tracked through analysis of viewing, response to the DRTV commercial and subsequent purchase via the scanned shopping baskets. The author may not have been an ideal panellist due to the lack of dedication to the scanning tasks, but the household concerned was able to receive both HTV Wales and West and occasional 'channel hopping' did indeed reveal different versions of some commercials being transmitted at the same time!

Source: O'Malley, Patterson and Evans (1999).[8]

Continuous market research

Continuous market research is a means of discovering marketing trends by taking a series of samples over an extended period of time. Chisnall (1997)[9] identifies the primary means of conducting continuous market research:

- *Consumer purchase panels*, which are the commonly-used panels, allow market research companies to track consumer purchases and usage. As we have seen, the widespread use of hand-held electronic scanners to capture barcode data has revolutionised the recording, gathering and dissemination of purchase panel data. Electronic data capture and transfer allows purchase data to be collected daily, providing market research companies with almost instantaneous feedback on consumers' responses to marketing initiatives.

- *Telephone panels*, based on regular telephone interviews with a panel of members, are also commonly used to gather market data in both consumer and industrial markets. Central telephone interviewing facilities using CATI are now common.

- *Store audits* provide purchase information from retail outlets. Because sales figures from the factory do not accurately reflect consumer demand, the store audit is an important mechanism for tracking sales promotions, forward stocks and prices as well as actual purchases. Information can be gathered using hand-held barcode scanners, but the trend is to obtain information directly from the electronic point-of-sale (EPOS) equipment at the checkout desk.

Although not always categorised under the heading of continuous market research, omnibus surveys consist of a series of short questions from different clients who

Table 4.2 Global market research companies

Rank	Company	Headquarters	Research revenue (US$m)
1	ACNielsen	USA	1,577
2	IMS Health Inc.	USA	1,131
3	Kantar Group	USA	928
4	Taylor Nelson Sofres	UK	709
5	Information Resources Inc.	USA	531
6	VNU Inc.	USA	526
7	NFO WorldGroup Inc.	USA	470
8	GfK Group	Germany	444
9	Ipsos Group SA	France	304
10	Westat Inc.	USA	264
11	NOP World	USA and UK	246
12	Aegis Research	USA and Hong Kong	232

Source: Esomar (2001).[10]

share the costs of the survey. Leading providers of omnibus surveys include BMRB in the UK, and Gallup and NOP throughout Europe. Again, the trend is increasingly for these omnibus surveys to be carried out by telephone. One notable European omnibus survey is CAPIBUS Europe, which surveys 5,000 adults per week across the UK, France, Italy and Spain. As the name implies, the omnibus uses computer-assisted personal interviewing to deliver results in less than four weeks. In Hong Kong, Taylor Nelson Sofres runs a regular monthly telephone omnibus survey with over 1,000 consumers.

Continuous market research – the international dimension

Continuous market research is today conducted by a number of global research companies, such as those in Table 4.2.

Despite the global nature of these research companies, continuous research is still conducted in a relatively fragmented fashion. Most countries are still researched as discrete markets and many large research companies such as IRI and GfK still cover only a few European countries. The European Society for Opinion and Marketing Research (ESOMAR) is attempting to harmonise the way research is carried out across Europe. For example, an 'adult' is defined in Germany as somebody who is 18 or over, while in other countries the age definition is as low as 12, making it difficult to conduct meaningful Europe-wide marketing research.

If we examine how Taylor Nelson Sofres conducts continuous market research into public opinions, we realise that European market research is still conducted on national lines rather than on a pan-European basis (*see* Exhibit 4.6). However, it is also clear that the cost and sophistication of continuous market research is driving research companies like Taylor Nelson Sofres to consolidate its research market across Europe.

> ### EXHIBIT 4.6
>
> **POLITICAL RESEARCH ACROSS EUROPE**
>
> Political research is one of Taylor Nelson Sofres's specialities. Many of our companies have been given the vote of public confidence by local political parties, TV and radio companies, unions and the written press when it comes to monitoring public opinion, measuring trends and gauging attitudes and carrying out estimation polls during elections:
>
> - *Belgium – Dimarso.* Dimarso launched its political research activities in 1963 and today is the leader in Northern Belgium in this sector.
>
> - *Denmark – Gallup.* Gallup A/S is one of the oldest (60 years) and well-known market research institutes in Denmark. 96 per cent of Danes equate Gallup with opinion polling and market research.
>
> - *France – Sofres.* Sofres is now the leading political and opinion pollster in France. Over 130 surveys are conducted yearly covering a wide range of subjects influencing the population's opinion.
>
> - *Germany – Emnid.* Emnid started its polling activities as early as 1945, and enjoys an excellent reputation in political research in Germany, with long-standing relationships with the cable TV company NTV and with the magazine *Der Spiegel*.
>
> - *Italy – Abacus.* Abacus's political research activities really took off in 1992 with the national elections. In 1996, a weekly TV programme called *Moby Dick* on Italia Uno was launched and has contributed largely to Abacus's reputation for political research in Italy.
>
> - *United Kingdom – Harris.* Harris Research first worked for the Conservative Party in 1966 and now has a panel of 150 MPs which is consulted six to seven times a year, giving direct access to parliamentary opinion across a wide range of issues.
>
> *Source*: Taylor Nelson Sofres website (www.tnsofres.com, 1999).

Other primary research applications

Advertising research

Advertising research is used to evaluate the effectiveness of advertising as a means of communication and persuasion, and can be categorised under three broad headings:

- *Advertising content research* is used at two stages in advertising: pre-publication, where individuals or groups are invited to view 'mock-up' advertisements and are tested on their degree of recall of specific aspects of the advertisements, and post-publication, where unaided (spontaneous) recall and aided (prompted) recall of advertisements are also measured.

■ *Advertising effectiveness research* aims to evaluate the degree of success achieved by advertising through different media. Tracking studies are typically used to identify the effectiveness of marketing research.

■ *Advertising media research* attempts to improve the efficiency of advertising by analysing the media available for promoting products and services. Aspects of advertising media research include press readership measurement, television and radio audience measurement, as well as cinema and poster research measurement. More recently, marketing research companies have been attempting to get to grips with measuring the effectiveness, or reach, of internet advertising.

Television audience research – the use of peoplemeters

In the UK, the Broadcasters' Audience Research Board (BARB) dominates much of the television advertising media research. BARB commissions both quantitative audience research for measuring audience size, and qualitative research for measuring audience reaction. Across Europe, television audience research methods are becoming more automated, harmonised and standardised.

Nowadays, most measurement is conducted using electronic systems including peoplemeters, as discussed earlier, which record the television viewing habits of sample households (*see* Figure 4.8). The peoplemeter is a device that provides television viewers in a household with their own individual 'buttons' to press each time they enter and then leave the room. How many people are likely to keep this up for months and years? Maybe those who do are not necessarily representative of the consuming population other than in the usual recruiting demographic or geo-demographic profile characteristics. Peoplemeters still rely on individuals to record accurately the times that they leave the room or stop watching the television, so some margin for error exists in the audience data collected by these devices.

However, the replacement of the paper-based diaries with electronic measurement has made a significant impact on the quality and accuracy of television audience measurement. A move to complete automation of television audience measurement may still be some years away, primarily for considerations of cost.[11] The next generation of people meters is essentially a digital camera that stores the image of each panellist and is able to detect who is in the room at that time. This is called the 'passive peoplemeter' but it is not a full video camera so behaviour while in the room is not recorded!

Radio audience research

Given the greater number of radio stations available to listeners, radio audience research is more complex than television audience research. RAJAR (Radio Joint Audience Research) is the trade association for commercial radio stations in the UK. It gathers audience data from a panel of 150,000 respondents who use seven-day paper-based diaries to record the stations to which they listen. Interestingly, despite

The peoplemeters installed in the AGB panel homes are the proprietary TVM series of peoplemeters, developed and maintained for companies of the AGB Group, by the technological subsidiaries, AGB Tech, AGB Lab and AGB IT. The most widely-installed of these, is the TVM2, with more than 30,000 units installed world-wide. Over the last 3 years, the TVM4, incorporating the latest technology, capable of measuring any type of broadcasting; including digital and analogue, free to air, cable and satellite, time shift viewing and teletext usage and can be applied for the measurement of personal television products, has been installed in Australia, United Kingdom, Italy, Serbia, Ukraine, Croatia & Cyprus. During 2003, Greece, Dominican Republic, Mexico & Hungary will either be increasing their panel or replacing older generation TVM meters with TVM4 meters. Today more than 25,000 TVM4 meters are installed in AGB panel households, providing excellent proven results.

Figure 4.8 Peoplemeters from AGB
Source: AGB website (www.agbgroup.com, 2003).

the variety of commercial radio stations available in major cities like London, listeners typically listen to fewer than three stations a week. Radio research has not yet embraced the electronic meters used in television research, mainly for reasons of cost, despite the fact that such meters have been used in the USA, in conjunction with paper diaries, for many years.

Public relations research

As Exhibit 4.7 shows, the measurement of the effectiveness of public relations (PR) is an imprecise science, typically involving the measurement of the number of words or column inches that are generated as a result of a press release or similar PR initiative. IT is beginning to make inroads in this area of marketing, although the technology is still relatively immature. Much of the so-called 'text-mining' technology is based on neural network technology that allows words, the structure of sentences and inflections to be analysed to determine the degree of satisfaction that customers or commentators have with a particular product or service. Apart from automating the task of assessing hundreds of separate articles, a greater consistency is achieved through the use of information technology – when analysed manually, different analysts can take different interpretations of the words in a press article.

One measurement system in the motor market comes from the company Millward Brown. Its 'Precis' service (www.mbprecis.com) combines several variables to form an

EXHIBIT 4.7

THE POWER OF PR

Words in print have been analysed since Caxton invented the press. In fifteenth-century Sweden, the appearance of the heretical *Books of Zion* led to an assessment of their religious orthodoxy in probably the earliest attempt at media evaluation upon which the lives of the publishers turned. Yet even in today's world of media sophistication, the means of assessing the value to a company of news pieces, articles and features, often rises little above the measurement of column inches or the size of a headline. 'Given the increasing amounts of money that is spent on this kind of public relations, which runs into billions worldwide, it is remarkable that PR companies remain so crude in the justification and targeting of the spend', comments Adam Briggs, senior lecturer at the London Guildhall University. But the question is 'how'?

Part of the answer is found in leading-edge information technology. PR is nothing if not the management of human reactions, though this is all about intangibles such as 'the feel' of an article or comment. IBM's text-mining solution provides one example of how technology is now beginning to cope with analysis at this level. Electricité de France, the large utility group, has used IBM's solution to study public perception of its electrical car and nuclear power development programmes in press reports.

Source: Financial Times (2 September 1998).[12]

effectiveness index (called the 'media influence index'). As Figure 4.9 illustrates, this index is based on the weighted scoring of such variables as:

- publication, scored for delivery of target and its readership, using NRS (national readership survey) or TGI (target group index) data;
- position of the article within the publication;
- position of the article on the page;
- percentage of the page covered by the article;
- percentage of the page occupied by a photograph;
- columnar spread of the article;
- journalist.

In Figure 4.9 the media influence index shows positive, negative and indifferent exposure for each of several specific characteristics of a particular car model. The right-hand graph shows a separate bar graph for each individual journalist and the media influence index that they personally achieve.

A new service is being offered by Thomson Intermedia via their GfK consumer panel and a quantitative model of press release effectiveness developed by Paul Harris of Thomson Intermedia.[13] The variables include size of message, circulation

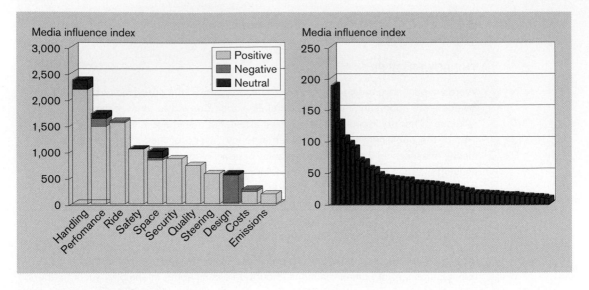

Figure 4.9 Media influence index for a press release about a car
Source: Evans and Fill (2000).[14]

and readership figures for the publication, estimation of positive or negative impact, relationship with news or feature article, journalist, and number of mentions of the company or product.

A further consideration revolves around the power of technology and the resulting temptation to rely – perhaps over rely – on it. Much database data, such as transactional and profiling data, provides valuable information on who is buying what, when, how and where, but it is qualitative market research that can get beneath the surface even further and discover the reasons 'why' behaviour is as it is.[15] Research amongst direct marketers reveals an emphasis on 'testing' (experimentation) with, in relative terms, little qualitative research.[16,17]

Linking research databases: T-groups

Recognising this danger, some marketers are linking their databases with more traditional market research data. In this way, for example, consumer panels are linked with geo-demographic or lifestyle databases. Such linking is referred to as a 'T-group'. The 'T' means that 'horizontally' database data provides tremendous breadth of data over millions of consumers, but the 'vertical', from market research (for example from panels), provides greater depth of information over a period of time (because panels are 'continuous' data sources). Figure 4.10 summarises the characteristics of the T-group.

It was from such research that the claimed levels of purchasing in lifestyle surveys have sometimes been found to be extremely over or under-represented in actual buying behaviour. One version of linking panel data with lifestyle database is the SMARTbase system developed by Taylor Nelson and Calyx – the former running a number of different consumer panels and the latter, lifestyle surveys.[18]

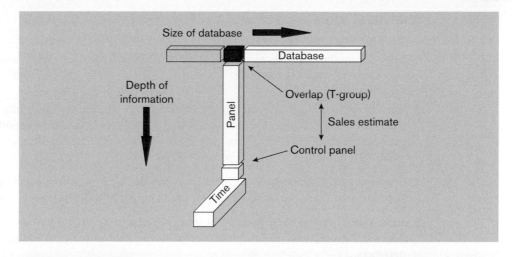

Figure 4.10 The T-group
Source: Cowling (1996).[19]

Using technology to analyse information

Providing faster statistical analysis

Statistics, or quantitative methods, have been used for many years in the analysis of market research data. However, the increasing power and decreasing costs of personal computers have more recently placed many of the more sophisticated statistical tools in the hands of marketing managers. The subject of statistics is beyond the scope of this book but the main categories, and some of their applications, are:

- *Multivariate methods*, which attempt to analyse the relationships between different marketing variables. Sub-categories include factor analysis, cluster analysis and multidimensional scaling techniques such as conjoint analysis, a consumer research technique for finding correlations between variables. Conjoint analysis was used by Novotel to examine the trade-offs that consumers make when they compare different aspects of hotel accommodation, such as size of room or bed versus type of television.[20]

- *Regression techniques*, including multiple regression, are often used in customer segmentation and sales forecasting.

- *Artificial intelligence*, including expert systems and neural networks, is used for market pricing and media planning.

- *Statistical decision theory*, sometimes referred to as stochastic methods, is used to optimise sales forces and call centre staffing, and for optimising pricing decisions.

Analytical tools

A variety of analytical tools are available to conduct statistical analysis. Some of these tools include:

■ *Spreadsheets and other decision support systems (DSS).* The most commonly used market research analysis tool is the humble spreadsheet. Spreadsheet software packages such as Excel and Lotus 1-2-3 have become the standard mechanism by which all marketing managers perform basic analysis.

■ *Geographic information systems (GIS).* These are decision support systems used for visualising and analysing geographical data (*see* below).

■ *Data mining and neural networks.* For more sophisticated analysis, several other decision support systems are available, including data mining and neural networks.

Geographic information systems (GIS)

GIS are computer systems that store, retrieve, display and manipulate geographically based information. In the past they were expensive and cumbersome systems that were rarely used outside the central planning departments of companies. Nowadays they have moved closer to the sharp end of the business and bring a wide range of various marketing data to the fingertips of the marketing manager. The main characteristic that distinguishes GIS from other systems is the ability to point and click on a particular area of the PC screen to obtain a range of information that has been assembled for that particular geographic feature. Typically, GIS allow at least four, but frequently many more, different layers of information to be overlaid in the same picture:

■ maps and other geographically based information

■ geo-demographic information from census information and electoral registers

■ internal information on customers

■ other internal market information such as sales force territories, store catchment areas, newspaper, television and other media boundaries.

Additional layers of information can also be added. More sophisticated GIS include global positioning system (GPS) satellite receiver information. For example, software from companies like Cyantel (www.cyantel.com) allows fleet management, haulage and delivery organisations to attach GPS transmitters to their vehicles, allowing each vehicle to be tracked and its position monitored and shown on a PC using a standard internet browser. Nowadays, advanced GIS systems have GPS connectivity bundled into their products, either as a basic feature or as an additional service.

GIS also have a variety of uses in marketing research. For example, Levi Strauss uses GIS to analyse sales and shipments by area and to make predictions on future sales, market potential and customer trends. The supermarket chain Tesco uses it for analysing changes in population, income and road and rail locations, so that it can plan the locations of its large stores more effectively. Halfords also has a system for analysing local demand (*see* Exhibit 4.8 and Figure 4.11).

EXHIBIT 4.8

GAINING LOCAL INSIGHTS

Halfords has over 400 stores and is the leading retailer of motor parts and bicycles in the UK. Halfords started working with information specialists CACI on a project basis using CACI's geographic information system, InSite. CACI produced definitions of Halfords' retail catchment areas, which they then used to examine the relationship between sales and demographics. Among the many applications of using InSite, it has provided Halfords with a tool for analysing their complete portfolio of stores and the consumer characteristics of each of their store catchments. This has enabled Halfords to identify gaps for new out-of-town outlets and expand their store base.

'As the retail market grows more and more sophisticated and competitive, so the demands we must make on our market analysis tools increase. InSite has proved itself to be more than able to meet our complex consumer analysis requirements, and it is now an integral part of our store evaluation process,' according to Richard Nixon, head of property at Halfords.

Source: CACI website (www.caci.co.uk, 2002).

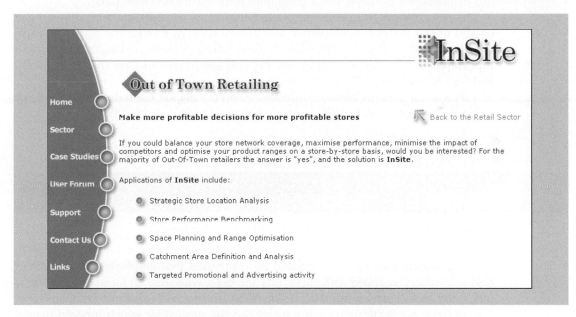

Figure 4.11 CACI's InSite offering for out-of-town retailing
Source: InSite website (www.insite.info/retail3.htm, 2003).

Data mining tools

A number of dedicated data mining tools are available for analysing databases. One such product is VIPER, developed by Brann Software and now marketed by SmartFocus of Bristol. This tool allows fast linking and analysis of different databases. Figure 4.12

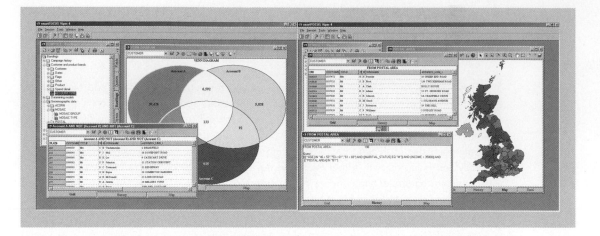

Figure 4.12 SmartFocus VIPER database interrogation
Source: SmartFocus VIPER software.

shows a printout from VIPER-processed queries on a lifestyle database, linked with a geo-demographic database and a geographical information system (GIS).

The objective might have been to select those customers (name and address) who possess financial services companies' accounts of types A, B or C. The graphical print-out of the model combines data from all the databases interrogated and shows in both topographical form where these people live and also in tabular form the actual names and addresses of the individuals concerned.

VIPER is not the only database interrogator on the market but it does reflect the sort of capability that is now available on a relatively standard desktop PC.

Summary

Market research used to be dominated by companies that employed large teams of field researchers equipped with clipboards and pens, who were set loose on the general public to conduct face-to-face interviews. Today, information technology, the internet and software applications have revolutionised the process by which modern market research is conducted. Done correctly, market research can provide insights on consumer behaviour and help make more effective marketing investment decisions. It is also now possible to gather information on customers behaviour on a more continuous basis, rather than in the past when market research tended to give picture from a snapshot in time. Successful companies will be those that best utilise the new tools to understand their customers needs and to meet those needs. However, technology-driven data and 'testing' should not become surrogates for more effective insight gained from traditional (especially qualitative) research.

Case study

Starbucks and Japan

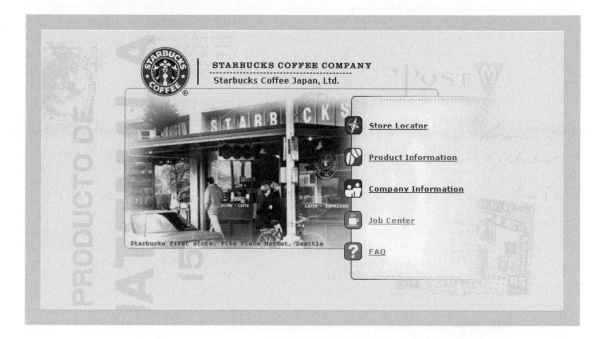

Figure 4.13

Japan is famous as a tea-drinking nation. However, it is also the third largest importer of coffee and the seventh largest coffee retail market in the world, snapping at the heels of more traditional coffee lovers, including the Italians, according to global market analyst Euromonitor. When Starbucks opened its first Japanese coffee store in Tokyo's fashionable Ginza shopping district in 1996, it was an overnight sensation. Seven years and 467 Starbucks stores later, Japan is Starbucks' biggest foray outside the USA.

Starbucks' expansion has been aided by the sophisticated use of market research and geographic information systems (GIS) technology to segment its market and choose retail site locations. According to Cyndie Horwat, Starbucks' vice president of store development, 'Early on, a relatively small number of people participated in new store decisions. So, while we valued location analysis, it was more experiential than systematic. As we continue to grow, we have more people making those decisions, and the analysis had to become much more formalised. Additionally, now that we're ramping up our numbers, we need to ensure that our people are being efficient and effective in where they are looking in the first place. By 2000, we were opening more than 400 company-owned stores a year. That type of a ramp up makes it necessary for us to do location analysis.'

But traditional location analysis techniques are not as easily applied to a country like Japan. According to Horwat, 'I think the largest challenge we face is the availability and accuracy of data. Internationally there is not a countrywide collection of address information. In addition, the systems available to use those data vary. Because we've developed strong approaches domestically we foresee a great opportunity in implementing those approaches with comparable data and comparable systems.'

A Starbucks spokesman agrees. He says that the real issue for Starbucks has been that there is no central place to get information about data availability in certain countries, whether demographic or consumer data or simple geographic boundary files. ESRI doesn't supply it for every market. Claritas, although it has a strong presence in many markets, doesn't have one clearinghouse. CACI is represented in a lot of markets, but doesn't have a clearinghouse. Starbucks' partners in Japan use a system that is not available in the USA and it was hard for them to have comparability in their research. For example in an analysis at the county level, county has a different meaning in the USA than it does in England or in Japan.

Starbucks faces big rivals in Asia. According to a 2003 report by market research specialists Euromonitor, Japanese players lead the fresh coffee sector. The top four players, UCC Ueshima Coffee, Key Coffee, Art Coffee and Unicafe, account for over half of fresh coffee retail sales. UCC is one of the oldest coffee suppliers in Japan and continued to lead the fresh coffee sector in Japan in 2002, with its well-established brands UCC and Crestia. UCC is one of the largest integrated coffee producers in Japan.

Japan's coffee market is expected to continue to grow steadily over the next 5 years, according to Euromonitor. Females are Japan's main coffee consumers and many have learned about the variety of fresh coffee from their experience with Starbucks. Indeed, the desire to repeat the 'real' coffee experience at home has helped boost retail sales of coffee and coffee accessories over the past few years, with the trend expected to continue. However, that potential is likely to be constrained by a limited consumer base – the target consumers of fresh coffee are young female consumers within the 25–39 age group. The Starbucks formula has worked well with females but male consumers are still regular drinkers of instant coffee.

Sources: *Euromonitor* (12 August 2003);[21] *Business Week* (9 June 2003);[22] *Business Geographics* (2002)[23] and authors' own research.

Case study questions

1 'I think the largest challenge we face, is the availability and accuracy of data.' Discuss.

2 How would you segment the coffee-drinking public in Japan?

3 How does the research company Euromonitor segment the market?

4 Can Starbucks hold off the challenge of its Japanese competitors? Conduct your own internet-based research to back up your answers.

Questions and exercises

Questions

1 Describe three internal data sources.

2 How has technology changed secondary data collection?

3 Assess the advantages and disadvantages of technology-enabled observation over traditional manual observation.

4 How would a business conduct continuous market research?

5 Describe how technology can be used to analyse information.

6 Briefly describe three methods of conducting advertising research.

Online exercises

1 Assume you are marketing manager for a major Japanese car manufacturer. You are planning to launch a new sports utility vehicle (SUV) into the European market. Using online sources prepare a competitive profile for one competitor of your choice in one European country. This should include: a) name of competitor; b) names of SUV models sold; c) key price points of models sold; d) key selling points of competitive models; e) some customer or trade reports on the models.

2 Access Doubleclick's website (www.doubleclick.com). Assume you are working for a major drinks company and that your line manager, who is in charge of market research, has asked you to prepare a feasibility report on using Doubleclick's services. Make a recommendation on whether you should employ Doubleclick's services.

References

1 Evans, M. (2000). 'Market information and research', in Blois K. (ed.) *The Oxford Textbook of Marketing*. Oxford: Oxford University Press.

2 Mitchell, A. (1996). Interview transcribed from BBC Radio 4 *You and Yours*.

3 Chisnall, P. (1997). *Marketing Research*, 5th edition. London: McGraw Hill.

4 Belsie, L. (2002). 'Preference profilers: we know what you bought last summer', *Christian Science Monitor*, 28 May.

5 Crawford, C.M. (1970). 'Attitudes of marketing executives toward ethics in market research', *Journal of Marketing*, Vol. 34, No. 2.

6 Loscher, D. (2001). 'Exploding some online myths', *Marketing*, September.

7 Miller, J. and Lundy, S. (2002). 'Test marketing plugs into the internet', *Consumer Insight*, Spring.

8 O'Malley, L., Patterson, M. and Evans, M. (1999). *Exploring Direct Marketing*, London: Thomson Press.

9 Chisnall, *Marketing Research*.

10 Esomar (2001). *Esomar Annual Survey of the Market Research Industry*, www.esomar.nl

11 Ephron, E. (1999). 'Let them eat peoplemeters?', *Advertising Age*, 31 May.

12 Vernon, M. (1998). 'Key role for IT in the marketing mix', *Financial Times*, 2 September.

13 Thomson Intermedia (1999). DART, www.thomson-intermedia.com

14 Evans, M. and Fill, C. (2000). 'Extending the communications process: the significance of personal influencers in the UK motor market', *International Journal of Advertising*, Vol. 19, No. 2.

15 Mouncey, P. (1996) and Mouncey, P. (1997). IDM Symposium, transcription of presentation, 11 June.

16 Evans, M. and Middleton, S. (1998). 'Testing and research in direct mail: the agency perspective', *Journal of Database Marketing*, Vol. 6, No. 2.

17 CMS (1998). *Precise Makes Sense of Media*, London: CMS.

18 Walker, J. (1996). 'SMART move but will it deliver the goods?', *Precision Marketing*, 6 May.

19 Cowling, A.B. (1996). 'Big issues for the next five years: data fusion, reach the parts others don't', IDM Symposium, May.

20 Wittink, D.R., Vriens, M. and Burhenne, W. (1994). 'Commercial use of conjoint analysis in Europe: results and critical reflection', *International Journal of Research in Marketing*, Vol. 11, No. 1.

21 Euromonitor archive, 2003. 'Japan: a nation of coffee lovers', www.euromonitor.com/article.asp?id=1584, 12 August.

22 Holmes, S., Kunii, I.M., Ewing, J. and Capell, K. (2003). 'For Starbucks, there's no place like home', *Business Week*, 9 June.

23 Francica, J. (2002). 'Location analysis tools help Starbucks brew up new ideas' www.geoplace.com/bg/2000/1000/1000ntv.asp.

5

Creating customer insight

Learning objectives

Once you have read this chapter you will:

■ understand the role of customer segmentation in generating customer insight;

■ appreciate how technology is creating new approaches to customer segmentation;

■ understand the concept of data warehousing;

■ understand how to use data mining techniques to find hidden customer insights;

■ appreciate the importance of creating a knowledge organisation to share customer insights throughout an organisation;

■ understand the role of intranets and extranets in organisations.

Contents

DATA WAREHOUSING AND DATA MINING

- The data warehouse
- Lower-cost solutions – the data mart
- Data mining techniques
- Getting results from data mining software
- Creating a data mining capability

CREATING A KNOWLEDGE ORGANISATION

- The value of a knowledge organisation
- The use of intranets and extranets
- Tools employed by knowledge-based organisations

SUMMARY

CASE STUDY

Introduction

One of the most talked about topics in marketing today is that of customer insight. Also referred to as business intelligence, it is the capability that companies need to create in order to 'sense' what their customers want and need, and adapt their products and services to those changing customer needs. Our starting point is the well-developed concept of customer segmentation. This is the cornerstone of any good marketing plan and we will see how technology now allows us to become increasingly more sophisticated in the way we segment our customers. One of the ways we can segment more effectively is through the use of data warehousing and data mining technology, which allows us to gather data on our customers and then look for relevant correlations in the data. The final topic that we review is the concept of the knowledge organisation. Companies are realising that it is not the amount of data that they collect that is important but the way their organisation acts on that data. This ability to act on data can be defined as knowledge in its widest sense and organisations have realised that they must actively manage their knowledge resources. Let us start by looking in more detail at customer segmentation.

Using segmentation to generate customer insight

The difference between information and understanding

An important thing to keep in mind is the difference between information and understanding. According to Piercy and Evans (1999)[1] 'The importance of market sensing, or market understanding by managers, is more than merely sophisticated marketing research or technology-driven marketing information systems'. As marketing people we are continually being bombarded by additional information: the challenge is in converting that information into customer insight and understanding. Piercy (2002) has developed a useful framework for converting information into understanding (*see* Figure 5.1).

Traditional approaches to customer segmentation

Segmentation involves identifying sizeable groups of customers with similar buying needs and characteristics. By identifying and understanding the major segments in any market, organisations can develop more appropriate product and service offerings targeted at particular customer groups. All decisions on the marketing mix are then made with the specific customer segment in mind, in contrast to a mass marketing approach where all customers are treated in a similar fashion.

Traditional approaches have been based on segmenting customers into distinct groups based on geographic, demographic and socio-economic information (*see* Table 5.1). Geo-demographics are not just a combination of these variables; they are based on census data that is cluster-analysed according to the variables included. These variables are the starting point for any traditional segmentation approach, such as the one used by Halifax Bank in Exhibit 5.1.

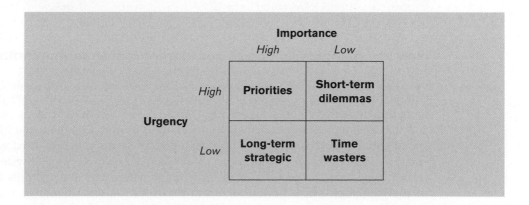

Figure 5.1 Marketing information priorities
Source: Piercy (2002), reprinted by permission of Butterworth-Heinneman.[2]

Table 5.1 Traditional segmentation variables

Key geographic variables	Key demographic variables	Key socio-economic groupings
Country	Age	A – professional/senior managerial
Region	Education	B – middle managers/executives
Population density (urban, rural etc.)	Family	C1 – junior managers/non-manual
Climate	Income	C2 – skilled manual
	Occupation	D – semi-skilled/unskilled manual
	Religion	E – unemployed/state-dependent
	Sex	

EXHIBIT 5.1

EXCLUSIVE PLASTIC

Halifax, the UK bank, joined the select band of credit card issuers hoping to woo rich customers with prestigious 'black cards'. Its Carbon credit card is aimed at customers earning more than £75,000 a year. Like all 'black cards', Carbon is offered by invitation and will not be sold in branches. Carbon, which costs £175 a year, follows the launch of NatWest's Black card earlier in the year.

The new breed of card is designed to give executives an exclusive slice of plastic in their wallets, now that gold and platinum cards have been devalued. Capital One, for example, offers its platinum card to applicants with a minimum salary of just £10,000. Card companies believe there is a large market for 'black cards', primarily among the almost 400,000 people in the UK who earn more than £100,000 a year.

Source: Financial Times (14 September, 2002).[3]

Increasing sophistication of geo-demographic segmentation

One of the more significant events in moving from generalised customer profiles to more individualised approaches was the commercial availability of census information and the development of geo-demographics analysis from it. Geo-demographics represents a combination of geography and demography and is generally used with reference to neighbourhood classifications, usually linked to the postcode system. It is a classification based on people's characteristics and where they live, typically then used to analyse patterns in behaviour. From the 1981 UK census, some 40 variables were analysed and the emerging clusters of households led to the creation of 39 neighbourhood types in the first geo-demographic system in the UK, called ACORN (A Classification of Residential Neighbourhoods). Compare this with the leading alternative of the time – social grade – which classifies the entire population into just six groups on the basis of a single variable (occupation of the chief income earner in the household). Whereas these traditional profiles are often based on sample surveys of approximately 1,000, the marketing industry now has access to census data on 58 million people. Names and addresses cannot be revealed from the census, but the statistics for enumeration districts (EDs) are made available (EDs typically constitute 150 households). Such data can be linked with the postcode database (there is one postcode for approximately 15 households) and when used with the electoral register (another database), it is possible to identify individual households and their characteristics.

ACORN now consists of 54 different neighbourhood types, some of which are outlined in Table 5.2.

The basic rationale behind geo-demographics is that 'birds of a feather flock together', making neighbourhoods relatively homogenous. An easy criticism in repost is that 'I am not like my neighbour'. However, geo-demographics have proved to be reasonably robust overall.

Companies can also use classification systems such as ACORN to profile their own customers into distinct segments. From a given list of names and addresses (from the company's own customer database, for example), information services organisations can identify the major segments or profiles within the database, which will allow them to seek out the best target market and cross-sell to customers (*see* Exhibit 5.2).

EXHIBIT 5.2

DRAWING BLOOD IN SCOTLAND

Among the non-corporate users of geographically-based marketing information supplied by specialised software groups is the Scottish National Blood Transfusion Service (SNBTS). SNBTS has five regional transfusion centres which collect blood from 300,000 donors annually. SNBTS needs 40,000 new donors per year – that's 770 per week – so it turned to the information specialists CACI when it wanted to find the answers to three questions:

- Which types of people have a high propensity to give blood?

- Where are these types of people located in each of the five SNTBS regions?

- How do we plan and set targets for developing the performance of each of the five regions?

CACI profiled the SNTBS database of donors using the Scottish*ACORN population classification, for each of the five regions. Only the donors' postcodes were used for the analysis to ensure confidentiality. In general terms, the profiling established that the overall SNBTS donor profile is fairly affluent, with Scottish*ACORN groups A (affluent consumers with large houses), B (prosperous home-owners) and D (private tenements and flats) being particularly prominent.

Source: CACI website (www.caci.co.uk, 1999).

Table 5.2 ACORN profiles based on the 1991 census

Category and label	Description
Category A, Group 1 Wealthy achievers, suburban areas	The majority of people in this Group live in a large detached house and have access to two or more cars. They are typically well-educated professional people, the corporate managers in their middle age, enjoying the fruits of their labour. These are the consumers with the money and the space to enjoy very comfortable lifestyles.
Category A, Group 2 Affluent greys, rural communities	This Group covers Britain's better-off farming communities – residents here are 12 times more likely than average to be involved in agriculture. Many are self-employed and work long hours. The very high incidence of visitors and households that are not the main residence show that these areas also include many holiday homes.
Category A, Group 3 Prosperous pensioners, retirement areas	The better-off senior citizens in society are to be found in Group 3. Living in flats, detached houses or bungalows, these are old people who can enjoy their retirement in pensioned comfort after their professional or executive careers. They are likely to own their home outright, so they have the disposable income to enjoy themselves.
Category B, Group 4 Affluent executives, family areas	These are the well-qualified business people, successfully juggling jobs and families. There are many working women in this Group. With mortgages, young children and often two or more cars to support, these busy people need their incomes but aren't having too hard a time making ends meet. They are likely to have large, modern detached houses and generally enjoy a good standard of living.
Category B, Group 5 Well-off workers, family areas	In a wide range of well-paid occupations, people in Group 5 are likely to be in couples, often with children aged 0–14. Both Mum and Dad are working hard to pay off the mortgage on their detached or, more probably, semi-detached home. While they are not as highly qualified as people in Group 4, they still have an agreeable lifestyle, often with more than two cars per household.
Category C, Group 6 Affluent urbanities, town and city areas	These are the young couples or single people starting out in life, a few years and a couple of children behind the people in Group 4. They tend to live in flats, terraced houses or bedsits. There are quite a number of students in this Group. Car ownership is average, reflecting the urban setting.
Category C, Group 7 Prosperous professionals, metropolitan areas	People in Group 7 share many characteristics with Group 6. However, they live in more cosmopolitan areas with a high ethnic mix. They take the train or underground to the office each day, working long hours in fairly senior roles and make the most of their high qualifications.
Category C, Group 8 Better-off executives, inner-city areas	These are well-qualified people, over a third of whom are single with no dependants. The age profile here is younger than for Groups 6 and 7 and there are many more students and other characteristics of academic centres. This Group also has a relatively high proportion of professionals and executives and shares many of the cosmopolitan features of Group 7.
Category D, Group 9 Comfortable middle-agers, mature home-owning areas	Mr and Mrs Average are to be found in these areas – they are close to the national 'norm' on just about every key characteristic. Living in a detached or semi-detached house with at least one car and likely to be an older married couple, Group 9 represents middle-of-the-road Britain. They are not particularly well-off but have few problems with unemployment or health.
Category D, Group 10 Skilled workers, home-owning areas	People in this Group are likely to be found in manufacturing areas, working in skilled occupations. They tend to live in terraced homes and are more likely to be couples with children aged 0–14. Most are home-owners and the majority are buying with a mortgage. Although not quite as comfortable as Group 9 – car ownership is lower – people in these areas are also around the midpoint on the social ladder.

Table 5.2 (cont'd)

Category and label	Description
Category E, Group 11 New home owners, mature communities	These areas are characterised by people who have bought up their semi-detached or terraced council houses. They are likely to be older couples, often pensioners. Those still at work tend to be involved in craft or machine-related occupations. Unemployment is only slightly above the national average.
Category E, Group 12 White-collar workers, better-off, multi-ethnic areas	The relatively high incidence of people from diverse ethnic groups – especially Afro-Caribbean and Indian – characterises these multi-ethnic family areas. Accommodation tends to be either terraced houses or flats. Unemployment is slightly higher than in Group 11, but overall living conditions are reasonable.
Category F, Group 13 Older people, less prosperous areas	These are the areas of older couples aged 55+ who find the going quite tough. The incidence of limiting long-term illness is high. The majority do not have a car. People are generally living in small terraced houses or purpose-built flats, typically from housing associations. Those still at work tend to be in manual or unskilled occupations; unemployment is above average.
Category F, Group 14 Council estate residents, better-off homes	These areas are typified by young couples with young children. Housing tends to be council or housing association terraces, often with cramped living conditions, though families tend to be better off than those in other Groups in this Category. Unemployment is relatively high and there are many single parents.
Category F, Group 15 Council estate residents, high unemployment	Group 15 has a greater ethnic mix and higher unemployment than Group 14. This Group has an older age profile and the highest incidence of limiting long-term illness – almost double the national average. People live mainly in purpose-built council flats. Car ownership is lower in these areas than anywhere else.
Category F, Group 16 Council estate residents, greatest hardship	Two key features characterise this Group: single parents and unemployment, both of which – at roughly three times the national average – are higher in this Group than in any other. Overall, living conditions are extremely tough. There are lots of young and very young children, with large households in small council flats.
Category F, Group 17 People in multi-ethnic, low-income areas	The greatest ethnic mix in Britain is found in this Group, especially of Pakistani and Bangladeshi groups, which account for over 40 per cent of the population. Single parenting and unemployment are very high. Many people are living in extremely cramped conditions in unmodernised terraced housing or council flats. While these areas are relatively poor, there is evidence to suggest small pockets of more affluent residents.

Source: © CACI Ltd.; 1999 source: ONS and GRO(S). © Crown copyright 1991; all rights reserved.

There are 'me-toos' of the original ACORN system. Richard Webber, who created ACORN, set up one of the competitors after he left CACI to join Experian and developed MOSAIC, which analyses the census data in conjunction with a variety of data sources, including county court judgments (CCJs), electoral roll and Royal Mail data. Nor are geo-demographic systems restricted to the UK, and there are a number of similar systems around the world. In other European countries similar systems exist, for example, under the names Geo Market profile and Omnidata. Several geo-demographic companies now operate throughout many European countries, such as Experian with its MOSAIC brand (*see* Figure 5.2).

However extensive the census becomes, the major limitation of census data relates to the difficulties associated with updating information, particularly because in the UK the census is only carried out every ten years. Experian has reallocated approximately

Figure 5.2 The MOSAIC brand in Europe
Source: Experian website (www.experian.com, 2003).

7 per cent of postcodes and has six name changes in the MOSAIC typology, both as an update and to improve clarity of meaning. There are suggestions that annual updates might be based on survey research, especially of the 'lifestyle' type that is discussed in the next section.

There are also issues concerning privacy. In November 2001 a member of the public won his case against Wakefield Council after that council had not been able to confirm that his electoral roll data (name and address) would not be supplied to third parties without his consent, such as marketers.[4] The consequence of this is that an opt-out option is being added to the electoral roll, which should help to alleviate privacy concerns at the same time as shifting marketing paradigm in yet another direction – 'permission marketing'. Perhaps customers will give permission to specific organisations to use their details for specified purposes.

Using new approaches to customer segmentation

The move from macro-segmentation to micro-segmentation

Traditional geo-demographic approaches can be described as macro-segmentation. Because geo-demographics are based on census data, there is the corresponding criticism of such macro-segmentation systems. In addition, sophisticated as geo-demographics are (certainly compared with the simplicity of age, gender and occupation – the main variables of the demographic alternative), the approach is essentially the same – that is, it 'profiles' people. It does not explain why people behave as they do and neither does it provide individualised information on what people buy. Even with the availability of good geo-demographic information, the marketing manager still faces the problem that the smallest neighbourhood unit that a system like ACORN can define consists of about 150 households. Two customers in the same segment (or even two people who live next door to each other) are likely to have different tastes, attitudes and purchasing behaviour. In addition, reliance on data from a national census that is carried out once every ten years has been seen as a drawback to the traditional geo-demographic segmentation approach.

Ultimately, geo-demographic segmentation is based on census data and is limited to providing an aggregate picture of the characteristics of people living in a particular district, rather than of the individual. These limitations are, to a great extent, addressed by newer micro-segmentation approaches, outlined below. They include:

- lifestyle research
- the use of transactional data
- biographics (a fusion of the above).

Lifestyle research

The main recent development in lifestyle research and segmentation is the lifestyle survey. These surveys are designed by companies such as Experian and essentially ask respondents to check those responses that apply. Figure 5.3 demonstrates some typical questions in these lifestyle surveys.

Figure 5.3 reflects just a portion of typical lifestyle surveys. Many more questions are included, covering claimed buying behaviour across many different product and service categories. Some questions will be sponsored by specific companies – for example, a car insurance company might sponsor a question asking for the month in which the car insurance is renewed. Because these surveys are not anonymous, the data will be filed in a database by name and address of respondent; it is then likely that in the month prior to that respondent's renewal date they will receive direct mailings soliciting defection to the sponsoring company.

Please indicate your marital status:

Single ☐   Married ☐   Divorced/separated ☐   Widowed ☐

What is your name and address? . . . .

What is your partner's name? . . . .

Holidays:
How much are you likely to spend per person on your next main holiday?

Up to £500 ☐   £501–£999 ☐   £1,000–1,499 ☐   £1,500–£2,000 ☐   £2,000+ ☐

In which country are you likely to take your next main holiday? . . . .

In which month are you likely to take your main holiday? . . . .

Figure 5.3 Contemporary 'lifestyle' research

Although the industry has claimed there is now a lifestyle census, the reality is somewhat different. Admittedly a large number of individuals (around 20 million in UK) have responded, but the survey is, by definition, a self-selected sample and it is known that some respondents do not tell the whole truth in completing the questionnaire.[5]

During the 1990s the increasing use of these new micro-segmentation methods sparked a fierce 'geo-demographic versus lifestyle' debate. Now both proponents accept that the combination of both approaches offers a more complete solution than either approach on its own. For example, Lifestyles from CACI (www.caci.co.uk) and PRIZM from Claritas (www.claritas.com) (*see* Exhibit 5.3) are among a number of targeting systems that combine the individual detail of lifestyle data with the solid foundation of census information and the statistical reliability of market research to give more targeted marketing solutions.

Another recent segmentation tool from CACI, called People*UK, goes further by assigning individuals to a particular category based on more than 300 geo-demographics, lifestyle and life-stage characteristics. People in the same household can be categorised and targeted differently using this technique.

The use of transactional data

Advances in information technology have enabled marketers to gather large amounts of data on customer behaviour and use that data to segment customers based on such variables as:

EXHIBIT 5.3

WHITE HOT GOODS

Hotpoint had invested in a bespoke point-of-sale display specifically for a new out-of-town superstore, the first for the retailer outside its traditional geographical area. The display showed Hotpoint's product portfolio across a range of price points, but sales through the store were running at 9 per cent lower than elsewhere and a lower average price per sale was being achieved. Hotpoint and the retailer were keen to address this problem and work together to increase product sales through the store, raise the average value per sale and ensure the product range reflected the profile of customers. To achieve this, they needed to attract a more affluent customer than normal for the retailer.

Using PRIZM, Claritas's segmentation system, customer groups were identified that matched the profile of Hotpoint's existing customers. These more affluent, established families with children at home were the type the retailer needed to attract. A catchment area was created around the superstore, highlighting the location of those who matched the target profile. The retailer prepared a direct mail pack offering a free video cassette for those consumers who visited the store, and additional offers were available if they purchased a Hotpoint appliance. The offer was sent to 40,000 homes.

From past experience, the retailer anticipated a 1 per cent response rate. The actual response was 5 per cent, with 2,000 customers visiting the store. As a result of the joint initiative, significant sales were generated. Hotpoint products accounted for 27 per cent of all white goods purchased at the store, with an average value 16 per cent higher than the average achieved for white goods sold overall. The initiative is now being rolled out to ten more superstores.

Source: Claritas website (www.claritas.co.uk, 1999).

- product usage
- repeat purchasing rates
- purchasing patterns.

The increasing use of electronic point-of-sale (EPOS) information is providing companies with detailed information by individual customer. In the food retailing industry, product purchasing information gathered through EPOS systems is combined with personal information that customers provide when they sign up for loyalty schemes, giving the retailers an understanding of how their customers buy products from their stores and how those purchasing patterns change over time. Why they buy as they do might be inferred from such data, but the data in itself will not provide the answer, as discussed in our coverage of market research.

Retailers are also capturing transactional data at point of sale via loyalty card schemes – for example, Tesco, Safeway and Sainsbury. By the end of 2002 Tesco had identified 100,000 different segments, each of which was targeted differently.[6] By knowing what individual consumers buy, the retailer might be able to target them with relevant offers, while the consumer saves money in the process.

Biographics – a fusion of lifestyle research and transactional data

Now that transactional data is at the heart of many databases, overlaid with a multitude of profile data, we are perhaps moving into the era of biographics – the fusion of profile and transaction data. Indeed, the ability to match names, addresses, purchasing behaviour and lifestyles all together on to one record allows companies to build a model of someone's life. By linking a number of different databases, companies can (and are beginning to) match individual customer data to credit history, actual purchasing behaviour, media response, and the frequency and monetary value of purchases. The data is certainly available to profile the life of an individual, but is the technology capable of supporting biographics? This question leads us to the discussion of data warehouses and data mining.

Data warehousing and data mining

The data warehouse

Over the past few decades the sources of market research and the amount of data on customers and customer transactions have increased enormously (*see* Figure 5.4).

As information becomes cheaper to warehouse and as companies integrate their information systems, the trend is set to continue unabated. Benetton, the fashion retailer, is linking its point-of-sale terminals in 7,000 shops and five continents. Throughout the 1990s many other large organisations started to examine the way in which this market data was reported and used. The oversupply of data and the undersupply of good management information prompted these companies to investigate how technology could be used to provide better decision-making information. The technical solution is the data warehouse, a very large database that holds operational, historical and customer data and makes it available to marketing managers for decision making and analysis. It is designed to help marketing managers make better decisions by analysing summarised snapshots of financial and marketing performance.

The retail industry, which uses large amounts of bar-code data from checkouts to provide accurate purchasing information, provides one of the best examples of the data warehousing concept in action. Many supermarket chains have integrated their entire ordering, stocking and replenishment systems with their checkout systems, allowing significant amounts of data to be used for marketing purposes (*see* Exhibit 5.4).

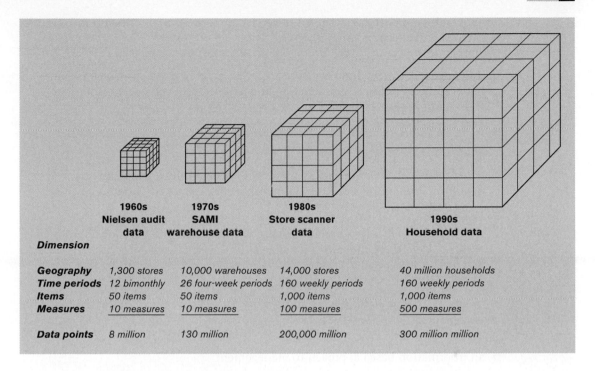

Dimension	1960s Nielsen audit data	1970s SAMI warehouse data	1980s Store scanner data	1990s Household data
Geography	*1,300 stores*	*10,000 warehouses*	*14,000 stores*	*40 million households*
Time periods	*12 bimonthly*	*26 four-week periods*	*160 weekly periods*	*160 weekly periods*
Items	*50 items*	*50 items*	*1,000 items*	*1,000 items*
Measures	*10 measures*	*10 measures*	*100 measures*	*500 measures*
Data points	*8 million*	*130 million*	*200,000 million*	*300 million million*

Figure 5.4 Growth of market data
Source: Accenture (1998).

EXHIBIT 5.4

A TRILLION TIMES MORE DATA

Club cards are but one source of a veritable ocean of information washing over most companies these days. Crawford Davidson, director of Club Card at Tesco in the UK, estimates that many companies now possess one thousand trillion times (yes) as much information as they did 12 years ago. EPOS data information from sales promotions, records of phone calls, e-mail logs, analysis of visits to websites – every transaction a company has with the outside world can now be stored and analysed.

Source: Financial Times (28 May 2002).[7]

Despite the high costs involved, data warehouses have proved successful in several aspects of the marketing function. Notable early proponents in the UK included Tesco, British Airways and Barclays Bank. At Fingerhut, the US-based marketing company, the data warehouse holds the equivalent of 3 billion pages of data on more than 30 million customer households. Fingerhut tracks up to 2,000 data elements, including demographics, buying patterns and preferences, credit history and even hobbies, anniversaries and birthdays.[8] The US research company Datapro cites several examples of successful data warehouse initiatives:

■ *Category management*. Data warehouses can help retail product managers gain a better understanding of consumer buying patterns and consumer response to their promotions.

■ *Claims analysis*. Insurance and healthcare firms use data warehousing applications to control costs and provide better customer service.

■ *Financial and market planning*. Many organisations gather and collate financial data from different sources in order to carry out product costing and customer-profitability analysis.

■ *Rate management*. Telecommunications companies use data warehouses in their efforts to determine the most profitable and competitive rates for cellular, local and long-distance calls.

In general, data warehouses are appropriate for companies exhibiting the following characteristics:

■ an information-based approach to management

■ involvement in highly competitive, rapidly changing markets

■ a large, diverse customer base

■ data stored in different systems.

Lower-cost solutions – the data mart

Data warehousing systems are usually built to meet the specific requirements of an entire corporation. They are expensive and it can take several years to migrate all the customer information from the old computer systems into the warehouse. In many cases data warehousing projects can cost in excess of $10 million over a three-to-five-year implementation period.

Given the high costs and long timescales involved, many companies question whether the benefits are sufficient to justify the cost. One solution is to scale down the scope and coverage of the project, confining the activities to, say, a single department with less data and less complexity. Data warehouses that are built on a relatively small scale are termed data marts. A data mart cannot do everything a data warehouse can, but it can be implemented at a fraction of the cost, typically less than $1 million. Rather than gathering all the company's information into a single warehouse, a small, cleaned-up subset of data is held, often at a summary level. Typically a data mart is designed for a smaller number of users, which reduces the implementation costs and means that it can be built using off-the-shelf computer packages. Companies like Bulmer in the UK have moved to a combination of data warehouses and data marts (*see* Exhibit 5.5).

EXHIBIT 5.5

GOING TO THE MART

HP Bulmer, the cider company, has since 1991 made a capital investment of £2 million a year in its IT system development and replacement programme. Bulmer decided to introduce a data warehouse to smooth the transition between old and new technology. Dr Martin Wynn, Bulmer's information technology director, says: 'Old and new systems are different not only in the technology they use but in the way they define things such as products, supplies and customers. As we switched over we wanted to draw data from both systems. The warehouse gave us information in a meaningful form that we could not get otherwise.'

Dr Wynn says: 'We can see how information changes from day to day, week to week and month to month. It helps us direct our sales effort.' Staff have been trained, with the 35 national account managers going through a two-year programme that has transformed the way they use computers. The warehouse has broken down barriers between departments, so that finance and sales staff look at the same data and understand each other's problems.

Source: *The Times* (data warehousing supplement, 5 June 1996).

Data mining techniques

Antoniou (1997)[9] defines data mining as a 'process of extracting hidden or previously unknown, comprehensible and actionable information from large databases'. Although there is currently no agreed classification scheme for data mining techniques, we can group the more popular techniques into the following types:

- *Inductive reasoning.* This is the process of starting with individual facts and then using reasoning to reach a hypothesis or a general conclusion. In data mining inductive reasoning, the facts are the database records, and the hypothesis formulation usually takes the form of a decision tree that attempts to divide or organise the data in a meaningful way. Decision trees are not suitable for all kinds of problems. Some decision-tree-based tools have problems dealing with continuous sets of values, like revenue or age, and may require that these values be grouped into ranges. For example, grouping ages 16 to 23 together may hide a significant break that might occur at age 20. Tools like Darwin from the data mining company Oracle Corporation avoid this problem by using techniques to cluster the data first.

- *Artificial neural networks.* The concept behind neural network technology is that a computer can be 'trained' to solve a problem in a similar fashion to a human brain, by recognising familiar patterns. While conventional computers have to be programmed with very specific instructions, neural computers do not require the same explicit instructions. Instead, they adapt their responses based on previous problems and solutions that are given to them. The systems 'learn' from these problems and, after a sufficient 'training' period, can offer a solution to a new problem. At present, the most commonly used applications of neural networks are in the areas of micro-marketing, risk management and fraud detection.

- *Data visualisation.* This refers both to the creation of visual images of things that we are unable to see, and to a way of displaying qualitative and quantitative data at a glance.

- *Memory-based reasoning.* Another artificial intelligence technique, memory-based reasoning classifies objects in a similar way to human intelligence – comparing attributes with those of other objects recalled from memory. Tools that use memory-based reasoning classify records in a database by comparing them with similar records that have already been clustered or classified.

Another way of looking at these techniques is to distinguish 'verification-driven' approaches from 'discovery-driven' approaches:

- *Verification-driven* involves extracting information to validate a hypothesis postulated by a user.

- *Discovery-driven* refers to the digging around in databases in a relatively unstructured way with the aim of discovering links between customer behaviour and almost any variable that might potentially be useful.

There is a parallel with market research versus environmental scanning, because the former focuses on specific problems and the latter has a wider ranging brief to identify anything in the marketing environment that might have a relevant impact upon the marketing operation. Marketers investigate a variety of marketing modelling approaches based on their database data. For example some examine consumers' individual biorhythms and star signs as predictors of their purchasing patterns.[10,11]

Getting results from data mining software

So, with the aid of a good database of information and some good analytical tools with which to query the database, companies can 'mine' for hidden information that can be used for marketing purposes. Companies that mine their data are looking for new correlations that may help them gain some insights into customer behaviour and thus competitive advantage in the marketplace. In insurance, for example, it has long been recognised that female drivers are a lower risk than their male counterparts and can be offered cheaper car insurance premiums. Data mining is used to find further sub-segments of female drivers with different price and risk profiles. Instead of providing a standard premium to women in the same age category, insurers can now price differently in order to retain their most profitable customers or encourage customers who are likely to be unprofitable to go elsewhere. The coverage of market research in Chapter 4 included an example of a data mining software product called VIPER. Exhibit 5.6 provides another example of a Californian company that turned to data mining to protect market share by getting to know its customers better.

Today, there are hundreds of different data mining tools available commercially. Some of the more established products from international companies can be seen in Table 5.3.[12]

EXHIBIT 5.6

MINING FOR A FEW GOOD CUSTOMERS IN HOLLYWOOD

Louise's Trattoria was hardly the place to be seen in the late 1990s. The Los Angeles-based restaurant chain was bankrupt and losing sales at a rate of 10 per cent a year, with few repeat customers. It had an unwieldy 62-item menu, a focus on heavy Italian offerings, outdated décor and an inefficient organisational system.

Fast forward three years and a lot has changed. A revamped Louise's is now upscale enough to attract the likes of Barbara Streisand, Jim Carrey and other Hollywood celebrities. How did Louise's new management orchestrate the turnaround? With hard work and one secret ingredient: a data mining initiative that uncorked the demographic make-up, along with their likes and dislikes, of Louise's best customers. The analysis, using a data mining solution from Gazelle Systems, created in-depth customer profiles, including demographic and psychographic information of the chain's top 500 customers, using point-of-sale credit card data. Gazelle's GAZ Reports showed that many of the chain's patrons were far more affluent than it had assumed – busy, health-conscious people with an affinity for fine wines, international travel and adventurous eating. Acting on the information provided in his customised GAZ Reports, CEO Fred LeFranc created a new 'California-Italian' restaurant featuring a revamped menu with lighter, Asian-influenced dishes along with Italian fare; redesigned interiors with open kitchens, patios, and an airy, open dining space; and a customer-convenient takeout and delivery service with internet and fax ordering capabilities.

Knowing more about his customers also enabled LeFranc to design cost-effective direct marketing campaigns (both e-mail and direct mail), select appropriately targeted community sponsorships, and create appealing loyalty and gift certificate programmes.

Sources: Earthweb website (www.itmanagement.earthweb.com, 2003); Gazelle website (www.gaz.com, 2003).

Table 5.3 Leading data mining products

Product	Company	URL
BusinessMiner	Business Objects	**www.businessobjects.com**
Scenario	Cognos	**www.cognos.com**
Intelligent Miner	IBM	**www.ibm.com**
Darwin	Oracle Corporation	**www.oracle.com**
Clementine	SPSS	**www.spss.com**
Enterprise Miner	SAS Institute	**www.sas.com**

EXHIBIT 5.7

LACK OF INSIGHT

When supermarket chain Safeway first launched its ABC loyalty card in the UK, it was a major event for the company. At the time, such cards were being hailed as a new dawn in retailing. The vision was of nano-targeted offers, as Safeway, with its wealth of consumer insight, would be able to write to customers offering them relevant new products, advising them that their toilet paper was just about to run out and incidentally wishing their third child 'Happy Birthday'. In 1999, just three years later, the card was withdrawn.

The problem was, says David Wright, then head of loyalty at Safeway, that the company had spent £30 million developing the card, £50 million a year maintaining it, but had just five staff to analyse the data and four to develop new offers for 20 million cardholders. 'They failed to understand that so much data needed a new approach. It not only required extra resources, it could potentially transform practically every element of the way that the company communicated with the public. Quite simply, their approach was not sufficiently creative. As a result, the ABC card turned into little more than a sophisticated money-off scheme – one that was totally at odds with the values of the brand' he says.

Source: *Financial Times* (28 May, 2002).[13]

Creating a data mining capability

While fast computing, efficient databases and high-speed networks are important elements of the data mining infrastructure, a variety of non-technical factors must be put in place as well. These include:

- methods for identifying, locating and extracting good-quality, relevant data for analysis;
- tools and techniques for identifying patterns and relationships in the data;
- statisticians and analysts to prepare the data, carry out the analysis and interpret the results;
- the presentation of relevant relationships mined from the data so that management and marketing decisions can be taken.

Exhibit 5.7 outlines why some data mining efforts fail for non-technical reasons. Underpinning at least some of the failures is what we refer to as the 'skills gap'. In research to explore the impact of IT on both marketing and marketers, some significant gaps were discovered in marketers' skills: 'Marketers should develop IT/new technology skills – (maybe via "junior mentors" – younger people who are "IT savvy" and who can educate their senior colleagues). We cannot influence the development and usage of IT within companies unless we know something about it.'[14]

Indeed, Carson (1999)[15] interviewed a group of leading US marketing practitioners and concluded that analytical skills and statistics topped the list of 'areas in which their education was lacking'. Businesses are demanding more accountability than ever before, making it essential for marketers to 'know how to do the numbers and prove their financial contribution to the bottom line'. Marketing academics must consider the implications of this for their own course design and delivery. As marketing is increasingly driven by marketing databases and strives to achieve a degree of personalised and interactive customer relationship management, marketing students would benefit from being able to deal with customer modelling and database analysis. Already we are seeing non-marketers taking over some of this ground and, for example, losing control of websites, as reported by the CIM (Chartered Institute of Marketing) in their *Marketing Trends Survey*.[16]

Creating a knowledge organisation

The value of a knowledge organisation

Many companies underestimate the knowledge that is held within their organisations. Academics have attempted to put a value on knowledge capital of pharmaceutical and chemical companies:

- *Merck's* knowledge capital has been estimated at $48 billion, thanks to its 'knowledge-intensive' pipeline of new products. Merck has annual sales of $24 billion.

- *Bristol-Myers Squibb's* knowledge capital of $30 billion compares to its annual sales of $17 billion.

- *Du Pont's* knowledge capital of $26 billion compares to its annual sales of $40 billion.[17]

Another reason for the focus on the value of knowledge capital is that the loss of corporate knowledge and the creation of corporate memory are finally being recognised as major management, and marketing, issues. It is a topical subject in the USA and has recently moved up the management agenda in Europe. The reason for the concern stems from the fact that managers are spending fewer years with the same company before moving on to their next job or career. According to Pencorp, the number of UK managers who have more than six years tenure with their current company has decreased from more than 60 per cent in the 1950s and 1960s to less than 20 per cent in the 1990s.[18]

With so few long-term employees in our organisations today, it is little wonder that senior managers are looking for new methods of capturing vital knowledge even when the original source of the knowledge has moved on to another job or another company. Exhibit 5.8 provides an example of a UK company using a combination of internal and external databases to improve its long-term corporate memory.

EXHIBIT 5.8

NUCLEAR MEMORIES

Information is the lifeblood of British Nuclear Fuels Ltd (BNFL), one of the world's leading nuclear energy services companies. In an industry where safety is paramount, it is the job of the information services team – known as IRS – to provide the information needs of thousands of professionals company-wide. A team of 11 IRS professionals ply their trade at BNFL, supplying a wide range of resources to colleagues worldwide. Michelle Byron is the IRS team leader for three BNFL sites (Springfields, Sellafield and Berkeley), while her colleague Diane Reeves looks after Risley on the outskirts of Warrington. Following an audit of the business's information usage in 1998, which concluded that all requests for business critical information had to go through the IRS department, the growth of the internet at desktop level has dramatically increased across BNFL's sites in the UK. In an average month, the IRS team handles 230 queries from across the company concerning all manner of topics. The prevailing themes, unsurprisingly, are the nuclear and energy industries, which account for one third of all queries lodged with IRS.

The IRS department has access to a number of external specialist databases, including Dialog, which are used for answering 60 per cent of queries, as well as access to an in-house database that contains details of BNFL documents. IRS staff also provide a corporate memory function and a records management/knowledge preservation programme.

Source: Dialog website (www.dialog.co.uk, 2003).

The speed at which knowledge is shared around an organisation has become a key differentiating factor between the excellent organisations and the mediocre. A central role in the dissemination of knowledge around organisations is played by technologies such as intranets and extranets.

The use of intranets and extranets

There are a number of enabling technologies that allow organisations to share information and knowledge more easily between employees. During the 1990s local area networks (LANs) linked PCs within the same building or on the same floor of a building. Employees located in different buildings or different cities could also be linked by using a wide area network (WAN), which links several LANs together.

More recently, companies have turned to intranet and extranet technology to link people electronically. While the internet is a global public medium, there are also private versions of the internet that can only be accessed by employees of one organisation and are protected by passwords and other security features. These intranets can also link to the outside world by connecting to the internet, but they are primarily for internal use within a company. Marketing managers tend to use intranets for:

■ publishing corporate documents, such as product literature, marketing literature, annual reports, newsletters, price lists, manuals and corporate policies;

■ providing access to searchable directories, such as corporate phone books, addresses, calendars, departmental diary systems and schedules;

■ distributing software to a wide number of users, for example issuing updates of quotation software to life assurance and pensions sales representatives;

■ connecting large numbers of employees in various geographic locations by means of electronic mail.

When these networks are extended to the company's trading partners over secure connections they are known as extranets. As Exhibit 5.9 points out, these private networks, which are based on the same technology and software as the internet, are becoming increasingly popular for sharing and disseminating information.

EXHIBIT 5.9

ROCHE ON ALERT – VIA EXTRANET

Hoffman-La Roche Pharmaceuticals Division is one of the world's largest pharmaceutical companies, developing, producing and marketing cost-effective drugs to combat human diseases. Roche Discovery Welwyn is one of six research centres at Pharmaceuticals Division and employs 340 scientists.

Roche decided to implement an online information service, delivered to the desktop of every scientist. It examined a number of options and eventually selected a customised version of DataStar Web from the Dialog Corporation. DataStar Web provides access to 350 databases using internet technology. Roche selected DataStar Web because:

• the product interface could be customised according to the specific requirements of Roche users;

• security was a key issue – Roche wanted to use a dedicated secure network (an extranet) rather than the commercial internet;

• Dialog Corporation offered a fixed price scheme, allowing the information department to predict costs and adhere to budget.

'Being able to access databases directly from the desktop has made the whole research process much faster and more streamlined for the users', said Sue Jackson, Roche Discovery Welwyn's head of information. 'But an even more exciting change has been the introduction of the alerting system, which enables them to receive automatic updates about specific areas of research, without them having to do the running themselves.'

Source: Dialogue Corporation website (www.dialog.com, 1999).

Tools employed by knowledge-based organisations

Intranets and extranets provide the mechanisms for disseminating knowledge throughout the organisation. But what tools are used to store and manipulate such knowledge? In general, there are three generic groups of technology tools employed by knowledge-based organisations:

- knowledge repositories
- groupware applications
- knowledge management systems.

Knowledge repositories

According to Davenport, De Long and Beers (1998),[19] there are three types of knowledge:

- *External knowledge*, which relates to competitive intelligence and other information that often lies in the heads of individuals rather than in a structured, searchable format.

- *Structured internal knowledge*, which includes information such as research reports that can be categorised and made available to others.

- *Informed internal knowledge*, such as discussion databases and other information like 'lessons learned' that are typically in a semi-structured format.

It is the first category that knowledge repositories are designed to manage. In essence, a knowledge repository is an electronic library that consists of a series of database tools and indexing systems. However, the most important component is arguably not the technology but the 'librarian' function that must be put in place to manage the repository. Unfortunately, many companies that attempted to create world-class knowledge repositories have ended up with what were referred to within the organisations as 'data dustbins'!

Groupware

Liebowitz (1999)[20] defines groupware as 'software that allows two or more people to communicate and collaborate across geographic and temporal boundaries'. Groupware provides rich content and interactivity using presentations, discussion databases and shared audio or video files. Examples of groupware include Banyan's BeyondMail, ICL's Teamware, Novell's Groupwise and the most popular and best-selling groupware product of all, Lotus Notes™ from IBM (*see* Figure 5.5).

Knowledge management systems (KMS)

Knowledge management systems are programmes such as expert systems and intelligent agents that allow non-experts to make decisions comparable to those of experts,

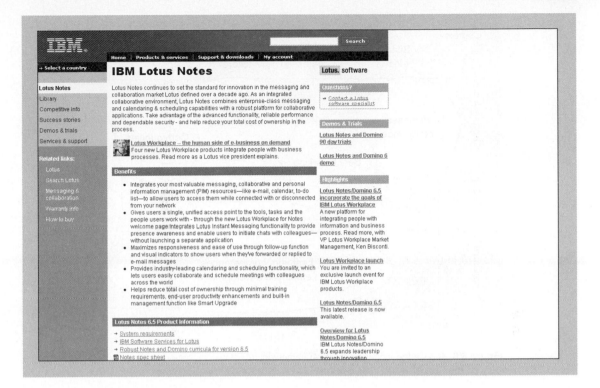

Figure 5.5 Lotus Notes

Source: Lotus website (www.lotus.com/products/product4.nsf/wdocs/noteshomepage, 2003).

centres employ KMS to allow relatively untrained agents to troubleshoot customer problems. Compaq's European technical customer services centre in Dublin employs such a system to help answer a variety of complex technical questions that customers have about Compaq products. The duties of the call centre agents include the creation of 'solutions' to common technical problems that customers have with different products. The solutions can be accessed by any member of the product team when a customer calls. Compaq's KMS is very sophisticated – re-use rates of the solutions are constantly monitored to ensure high-quality solutions are entered into the database, and the solution sets are used as the basis for training and monitoring technical capabilities of the team members.

Knowledge management frameworks

Unfortunately, many companies see a software package as all that is required to achieve the sharing and transfer of knowledge across functions, departments and partners. But if the management of this resulting knowledge is not integrated and shared across relevant organisational functions, there is little chance of there being sustainable relationship marketing. Knowledge management is a framework for moving data-driven marketing to a more strategic position within the broader CRM paradigm. The marketer needs to be less insulated from other functions and even from the informational advantages and consequences of data shared with other organisations. For example, Depres and Chauvel (2000)[21] distil literature from academics, consultants

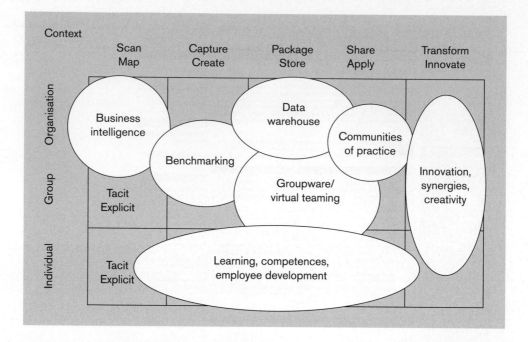

Figure 5.6 Knowledge management (KM) framework
Source: Depres and Chauvel (2000).[22]

and to other functions in the organisation, even outside the marketing function. In Figure 5.6 knowledge is measured on the vertical axis, while the horizontal axis provides a 'process' that essentially reinforces the importance of 'sharing'.

Summary

Good customer segmentation is critical for good marketing planning. We saw in this chapter how technology now allows us to become increasingly more sophisticated in the way we segment our customers and new databases allow us to perform geo-demographic segmentations with greater precision. In addition, new approaches such as micro-segmentation, psychographics and the use of transactional data are allowing even more sophisticated approaches to segmentation. The development of data warehouses and data marts gives us the ability to store and analyse large amounts of data on our customers. Good data mining techniques and software are vital for uncovering the customer insights from the data we have stored. Finally, it is important to create a knowledge organisation. It is not the amount of data that an organisation collects that is important but the way their organisation uses that data. Organisations have realised that they must actively manage their knowledge resources.

Case study

DISCO (A ROYAL AHOLD COMPANY)

Figure 5.7

Company profile

Disco was founded in 1961 and is a leading supermarket chain in Argentina, operating more than 200 stores with the brands Disco, Ekono, Súper Vea, Gonzalez, Americanos and Pinocho. These stores are located in five regions in the most densely populated areas in Argentina, and have a total selling surface of approximately 300,000 square metres. The company is controlled by Disco Ahold International Holdings NV, a joint venture between the retailing giant Royal Ahold of the Netherlands and local banking group Velox. The link with Ahold is easy to understand, but what do supermarkets have to do with financial services? Just about everything, as the Grupo Velox has shown.

The Banco Velox focuses its corporate banking activities on small and medium-sized suppliers of the Disco supermarket chain. The bank also supports the group's retailing operations through its consumer finance division, Credcuotas, while its retail banking operations are closely tied to the Disco supermarket. As Velox's executive director, Luis Maurette, explains: 'As an overall concept, Banco Velox will be present wherever there are Disco supermarkets. The target of our retail activities are the clients of Disco's successful loyalty programme DiscoPlus'. Maurette also mentions that 'the bank has strategic alliance agreements with Visa credit cards and Link, a major network of ATMs in Argentina'.

The economy in Argentina

Argentina has suffered a dramatic contraction of its economy in the last few years. This economic downturn started in 1998 and extended over 14 consecutive quarters, with 2001 ending with a considerable deterioration in the main economic indicators. Manufacturing levels and unemployment (nearly 25 per cent) reached the highest historical levels by the end of 2001. For the fourth consecutive year, Argentina's gross domestic product fell at the rate of 4 per cent. The supermarket industry was also affected by the crisis. The severe contraction in activity has translated into a significant reduction in investment by the main supermarket operators in Argentina. For the third consecutive year, food and non-food consumption fell, reaching an aggregated decrease since 1998 of 16 per cent and 43 per cent respectively.

Disco and technology

In his annual reports, the chairman constantly refers to the fact that 'Disco means technology' and that 'the company's strong conviction on information system development and the constant search for new technological solutions place Disco in a privileged position in the face of the business requirements generated by the businesses'. During 2001 and 2002, Disco invested significantly in operations, store formats and technology: 'The development of the Disco and DiscoVirtual concepts in the service segment and SuperVea and PlazaVea in price are clear examples of the implementation of this strategy. These as well as other actions performed in other areas, such as category administration, home shopping through DiscoVirtual on the internet, launching of the new payment method VALIDA for PlazaVea, the relaunch of Discocard, implementation of new services such as Discopago and Discocheck, confirm once again its leadership in the local market.'

Disco's electronic offerings

Disco has become the country's leading e-commerce player, and since launching online delivery in 1997 its online sales have grown to $40 million. That is about half of all of Peapod's (another unit of Royal Ahold) sales in the much more affluent US market. Total e-commerce sales in Argentina are about $150 million in 2001, compared with $150 billion in the USA. (Research suggests that only about 5 per cent of Argentines use the internet, as opposed to 60 per cent of the US population.) Disco has built the business without the massive customised warehouses and automated distribution systems that cost US companies like Webvan hundreds of millions of dollars.

Instead, it based the operation on a service that Disco has offered for decades: home delivery. In 2000 about 25 per cent of Disco's $2.5 billion in sales were delivered. Disco made good use of all the local and international tools available as a result of the association with Royal Ahold and the participation in its different global programmes. For example, by the end of 2001, Disco operated the following electronic-based services:

- *DiscoVirtual*. This tool enables customers to do their shopping online without leaving their homes. The system, among the first in Argentina, thus enables users to shop using their computers. While shopping, customers walk along the supermarket, where they can see the products, including their pictures and prices; they can also see the TV ads for the products and once they have finished shopping they can chose the means of payment and the delivery time. The connection may be established by Disco's web page on the internet or using a modem through Disco's customer service phone numbers (Disco provides users of this system with CD-based software). This service is supplemented with Disque, where customers may use the toll-free service for placing their orders via phone or facsimile.

- *In-store banking*. This service is rendered by Banco Velox inside the supermarkets. The stands include ATMs whereby Banco Velox is near its customers through Disco. In-store banking is a highly valued service contributing to increase loyalty between customers and Disco.

- *DiscoPlus*. Disco's frequent-buyer programme was launched by in 1996 under the 'Shop as always, win as never before' motto. It provides customers with the possibility of wining many prizes by accumulating points obtained through purchases. The purchases are stored in an online database including customer shopping preferences, making it an exceptional tool for improving Disco's product, service, and price quality and assortment according to customers' needs. The programme is available in all Disco stores.

The success of DiscoPlus

By early 2002 DiscoPlus's frequent-buyer programme had more than 3 million participants, making it the most successful scheme in Argentina. DiscoPlus's record of customer growth since its introduction in 1996 is impressive:

- 2001: 3.0 million
- 2000: 2.6 million
- 1999: 2.1 million
- 1998: 1.5 million.

Mining and warehousing customer data

Disco needed to analyse the information gathered from its customers through all its electronic offerings but primarily through DiscoPlus. Disco held more than 900 gigabytes of information, including all its databases and data warehouses. For this reason, the company felt it necessary to develop a data mining model that would be helpful to increase the business value for the users and would allow Disco to increase the value of this infrastructure. Disco completed an analysis of the segments of customers who were members of the DiscoPlus programme in Buenos Aires. The aim was to divide the customer portfolio into groups based on their shopping frequency, tendencies and ticket amounts. The availability and use of additional information on customers, combined with the application of clustering techniques, allowed the company to identify differentiated customer groups. These could be used to gain a better understanding of customers' behaviour and to design marketing actions that were more appropriate to each profile. The final objective was to achieve a better understanding of the customer base being analysed.

Technology solution

Disco had to build a system that allowed the items of each ticket issued by over 200 branches across the country to be stored online in a central database or data warehouse. This database had more than 2 billion records, with over 900 gigabytes of stored information in 2001. For the operation of this system, Disco implemented a data mining solution on a Microsoft platform. Since then, the company has been obtaining 'knowledge' with added value, making better use of the data available in the data warehouse. The system implementation was completed in one month, and it was initially done in the customer relationship management (CRM) area within the marketing department.

Disco needed a tool to analyse the information gathered in its databases. 'As our data warehouse was based on Microsoft, we thought that it would be most natural and appropriate to use the new possibilities offered by the data mining techniques that come with the analysis services of Microsoft SQL Server 2000 Enterprise Server', said Horacio Díaz, data warehousing project leader of Disco. With this implementation, Disco took its first steps in the application of advanced data mining processes for better use of the data available in its data warehouse. 'The data mining processes will allow us to create more business value through the adoption of several actions – such as tailoring communications to each profile or undertaking specific promotions for interest groups – on the grounds of the new business knowledge we are obtaining', concluded Díaz.

Sources: Disco website (www.disco.com, 2003); *Disco Annual Report 2001* (www.disco.com/ar); *The Standard* (30 April 2001);[23] Microsoft website (www.microsoft.com).[24]

Case study questions

1 What do supermarkets have to do with financial services?

2 Why is technology so important for a supermarket chain like Disco?

3 Why was Disco successful in its online offering while companies like Webvan were not?

4 Why did Disco find it necessary to develop its data mining model? What are the benefits?

5 Why do supermarket chains like Disco want to identify different customer groups?

Questions and exercises

Questions

1 Why is customer segmentation so important to creating customer insight?

2 What are the advantages of micro-segmentation over macro-segmentation?

3 Why would a company embark on a data warehousing initiative?

4 Describe and discuss the issues that companies face if they decide to undertake a data warehouse or data mining initiative.

5 Conduct a search on the internet to find out what types of organisation provide data mining software and data warehousing solutions.

6 Why is corporate knowledge so important in the early twenty-first century?

7 'It is not the amount of data that an organisation collects that is important but the way the organisation uses that data.' Comment.

Online exercises

1 Visit Claritas's website (www.claritas.co.uk). Comment on how the company can help businesses segment their customers.

2 Visit the website of Cognos (www.cognos.com). Review their product BusinessMiner and write a short note on its advantages and potential drawbacks.

References

1 Piercy, N. and Evans, M. (1999). 'Developing marketing information systems', in Baker, M. (ed.) *The Marketing Book*, 4th edition. Oxford: Butterworth-Heinemann.

2 Piercy, N. (2002). *Market-Led Strategic Change: Transforming the Process of Going To Market*, Oxford: Butterworth-Heinemann.

3 Berwick, E. (2002). 'Halifax launches exclusive plastic,' *Financial Times*, 14 September.

4 Acland, H. (2001). 'Ruling puts DM industry firmly on back foot', *Marketing Direct*, December.

5 Evans, M., Mitchell, S., O'Malley, L. and Patterson, M. (1997). 'Consumer reactions to supermarket loyalty schemes', *Journal of Database Marketing*.

6 Marsh, H. (2001). 'Dig deeper into the database goldmine', *Marketing*, 11 January.

7 Benady, A. (2002). 'Better targeted briefs', *Financial Times*, 28 May.

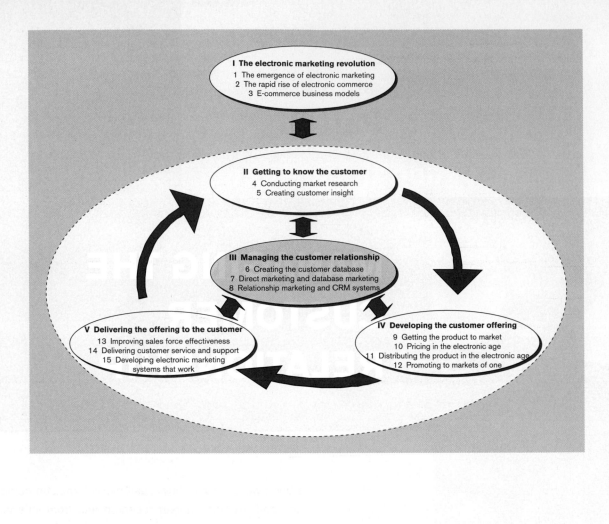

I The electronic marketing revolution
1 The emergence of electronic marketing
2 The rapid rise of electronic commerce
3 E-commerce business models

II Getting to know the customer
4 Conducting market research
5 Creating customer insight

III Managing the customer relationship
6 Creating the customer database
7 Direct marketing and database marketing
8 Relationship marketing and CRM systems

V Delivering the offering to the customer
13 Improving sales force effectiveness
14 Delivering customer service and support
15 Developing electronic marketing
   systems that work

IV Developing the customer offering
9 Getting the product to market
10 Pricing in the electronic age
11 Distributing the product in the electronic age
12 Promoting to markets of one

6

Creating the customer database

Learning objectives

Once you have read this chapter you will:

- understand the nature and role of marketing information systems (MkIS);
- understand the central role that the customer database plays in a marketing information system;
- understand the steps required to build an effective customer database;
- appreciate how the customer database can become a key strategic resource.

Contents

There are typically two uses of customer information: strategic and tactical. Strategically, the database can be used for:

■ changing the basis of competition

■ strengthening customer relationships

■ overcoming supplier problems

■ building barriers against new entrants

■ generating new products.[20]

We will see shortly how customer databases typically go through several stages of evolution or development before they end up as strategic organisational assets. Tactical uses are essentially operational and analytical. The distinction is an important one, as we will see when we discuss the design and development of customer databases.

The central role of the customer database

While an organisation may have many different kinds of operational systems, the key source of information is the customer database. This database plays a central role in integrating the information within an organisation (*see* Figure 6.1).

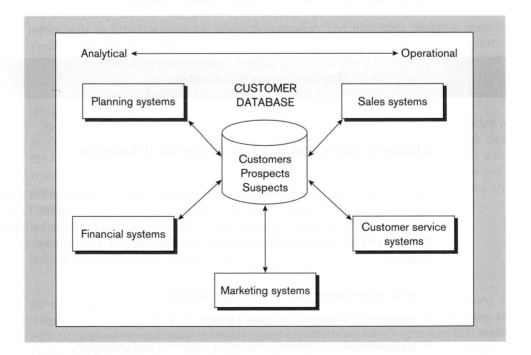

Figure 6.1 The central role of the customer database

Note from Figure 6.1 that:

- the customer database may contain information on potential as well as existing customers;

- although the database is shown as a single entity, in practice companies find that they have customer data stored in several databases, each of which is used for different purposes;

- the customer database is depicted as supporting a variety of operational and analytical systems (we will shortly examine these in more detail);

- customer information that is required for analytical reasons is often downloaded into separate stand-alone databases that are designed specifically for purposes such as data mining.

Operational and analytical uses

By operational uses, we mean the day-to-day support of the business. Examples include:

- a customer service representative of an electricity company accessing a customer's account details in order to answer telephone queries;

- a bank teller accessing a customer's current balance to decide whether or not to make a cash advance;

- a hotel receptionist keying in a customer's name to find out which room the customer has been booked into.

Analytical uses include the research of historic and transaction data to create or adjust a particular product offering or promotion. For example:

- the selection by an electricity company of the most appropriate customers for a mailshot to promote and sell home heating appliances;

- the analysis of a bank's customers to identify the most profitable segments;

- the analysis by a hotel manager of the home addresses of customers to measure the effectiveness of a particular advertising campaign.

Recency, frequency and monetary value (RFM)

Most of these types of analysis fall into one of three categories commonly referred to as RFM (recency, frequency and monetary value). Recency is an important concept. The drinks company Seagram has a worldwide database policy that restricts customer information on the database to that which is both recent and relevant. Names will not get on to the database in the first place unless they pass certain criteria. Similarly, if customers stay on the database for too long without responding to any offers, they are removed.[21] This raises another issue, namely 'exclusion' of some customers. It makes

EXHIBIT 6.3

WHISKY DRINKERS

Highland Distillers recently made a strategic marketing decision. It reviewed the promotion of its Macallan whisky brand and decided to switch its entire advertising budget into direct marketing. It built a database of 100,000 of its more frequent drinkers (those who consume at least five bottles a year), mailing them every few months with interesting facts about the brand, whisky memorabilia and offers. 'It's not a hard sell at all but we've found it's a great way to strengthen our relationship with customers and retain their loyalty in a fairly price-sensitive market', says Jason Craig, Highland Distillers' direct marketing and internet manager.

Source: Financial Times (24 July, 2002).[22]

sense for businesses to concentrate on those customers who contribute most in terms of sales and profit, but if too short-term a view is taken, certain customers who are likely to become higher spenders in the near future might be deselected because of lower spending.

Frequency and monetary value are related characteristics and good marketing analysis allows targeting based on customer profitability. Many companies can target their marketing messages exclusively to their most profitable customers (*see* Exhibit 6.3).

Other drinks manufacturers have followed a similar approach to Highland Distillers. In 2001 Campbell's Distillery (part of Pernod Ricard) ran a direct marketing campaign inviting 'frequent' consumers of its own brand Aberlour Whisky to:

Visit www.aberlourgold.com and nominate five of your friends or relatives who share your appreciation of the finer things in life. As soon as all five have given a positive response to your e-mail invitation then you will automatically be entered into our unique prize draw. The potential rewards include full board and lodging at one of the finest country house hotels in Scotland, a guided tour of the world-famous Aberlour distillery – where you can sample our award-winning single malt whiskies – plus a total of £1,000 spending money for the successful entrants.

While the AberlourGold website is no longer active, the company continues to maintain a strong internet presence that is used for a combination of marketing and sales activities aimed primarily at its frequent customers (*see* Figure 6.2).

As well as identifying volume segments and best prospects, the RFM information also contributes to the calculation of 'lifetime value' – another of the marketer's cornerstone measures. 'Lifetime' is perhaps a little of an overstatement – it does not mean the lifetime of the customers, but rather a designated period of time during which they are customers of your organisation. Sometimes marketers might only use a 'lifetime' period of three years, so it would probably be better to refer to 'longtime' value analysis. Whatever period is chosen, however, the value of the customer to the organisation in sales and profit terms over a period of time is an important concept in electronic marketing.

Figure 6.2 Marketing Aberlour whisky to frequent customers
Source: Aberlour website (www.aberlour.com, 2003).

Developing the customer database as a strategic asset

Shaw and Stone (1988)[23] believe in a four-stage process of development of the marketing database:

■ In *Phase One* the database is merely a sales database originating from accounting systems and focusing more on product sales rather than customers.

■ *Phase Two* is where there are often multiple databases for different sales territories or retailers. Although they may be used effectively within the sector they cover, there can be an overlapping of effort due to lack of communication and coordination. For example, customers might receive direct mailings from the same company, but different and even conflicting ones from different parts of that organisation. This problem of poor integration and limited strategic use of the database is quite widespread – organisational structures often mean that direct marketing is separate from functions such as sales and public relations, with each trying to maintain its own integrity by keeping vital information (even customer lists) to itself (Evans and Fill, 2000).[24]

▪ *Phase Three* sees more of a customer focus, with a single database coordinating all communication with customers. Analysis is according to profiles, transactions and other relevant factors, to determine how to target segments and individuals effectively.

▪ In *Phase Four* there is true integration, when different organisational functions, not just marketing, are linked with the marketing database.

In parallel with this analysis, Parkinson (1994)[25] identifies three levels of IT application within marketing, concerned with:

▪ the management of transactions

▪ profiling, targeting and developing effective direct marketing

▪ marketing productivity analysis, modelling (discussed later) and their link with strategic planning.

If the organisation is not truly customer-orientated (a theme of this chapter) then the marketing database will only have a tactical role. If used strategically, then the customer database can play a central role in building a relationship with the customer. We discuss the trend toward relationship marketing in a later chapter. However, if the marketing database is used merely tactically, its nature does not need to refer greatly to corporate strategy or organisational structure (Cook, 1994).[26] Under such circumstances, it is more concerned with 'the next event' than with a longer-term view of customers. Bigg (1994)[27] and Cook suggest that it is actually more usual for organisations to employ the database at the tactical rather than at the strategic level.

Developing the customer database

Identifying the sources of customer information

Customer information can be sourced from within the company or purchased from external sources (*see* Table 6.1). The most useful sources of customer information are often the internal systems within an organisation. Additional external information and customer lists can be sourced from list brokers such as Mardev (part of the Reed Elsevier group) or Dudley Jenkins (part of the Wegener group – *see* Exhibit 6.4). These increasingly international list brokers sell customer lists to clients at a typical rental charge of several hundred euro per thousand names. Most lists are supplied in a consistent format to facilitate de-duplication and data cleansing. In the UK such lists can be checked against the Mailing Preference Service (MPS) to exclude those who do

Table 6.1 Internal and external sources of customer data

Internal sources of data	External sources of data
Accounts/general ledger	Census data (the underpinning of geo-demographic systems)
Customer application forms	External lists from list brokers
Customer complaints	Market research (specially commissioned)
Customer enquiries	Records from sister companies or trade associations
Customer information files	Directory publishers
Market research (existing)	Credit referencing data
Merchandising statistics	
Promotional campaigns	
Service reports	
Warranty cards	
Transactional data	

EXHIBIT 6.4

DUDLEY JENKINS GOES DUTCH

Dudley Jenkins was the first UK company to trade customer lists. It was founded in 1970 and is now well into its fourth decade of business. As a leading UK list broker, it supplies over 100 million names each year to over 200 different clients such as the Royal Bank of Scotland and Pitney Bowes. Having played a major part in the consolidation of the UK direct marketing industry, Dudley Jenkins was itself acquired in 1999 by Wegener, the Dutch-based group with more than 40 companies in the information, direct marketing and media industries.

Source: Dudley Jenkins website (www.dudleyjenkins.co.uk, 2003).

not wish to receive unsolicited mail. There are other 'preference' services, some of which are subject to legislation. The Telephone Preference Service, for example, comes under data protection legislation in the UK and companies are required to clean their databases against this list of individuals who have registered to be excluded from outbound cold calling.

The sources of customer data are expanding rapidly and data fusion facilitates overlays of connecting data, ranging from the census and electoral roll to lifestyle survey data, transactional data and even genetic data. The latter is subject to a moratorium at the time of writing, but it is clear that financial services companies would be keen to identify potential poor risks for insurance policies on the basis of genetic disease in the prospect's family history.

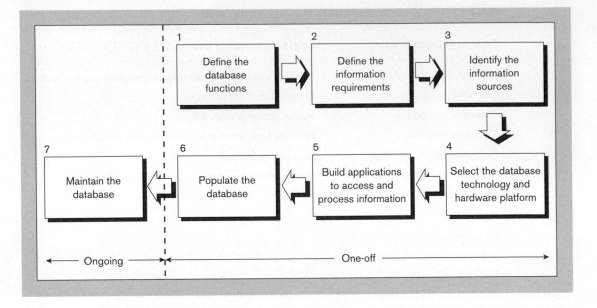

Figure 6.3 Seven steps to developing a customer database

Seven steps to developing a customer database

There are seven steps that should be followed in designing a customer database (*see* Figure 6.3). The first six steps need to occur only once, while the final step, maintaining the database, is an ongoing activity.

Step 1 Define the database functions

The first question to ask when deciding to build a customer database is: 'What do I want this database to do?' This may seem obvious, but it is fundamental to the success of any customer database initiative. The design of the customer database, and how data is held on it, will depend on whether the database is used primarily for operational or analytical purposes.

Operational applications have different demands, such as quick response time for accessing transactional or account data. If an electricity company is to provide good customer service, the customer service representative (CSR) needs to be able to access that customer's latest account details within a matter of seconds, just by keying in the customer's name or address. The same operational system is probably also used to send out the monthly or quarterly bills, but may be of limited use in analysing trends, selecting customer groups for a mailshot or for analysing electricity consumption across different geographic areas. For marketing analysis, a much wider set of data will be required and that data needs to be organised in a different fashion. Processing power to crunch through millions of calculations per second may be more important than fast access to individual items of information.

Thus the design and organisation of a customer database are critically dependent on its primary purpose. IT departments may be more focused on the operational aspects of systems, which can lead to the development of marketing systems that fail to meet the expectations of the marketing and sales staff. The onus is on the marketing department to communicate clearly its requirements to the IT department.

Step 2 Define the information requirements

There are two approaches that can be taken when defining the information to be held on the customer database. The first is to focus on a small amount of key customer information that can be used to make marketing decisions. The second approach is to capture as much information as possible and then start looking for trends within the data. This is the data mining approach, where an organisation creates a large data warehouse that is analysed to identify meaningful trends. To determine the most appropriate approach to take, the following questions should be asked:

- *What data do we really need?* Regardless of the approach taken, there are key elements of information that the marketing manager must have. Typically, marketers require data on customer name, address, age, profession and income. Other information on nationality, language spoken and personal hobbies may be useful, but often of secondary importance.

- *Does the data support our marketing segmentation strategy?* As organisations become more sophisticated in targeting specific market segments, it becomes more important to capture data to support these segmentation strategies.

- *How easily can the information be updated?* Keeping customer data up to date is critical. If data changes regularly and cannot be easily updated, it may not be worth the cost of obtaining it.

- *Should the database include prospective customers?* Marketing managers must decide whether to limit the database to existing customers or extend it to include information on prospective customers.

Step 3 Identify the information sources

Having defined the information required, the next step is to identify how the information will be acquired and updated on an ongoing basis. Customer information can be sourced from within the organisation or from third parties. While the purchase of mailing lists is still a popular method of finding potential new customers, the effectiveness of using such lists for direct marketing can be poor. Unless carefully targeted, response rates are often low and the cost of generating a sale can be higher than traditional methods of advertising. Typically, the best sources of customer data are from internal sources, but such data is often enhanced by combining it with additional data from external sources. A 1997 survey by the Direct Mail Information Service (DMIS) in the UK found that 53 per cent of companies matched their internal data with external geo-demographics and 57 per cent with external lifestyle profiles.[28]

Step 4 Select the database technology and hardware platform

There are several different ways in which data can be held in a database. The choice of database technology and database management system depends on the uses that are intended for the database. A relational database is likely to be the preferred database solution for the vast majority of applications. The main advantages of relational databases are faster processing speeds and the flexibility to create more complex queries to determine relationships between data. The selection of a hardware platform will depend on a number of factors, including the existing hardware, the number of customers and the number and location of potential users. Designing the right technical solution is not a trivial exercise and can be very expensive if the wrong decision is made (*see* Exhibit 6.5).

Step 5 Build applications to access and process information

Once the technology has been selected, the applications to utilise the information held on the customer database can be built. We will examine database marketing applications in more detail in the next chapter.

EXHIBIT 6.5

WEBHOUSE HITS THE TECHNOLOGY WALL

Priceline.com affiliate WebHouse Club had a short life. It launched at Halloween 1999 and shut its doors in October 2000. The private company, which licensed the name-your-price model and received $179 million in financing from Priceline founder Jay Walker and more than $360 million all told, was unable to raise enough capital to build a national network to sell groceries and gasoline. In its first few months WebHouse amassed two million customers – a half-million for the gas business alone in just 12 weeks.

On the technology front, it was decided that all the various Walker enterprises – Priceline, WebHouse, Perfect YardSale and others – would share the customer database (Oracle software running on Sun Microsystems Unix boxes). That way, customer data had to be entered only once and could eventually be accessed by all the enterprises. Sounds good in theory. Trouble was, each business had different approaches for entering and accessing this information, introducing a litany of operational problems and breakdowns. By early 2000 the national rollout had to be delayed for a month because the platform broke down so often. Key retailers such as Winn-Dixie Stores had to pull back deployment to give the website breathing space.

How ironic that such a bold enterprise would fall victim to religious zealotry over the choice of technology, when Walker himself repeatedly avowed: 'We're a marketing company, not a technology company.'

Sources: *The Industry Standard* (16 October 2000);[29] *Business 2.0* (December 2000).[30]

Step 6 Populate the database

The task of populating a customer database is a major exercise and poor quality customer data is the primary reason for most database marketing failures. Much of the required information on existing customers is already held in paper or electronic format within the organisation, but a major problem is the number of different locations where such information can be found. In organisations such as banks and insurance companies, older ('legacy') computer systems are often organised on a product, rather than a customer, basis. In other words, if Joe Bloggs has a current account, a savings account, a credit card and a pension with the same financial institution, it is entirely feasible that his details are held on four different databases. When data is consolidated on to one central database, it is likely that four separate entries will be made for Joe Bloggs. When a mailshot is planned, it is also entirely possible for Joe Bloggs to receive four separate pieces of direct mail. Apart from the additional cost, such unnecessary communication will leave Joe Bloggs with a less than favourable impression of the company.

Software can be purchased to assist in the 'de-duplication' and merging of customer records so that there is only one record for each customer on the database (*see* Exhibit 6.6). However, such software is not foolproof. In some instances there is no alternative to contacting large numbers of customers to obtain or confirm their details. Several creative techniques can be employed to persuade the customer to divulge such personal information. Many companies on the internet ask their customers to provide, or update, their own information. Whichever approach is used, the exercise of populating the database will take time and require considerable resources.

Step 7 Maintain the database

Once marketing managers are satisfied with the quality of the information in the database, an ongoing maintenance activity is required to keep it up to date, otherwise its effectiveness as a marketing tool diminishes quickly. As Curtis (1996)[31] states: 'The database is a living breathing thing that requires constant attention – you can't just build it and say "that's it"'.

This maintenance activity is a major task that is compounded by errors caused at data entry. A competent data entry clerk might have an error rate of between 2 and 4 per cent, while the incidence of errors from people entering their own customer details over the internet can be significantly higher. Births, deaths, marriages and changes of address can alter between 8 and 12 per cent of the information in a database in any one year. In the UK, the Royal Mail has been changing an average of 5 per cent of its postcodes annually.[32] It only takes a few years for the integrity of customer information in any database to degrade to a level where its usefulness becomes questionable. Incorrect or out-of-date information is costly, and can drive customers away rather than enhancing the relationship (*see* Exhibit 6.7).

Ideally, companies should regard all contacts with a customer as an opportunity to update the customer's details on the database. For example, if a customer walks into a bank branch to open up a new account, all the relevant details should be entered on to the database at the point of contact with the customer, and any existing information that the bank may have on the customer should also be verified at the same time. In reality, few organisations can claim to have up-to-date information on their

EXHIBIT 6.6

KEEPING AN EYE ON DATA QUALITY AT ALLERGAN

Companies within the pharmaceutical industry are under a great deal of pressure to merge customer and business information from multiple sources, consolidate data for multiple brands and integrate disparate systems and organisational views of the customer. Key drivers in the USA include consolidation within the healthcare industry; third-party data sharing with other healthcare constituents, including health maintenance organisations (HMOs), preferred provider organisations (PPOs), third-party prescription services and hospitals and doctors' offices; as well as the 1997 decision by the Food and Drug Administration that allows drug manufacturers to market their products directly to consumers.

One such specialty pharmaceutical healthcare provider is Allergan, which uses a data quality application called Trillium from the customer relationship management (CRM) company Harte-Hanks. In April 2002 Allergan, which develops and commercialises products for the eye care, pharmaceutical, ophthalmic surgical device, over-the-counter contact lens care, neurological and dermatological markets, decided to use Trillium for its global data quality needs. Allergan will use Trillium to standardise, de-duplicate and integrate data from many sources, including sales, customer and marketing data, for inclusion into its data warehouse. Trillium will also provide the foundation for enabling CRM initiatives and supply chain management in future phases of its rollout at Allergan. The Trillium software consists of four core modules:

- *Converter* – a data investigation, transformation and analysis tool used for data conversions and reengineering.

- *Parser* – a processing engine for data cleansing, elementising and standardisation.

- *Geocoder* – an internationally certified module for postal and census geo-coding and address verification and standardisation.

- *Matcher* – a module designed for relationship matching and record linking.

Sources: Harte-Hanks website (www.harte-hanks.com, 2003); Trillium website (www.trilliumsoft.com, 2003).

customers. Consider the following case of a European bank[33] that carried out an analysis of the quality of its customer information:

- ▪ 10 per cent of accounts in the customer database did not have a valid name

- ▪ 13 per cent did not have a full address

- ▪ 47 per cent did not have a title/sex for the customer

- ▪ 55 per cent did not have a marital status

- ▪ 72 per cent did not have a home phone number

EXHIBIT 6.7

DEAD MEN'S BLUES

One of the problems with data is that some of it is nearly always 'dirty' – in other words, wrong. Data goes out of date fast, as customers change address, clients change jobs, orders are cancelled. The constant struggle to keep data up to date inevitably leaves inaccurate bits floating around the system, while human error adds to the problems when details are wrongly keyed in or duplicated. Some results can be embarrassing. Everyone has experienced a moment of irritation or mild amusement on finding a piece of junk mail mis-addressed. Most people think no more of it. Occasionally, though, it may cause serious offence. Take the case of Marion Hearman of Reading, who was shocked to receive through the post a mock newspaper whose front page showed her husband, who had died six months before, winning a prize. The READ Group, which runs a bereavement register so companies can check their databases against deaths, estimates that British businesses waste more than £33 million a year sending marketing material to dead people.

Source: Financial Times (28 May 2002).[34]

- 75 per cent did not have a date of birth
- 77 per cent did not have a occupation
- 85 per cent did not have a record of the number of dependent children.

The percentage of customer records where all eight fields were completed was extremely low and, with complete information on only a few per cent of all customers, the effectiveness of the bank's customer database was seriously compromised.

Treating the customer database as a strategic resource

Customer information provides organisation knowledge

Many organisations are realising that in an increasingly competitive market it is information on their customers that can be a differentiator. DeTienne and Thompson (1996)[35] believe that 'The customer database is an opportunity for organisations to mechanise the process of learning about customers'. Furthermore, this needs to be iterative because 'The database transcends the status of a record keeping device and becomes an implement of ever-increasing organisation knowledge'.

In this sense, the marketing database can focus on a whole range of different categories – for example new prospects, best prospects, loyals and so on – which can essentially be boiled down into acquisition or retention strategies. Retailers, for example Tesco, Safeway and Sainsbury, capture transactional data at point of sale via loyalty card schemes. By 2002 Tesco had analysed their customer database and identified 100,000 different segments – each of which were targeted differently. The company analysing the Tesco data is Dunn Humby; Clive Humby (1996)[36] has described the interrogation of data and stated that it is not worth including 'everything' as there is always the danger of 'paralysis by analysis'. He goes on to suggest that 'It is not the detailed transaction data that is of interest, but patterns in transactions, such as an increasing balance over time of the range of products purchased'.[37]

Customer transactions and customer relationships

Gronroos (1990)[38] indicates that there are several strategies open to marketers, along what he calls the 'marketing strategy continuum'. At its extreme, transactional exchange involves single, short-term exchange events encompassing a distinct beginning and ending. Consumer goods firms with mass markets and little contact with their ultimate customers are most likely to place themselves at this end of the continuum. At the other extreme, relational exchange involves transactions linked together over an extended time frame. These exchanges trace back to previous interactions and reflect an ongoing process. Gronroos suggests that most consumer goods companies are more likely to be on the transaction end of the continuum. Despite this, there have been many attempts to apply relationship marketing concepts to consumer markets. The main elements come from research in industrial marketing, which indicates that relationships are complex, long-term in nature, and mutually beneficial.

It is the customer database that is at the heart of the relational exchange. Although it can merely be used as a list from which to target customers via direct marketing activity, it can alternatively provide a wealth of information on the market and on customers within it. In this context, the database provides information for both planning and analysis purposes: the database can be analysed for the most attractive segments, for campaign planning and predicting campaign response. So, it is clear that whichever techniques are chosen to update customer information, company employees must be encouraged to recognise the value of the customer database and the data held on it. Such data is an important strategic asset.

The need for a change in mindset

A mindset and attitude change is required in most companies before employees will treat every contact with the customer as a means of improving the level of information held on that customer. Often, there is no incentive to log a customer telephone call or ask all those questions when a new customer walks in the door. Frequently, major process and procedural changes are required to ensure that each customer contact can be captured without hindering or slowing down the transaction. For example, many airlines have loyalty schemes. However, when a customer arrives at the check-in counter, there may be another half a dozen people in the queue and the last thing that the check-in clerk (or the person in the queue who is already late for a flight) needs is the additional delay of accepting the loyalty card and typing the details into the system. One answer is to have self-swipe mechanisms for customers to record their own flights, or to implement a system for recording the flight when the ticket is purchased rather than when the boarding card is issued. Another is to embrace the power of the internet and allow customers to check, and update, their own details online. It is not uncommon nowadays for companies to pay their customers to provide more detailed personal information, which can be used to improve the subsequent marketing messages via the internet. This 'permission marketing' approach is gaining ground as a possible solution to consumer privacy concerns and also a way of reinforcing the organisation–customer relational paradigm (Westin, 1967).[39]

This last point is the focus of a later chapter on relationship marketing, but it is worth mentioning here because it can be argued that technological developments in the collection and use of marketing information have led to a change in the marketing paradigm itself – away from transactional marketing and toward relationship marketing (Evans et al., 1998).[40] This relationship marketing paradigm is concerned with all activities directed towards attracting, developing and retaining customer relationships.

Summary

An effective marketing information system is the cornerstone of any successful marketing department. In many cases it will use information from other systems in the organisation and also from external sources. However, the key component of any MkIS is the customer database, which can have both operational and analytical uses. The key steps in developing a customer database are deciding what type of information is necessary and ensuring that the data can be kept up to date. Many customer databases are over ambitious: not only do they not use much of the information that they gather, but the quality of the data becomes very suspect over time. Finally, customer information is a key strategic resource and should be managed accordingly.

Case study questions

1 Why did Marks & Spencer Money (M&SM) need to upgrade its customer database?

2 What benefits has the new customer database brought to M&SM?

3 Use the internet to investigate the capabilities of the software products that M&SM chose for its database solution (Affinium Campaign, Enterprise Miner, MicroStrategy).

4 How can M&SM use the customer database to improve its relationship with customers?

5 Did M&SM follow the seven steps for developing a customer database?

Questions and exercises

Questions

1 Describe a marketing information system.

2 Why is a customer database central to any marketing organisation?

3 Discuss the steps in developing a customer database.

4 Why is it so important to keep customer data up to date?

5 Provide an example of an internet site that encourages, or pays, its customers to update the information held on them.

Online exercises

1 You are working as a marketing analyst for one of the top five UK banks. Access the site of www.dudleyjenkins.co.uk. Review the information on the site and write a short note to your marketing director outlining the opportunities if any of using the services of Dudley Jenkins.

2 Access the website of Similarity Systems (www.similaritysystems.com). Write a short note on how Similarity's ATHANOR product suite of data quality management tools (Designer, Runtime and Realtime) can be employed in the seven stages of developing a customer database. How does ATHANOR help maintain the quality of customer data in a customer database?

References

1 Kohli, A.K. and Jaworski, B.J. (1990). 'Market orientation: The construct, research propositions and managerial implications', *Journal of Marketing*, Vol. 54, No. 2.

2 Jaworski, B.J. and Kohli, A.K. (1993). 'Market orientation: antecedents and consequences', *Journal of Marketing*, Vol. 57, No. 3.

3 Narver, J.C. and Slater, S.F. (1990). 'The effect of a market orientation on business profitability', *Journal of Marketing*, Vol. 54, No. 4.

4 Slater, S.F. and Narver, J.C. (1995). 'Marketing orientation and the learning organisation', *Journal of Marketing*, Vol. 59, No. 3 (July).

5 Piercy, N. (2002). *Market-Led Strategic Change: Transforming the Process of Going To Market*, Oxford: Butterworth-Heinemann.

6 Piercy, N. and Evans, M. (1999). 'Developing marketing information systems', in Baker, M. (ed.) *The Marketing Book*, 4th edition, Oxford: Butterworth-Heinemann.

7 Marshall, K.P. and LaMotte, S.W. (1992). 'Marketing information systems: a marriage of systems analysis and marketing management', *Journal of Applied Business Research*, Vol. 8, No. 3, Summer.

8 Talvinen, J.M. and Saarinen, T. (1995). 'MkIS support for the marketing management process: perceived improvements for marketing management', *Marketing Intelligence and Planning*, Vol. 13, No. 1.

9 Harvey, F. (2002). 'Let's get personal again', *Financial Times*, 28 May.

10 Kotler, P. (1999). *Marketing Management: Analysis, Planning, Implementation and Control*, millennium edition, New Jersey: Prentice-Hall.

11 Harvey, F. (2002). 'Let's get personal again', *Financial Times*, 28 May.

12 Evans, M. (1998). 'From 1086 and 1984: direct marketing into the millennium', Special Issue of *Marketing Intelligence and Planning on Direct Marketing*, Vol. 16, No. 1.

13 Fletcher, K. and Peters, L. (1996). 'Issues in consumer information management', *Journal of the Market Research Society*, Vol. 38, No. 2.

14 Market Research Society. (1997). *Code of Conduct*, London: Market Research Society.

15 Evans, M., O'Malley, L. and Patterson, M. (1996). 'Direct mail and consumer response: an empirical study of consumer experiences of direct mail', *Journal of Database Marketing*, Vol. 3, No. 3, pp. 250–61.

16 O'Malley, L., Patterson, M. and Evans, M. (1997). 'Intimacy or intrusion? The privacy dilemma for relationship marketing in consumer markets', *Journal of Marketing Management*, Vol. 13, No. 6.

17 Patterson, M., Evans, M. and O'Malley, L. (1996). 'The growth of direct marketing and consumer attitudinal response to the privacy issue', *Journal of Targeting, Measurement and Analysis for Marketing*, Vol. 4, No. 3.

18 www.ascet.com

19 Klitsch, J. (1997). 'Databases put the direct in direct marketing', *Journal of Health Care Marketing*, Vol. 17.

20 Fletcher, K., Wheeler, C. and Wright, J. (1990). 'The role and status of UK database marketing', *Quarterly Review of Marketing*, Autumn, pp. 7–14.

21 Curtis, J. (1996). 'Sorting out the wheat from the chaff', *Precision Marketing*, 5 February.

22 Murphy, C. (2002). 'Catching up with its glitzier cousin', *Financial Times*, 24 July.

23 Shaw, R. and Stone, M. (1988). 'Competitive superiority through database marketing', *Long Range Planning*, Vol. 21, No. 5.

24 Evans, M. and Fill, C. (2000). 'Extending the communications process: the significance of personal influencers in the UK motor market', *International Journal of Advertising*, Vol. 19, No. 2.

25 Parkinson, S. (1994). 'Computers in marketing', *The Marketing Book*, Oxford: Butterworth Heinemann.

26 Cook, S. (1994). 'Database marketing: strategy or tactical tool?', *Marketing Intelligence and Planning*, Vol. 12, No. 6, pp. 4–7.

27 Bigg, A. (1994). 'Techno tactics', *Campaign*, 8 July.

28 DMIS (1997). *Consumer Databases: A Study of External Lists and In-House Database Usage*, London: DMIS.

29 Abramson, R. and Hammer, B. (2000). 'Priceline on the ropes', *The Industry Standard*, 16 October.

30 Mott, S. (2000). 'Trial by fire', *Business 2.0*, December.

31 Curtis, J. (1996). 'Sorting out the wheat from the chaff', *Precision Marketing*, 5 February.

32 Reed, D. (1996). 'Power merge', *Marketing Week*, 12 July.

33 O'Connor, J. Unpublished research.

34 Harvey, F. (2002). 'Dead men's blues', *Financial Times*, 28 May.

35 DeTienne, K.B. and Thompson, J.A. (1996). 'Database marketing and organizational learning theory: toward a research agenda, *Journal of Consumer Marketing*, Vol. 13, No. 5, pp. 12–34.

36 Humby, C. (1996). 'Digging for information', *Marketing*, 21 November.

37 Humby, C. (1996). 'Opening the information warehouse', *Marketing*, 18 September.

38 Gronroos, C. (1990). 'Relationship approach to marketing in service contexts: the marketing and organisational behaviour interface', *Journal of Business Research*, Vol. 20 (January).

39 Westin, A. (1967). *Privacy and Freedom*, New York: Atheneum.

40 Evans, M., O'Malley, L. and Patterson, M. (1998). 'Relationship marketing and privacy issues: building bonds or barriers', *Journal of Database Marketing*, Vol. 6, No. 1.

7

Direct marketing and database marketing

Learning objectives

Once you have read this chapter you will:

- appreciate how direct marketing and database marketing have evolved;
- understand how database marketing adds value and can be used to improve marketing performance;
- become familiar with direct marketing categories and trends;
- understand new tools in direct marketing such as e-mail and SMS messages;
- appreciate the importance of data privacy;
- become familiar with the likely future direction of direct and database marketing.

Contents

DIRECT MARKETING IN THE INTERNET AND WIRELESS AGES

- ■ E-mail marketing
- ■ SMS and MMS marketing
- ■ Electronic direct marketing in the future

DATA PRIVACY

- ■ Mounting customer concern
- ■ Use of census data
- ■ Other concerns about Big Brother

ADDRESSING DATA PRIVACY CONCERNS

- ■ The need for awareness
- ■ Data privacy legislation
- ■ Self-regulation guidelines for businesses

THE FUTURE OF DATABASE AND DIRECT MARKETING

- ■ The 'myth of database marketing'
- ■ The database marketing skills gap

SUMMARY

CASE STUDY

Introduction

Having looked at how we build the customer database in Chapter 6, we now examine how we can apply this knowledge. One way we use this information is through direct marketing and database marketing. Unlike a TV or magazine advertisement that is broadcast to a wide audience, direct and database marketing campaigns are targeted at specific customers on a one-to-one basis. There are increased opportunities and challenges to this approach. The opportunity is that people respond better to a more personalised approach: if you meet someone and you greet them by their first name, it creates a very positive impression. The downside is that if you get it wrong, it likewise creates a negative impression. As organisations often have thousands or even millions of customers it is necessary to have systems and databases to record correct customer information. Thus any attempt to develop a direct marketing or database marketing campaign will require a good understanding of the technology and how it can be used effectively.

We begin with a general discussion of the origins and evolution of direct and database marketing, before examining the trends in both. We then devote a significant section of this chapter to discuss data privacy issues, which affect how we store and use data on our customers. We need to be aware of the guidelines and legislation that have been put in place to protect the privacy of consumers. We finish with a perspective on the future of direct and database marketing. Let us begin by looking at the evolution of direct and database marketing.

The evolution of direct and database marketing

The origins of direct marketing

Direct marketing is not new in concept. The first proponent of direct marketing is sometimes cited as the Bishop of Chartres in 1194 when he requested money from English and French noblemen to rebuild his cathedral (Evans, 1998).[1] Other early examples include Aldus Manutius, who published a book catalogue in Venice in 1498, and William Lucas, who published a gardening catalogue in England in 1667. A variety of other mail-order catalogues and clubs appeared throughout the eighteenth and nineteenth centuries, especially in Europe and the USA. In fact, there was a significant growth in the USA in particular during the 1800s because of rising demand for goods from isolated communities that could be serviced by the improving distribution and postal systems (IDM, 1995).[2] The mail-order industry in the UK also grew on the basis, initially, of 'savings clubs' (for example Christmas clubs) and this was extended to credit availability, so a major motivation in the UK revolved around financial considerations. The development of sophisticated 'credit referencing' can be traced back to this era and is a significant factor in the growth of current direct marketing (explored later).

The concept of direct marketing is simple. Instead of broadcasting a mass-marketing message through television or print to a wide number of people, a customised message is sent on an individual, direct basis to a much smaller number of people who are more predisposed to listening to the message and buying the product or service. In comparison, mass marketing is untargeted and can be much more expensive. National television advertising is one of the most expensive forms of marketing and is entirely inappropriate for many organisations that target relatively small or niche markets.

Direct marketing has probably been the most significant development in marketing in recent years, not least due to the rapid growth in the use of databases in marketing (as discussed in the previous chapter). This has also contributed to the paradigm shift from transactional marketing based on the 'marketing mix' approach created by Borden (1964)[3] and popularised into the 4Ps by McCarthy (1960),[4] to the notion of retention strategies within a relationship marketing context. Today, the term direct marketing is often used interchangeably with the term database marketing and, more recently, the use of such terms as relationship marketing and customer relationship management have also become commonplace. How then should we define database marketing?

What is database marketing?

Database marketing can be defined in a number of different ways. DeTienne and Thomson (1996)[5] give a broad definition of database marketing:

> Database marketing is the process of systematically collecting, in electronic or optical form, data about past, current and/or potential customers, maintaining the integrity of the data by continually monitoring customer purchases and/or by inquiring about changing status and using the data to formulate marketing strategy and foster personalised relationships with customers.

Exhibit 7.1 provides an example of how one company has developed a marketing database that is the central corporate tool for managing not only its direct marketing campaigns but its entire customer relationship process.

EXHIBIT 7.1

BMW'S HIGH-TOUCH MARKETING DATABASE

In 2000 BMW built a robust customer and prospect database designed to:

- provide a comprehensive view of the automotive and financial services BMW customer;
- deliver short-term, incremental revenue through opportunistic marketing programmes;
- increase customer loyalty through understanding and ability to deliver relevant, timely communication;
- secure BMW's place in its customers' lives by identifying which households are good targets for additional BMW purchases.

BMW now has a central system of measurement (the BMW Report Centre monitors communications and response from prospects and customers) and has the ability to view prospects as well as customers. BMW can now view the full shopper-owner cycle from first point of contact, through sale and cross-sale. The new marketing database contains a broad range of information on the BMW consumer, including campaign, response and financial service data. The 190 individual and household data points allow a full view of the BMW customer and help deliver smarter targeting for up-selling and cross-selling.

Source: MSDBM website (www.msdbm.com, 2003).

Benefits of database marketing

Linton (1995)[6] defines a number of ways in which database techniques allow marketing managers to improve performance:

- increased understanding of customers

- improved customer service

- greater understanding of the market

- better information on competitors

- more effective management of sales operations

- improved marketing campaigns

- better communication with customers.

Increased understanding of customers

Even where companies have built a customer database, it is surprising how few analyse their databases for answers to questions such as:

- How many customers do I have?

- What products are they buying?

- Which segments do those customers fit into?

- Which delivery channels do they prefer?

- Which customers can I not afford to lose?

A marketing database that allows marketing managers to understand their customers is the first step towards building long-term relationships with them. By knowing what individual consumers buy, the retailer might be able to target them with relevant offers, while the consumer saves money in the process, so over time there is more scope for relational development (Evans, 1998).[7]

Improved customer service

One of the most common applications of database marketing is customer service, where it can be used for a wide variety of operational functions, including:

- *Enquiries.* Enquiries can be supported through marketing databases that allow access to a variety of customer, product, price and transaction information.

- *Complaints.* Complaints handling is typically supported through the use of databases that categorise, monitor and track customer problems.

▓ *Helpdesk facilities.* Helpdesks allow customers to phone a central telephone number for answers to commonly asked questions and solutions to commonly encountered problems.

In most cases, these customer service applications are provided both in face-to-face situations and via a telephone service. The use of marketing databases in supporting telephone-based customer service activities is examined in more detail in Chapter 13.

Greater understanding of the market

In Chapter 4 we examined the use of information technology in marketing research. The integration of marketing research data with other information on the marketing database allows companies to answer strategic questions such as:

▓ What direction should we take with new product development?

▓ Which new delivery channels should we be experimenting with?

▓ Which new markets should we be expanding into?

These issues can be taken further and related back to the concept of data fusion that we introduced in Chapter 5. Much database data, such as transactional and profiling data, provides valuable information on who is buying what, when, how and where, but it is market research that can get beneath the surface even further and discover reasons why behaviour is as it is. As a result, some direct marketers are linking their databases with market research data. As we mentioned in Chapter 4, consumer panels are linked with geo-demographic or lifestyle databases in T-groups.

Thus direct marketing has much to gain from turning to more traditional market research, not as a substitute for the highly measurable and accountable testing methodology, but to create a valuable 'gestalt' (Evans, 1998).[8]

Better information on competitors

According to Linton (1995),[9] competitor assessment is easily overlooked and very often is not captured in a formalised way. The integration of competitor information into a marketing database, rather than in the heads of individual marketing managers, will allow the following questions to be answered with greater speed and accuracy:

▓ Who are our main competitors by product or market segment?

▓ How have their market shares changed in recent weeks/months/years?

▓ What is their pricing structure and what impact have price changes had on market share?

▓ How much are our competitors spending on promoting their products and services?

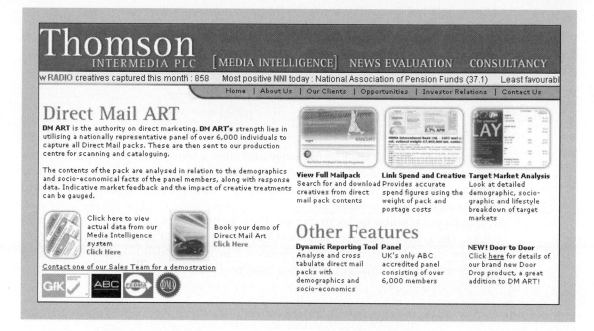

Figure 7.1 Direct Mail Art (DM ART) from Thomson Intermedia

Source: Thomson Intermedia website (www.thomson-intermedia.com, 2003).

The formal analysis of competitor activity and the impact of marketing decisions taken by competitors will enable the marketing manager to make better-informed decisions and have a clearer understanding of the likely impact of those decisions.

Related to this, and to the above discussion of market research and T-Groups, is the further use of consumer panel data. For example there are consumer panels run by Thomson Intermedia (DM ART – *see* Figure 7.1) and by ACNielsen (MMS) that provide details of competitors' direct mailings.

This is an interesting development because it destroys the 'privacy' of mailings. Previously, these were more private than, say, mass media advertising because they were hidden from the view of competitors by being within envelopes and distributed through letter boxes rather than more overt media. Now, however, panel households collect all their direct mailings and the agency concerned scans it into computer formats and analyses the profile of recipients of all direct mailings within different product markets, for any company to purchase – to see what sort of campaigns their competitors have embarked upon, when and to whom.

More effective management of sales operations

Another major area of operational support that is enabled by database technology is the management of sales operations. We examine in more detail the use of marketing databases within sales in Chapter 13, but a sample of sales activities that are supported through marketing databases includes:

- managing the performance of different sales representatives
- managing customer contacts and client portfolios
- demonstrating product features and providing quotations
- capturing and fulfilling customer orders.

Improved marketing campaigns

The management of marketing campaigns involves a series of steps from initial analysis and planning through to the subsequent monitoring of those campaigns. These steps are depicted in Figure 7.2, which also shows the different technologies used to support each stage of a campaign.

Database marketing tools can improve the effectiveness of running marketing campaigns. The Global Consumer Finance (GCF) division of GE Capital claims that a new customer database system that it implemented in 2001 helped it reduce the time to execute marketing campaigns in Austria from twelve to two weeks.[10]

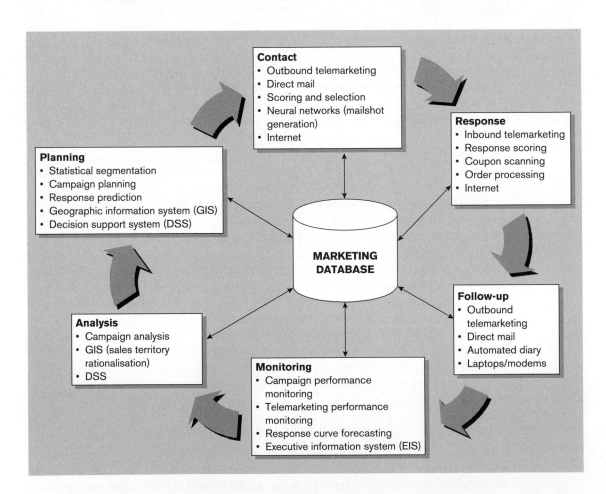

Figure 7.2 Database marketing in the management of marketing campaigns

EXHIBIT 7.2

BEANZ–DIRECT

In 1994 the British division of Heinz, an American food giant, abandoned conventional ads for individual products such as ketchup and baked beans in favour of database-driven direct marketing. By combining its existing 1 million names (gathered from people who had responded to previous offers on tinned goods) with lists of similar households bought from brokers, Heinz has built up a database of 4.6. million people to send a copy of *At Home*, a free magazine of recipes which also promotes its products. Heinz will not give figures, but says that the strategy has paid off.

Source: *The Economist* (23 August 1997).[11]

Better communication with customers

It is sometimes forgotten that communication is a two-way process. All too often, marketing managers mistake the periodic mailing of promotional material for a meaningful and relevant dialogue with customers. Marketing databases should be used for issuing customer communications at appropriate times, such as in the case of Heinz's *At Home* magazine in Exhibit 7.2. Where marketing databases are used to support customer service representatives (CSRs) in call centres, they should also be capable of reminding CSRs of all previous customer contacts, whether that contact was by mail, telephone or in person.

The evolution and future of database marketing

Database marketing has evolved from unsophisticated direct mail or telemarketing lists where all that was required for a campaign was a list of addresses or telephone numbers. In the early days, the large amounts of junk mail arriving at people's homes caused many consumers to switch off and ignore further mailshots. The route to more effective direct marketing campaigns was through better customer information, to increase the relevance of the offer, and better management of the communication between the company and the customer.

Despite the practical difficulties of building a sophisticated database marketing operation, the customer database is the greatest single application of technology within marketing. The rapidly declining costs of computer hardware and software during the 1970s and 1980s have increased the attractiveness of database marketing. The cost of storing and accessing a single customer name on a database dropped by a factor of a thousand during these two decades alone, resulting in a massive shift towards the importance and use of database marketing. Nowadays, companies are becoming much more precise about the type of potential customer to whom they will mail, and the size of mailshots is reducing correspondingly, while the effectiveness, or response rate, from these mailings is also increasing.

There have been both demand-side and supply-side reasons for the growth of the direct data-driven approaches within marketing (Evans et al., 1996).[12] Let us now examine these reasons, starting with demand-side factors.

Demand-side factors

There have been changes in market behaviour and also changes in the effectiveness of traditional media. Some of the more significant changes in market behaviour include:

- *Fragmentation and demassification.* In terms of markets, it is clear that fragmentation has taken place and markets have become demassified. These major trends have aided the growth of direct marketing. This is manifested in greater pluralism within society, evident in the high street where pluralism in clothing styles is observable. The Henley Centre (1978)[13] predicted this trend as far back as the 1970s when it discussed household behaviour as being 'cellular' rather than 'nuclear' – households were beginning to do things together less and less and beginning to behave more independently. Thus families were not eating together as often, they had TV and sound systems in their 'own' rooms and whereas it used to be typical to have one large 'family-sized' packet of cornflakes in the kitchen, it was becoming more likely that each household member would have a packet of 'their' cereal in the cupboard.

- *Increase in the number of working women.* There has also been an increase in the number of working women, many of whom are joining their male counterparts in seeking time-saving purchasing methods, such as direct mail and telemarketing. Working women are also more independent and contribute to the greater number of smaller households, which require narrower targeting.

- *Divorce rates and other social changes.* The divorce rate has risen and with it the number of small and single households – affecting both sexes. This also means that more men are deciding which washing powder they will buy and more women are buying cars and pensions for themselves. The continuing trend away from cash as the means of payment to credit, debit and smart cards, through the post and over telephone and internet cables, has enabled purchase behaviour to take place when the customer wants it – 24 hours per day and from the armchair, office phone, laptop computer or mobile phone.

Companies have also become disillusioned with more traditional promotional media over recent years. Market fragmentation has resulted in diminishing audiences for individual media, media costs have soared and consumers are suffering from 'clutter'. Although above-the-line advertising (such as TV advertising, for which advertising agency commission is payable) is targeted at specific audiences – the UK audience for a late night Friday show on Channel 4 is unlikely to have the same composition as one for a Wednesday afternoon on BBC2 (or if it has, the audience might not be in the same frame of mind) – the targeting is still of the 'shotgun' variety rather than the 'sniper's rifle' that is possible through direct marketing. Audiences are fragmenting as more TV channels appear (satellite and cable) along with more newspapers and magazines – all with advertising space to fill. Furthermore, consumers are not helping the advertiser by video recording TV programmes and 'zapping' the commercials (Kitchen, 1986).[14] Direct marketing is seen to have the potential to overcome the difficulty of this 'clutter' because the message can be personalised. Together, the trends have created a demand for more effective targeting.

Supply-side factors

The supply side on the other hand is concerned with changes in information about customers (based on much more sophisticated research) and also on technological improvements that have facilitated the collating and analysis of huge amounts of detailed and personalised information. It is clear that there has been a tremendous increase in the availability and collection of personalised customer data. This is based, in part, on the relative decline of demographic segmentation variables, due to their lack of explanatory depth and their relatively broad targeting capabilities. The typical market profiling according to age, gender and social grade gave way to parallel profiles in psychographic and geo-demographic terms (*see* Chapter 4). Indeed, the rise of psychographics and geo-demographics have added to the decline of demographics because of their potential abilities to understand target customers in greater detail, even individually, and to target them equally specifically.

The future direction of database marketing

The availability of more individual-specific data coupled with technological facilitators is leading to the targeting of individuals based on what we know of their interests and characteristics. The means for storing and retrieving such individual data is the marketing database and it is this that is at the heart of much direct marketing. The main focus, of course, should still be the customer, but increasingly marketers are using profile data (such as geo-demographics) and behavioural data (such as trans-actional data) to understand their customers and certainly to target their marketing activities (in terms of the 'best' prospects). It could be argued, though, that this wealth of data, good as it can be for identifying who buys what, when, and how, is not a true surrogate for understanding why customers buy as they do (Evans, 1999).[15] Indeed, Mitchell (2001)[16] has even quoted a director of a major UK supermarket as saying: 'We have given up trying to understand our customers'.

However, what is clear is that using transactional and other personal customer data allows companies to 'sense and respond' rather that spend time and resources developing theories and testing them out. It also, however, raises concern over marketing's new direction. Where is the role of more qualitative research that has a well-proven track record in providing explanations for how and why customer behave in the way they do?

Direct marketing

Direct marketing categories

Telemarketing and direct mail are sometimes thought of as the main, or only, forms of direct marketing. However, many traditional forms of marketing have a direct marketing component. According to the Direct Marketing Association (DMA, www.dma.org) in the UK, the different types of direct marketing are:

- *Telemarketing.* With the continued growth in special-number usage (for example 0800, 0500 and 0808 numbers in the UK and 1–800 numbers in the USA) and the growing trend for call centres to become customer contact centres handling 'outbound' as well as 'inbound' calls, telemarketing is now the major form of direct marketing in the UK. On average, UK households now receive an average of three telemarketing calls per month.

- *Direct mail.* Interactive electronic alternatives such as e-mail are on the increase, but direct mail is still a cornerstone of the direct response industry.

- *Direct response TV.* Direct response television continues to grow in popularity, led by the financial services industry. Interactive TV advertising remains a small component of direct response TV.

- *Database list marketing.* The purchase and rental of database lists has now become commonplace in direct marketing.

- *Door-to-door.* The traditional marketing and selling of products by visiting consumers' homes continues to be a significant component in the direct marketer's arsenal.

- *Inserts.* Inserts in newspapers and magazines are also traditional direct marketing tools.

- *National press.* While most national press advertising has some element of direct response, only a quarter of all such advertising can truly be regarded as direct response.

- *New media.* Internet advertising has risen from nothing in the mid-1990s to become a significant force in direct marketing, despite the dot-com bust. E-mail is the primary form of new-media direct marketing, which also includes internet banner advertisements and SMS messages.

- *Magazine direct response.* Response advertising shows a similar profile to national press advertising – most have a direct response element but true direct response advertisements account for approximately one quarter of the total.

- *Contract magazines.* Contract magazines are a direct form of communication between manufacturers and their customer about their products and services.

- *Direct response radio*. Approximately half of radio advertising has some form of call to action.

- *Regional press direct response*. Regional press tends to be more traditional, with true direct response advertising accounting for 8 per cent of all advertising in the regional and local press in 2001.

- *Outdoor/transport*. Direct response posters now account for approximately 20 per cent of all outdoor/transport advertising.

Direct marketing expenditure in the twenty-first century

Direct marketing has gone through a series of peaks and troughs over the past 50 years. Its golden age was the 1950s, in the form of mail-order catalogue selling in the USA as the post-war boom drove consumer spending. However, this golden age was coming to an end in the 1960s and 1970s as competition from television intensified. During the 1990s direct marketing saw a major resurgence again. The forces behind the re-emergence of direct marketing over this decade were:

- *Fragmentation of advertising media*. The arrival of commercial television may have heralded the decline of direct marketing in the 1960s, but commercial television itself came under fire in the 1990s from a variety of different cable and satellite channels. Advertisers began to understand what Livingston and Schober (1995)[17] refer to as the 'dishwasher powder effect' – why advertise dishwasher powder on television if 85 per cent of households do not have a dishwasher and if direct marketing can help you identify the 15 per cent who do?

- *Increasing retailer power*. The increasing power of retailers and the success of own brands have made it more and more difficult for manufacturers to gather information and develop relationships with their customers. An increasingly effective means of bypassing the manufacturer and gaining the 'mindspace' of the end-customer is via direct marketing.

- *Declining brand loyalty*. The product proliferation that we discussed in Chapter 1 has done little for brand loyalty. Direct marketing can help win back that brand loyalty by keeping a particular product or service in the consumer's mind on a regular basis.

- *Search for long-term customer relationships*. Not all customers are profitable. And those that are often only become profitable after the company has recouped the costs of recruiting them in the first place. Companies are beginning to understand the desirability of retaining customers and maintaining their loyalty. Regular communication via direct marketing can help.

Today, the most widely used forms of direct marketing in the UK are telemarketing and direct mail which, according to the Direct Marketing Association (DMA), account for half of the £11 billion spent on direct marketing during 2001. Figure 7.3 provides a breakdown of expenditure by media type, showing the continued rise of electronic forms of direct marketing, particularly telemarketing and new media.

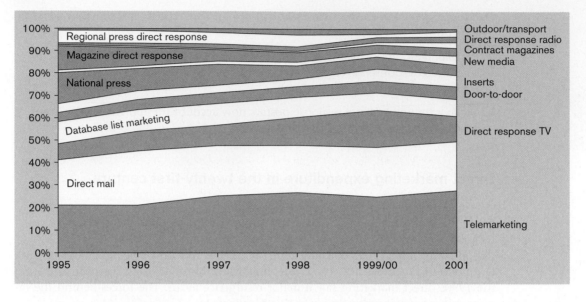

Figure 7.3 Direct marketing expenditure in the UK by media type (1995–2001)
Source: DMA (2002).[18]

Given that direct response television, radio and press will typically require listeners and readers to contact the advertiser by telephone or internet, these figures show the increasingly important role that such new media has in direct marketing, even if the actual expenditure on new media is still relatively low in overall terms. The DMA agrees, pointing to an increasing combination of new and old direct marketing techniques:

> Overall, the direct marketing industry is adapting and expanding to incorporate the challenge of new methods and channels whilst continuing to employ more traditional methods to greater effect. The future of the industry in the 21st century looks certain to bring more growth and gain greater investment from marketers.[19]

Direct marketing in the internet and wireless ages

E-mail marketing

The recent resurgence in direct marketing has been enabled by the increased productivity and processing power of information technology. As the technology continues to develop and marketers became more skilled in using it to its maximum advantage

EXHIBIT 7.3

E-MAIL ORDER

Argos, the pioneer of mail-order and catalogue retailing in the UK, publishes a total of 48 million catalogues each year – 36 million of its main catalogue (over 950 pages and growing) and 12 million 'Argos Additions' catalogues (over 700 pages). Two editions are printed for each – Spring/Summer and Autumn/Winter. Argos offers customers a multi-channel approach to shopping, via stores, through the website and over the telephone.

Argos launched its first e-mail marketing campaign in 2002 as part of its 'Get Set for Summer' promotion. The promotion ran alongside a TV advertising campaign. An Argos spokeswoman said: 'New e-marketing tools are emerging all the time. We are looking forward to seeing the results of this campaign as this is the first time we have been able to replicate the above-the-line TV advertising in a marketing e-mail, as well as incorporate dynamic content to cope with the flexible nature of our product offers.'

Source: Argos website (www.argos.co.uk, 2003); Inbox website (www.inbox.co.uk, 2002).

to target key customers, it will continue to grow in importance. The internet provides companies with a new and richer source of customer information with which they can target selective audiences. Today, many websites will gather significant amounts of customer data in return for free information or other services. This personal information can subsequently be used by those companies (or others to whom the information is sold) for direct marketing. The medium for many of these direct marketing campaigns is by e-mail. Already, companies like Argos in the UK have started to apply modern e-mail marketing techniques to revive the stagnant old mail-order businesses that once dominated direct marketing (*see* Exhibit 7.3).

Similarly, an e-mail newsletter written by Japanese Prime Minister Junichiro Koizumi broke subscription records when it was launched in 2001. The newsletter, entitled 'Lion Heart' in reference to Koizumi's mane of wavy hair, gained about a million subscribers within a week of its launch. The research group GartnerG2 found in 2002 that more US businesses were using e-mail marketing campaigns than traditional direct mail, primarily because of the disparity in cost between the two media ($5–7 per thousand for e-mail versus $500–700 per thousand for direct mail).[20]

SMS and MMS marketing

E-mail is increasingly used to target consumers: by 2001 expenditure on internet direct marketing had increased from zero to nearly 5 per cent of total UK direct marketing expenditure. In addition, experiments are now being made with newer forms of direct marketing using wireless and mobile phone technology (*see* Exhibit 7.4).

EXHIBIT 7.4

ASIA RULES THE SMS ROOST

When it comes to the wireless future, Asia rules the roost. Japan recently launched its 2.5G mobile telephone based on its i-mode standard. China is the world's largest mobile phone market. The Philippines sends more SMS messages than anyone else. Hong Kong, Korea, Taiwan and Singapore all have mobile phone penetration rates in excess of 50 per cent. Whichever way you turn, Asia has switched on to mobility. And where the consumer leads, the marketing dollars follow. Heineken is currently the global poster pin-up of SMS and it cut its teeth in Australia and China. Singapore has just seen the world's first conversation-based SMS marketing campaign. Location-based marketing services are just round the corner according to Hubert Ng, CEO of Hong Kong mobile telco CSL. Wherever you look there's something in the air – and that something is increasingly going to be an SMS marketing message with your name on it. British music retailer HMV is already experimenting with location-based SMS marketing in its domestic market. If you opt in to a 'promotion finder' service you receive special offers whenever you are within 500 metres of an HMV store. Similar services will be coming your way soon. So do you have a wireless marketing strategy yet?

Source: Mobile Commerce World (15 December 2001).[21]

There are more than 500 million GSM (global system for mobile communications) users in the world capable of receiving text messages using short messaging service (SMS) technology. These individuals generally carry their phones with them wherever they go, and when they receive a message they have to open it first before being able to delete it. Marketing opportunities do not come much better than that. In the future, sophisticated wireless marketing may become genuinely interactive, allowing personalised one-on-one conversations with a target audience, but for the moment, SMS is still in the experimentation stage. A 2002 survey in the UK from the DMA[22] found that:

- 60 per cent of respondents are currently running e-mail marketing campaigns;

- of these, notably, 16 per cent of marketers are using e-mail marketing more than direct mail, with 30 per cent electing to use e-mail marketing rather than telemarketing;

- 55 per cent are using e-mail marketing more than SMS.

With the arrival of newer generation mobile handsets, a new marketing medium is beginning to open up through the use of multimedia messaging service (MMS) technology. MMS is basically an upgrade of text messaging that allows pictures and images to be sent via a mobile phone. Mobile telecommunications companies like Vodafone (*see* Figure 7.4) have a vested interest in the promotion of SMS and MMS technologies for marketing purposes, since they drive up the traffic on their networks.

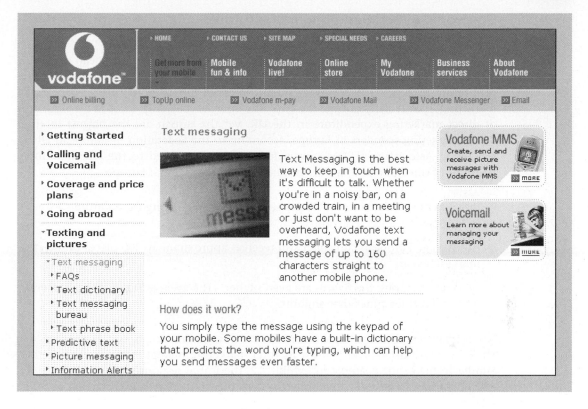

Figure 7.4 Vodafone's SMS and MMS offerings

Source: Vodafone website (www.vodafone.com, 2003).

It remains to be seen how SMS and MMS marketing will fare. Avon is targeting teenage girls with text messages to go to their website for further interaction, relationship building and of course sales.[23] A concern here could be the unscrupulous targeting of children. An extension of this is the targeting of prospects in real time. For example, the popular film *Minority Report* demonstrates a likely scenario: customer profile and transactional records are accessed in real time as that customer is recognised via biometrics (such as retina recognition) as they enter or just pass close to a store; relevant offers are then transmitted to that customer while in or near the store. Satellite and third-generation (3G) telephony technology can provide this sort of real-time location-based targeting.

Will we also see everyday household items linking us digitally with companies? For example, the humble fridge, linked to the internet, could become an important medium for uploading stock levels of yoghurt to the local supermarket, so that (EDI-style) orders are placed and subsequently delivered. The same internet link could download recipes and other food and kitchen products and services to the location at which they would be most relevant.

Electronic direct marketing in the future

According to DoubleClick (www.doubleclick.com), almost half of European marketers used online marketing tools in 2002. However, it should also be noted that the online or internet market is still relatively small compared to traditional methods of direct marketing – particularly outside the USA. The internet may only account for 5 per cent of direct marketing expenditure in the UK, yet the British are the biggest internet direct marketing spenders in Europe, according to the Federation of European Direct Marketing Association (FEDMA, www.fedma.org). Compared to the UK, traditional methods of direct marketing still dominate across continental Europe:

- direct mail still accounts for 70 per cent of direct marketing expenditure in Europe;

- the average European consumer still receives approximately 200 pieces of direct mail each year;

- in some countries, the figures are even higher – the average Dutch person receives more than three times that amount.

Nor is it always advisable to put all eggs in the direct marketing basket. Some years ago Shell Denmark decided to redirect its total marketing budget into direct marketing. Similar to the Heinz example in Exhibit 7.2, the initial response was excellent. However, brand awareness eventually declined to the point that it was starting to affect sales.[24]

Yet such analysis misses the important point that all forms of direct marketing involve the collation and use of customer data, regardless of the media by which the marketing message is ultimately delivered. The fact that direct mail is more prevalent than e-mail is less relevant than the trend towards more and more customer information being collated into larger and larger customer databases. This trend is the source of much concern and debate. Are consumers sufficiently protected from companies who can abuse this information? What limitations should be put on the use of customer data? And are special rules required for the internet, wireless and other emerging technologies?

Data privacy

Mounting customer concern

Consumers are becoming increasingly concerned about the amount of information that is being gathered on them and how this information is used. Concerns will continue to grow as the internet, regarded by some as the world's biggest data collection agency, increases its reach. Small programmes known as 'cookies', downloaded to the hard disks of computers used by internet users, can be used to trace a surfer's path through the internet and pass this information back to the website owner. Few websites that gather customer data (either directly by requesting customers to register to use their site or indirectly through the use of cookies) tell their visitors what they gather and how they use it. In 1999 it was also revealed that Intel's computer chips and Microsoft's software transmitted unique identification numbers whenever a PC was logged into the internet, potentially allowing consumers' internet activities and transactions to be tracked and monitored.

As a consequence, database marketing has attracted privacy concerns. Information privacy is perhaps the major issue in terms of wider social implications and refers to the ability of individuals to determine the nature and extent of information about them being communicated to others (Westin, 1967).[25] The dilemma is one of balancing consumers' rights to control access to their personal information and companies' rights to information access for business purposes (Simitis, 1987).[26]

Three quarters of a sample of 200 companies were not prepared for the new data protection legislation of 1999 (GB Information Management, 1999).[27] This lack of awareness is a concern because it suggests companies are more concerned with today's campaigns and, perhaps, feel the new legislation is not particularly important. This last point was demonstrated at the FEDMA Council Day in 1998. During a presentation by the legal director, an off-the-cuff and unscripted remark was made to the effect that the new legislation being introduced throughout the European Union (EU) was 'a solution looking for a problem'. There was spontaneous applause from the audience, which was composed almost entirely of senior direct marketing practitioners from several member states. This is a reflection of the attitude the industry might sometimes be seen to possess. It is further reinforced by the title of a paper in a practitioner-based direct marketing journal: 'Beating the data protection registrar!' (Dineen, 1999).[28] So data protection legislation is sometimes seen to be a hindrance to how direct marketing campaigns are run.

However, activity at a grassroots consumer level has also been on the increase, particularly in the USA. For example, when Benetton announced in 2003 that it was introducing radio frequency identification (RFID) tags on clothes in its Sisley range, the reaction from consumer groups was swift and furious (*see* Figure 7.5 and the case study at end of the chapter).

Use of census data

Taking privacy and data protection issues further, and again beyond the 'campaign' level, it is useful to explore briefly one of the main sources of data that was a major initiator of the direct marketing explosion: the commercial use of the census data.

Although names and addresses cannot be revealed from the UK census, the statistics for enumeration districts (EDs) can. As we discussed earlier, such data can be linked with the postcode database (there is one postcode for approximately 15 households) and with the electoral register (another database), making it possible to identify individual households and their characteristics. One of the recent debates is between the Data Protection Commission's position that the electoral roll was not collated for marketing purposes and should not therefore be used in this way, and on the other hand the marketing industry, which argues for freedom in its use. Recent court cases have upheld the position of the information commissioner and there are now two electoral rolls, one being the 'opt-out' version.

Figure 7.5 Consumer boycott against Benetton
Source: CASPIAN website (www.boycottbenetton.org, 2003).

Clearly, without the electoral roll it is more difficult to identify individual households from census data. One study by Denny (1999)[29] suggests that a ban on using electoral roll data could cost advertisers £55 million per year, because 'The cost of not having access to the electoral roll would be five pence per [mail] pack'.

Other concerns about Big Brother

A further area for potential 'social responsibility' concern is the purchase of marketing data by government departments. The information specialists CACI, for example, has an entire department dealing exclusively with government contracts for ACORN and related products. Geo-demographic systems use an increasing range of financial data sources to overlay census, housing and demographic data, and the resulting 'financial' ACORN and MOSAIC products can be of potential value to the UK Inland Revenue (for example) to check financial details and trends against tax returns from those they want to investigate further.

The UK Inland Revenue is also able to access individualised transaction data from supermarket loyalty schemes for those cases of potential tax fraud that it investigates (Key, 2000).[30] Claimed levels of poverty on the tax return can be compared with actual purchase behaviour. Would consumers be so willing to sign up for these schemes if this was known?

The UK government has been interested in loyalty scheme data for another purpose. The idea was to track consumers' food consumption patterns with a view to assessing the impact of genetically modified foods (Hansard, 1999, Parker, 1999).[31,32] Is this the point beyond which the use of personal data, supposedly for marketing, becomes unacceptable – or is it entirely justified to use such data to investigate a serious health issue of public concern? Could it be that government has been content to provide the marketing industry with space to collect, fuse and mine data from a variety of sources and then for various departments to buy or take what they can use for reducing fraud and for other instances of social (individualised) monitoring?

Sharing of data is also an issue. Mail Marketing, for example, is to share some of its lists with a US list company Infocore (Wood, 1998).[33] However, the EU Data Protection Directive prevents all member countries from exporting personal information to countries that do not have adequate data protection, which includes the USA, in the view of the EU. As the EU information commissioner has said: 'Businesses exporting data must be satisfied that they comply with the law – otherwise I will simply prevent the activity'.[34]

The possible acquisition of genetic data is another concern (Specter, 1999),[35] with perhaps even more serious ethical issues. The accessing of individual medical records might be considered an invasion of privacy if information that is understood to be confidential between doctor and patient is shared with financial services companies. In a survey of 3,000 UK households:

- 75 per cent were against genetic tests for insurance underwriting;

- 85 per cent were against insurance companies rejecting applicants on the basis of genetic tests;

- 78 per cent were opposed to insurance companies charging higher premiums on the basis of genetic tests.

Indeed, 68 per cent of the sample thought that this use of genetic data should be prohibited by law (Borna and Avila, 1999).[36] Introna and Powlouda (1999)[37] report that medics have also expressed concern. The logical extension of the scenario is that those who do not need insurance will be insured and the rest will be excluded.

An outcome of data mining is the identification of specific customers' contribution to profit. Segmentation is often based on this, leading to 'gold', 'silver' and 'bronze' levels of purchasing (Beenstock, 1999).[38] However, might the less privileged become disaffected when they realise that others are being presented with the 'better' offers? There are signs that this has been recognised by government – a social exclusion department has been established in the UK and is concerned about banks closing branches in favour of direct approaches because of potential exclusion effects within some sections of the community. In the USA the Community Reinvestment Act is supposed to prevent banks from closing in poor neighbourhoods, so perhaps there are signs of the tide turning with respect to these sorts of wider social responsibility issues, but at a political rather than at a marketing level.

Data privacy legislation

The situation in Europe

The 1998 EU Data Protection Directive obliges all member states to update their data protection legislation to allow the 'processing' of personal data only where the individuals concerned have given their consent or where, for legal or contractual reasons, this processing is deemed to be necessary (for example, consumer credit legislation requires financial institutions to ask certain questions of any individual applying for a loan). Personal data processing is given a much wider definition in the directive than in most existing data protection legislation in operation around Europe. Individuals will also have the right to object to being targeted by direct marketing activities. The directive also lets EU citizens sue organisations that misuse personal data. As EU member countries enact their own national laws in accordance with the directive, the protection afforded to the individual will be increased, as will customers' understanding of their rights to privacy. These changes will pose particular issues for the holders and users of customer information, particularly where direct marketing activities are concerned.

US legislation

The USA may be further ahead in terms of internet usage than any other country, but in many respects its data privacy laws are less advanced. This has become of particular concern because of the increasing amounts of customer data that are being gathered, held and used in corporate data warehouses (*see* Exhibit 7.6).

The rapid expansion of commercial databases is helped by the fact the USA has no broad-based law governing how companies collect and use personal data about customers. While companies operating in the EU must comply with the sweeping Data Protection Directive, US corporations are governed instead by a patchwork of legislation covering specific sectors such as financial services, health and telecommunications. The Gartner Group has predicted that the USA will be squeezed into adopting more stringent data privacy regulations for the online world. The Health Insurance Portability and Accountability Act (HIPAA), effective in the USA since 2003, was developed in response to growing concerns about the privacy of personal health information in the information age. Marketers in the US life sciences industry now require written permission before they can use an individual's data for direct marketing purposes.

Legislation in other countries

Pressure to conform will grow as the trend toward privacy regulation gains momentum beyond the boundaries of the EU. Countries such as Brazil, Chile, Argentina and Canada, as well as several in Eastern Europe, are considering or have already implemented stringent, EU-style data privacy policies.

Data privacy in a post-September 11 world

In recent years, another dimension was injected into the debate – the need for national governments to protect themselves even at the cost of the data privacy of individuals. In a post-September 11 world, many governments have enacted legislation to limit data privacy (*see* Exhibit 7.7).

EXHIBIT 7.6

THE COSTS OF DATA PRIVACY AT WAL-MART

Wal-Mart, the world's biggest retailer, has created what analysts believe is the largest and most complex commercial database. The Arkansas-based company recently doubled the size of its central data warehouse, which can store and analyse more than 200 terabytes of information. A terabyte is 1,000 gigabytes or 1 million megabytes. Put another way, the Wal-Mart database could store all the books and records in the Library of Congress – 25 times over. Such scale is one of the more dramatic aspects of the rapid accumulation by companies of information about sales and customers – a trend causing anxiety among privacy advocates and politicians. While US corporate investment in information technology has in general slumped from the very high levels of the late 1990s, the cost of data storage has tumbled due to advances in computer hardware. This has made it economic for companies to increase substantially the amount of data they collect.

Stephen Brobst, chief technology officer at NCR's Teradata data warehousing division, said the hardware and software required to store 1 megabyte of data was currently 15 cents, down from $15 a decade ago. He predicted that the cost per megabyte would fall to 1 cent within five years. Companies such as Wal-Mart regard the ability to analyse huge quantities of information as a strategic asset. Its database is the foundation of a sophisticated system that enables the company to track and predict demand for consumer products.

Source: *Financial Times* (15 June 2002).[44]

EXHIBIT 7.7

EU DATA PRIVACY ON HOLD?

A bitter battle over the right to privacy and the use of new technology ended yesterday when the European parliament said telecommunications and internet companies could be obliged to keep information on their users for a 'limited period' for national security reasons. The measure, an amendment to a European Union (EU) directive on data protection, had worried human rights advocates, while some telecoms companies had complained of the cost of keeping extra information. But after pressure from EU member states in the wake of September 11, MEPs from the main right and left wing parliamentary groupings swung behind the change. The European Commission, which had initially proposed that normally data could only be stored 'for the purpose of billing and for interconnection payments', also accepted the change for fear that otherwise the legislation could be delayed for months.

Source: *Financial Times* (31 May 2002).[45]

Self-regulation guidelines for businesses

A recent survey from Georgetown University[46] examined the privacy practices at top commercial websites. The survey found that, while 93 per cent of websites collect personal information about visitors, only two-thirds give notification of how that information will be used. Worse, less than 10 per cent comply with the privacy protection standards outlined by the Federal Trade Commission (FTC). To meet the FTC standards, a site must do five things:

- notify users when data is being collected;

- give users a chance to 'opt out' of giving information about themselves;

- give users access to their information so they can correct it;

- provide adequate security for customer databases;

- provide access to a live customer contact.

These principles are being taken on board by the progressive marketing companies (*see* Exhibit 7.8) but there is clearly a long way to go before consumer concerns are addressed by the majority of companies gathering customer information over the internet.

One company that has been praised for its stance on protecting customer privacy is the McGraw-Hill group of publishing companies that operates more than 80 different websites. Its privacy policy is based on four principles that cover the main issues that customers face:[47]

- *Notice.* Tell prospective customers what information you're collecting and what you're planning to do with it. When it comes to collecting information, uncertainty is the enemy. If you keep people in the dark about what's happening to their private information, they'll imagine the worst.

- *Choice.* Adopt a policy with a procedure by which customers can choose not to have their information shared outside your company. It's a way of saying you recognise the information they've shared with you is, in important ways, still theirs.

EXHIBIT 7.8

PRIVACY AT NATIONAL EXPRESS

Our site provides an opt-in and opt-out facility so that you only receive information if you choose to. At any time you can access your account and change your status indicating whether you want to opt-in or opt-out of receiving marketing information. If you choose opt-in status, whenever we send you information, we will always give you the opportunity to request your details to be removed from our marketing list.

Source: National Express website (www.nationalexpress.com/p.cfm?n=pg-pri, 2003).

■ *Security*. Give the customer confidence that their information is safe from tampering, safe from theft, and safe from misappropriation and misuse.

■ *Review and correction*. Give customers a way to see what information has been collected from them, and a means to correct any errors in that data.

Other companies understand their customer sensitivities and try to address their data privacy concerns. Many have restricted the transfer of customer information outside their own organisations. Organisations such as the Red Cross, AT&T and Reader's Digest refuse to market their customer lists to other firms and others, such as the retailer Lands' End, will retain all customer information and rent out only the names. One large credit reporting agency, with 120 million names in its file, has also decided to stop providing mailing lists to direct marketers.

The future of database and direct marketing

The 'myth of database marketing'

Rosenfield (1998)[48] uses the term 'myth of database marketing' when talking about the gap between the promise of database marketing and its practice. A survey of the state of database marketing by Seller and Gray (1999)[49] confirms that such a gap exists by providing a sobering message that the practice fails, in many instances, to live up to the promise: 'Proponents of database marketing speak often and loudly of its role as a source of competitive advantage. Yet surveys of database practitioners show few companies realise significant advantages from their systems.'

While these comments are sobering, it is worth putting them into perspective. Marketing practitioners and students should recognise that database marketing is still at a relatively early stage of development. While direct marketing using mail-order techniques and bought-in lists has been with us for some time, the sophisticated use of customer database technology is a much more recent phenomenon. The fact remains that while such database technology is now cheaper than it ever has been, the management and marketing processes that are needed to accompany it are still relatively immature (*see* Exhibit 7.9).

The database marketing skills gap

We believe that the customer database is the most important technology enabler in marketing, and that database marketing will remain the cornerstone of sound marketing strategies into the future. This poses problems for some organisations. There is a skills gap between analysts who can analyse data but do not understand marketing segmentation models and marketing graduates who cannot analyse the data. Information for electronic marketing is now increasingly based on data-driven metrics and these require much more curriculum coverage than appears in most universities.

EXHIBIT 7.9

THE FUTURE OF DIRECT MAIL

Priceline.com's Jay Walker delivered a chilling speech to the audience of Direct Marketing Days New York, predicting the end of paper, printing and the post office. (This was before Priceline.com stock plunged from $162.50 to $1.37.) All marketing will be accomplished on the computer. Oh yeah? I hit the computer at 5 a.m. to finish this article and look what awaited me on AOL:

- cherryspop@exmai Best Insurance Rates Ever!
- bfsnaer2431a72@p Earn Extra Cash With A Free Online Casino. . . . 5057pDCO1-243AK14
- Lori.Anderson-re Congratulations Denys, Your Entry was Selected!
- Swttlkr923 All of the things you see on the Inter-net are logged!! 4434d
- ioffers@reply.mb What's Better Than FREE Satellite TV?
- freetermquote@pr Prepare yourself!
- foundmoney@consu dennyhatch, do we have your money?
- ESavers@usairway US Airways' Domestic E-Savers for Easter Weekend
- insurance_rep_19 Re: Lowest Term Life Insurance 199 sk9gg72
- kateanie@arabia. Get a FREE ADULT MOVIE!! 11673
- mortgagetou2Xtd4 We Have Mortgage Lenders Ready To Help You.
- Happy_Easter@cus Denys – EASTER ROSES ONLY $29.99 PLUS FREE CHOCOLATES!
- viqjzystfuxnrvay Viagra To Your Door bxymh
- UIO5363@MoscowOf Health care for Pennies, call our hotline today
- alerts@marketwat Bulletin: Andersen CEO Berardino resigns
- billmcnutt@chart Trade Mission to South America May 19–24
- mkaye@reply.mb00 Hey, there's a price on my head . . .
- health2002@yahoo Hgh: safe and effective release of your own growth hormone!18804
- chefscatalog_sup Save up to 70 per cent. CHEF'S Spring Clearance . . .
- R-8-722010-46686 14th Annual Card Forum and Expo – Register Now – Save up to $300
- duh@conspiracima women welcome to our casino
- mortgagelender23 We Have Mortgage Lenders Ready To Help You.
- adfxh@geography. DONT GO TO JAIL . . . Katmandu! 30385

- uenelnfy@yahoo.c Viagra Without A Doctor Appointment . . . 2357
- BigNews56833348@ Mortgage Information For You!
- mkaye@reply.mb00 Someone, pinch me
- DVD_Deals@custom Get 4 DVDs for $.49 each! Details Inside!
- poiuytf@msn.com *News Alert* Technology and Innovation take the Hassle out of Mortgages!
- stuboysen@earthl DMCNY 4/11 Luncheon – 'Winning Creative from Around the World'
- snoreless@nation Stop Snoring GUARANTEED!

Years ago, Maurice Chevalier crooned, 'Thank heavens for little girls'. Today I croon, 'Thank heavens for "Delete All"!' My prediction: direct mail will be around for a long, long time. And all the old rules apply.

Source: Target Online (2001).[50]

Data-driven marketing requires marketing curricula to equip graduates with appropriate skills and at least an understanding of the same language that data miners use. However, it is important to remember that metrics are not, and cannot, be a substitute for understanding and real insight (Evans et al., 2002).[51]

Summary

In this chapter we looked at how we use the information stored in customer databases through direct marketing and database marketing. These marketing campaigns are targeted at specific customers on a one-to-one basis. The benefit of this approach is that people respond better to a more personalised approach. The downside is that if you use incorrect information on a customer and get it wrong it creates a very negative impression. With thousands or even millions of customers at stake, having good systems is critical to being able to launch effective direct marketing or database marketing campaigns. We also discussed the importance of data privacy issues that affect how we store and use data on our customers. We outlined some of the guidelines and legislation that should be used to protect the privacy of consumers. We concluded with the observation that while database technology is now cheaper than it ever has been, the management and marketing processes that are needed to accompany it are still relatively immature. There are still huge opportunities for marketing people to apply sound principles of direct and database marketing.

Case study

Benetton

Figure 7.6

Philips and RFID technology

Radio frequency identification (RFID) chips are tiny radio transmitters that allow items to be identified and tracked at a distance. They are commonly used in warehouses for logistics purposes. Indeed, they are sometimes considered the future of inventory tracking. More recently, the application of RFID has been explored outside the warehouse. In one such experiment, Gillette, Wal-Mart and Tesco were working to install specially designed shelves that could read radio frequency waves emitted by RFID chips embedded in millions of shavers and related products. The Gap had another trial at one of its stores and found that sales rose by more than 5 per cent because in-store availability improved. Other companies have also been mulling over using smart tags for restocking, anti-theft and anti-counterfeit purposes.

One of the leading manufacturers of RFID devices is Philips Semiconductor, a division of Philips Electronics. In early 2003, it appeared that Benetton, which makes casual clothes and sportswear for men, women and children, would become Philips' next major customer to use RFID technology.

Benetton

A major attraction to Philips was the sheer scale of the Benetton Group. Today, Benetton is present in 120 countries around the world. Its core business is clothing: a group with a strong Italian character whose style, design expertise and passion are clearly seen in the fashion-orientated *United Colors of Benetton* and *Sisley* brands; in *The Hip Site*, the brand for teenagers; and in sportswear brands *Playlife* and *Killer Loop*. The Group produces over 100 million garments every year, 90 per cent of which are manufactured in Europe. Its retail network of 5,000 stores around the world is increasingly focused on large floor-space point of sale offering high-quality customer services and now generates an annual turnover of €2 billion, net of retail sales. The development of Benetton's commercial organisation has been supported by a major programme of investment in megastores, some of which are directly managed by the Group. These stores are characterised by their large dimensions, their prestigious locations in historic and commercial centres and by the high level of customer services they offer. The new Benetton megastores carry complete casual womenswear, menswear, childrenswear and underwear collections, as well as a wide selection of accessories, offering a full range of Benetton style and quality. As in the case of the commercial network, a constant commitment to innovation, a crucial factor for development, has always characterised the Group's business organisation, from communication to IT, from research into new materials to integrated logistics. Special attention is given to innovation in production, where all systems and equipment are totally renewed every 5 years. Benetton's production system is co-ordinated by a high-tech facility at Treviso, which is one of the most advanced clothing-manufacturing complexes in the world.

The Philips announcement

In March 2003 Philips Semiconductor announced that it would ship 15 million tags for use in Benetton's Sisley line of clothing. The company claimed that the initiative was 'the world's largest and most comprehensive item-level tagging implementation of RFID technology in the fashion industry to date'. According to the announcement, Benetton would weave the technology into the collar tags of clothes that cost at least $15 to keep track of them as they ship. The use of RFID would allow for a quicker and easier means of uploading to Benetton's inventory tracking system a box containing clothes of varying styles, colours and sizes all at once, as opposed to having to check in one piece at a time. As soon as readers were installed in stores, staff could ensure that each colour and size of each style was in stock and be able to locate items when a consumer has returned it to the wrong rack or shelf. Philips did not reveal the cost of the tags, but they were assumed to cost 25–50 cents, based on the order size. The tags incorporated a Philips I-Code chip, which operates at 13.56 MHz, stores 512 bits, and has a read range of 1.5 metres.

The benefits of RFID

The RFID technology offered Benetton a number of advantages, not the least of which was ease of use. Unlike a barcode scanner, which must be held directly in front of the item being scanned, employees with RFID receivers or shelves with the technology can scan entire boxes of items from a short distance. The technology would thus require fewer people to scan clothing items for inventory purposes. The tagging system could also save the company money by reducing theft. RFID tags can be programmed to set off an alarm if someone leaves a store without paying for an item. Similarly, the technology would make it harder for merchants to sell stolen or bootlegged versions of clothing in flea markets and other venues. Retailers who spot an item that they suspect is either stolen or illegally manufactured could check its origin using the tagging system. 'You can register [the garment] at the point of sale or register it through a computer', said Victor Chu, a fashion designer and technologist who runs his own company, MIL Digital Labeling. Chu, who has designed apparel for fashion gurus Ralph Lauren and Tommy Hilfiger, said piracy of high-end clothing and accessories by Prada, Gucci and Louis Vuitton is a 'big problem', for which RFID tags may be a solution. He also was not alarmed by privacy concerns that might arise when customers leave retail stores with activated RFID tags. 'It's a very local signal', Chu said. 'You would have to have the equipment to use it. It's not like a GPS tag. A GPS tag would be totally different, and that's expensive for Benetton clothing.'

Privacy issues with RFID

But RFID technology is not without its detractors. Even though the tags had a limited read range, it was known that some privacy groups were concerned about the possible abuse of the technology. Despite the obvious merits, Philips also knew the ability to track a product's movement might raise a disquieting concern about privacy. With RFID tags it becomes technically possible for marketers to obtain invaluable information on a host of consumer preferences, ranging from the clothes they like to the food they prefer. In addition, there are worries that such a technology could be exploited for government surveillance or be misused by hackers and criminals. Philips, on its part, had consistently reassured consumers that clothing could not be tracked outside the store or warehouse. The general feeling at Philips was that the privacy issue was overblown. Among other businesses, luxury clothing retailer Prada already embedded RFID inventory tags into its clothing.

The CASPIAN campaign

CASPIAN (Consumers Against Supermarket Privacy Invasion and Numbering), a US data privacy group, was one of the first to react to the Philips announcement. Within days it declared that it would oppose Benetton's plans to place radio tags into clothing labels and called for an immediate, worldwide boycott of Benetton. CASPIAN founder and director Katherine Albrecht, a Harvard University doctoral candidate and consumer privacy advocate, warned that Benetton's chips could be used for more than just unwanted advertising. 'Benetton could easily link your name and credit card information to the serial number in your sweater, in essence "registering" that sweater to you', she explained. 'Then any time you go near an RFID reader device, the sweater could beam out your identity to anyone with access to the database – all without your knowledge or permission.' She slammed claims that the devices were 'imperceptible to the wearer and remain in individual items of clothing throughout their lifetime'. Albrecht also claimed that the chips have already begun appearing in Benetton's 'Sisley' clothing line.

Although CASPIAN's comments were extremely strident and somewhat emotional, they could not be easily dismissed. Other commentators were also concerned. Mike Laird, an analyst with technology research and consulting firm Venture Development, said that 'the more companies that embed RFID tags in their products, the more likely it is for someone to drive by a home and say "Look what we've got in there. An HDTV is in there, and she wears Benetton". That's a huge concern.' Richard Smith, an internet privacy and security consultant said he was eerily reminded of a scene from the movie *Minority Report*, when Tom Cruise enters a department store and is welcomed by a billboard ad. But instead of scanning his eyeballs, as was done in *Minority Report*, his Benetton shirt would be scanned to identify him. 'It's extremely intrusive', Smith said of Benetton's proposed RFID system. 'The surveillance network would be initially built to sell clothes in the store but could be used for this other stuff. You don't need to build anything new for that.'

The *Minority Report* scenario is not far-fetched, according to a 2001 *Information Week* article in which RFID proponents have already predicted a seamless global network of millions of RFID receivers in airports, seaports, highways, distribution centres, warehouses, retail stores and consumers' homes. Privacy advocates fear that consumers will be bombarded with intrusive advertising since a history of customers' purchases and their identities would be linked with the tag even after they leave the store.

Benetton's response

Philips responded quickly to the impending marketing and PR problem. A Philips's spokesperson said that the tags 'have a feature that enables the retailer to disable the chip once a product has been purchased. This destroy command deactivates the chip and erases data stored on it, thereby granting the privacy of the buyer.' The 'self-destruct' command can be used at the discretion of the retailer and depends on the set-up of the project. Public concern and commentary continued unabated. Within a few weeks, Benetton decided a new approach was required. The privacy issue may have been overblown but the company cared deeply about its image in the marketplace. On 4 April 2003 the company clarified its plans regarding radio tags in an official company statement:

> Benetton Group, with reference to articles recently published in the press, declares that no microchips (Smart Labels) are present in the more than 100 million garments produced and sold throughout the world under its brand names, including the Sisley brand. Benetton, which has always been a leader in technological innovation in the clothing sector, is currently analysing RFID technology to evaluate its technical characteristics and emphasises that no feasibility studies have yet been undertaken with a view to the possible industrial introduction of this technology. On completion of all studies on this matter, including careful analysis of potential implications relating to individual privacy, the company reserves the right to take the most appropriate decision to generate maximum value for its stakeholders and customers.

A company spokesman, Federico Sartor, elaborated: 'The company has to date purchased only 200 RFID chips and is still studying whether or not it will use this technology to track its products'. Benetton said that there was a misunderstanding about its use of RFIDs, and while the company did not believe it was a major issue, concern in the financial markets regarding the cost of technology and its benefits caused the company to clarify its position. 'We are not using any RFIDs in any of our garments today', Sartor said, adding that Benetton has completed technology tests of radio frequency identification to help in the improvement of supply chain management, but it was still testing the economics of RFID and whether it was cost efficient to replace the barcode scanning technology that it currently used. Sartor declined to comment on the cost of using RFID in its inventory system, but said a decision concerning whether to use the technology would be made before the end of the year.

Sources: Benetton website (www.benetton.com, 2003); CASPIAN website (www.nocards.org/AutoID/benetton.shtml, 2003); *Wired Magazine* (12 March 2003);[52] *RFID Journal* (12 March 2003);[53] CNet News (12 March 2003);[54] CNet News (7 April 2003).[55]

Case study questions

1 Did Benetton make the right decision in early March 2003?

2 Put yourself in Mr Sartor's shoes at the beginning of 2003. How would you have planned the introduction of RFID tags in Benetton, even if only on a trial basis?

3 Visit CASPIAN's website. Do you believe their proposition about the use of RFID tags?

4 Conduct your own research on the internet. Are there any other well-known retailers who are using wireless technology for marketing purposes?

Questions and exercises

Questions

1 How can database marketing improve marketing performance?

2 Describe briefly the evolution of database marketing.

3 'Direct marketing is one of the oldest marketing concepts around.' Discuss.

4 What factors have driven the resurgence of direct marketing in recent years?

5 'SMS marketing is particularly effective for targeting younger audiences.' Discuss.

6 Why is data privacy of increasing interest to both consumers and governments?

7 What is meant by the 'myth of database marketing'?

Online exercises

1 QXL, the internet auction house, has a policy on consumer privacy. View it at www.qxl.co.uk and comment on how effective it is likely to be.

2 Access the site of the British Direct Marketing Association at www.dma.org.uk. What are the key benefits of a site like this to a small company considering launching itself into direct marketing?

References

1 Evans, M. (1998). 'From 1086 and 1984: direct marketing into the millennium', Special Issue of *Marketing Intelligence and Planning on Direct Marketing*, Vol. 16, No. 1.

2 IDM (1995). *Marketing Planning: Strategy, Planning and Analysis, Module 1*, Institute of Direct Marketing.

3 Borden, N. (1964). 'The concept of the marketing mix', *Journal of Advertising Research*, June, pp. 2–7.

4 McCarthy, E.J. (1960). *Basic Marketing*, Homewood, Illinois: Irwin.

5 DeTienne, K.B. and Thompson, J.A. (1996). 'Database marketing and organisational learning theory: toward a research agenda', *Journal of Consumer Marketing*, Vol. 13, No. 5.

6 Linton, I. (1995). *Database Marketing: Know What Your Customer Wants*, London: Pitman.

7 Evans, 'From 1086 and 1984'.

8 Evans, 'From 1086 and 1984'.

9 Linton, *Database Marketing*.

10 www.sas.com/news/success/gecapital.html

11 *The Economist* (1997). 'Hi ho, hi ho, down the data mine we go', 23 August.

12 Evans, M., O'Malley, L. and Patterson, M. (1996). 'Direct marketing communications in the UK: a study of growth, past, present and future', *Journal of Marketing Communications*, Vol. 2, No. 1.

13 Henley Centre (1978). *Planning Consumer Markets*, London: Henley Centre.

14 Kitchen, P. (1986). 'Zipping zapping and nipping', *International Journal of Advertising*, Vol. 5.

15 Evans, M. (1999). 'Direct marketing', in Kitchen, P. (ed.) *Marketing Communications: Principles and Practice*, London: Thomson Learning.

16 Mitchell, A. (2001). 'Playing cat and mouse games with marketing', *Precision Marketing*, 16 March.

17 Reed, D. (1995). 'Power merge', *Marketing Week*, 12 July.

18 DMA (2002). *Census of the Direct Marketing Association 2001–2*, www.dma.org.uk

19 DMA, *Census 2001–2*.

20 www3.gartner.com/5_about/press_releases/2002_03/pr20020319b.jsp

21 Smith, J. (2001). 'The big numbers game: wireless marketing', www.mobilecommerceworld.com, 15 December.

22 DMA, *Census 2001–2*.

23 *Precision Marketing* (2002). 'Avon adopts SMS strategy to push youth brands', 19 April.

24 Lindstrom, M. (2001). 'Cutting back without cutting yourself off', www.clikz.com, 2 October.

25 Westin, A. (1967). *Privacy and Freedom*, New York: Atheneum.

26 Simitis (1987). 'Reviewing privacy in an information society', *University of Pennsylvania Law Review*, 595.

27 GB Information Management (1999). Reported in 'Most firms ignorant of new data rules', *Marketing*, 20 May.

28 Dineen, A. (1999). 'Beating the data protection registrar', *Direct Marketing Strategies*, Vol. 1, No. 1.

29 Denny, N. (1999). 'Marketing success is judged by cash criteria', *Marketing*, 13 May.

30 Key, A. (2000). 'The taxman: snooper or helper', *Marketing Direct*, February.

31 Hansard (1999). House of Commons Debates, 3 February.

32 Parker, G. (1999). 'Tories accused of GM foods scaremongering', *Financial Times*, 4 February.

33 Wood, J. (1998). 'Mail marketing group to share leads with US firm', *Precision Marketing*, 15 June.

34 France, E. (1998). Reported by Davies, S. (1998), 'New data privacy storm threatens global trade war', *Financial Mail on Sunday*, 29 March.

35 Specter, M. (1999). 'Cracking the Norse code', *Sunday Times Magazine*, 21 March.

36 Borna, S. and Avila, S. (1999). 'Genetic information: consumers' right to privacy versus insurance companies' right to know: a public opinion survey', *Journal of Business Ethics*, Vol. 19.

37 Introna, L. and Powlouda, A. (1999). 'Privacy in the information age: stakeholders, interests and values', *Journal of Business Ethics*, Vol. 22.

38 Beenstock, S. (1999). 'Supermarkets entice the ultra consumer', *Marketing*, 15 April.

39 Davies, J.F. (1997). 'Property rights to consumer information: a proposed policy framework for direct marketing', *Journal of Direct Marketing*, Summer, Vol. 11, No. 3.

40 Hagel, J. and Rayport, J.F. (1997). 'The coming battle for customer information', *Harvard Business Review*, January–February.

41 Westin, A. (1992). 'Consumer privacy protection: ten predictions', *Mobus*, February.

42 *The Economist* (1999). 'The surveillance society', 1 May 1999.

43 Harvey, F. (2002). 'The full picture', *Financial Times*, 28 May.

44 London, S. (2002). 'Wal-Mart doubles size of its data warehouse', *Financial Times*, 15 June.

45 Dombey, D. (2002). 'EU deal agreed on internet privacy', *Financial Times*, 31 May.

46 www.msb.edu/faculty/culnanm/gippshome.html

47 www.mcgraw-hill.com/privacy.html

48 Rosenfield, J.R. (1998). 'The myth of database marketing', *Direct Marketing*, February.

49 Seller, M. and Gray, P. (1999). 'A survey of database marketing,' Centre for Research on Information Technology and Organisation, March, www.crito.org

50 Hatch, D. (2001). 'The evolution of direct mail', www.targetonline.com/doc/274805681805589.bsp

51 Evans, M., Nancarrow, C., Tapp, A. and Stone, M. (2002). 'Future marketers: future curriculum: future shock?', *Journal of Marketing Management*, Vol. 18, Nos. 5–6.

52 *Wired Magazine* (2003). 'What your clothes say about you', www.wired.com/news/wireless/0,1382,58006,00.html, 12 March.

53 *RFID Journal* (2003). 'Benetton to tag 15 million items', www.rfidfournal.com/article/articleview/344/1/1, 12 March.

54 CNet News, 2003. 'Benetton to track clothes with ID chips', http://news.com, 12 March.

55 CNet News, 2003. 'Benetton considers chip plans', http://news.com, 7 April.

8

Relationship marketing and CRM systems

Learning objectives

Once you have read this chapter you will:

- understand why relationship marketing has grown in importance in recent years;
- understand why customer loyalty and loyalty schemes have become common themes in marketing;
- appreciate the importance of customer lifetime value and customer retention;
- become familiar with the key principles of customer relationship management (CRM);
- appreciate the role that information technology has to play in relationship marketing.

Contents

- Rewarding customers for their loyalty
- Establishing a 'single customer view' for marketing, sales and operations

THE ROLE OF CRM TECHNOLOGY IN RELATIONSHIP MARKETING

- The power of technology to build or destroy relationships
- The truth about CRM systems
- ERP systems and data warehouses as enablers

SUMMARY

CASE STUDY

Introduction

Relationship marketing is a concept that has gained popularity in recent years. Companies are beginning to understand the value that customers, rather than products, generate for them. Consequently they are now striving to develop meaningful relationships with key customers and to manage those customer relationships more proactively. A more recent extension of this concept is customer relationship management (CRM). It is more embracing than relationship marketing as it seeks to manage the 'service encounter' with the customer, reward the customer for his loyalty and is based on a 'single customer view' for sales, marketing and operations. To implement CRM usually requires the support of integrated IT systems which can share information on customers across the organisation. To meet this need there are a large number of software packages developed that target the CRM market. However, as we will see later in the chapter, implementing CRM is not just about implementing a software package. It is also very much a mindset. Let us start by looking at the development of relationship marketing.

The rise of relationship marketing

Relationship marketing versus transaction marketing

Relationship marketing was originally introduced by Leonard Berry[1] in 1983 when he made the distinction between relationship marketing, which was based on the concept of developing a long-term relationship with a customer, and transaction marketing, which viewed the customer in terms of one-off transactions. In the same year Theodore Levitt[2] exhorted companies to leave behind the culture of selling, and instead move to a marketing culture based on proactive relationships with customers. So what exactly is relationship marketing? Gordon (1998)[3] describes it as:

> the on-going process of identifying and creating new value with individual customers and then sharing the benefits of this over a lifetime of association. It involves the understanding, focusing and management of on-going collaboration between suppliers and selected customers for mutual value creation and sharing through interdependence and organisational alignment.

Gordon makes some other observations about relationship marketing, stating that:

- *Relationships are the main asset of the enterprise* – not the machines that make the products, the products themselves, or even the intellectual capital inherent in people, patents or know-how, important though all these might be.

- *Relationship marketing affects the entire enterprise*. It is not just another layer on the marketing onion – it *is* the onion.

- *Relationship marketing is a process, not a programme*. As such, its work is never done as long as the customer has money to spend, a willingness to spend it, and a supplier that can profit from the expenditure.

We will examine these themes throughout this chapter, and also investigate how customer databases, the internet and newer electronic marketing applications such as e-mail, SMS and MMS are being used to build relationships with customers (*see* Exhibit 8.1).

Relationship theory and concepts

Relationship marketing involves trust, commitment, mutual benefit, adaptation and regard for privacy.[4] However, there is a degree of 'rhetoric versus reality' here. Consider the following advice to business:

> Relationship marketing . . . requires a two-way flow of information. This does not mean that the customer has to give you this information willingly, or even knowingly. You can use scanners to capture information, you can gather telephone numbers, conduct surveys, supply warranty cards, and use a data overlay from outside databases to combine factors about lifestyle, demographics, geographics, psychographics, and customer purchases.[5]

This, possibly commonplace, view would define relationship marketing as an oxymoron! And the supposed paradigm shift from focusing on one-off transactions is also dubious. It is interesting to remember that even in the 1960s and 1970s marketers were not concerned exclusively with one-off transactions: retention strategies such as the old Green Shield Stamps and indeed the entire branding process are clearly not concerned exclusively with acquisition. It is obvious that marketers want customers to return and spread goodwill about the product, brand or company.

EXHIBIT 8.1

BOLLYWOOD IN YOUR INBOX

If you're heading out tonight to see the latest Austin Powers film or perhaps a Bollywood blockbuster, there's a good chance you read some reviews online and booked your tickets over the web. UK cinema chains are dramatically stepping up their efforts to reach movie-goers via the internet, and are developing highly sophisticated databases so they can immediately alert you when your favourite film actor is next going to be appearing on the silver screen.

'Cinema chains and film distributors are getting more switched on to e-mail marketing and are finding out which consumers are coming to see their films', says Brooke Hunter, a director of new media agency Haygarth Direct. 'They're using their databases more cleverly to build relationships with their customers. We have built a database of cinema-goers and we know what genres of film they are interested in. If someone is interested in arthouse films, we're not going to send them information on Stuart Little,' she says.

Segmenting and targeting specific movie audiences is one of the chief preoccupations of the major cinema chains, who are desperate to foster customer loyalty. Recognising the surge of interest in Bollywood movies, Warner Village Cinemas has created a dedicated Bollywood microsite. There's also a quick introduction to the many different types of Bollywood movies that are playing. You can learn about Yash raj movies, which are love stories for hopeless romantics, and Muktha films, which specialise in forbidden love which dares to cross age-old caste divides. 'Bollywood is quite a hot thing at the moment, and the Asian market needs to be catered for', says Sarah Kelly, director of marketing and sales for Warner Village Cinemas.

The Odeon chain is equally enthusiastic about the marketing potential of new media and its ability to personalise communications. The Odeon already has a Wap-based ticket sales service and Luke Vetere, head of marketing for Odeon UK, is now keen to exploit the potential of SMS-based marketing. The cinema chain is setting up a service so punters can buy tickets on the move using SMS.

Source: *The Guardian* (12 August 2002).[6]

So is relationship marketing really that new? Many of the 'old' definitions of marketing often include relational constructs like that of Borch (1957):[7] 'Marketing means customer orientation – a true *alliance* with the fellow at the other end of the pipeline, but it insists upon a course of action of *mutual* benefit'. Indeed, the relational concept that proposes past, present and future interaction between organisations and customers and wider 'networking' issues was suggested by Wroe Alderson in the 1950s:[8] 'It means creating a pattern for dealing with customers or suppliers which persists because there are advantages on both sides'.

One of the 'new' ways of conceptualising this 'new' relational approach is to consider it analogous to human relationships, yet many studies are critical and conclude that the human relationship analogy is inappropriate.[9] Personalisation, in the form of sending relevant offers to named customers, is not the same as developing and maintaining a true relationship.

A recent approach that takes the relational interaction further is the modern variant of the old Green Shield Stamps strategy: the loyalty scheme. The next section provides the reasons for adopting this approach and then explores the theory that underpins these schemes.

Customer loyalty

Relationship marketing and the value of customer loyalty

Many commentators have stressed that relationship marketing is all about developing long-standing, meaningful relationships with customers. Long-term customers are more profitable for the following six reasons:[10]

- regular customers place frequent, consistent orders and, therefore, are less costly to serve;

- longer-established customers tend to buy more;

- satisfied customers may sometimes pay premium prices;

- retaining customers makes it difficult for competitors to enter a market or increase their market share;

- satisfied customers are a source of referrals of new customers;

- the cost of acquiring and serving new customers can be substantial.

This concept of long-term customers generating greater profits is supported by the classic analysis of Reichheld and Sasser (1990),[11] who computed the lifetime value of customers across a number of different industries. The financial basis for these claims is relatively simple, as can be seen from Figure 8.1 .

Figure 8.1 shows graphically how the lifetime value of a customer is a function of the acquisition costs in the first year and the profits that can be generated from that customer in each of the subsequent years. Customers who defect or switch after a year or two will show a negative lifetime value, while loyal customers will generate handsome returns. Reichheld and Sasser's analysis demonstrated that a 5 per cent increase in customer retention boosted profits by 35–85 per cent, depending on the industry in question. Yet many companies still do not appear to have learned this lesson. In subsequent research, Reichheld found that US companies lost half their customers within five years, half their employees in four, and half their investors in less than one.[12]

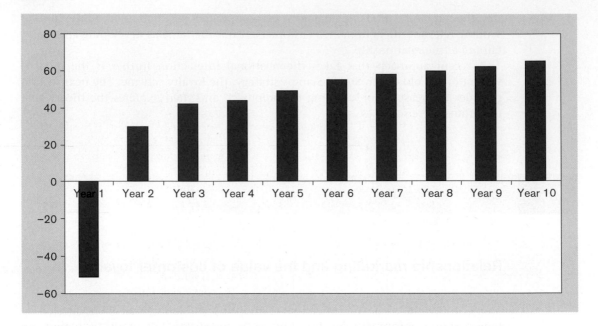

Figure 8.1 Annual profit per customer

As we have mentioned earlier in Chapter 6, 'lifetime value' is probably a bit of a misnomer – 'longtime' would be more relevant and the extent of repeat purchasing from the same company varies from sector to sector. To take an example, if a car company is only concerned with acquiring customers and does nothing to retain them, there is a fair chance that each customer who buys one of its cars this year will go on to buy from a different manufacturer next time. The value of the sale might be £10,000, but subtracting acquisition costs, production and other costs could mean a net profit of a just a few pounds. With a more dedicated retention programme, the company could expect that customer to buy one of its cars every third year for, per-haps, 12 years – and not just at £10,000, since as they progress through their life stages they may be able to buy more expensive models. So, with lower costs of retain-ing a customer than the initial acquiring cost, together with repeat buying and the prospect of up-selling over a period of time, the sales value could be as high as, say, £70,000 (£10,000 + £12,000 + £14,000 + £16,000 + £18,000).[13]

It is also an important fact that in many industries most of the profits are generated by a relatively small number of customers. This is particularly true in financial services, where the top 10–15 per cent of bank customers typically generate all the profits, while up to half of all customers are loss-making at any particular point in time.[14] As a result, many banks focus on providing a premium service to their wealthier and older customers. This phenomenon is also true in other industries. Airlines try to identify, satisfy and retain customers who are frequent fliers (*see* Exhibit 8.2).

The more discerning companies will also have procedures in place for attempting to win back lost customers that are worth regaining, and will actively attempt to rebuild the relationship. Customer exit interviews, or telephone calls, are an effective means of finding out what went wrong and potentially winning the customer back.

EXHIBIT 8.2

THE VALUE OF LOYAL AIRLINE CUSTOMERS

An effective customer relationship management (CRM) programme can not predict the future, but it can provide valuable insights into the travel patterns of customers and their lifelong value to the airline. Following the attacks on New York and Washington, those insights could be more valuable than ever. In the aftermath of the events of September 11, businesses have been urgently reviewing their travel policies and the travelling patterns of many people will alter for a time, if not permanently. The airlines which have already implemented sophisticated CRM have already started targeting customers to reassure them, while those which have not contacted their customers since September 11 do not have the channels to do so, according to Carlos De Pommes of McKinsey.

'Advanced' airlines such as Air France and British Airways will pull ahead, says De Pommes. 'They will refocus on specific markets and rack back on other expenses. In a downturn that's when you can gain market share.' The airlines that will trail behind are those which over recent years, says De Pommes, have failed to invest sufficiently in developing their CRM capabilities. Studies by McKinsey's global airline and CRM practices have shown that many airlines have no idea of the value of an individual customer to them. However, there are some which can identify with 60–70 per cent accuracy the lifetime value of a new customer. 'A large proportion of the value can be captured in modest time frames if top management gives CRM the necessary attention', De Pommes says.

British Airways has drawn on its customer base to send e-mails to Executive Club members from Rod Eddington, its chief executive, to offer reassurance about security. BA has a worldwide database, Ocean Wave, which includes details of 8.5 million passengers. BA is developing the project in-house and is consolidating all customer records to a single location. BA and other European airlines have been carrying out real CRM activities for 10 years in Europe, while in the US there has been activity for 20 years, says Mark Raskino of Gartner, the IT market analysts. 'The reduction in the numbers of people travelling as a result of the Gulf War was the first test for CRM', says Raskino. Those airlines which had made significant investments in technology were rewarded, he said. Many have bespoke systems which have been largely built internally.

Source: Financial Times (17 October 2001).[15]

The value (or myth) of customer loyalty schemes

Jones and Sasser (1995)[16] show that satisfied customers will still defect and that companies must strive to achieve 'completely satisfied customers'. They make the interesting distinction between true long-term loyalty and 'false loyalty', which is caused by factors such as:

- strong loyalty-promotion programmes, such as frequent-flier schemes;
- government regulations, which limit competition and reduce consumer choice;

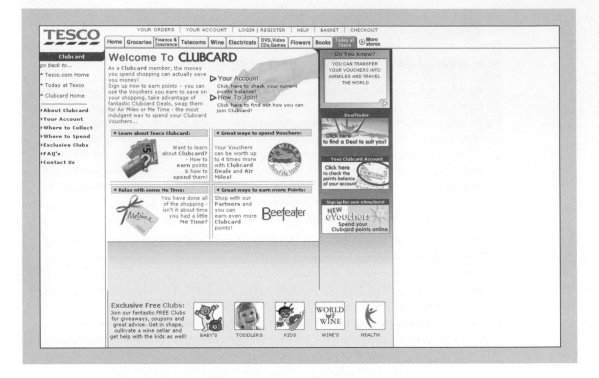

Figure 8.2 The Tesco Clubcard

Source: Tesco Clubcard website (www.tesco.com/clubcard, 2003).

- high switching costs, such as penalty clauses;
- proprietary technology, which limits alternatives.

The first example is perhaps the most interesting of all. It implies that marketing managers can delude themselves into thinking that a strong loyalty card scheme will, on its own, generate long-term customer relationships. Although loyalty schemes have been hailed as examples of relationship marketing, Hart et al. (1999)[17] found little evidence to verify this contention. On the one hand, a large proportion of consumers participate in these schemes. The high level of participation is supported by loyalty card ownership. Tesco's Clubcard (*see* Figure 8.2) was introduced in 1995 and has 10 million active participants. By 1997, all major UK retailers had their own loyalty schemes. The Nectar loyalty card (*see* Exhibit 8.3) claimed 14 million active participants within two months of its launch in 2002. On the other hand, research into loyalty schemes from a consumer perspective (Evans et al., 1997)[18] found that although these schemes have strong participation and are seen to be potentially money saving, this potential is not always fully realised. This sometimes produces switching behaviour between schemes, with a major factor being locational convenience: 'If you shop in that store anyway – it's a good idea' (C2D male, aged 28–35).

There is also a general feeling that the discounts themselves are not large enough; this is supported by an NOP survey that found that 43 per cent of non-cardholders thought the savings too small.[19] Another issue, if some customers are treated differently from others, is that marketing may be in danger of becoming anti-democratic and divisive.[20] The 80:20 rule (80 per cent of sales and profits typically come from

20 per cent of the customers) means that volume segments should be treated differently, but this again raises the issue discussed in Chapter 6 – deselection and exclusion.

Another issue for consumers is the view that schemes lock people into shopping in one place: they 'tend to tie you into one shop . . . people shop because of convenience' (BC1 male, aged 50+). It is interesting to note that marketers use the phrase 'locking-in customers' in a way that is positive to the marketer, but can be negative for customers. Promiscuity in shopping behaviour is also reflected in the estimated 3.2 loyalty cards that each UK consumer, on average, possesses.[21] It can be argued that there has been a shift from loyalty to a brand/company/retailer to loyalty to the scheme itself.[22] How much 'real loyalty' is there?

Concerns over revealing personal details were also uncovered in the research among consumers by Evans et al. Many participants (especially, but not exclusively women) did not like divulging personal details such as marital status, age, household numbers, telephone numbers, bank accounts, type of dwelling or home contents. This was seen as 'very intrusive' (C2D female, aged 20–7). There was even a degree of fear associated with this:

- 'Wouldn't give my personal details – not for a woman on her own' (BC1 female, aged 39–49).
- 'Elderly women are worried about others knowing they are on their own' (BC1 female, aged 39–49).
- 'There's no guarantee of confidentiality' (BC1 female, aged 50+).
- 'I don't like to give my address. In the old days you could trust people – not these days' (BC1 female, aged 50+).

On this 'trust' issue – a central construct of relationship marketing – it is worth referring to research conducted by the Henley Centre[23] and the Future Foundation,[24] both of which found consumers trust companies less today than in the past.

There is also some evidence that most loyalty schemes are little more than defensive measures in markets that are mature and competitive.[25] Miller (1998)[26] goes further and suggests that loyalty schemes are designed to make it hard for customers to leave, rather than trying to make them an advocate for a particular company, brand or product.

Despite these concerns about the true purpose and value of customer loyalty schemes, their popularity, at least in the eyes of the retailers, continues unabated. Supermarket chains, in particular, continue to revamp and update their loyalty card schemes to help revive interest among shoppers (*see* Exhibit 8.3).

Building customer loyalty and improving customer retention

Relationship marketing can only happen as part of a wider all-encompassing programme that puts the customer at the heart of the organisation and where processes are built, or redesigned, with the objective of pleasing and 'delighting' the customer. The critical point for marketers is that true customer loyalty does not result from the implementation of card schemes or from sales promotions. Marketers must work out what engenders loyalty in customers if they are to discover how to improve retention figures. Most marketing managers will have to work hard at this, as customers can be fickle and inherently disloyal. Marketing managers need to aspire to the levels of loyalty displayed by sports fans and other customer groups that display 'true loyalty'. Indeed,

EXHIBIT 8.3

THE BATTLE FOR CUSTOMER LOYALTY

The fiercely competitive battle to win the loyalty of consumers has heated up with the arrival of yet another loyalty scheme. Nectar, a loyalty card backed by Debenhams, J. Sainsbury, BP and Barclaycard, is trumpeting itself as the 'UK's most comprehensive reward programme'. It comes hard on the heels of a £50 million 'giveaway' by Air Miles, the British Airways-owned consumer loyalty scheme, and a similar promotion by Buy and Fly, a rival reward card operator.

But the proliferation of reward schemes has prompted some analysts to question whether there is enough room for them all. Air Miles, the best known loyalty scheme, says it redeemed more than £1 billion worth of air miles last year – enough, it claims, to have flown all its members round the world 37,000 times. It faces a battle to hang on to its popularity as the loyalty card market matures and the company is certainly not ignoring the threat posed by Nectar. Its £50 million giveaway, which has been running for a couple of weeks, looked to have been conceived to deflect attention from the new rival. 'It was a classic spoiler', said David Lyne, chief executive of Landround, the owner of Buy and Fly. According to Keith Mills, chairman of Loyalty Management UK, the company behind Nectar: 'We aim to have 50 per cent of the UK's population signed up in the first few months', he said. 'In Canada, a similar scheme we operate is used by about 70 per cent of the population, so we're confident of similar success here.' But are loyalty schemes still popular and do consumers stand to benefit from the increased competition? The schemes are of immense importance to retailers – Sainsbury's sales fell recently after the group parted company with Air Miles.

Source: Financial Times (12 September 2002).[27]

many sports companies have latched on to this. Manchester United mails out a glossy merchandise catalogue to a quarter of a million fans three times a year, while Chelsea dispatches its own version to around 200,000 fans.[28] US basketball clubs like the Phoenix Suns and baseball clubs like the Arizona Diamondbacks manage the relationships with their fans using sophisticated marketing and relationship management software.[29]

A 2002 McKinsey study[30] found that defecting customers were less of a problem than customers who change their buying patterns and that new analytical techniques were required to understand the motives that underpin customer loyalty. McKinsey found that life insurance and soft drinks customers tended to be extremely loyal to their chosen brands, but that products like internet service providers (ISPs), credit cards, retail bank deposits, mobile phones and clothes were much more susceptible to the vagaries of changing consumer behaviour. The study segmented the loyal customers into three 'loyalty profile' categories:

- deliberative
- inertial
- emotive.

EXHIBIT 8.4

LOYALTY AT THE HERTZ#1 CLUB GOLD PROGRAMME

One approach that sophisticated marketers take is to expand the deliberators' concerns from, say, price alone to include other factors. Well structured reward programmes often provide the kind of concrete process or relationship benefits that appeal to many deliberators. Hertz, for example, centrally stores all customer and payment data for the members of its #1 Club Gold programme, so that customers don't have to fill out repetitive forms every time they rent cars. In this way, Hertz encourages frequent travellers to base their decisions about which car rental company to patronise not only on price but also on the ability to save time.

Source: Coyles and Gokey (2002).[31]

Each category required a different set of tactical and strategic marketing responses. An example of such a response is shown in Exhibit 8.4.

Loyalty, in a relational context, should go beyond regular purchasing. Dick and Basu (1994),[32] in their conceptualising of the loyalty phenomenon, argue that 'relative attitudes' are also important. That is, loyalty depends not only on positive attitudes toward the store or brand, but also on differentiated attitudes toward the alternatives (*see* Figure 8.3). In other words, if a consumer is positive toward store A and not very positive towards B and C, then the consumer might indeed develop loyalty towards A. On the other hand if there are fairly similar positive attitudes toward A, B and C, then there is unlikely to be real loyalty. In this case the consumer might patronise a particular store regularly, but only due to factors such as convenience and familiarity.

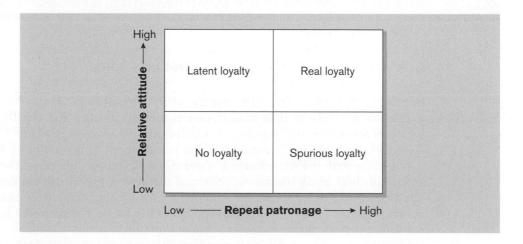

Figure 8.3 Loyalty framework
Source: Adopted from Dick and Basu (1994).[33]

EXHIBIT 8.5

MOTORISTS IN DISTRESS

Marketing managers in petrol retailing sometimes talk about motorists making 'distress purchases', but are really referring to drivers that are in danger of running out of petrol and fill up at any motorway station rather than their regular location. The assumption is that motorists are loyal to their regular petrol retailer. In actual fact, many motorists have no loyalty whatsoever – their 'regular' location just happens to be on the way to the office or the shopping centre.

This analysis is useful because it is an explanation of why apparent loyalty – at least regular patronage – might not be true loyalty at all (*see* Exhibit 8.5). Conversely, Dick and Basu's framework contributes to our understanding of why some consumers exhibit aspects of real loyalty without holding particularly strong positive attitudes toward that store. In this latter case the argument would be that a positive but weak attitude towards A might be accentuated by even weaker positive attitudes towards B and C.

Dick and Basu describe a situation in which relative attitude is low (there is little to choose between the alternatives) but which is also characterised by high store patronage; they describe this as 'spurious loyalty'. Alternatively, where there is low patronage but strongly differentiated and positive attitudes towards A, this is 'latent loyalty'. The expected high patronage in this case might be inhibited by co-shoppers' preferences, for example. When it comes to real loyalty itself, it is clear that they see this as where there is both high patronage and a positive attitude towards the store that is not matched by similarly positive attitudes toward alternative stores.[34]

Customer relationship management (CRM)

Customer relationship management principles

In practice, the most usual interpretation of the organisation–customer relationship is essentially a type of data mining that is used to identify and classify customer segments for differential targeting. It is unfortunate that many companies see a software package as all that is required. If the management of this resulting knowledge is not integrated and shared across relevant organisational functions, there is little chance of there being sustainable relational marketing. Knowledge management (or KM as it is sometimes termed) is a framework for moving data-driven marketing to a more strategic position. This is an approach that moves the narrower relationship marketing towards intra- and inter- company networks within the broader customer relationship management (CRM) paradigm.[35] Companies that are held up as good examples of customer relationship management (CRM) tend to do three things better than their competitors:

- they design and manage the 'service encounter' with the customer correctly;

- they reward the customer for their loyalty;

- they are based on a 'single customer view' for sales, marketing and operations.

Designing the service encounter correctly

Customer databases and other technology applications enable employees to provide a satisfying and consistent service encounter for the customer, regardless of the method that the customer chooses to interact with the organisation. For example, in a bank, it is important that:

- employees in the bank's call centre have an equal, or better, understanding of the bank's products than their counterparts in the branch network: this requires them to be given either the training or the computer systems support to explain product details to customers;

- branch staff are committed to capturing as much customer information as they can when new accounts are opened, so that a more complete picture of the customer can be created, which can be used in subsequent service encounters;

- staff are also committed to updating key elements of customer information on the bank's long-standing customers, since these customers are likely to be the most profitable;

- IT managers design customer service systems so that the 'interface' through the branch, telephone, ATM, kiosk or internet are consistent and have the same 'look and feel' (we will shortly refer to this as 'a single customer view');

- marketing managers view direct mail as part of an ongoing dialogue with the customer, rather than a one-off blitz to promote a specific product or service.

Consider also the role of inbound communication from customers. A phone call from a customer to change his address might just lead to a minor update on the database. However, if reasons for the change were explored, these might reveal a recent marriage. For a financial services company, for example, this would be a strategic trigger point for moving into the next stage of the family life cycle and could prompt the mailing of a 'marriage pack', including relevant mortgage and insurance offers.[36] A good CRM solution can achieve these objectives by providing trigger questions for the call centre agent. Training of those agents is vitally important, so that they appreciate fully the opportunity associated with different types of inbound calls.

Rewarding customers for their loyalty

The 'fewer than ten items' checkout in a supermarket is a good example of a 'service encounter' that has been well designed. The express lane removes a bottleneck for those customers who buy only a few items but who have to queue up behind several families with large trolley-loads of food. However, it is a poor example of rewarding loyalty, particularly the loyalty of those families who fill those large trolleys each week, every week when they shop. The concept that customers should be rewarded for loyalty was the driving force behind the many loyalty card schemes that have been introduced by airlines and supermarkets. One practitioner describes it as follows:

> It is important to reward customer loyalty . . . but we have to be careful not to bribe customers into loyalty. It's kind of like raising children. Once you start to 'bribe' your child, as in 'if you'll eat everything on your plate tonight you'll get a cookie', there is no ending to the bribe. This one-cookie-for-a-clean-plate trick works for a week or two, and then the bribe has to be increased to two cookies, or even three before the child will willingly complete his or her entire meal. Many marketers are making the same mistake when it comes to developing so-called loyalty programmes. The airlines were one of the first to make this error. Once one airline started to capture greater market share with a frequent flyer programme [FFP], everyone else added similar schemes. Now, practically all airlines offer some kind of a mileage programme. There is little differentiation between these programmes, and hence many passengers (and certainly most frequent flyers) are no more loyal to one airline than they were previously. Frequent flyers tend to belong to multiple programmes. And now with two or three major alliances being formed in the industry, it will be easy for everyone to belong to these two or three super league FFPs. So where's the point of differentiation? There isn't one![37]

Customers who become loyalty card holders end up on the loyalty scheme's customer database and become targets for communication and targeted marketing messages. The key point to remember is that such databases – in fact any customer database – must be used to reward customers, and not to put them off by indiscriminate use of direct mail (*see* Exhibit 8.6).

The country that is the most advanced user of direct mail in Europe is Germany, which also has the most stringent data protection legislation governing the sale or rental of customer data. With proper respect for consumer privacy, German businesses have been able to collect data from willing customers and use that data to sell more effectively and to improve customer satisfaction and loyalty.

EXHIBIT 8.6

VODAFONE PROMISES TO END JUNK MAIL

Vodafone is developing global customer database technology it claims will put an end to unwanted junk mail. As part of a global rebranding exercise, the telecoms giant is working on a technology capable of analysing data on all its customers across the 30 different Vodafone-owned networks worldwide. The initiative means Vodafone will be able to target customers according to their personal preferences. It will also lead to cost savings for the group.

'The software platform will analyse data in a uniform way across the group', said Jon Earl, investor relations manager at Vodafone. 'Customer data is our raw material, particularly with data services on the horizon. It will give a much higher level of personalisation and will mean our marketing won't spam customers with junk mail.'

Source: The Guardian (19 March 2001).[38]

Establishing a 'single customer view' for marketing, sales and operations

Now we come to the holy grail of relationship management: the creation of what is often referred to as the 'single customer view' – a customer database that has all relevant information pertaining to an individual that can be accessed in real time by any authorised staff member.

Marketing, sales and operations staff all need access to customer information for different purposes. As we have seen in Chapter 6, the gathering of such customer data into a single database can be a difficult enough task in small organisations. In large organisations, it becomes a very complex and sometimes impossible task (*see* Exhibit 8.7).

The reason for the complexity is that corporations have been capturing and storing significant volumes of customer information for years, and this information is typically stored in different databases, which can typically be categorised by process type such as customer service and billing, by channel type such as telephone and internet, and by product type.[39] As CRM has grown, a number of specialised consultancies and websites have been created to fill the growing need for information and research on CRM. A good example is CRMGuru (www.crmguru.com), a company that provides a wealth of information and articles on its site (*see* Figure 8.4).

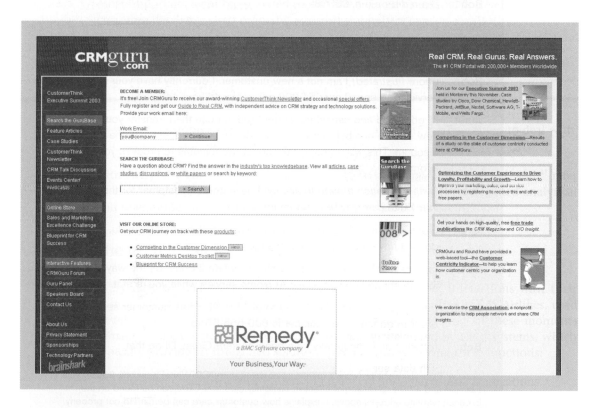

Figure 8.4 Real answers from CRMGuru

Source: CRMGuru website (www.crmguru.com, 2003).

EXHIBIT 8.8

DRIVING OUT THE CRM BENEFITS IN CHINA

Headquartered in Changchun, FAW-Volkswagen Automotive Company is a joint-venture collaboration between First Automobile Works of China and German auto-makers Volkswagen and Audi. FAW-Volkswagen, which pioneered modern car manufacturing in China, sells through regional dealers but was unable to get the direct customer feedback it needed to ensure superior customer service and gather market intelligence.

'The major business challenges we wanted to address were unresponsive customer service and slow reaction times', says Wang Qiang, senior manager of management information services. The IT challenges in support of these business issues were lack of real-time information, incomplete integration of data and processes, and a shortage of IT personnel. The company implemented a CRM system from the German software company SAP to improve customer service and gather more crucial knowledge about its customer base. 'We can now dramatically strengthen the relationship with our customers and integrate all customer service functions on a single platform, from the contact centre through sales, service, and marketing', says Wang. The CRM system was installed in six months and ten FAW-Volkswagen agents now work in the customer centre, handling approximately 800 inbound and outbound calls per day. The system provides inbound and outbound call processing, e-mail management and activity management to track, monitor and enhance all customer contacts. 'We can now respond to customer requirements quickly and correctly, so that they will be satisfied with our service and be more loyal to our company', Wang says.

Source: SAP website (www.sap.com, 2003).

■ *Customer service*, which increasingly involves sophisticated call centres or customer contact centres that carry out fulfilment processing, order-entry and field dispatch (*see* Chapter 14 for further discussion).

Exhibit 8.8 and Figure 8.5 provides an example of how Volkswagen implemented a CRM solution in China to allow the company's relationship with its distributors – across all three functions of marketing, sales and customer service – to be managed more effectively.

In theory, CRM applications require information from the full gamut of functions within the typical organisation. In practice, fully integrated CRM systems are still rare. Most companies have employed CRM systems as solutions for specific problems. Most pharmaceutical and life sciences companies are still only using basic CRM systems to reduce the costs of their sales and marketing functions, according to one survey in 2002.[42] The primary focus in these companies has been on the operational side of sales force automation and call centre automation, rather than the more holistic approach that most CRM proponents talk about. Indeed, many CRM companies – aware of the real objectives of their customers – focus heavily on the cost-savings opportunities offered by their products (*see* Figure 8.6: Siebel is the CRM software vendor to Travelport). However, the trends are for this focus to change. In future, life sciences companies are expected to deploy CRM systems for functions such as online channel development, customer analysis and campaign automation.

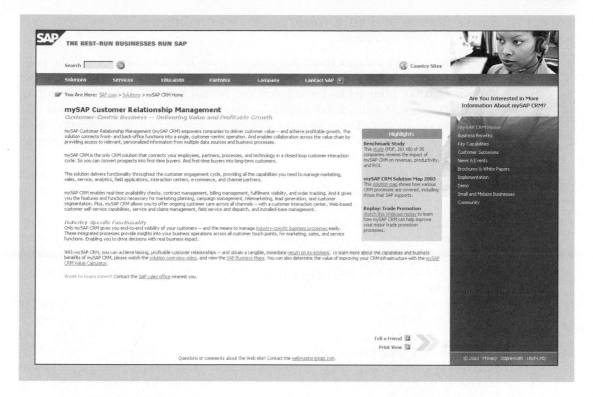

Figure 8.5 CRM offerings from SAP

Source: SAP (www.sap.com/solutions/crm, 2003).

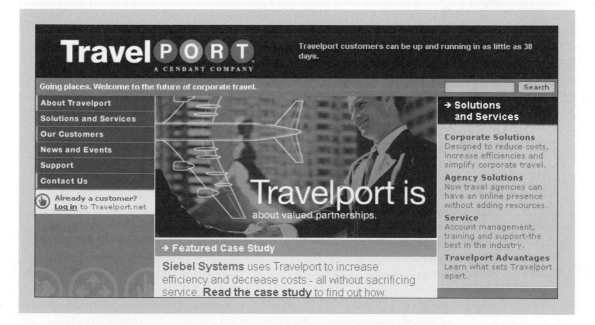

Figure 8.6 Using software to decrease costs

Source: Travelport website (www.travelport.com, 2003).

ERP systems and data warehouses as enablers

One of the primary reasons that CRM systems have not matured beyond the basic functions mentioned above is the technological difficulty of integrating data from disparate systems from across the corporation. Several different hardware platforms, operating systems, databases and applications are typically involved. Operational data is likely to stored in different formats. The company's inventory system may store data as 'male' and 'female', while the billing system might store the same information simply as 'M' and 'F'.

To overcome this technology barrier, companies will need better enterprise resource planning (ERP) systems and greater data warehouse functionality. The ERP system is the backbone of the internal information in most companies. A well-organised ERP system will hold general ledger, accounts payable, accounts receivable and other financial information in a consistent format and allow CRM applications to work more effectively. Similarly, a good data warehouse, or data mart, will allow the most relevant and up-to-date customer and transactional information to be used by the company's CRM systems.

A final point to make – if we really need to repeat it – is that technology is not the only enabler. In fact the most important factor is not the technology at all. Rather, it is the mindset of the people in the organisation that puts the customer first and engrains a customer-centric policy in the fabric of the organisation. Unfortunately, many CRM systems have failed to deliver any real value. Surveys by organisations as diverse as JD Edwards (a CRM software vendor), the Gartner Group (a technology research company) and Bain & Company (a consultancy) all point to the inability of most CRM solutions to deliver real benefits to the organisations that implement them.[43] Customer relationship management is still an immature science. However, today's marketers can at least learn from the mistakes of earlier pioneers and start to deliver the benefits that have long been expected from CRM systems (*see* Exhibit 8.9).

EXHIBIT 8.9

LEARNING FROM THE CRM FAILURES

There is evidence that companies are beginning to learn from the mistakes of the CRM pioneers. HSBC Bank, for example, has been ranked in the top 10 per cent of CRM companies in the UK, not least because the key elements – strategy, systems, data, people and processes – are moving forward together. Graham Flower, the bank's head of customer management, says that most CRM programmes are run out of marketing and finance departments, where the belief is that CRM is an IT problem, to be solved by installing the right computer system. 'As much by good luck as judgment, our conclusion was the opposite', he adds. 'Technology is just the enabler. As much as 80 per cent is in communication, training and culture. Just 20 per cent has to do with the technology.'

Source: Financial Times (28 May, 2002).[44]

Summary

Leonard Berry[45] introduced relationship marketing in 1983 when he made the distinction between relationship marketing, which was based on the concept of developing a long-term relationship with a customer, and transaction marketing, which viewed the customer in terms of one-off transactions. Relationship marketing involves an ongoing process of identifying and creating new value with individual customers and then sharing the benefits of this over a lifetime of association (Gordon, 1998).[46] The key point is that relationship marketing is a process, not a programme. Its work is never done as long as the customer has money to spend and there is a supplier that can profit from the expenditure. A more recent extension of relationship marketing is customer relationship management (CRM). We have seen how is more embracing than relationship marketing as it seeks to manage the 'service encounter' with the customer, reward the customer for their loyalty and is based on a 'single customer view' for sales, marketing and operations.

Implementing CRM usually requires the support of integrated IT systems that can share information on customers across the organisation. While there are a large number of CRM software packages, many of these systems have failed to deliver the value they have promised. This brings us to our final point, which is that technology is only an enabler in implementing CRM. The key success factor is the mindset of the organisation to put the customer first and to engrain a customer-centric philosophy in the organisation. Customer relationship management is still an immature science. However, we can learn from the mistakes of earlier pioneers and start to deliver the benefits that have long been expected from CRM.

Case study

Samsung Life Insurance

Figure 8.7

Korea's economic crisis in 1998 wreaked havoc on some businesses, causing an estimated 12 out of 30 top corporations to downsize by 20–50 per cent. Despite the turmoil across the country, one company managed to boost its assets to nearly $30 billion – Samsung Life Insurance Company. It is the largest insurance company in South Korea with a market share of over 40 per cent and a distribution network of about 2,000 sub-branch offices and about 60,000 agents. *Fortune* magazine currently ranks it fourteenth in the world.

The *ajuma* sales force

In South Korea, life insurance continues to be sold through a 200,000-strong *ajuma* (middle-aged housewife) sales force that dominates the industry's distribution channels. It remains the most powerful distribution channel today, accounting for about two-thirds of first-year insurance premiums. However, the traditional 'housewife' channel is being challenged and life companies are increasingly looking at diversification and more efficient alternative channels. Too many companies are solely dependent on the *ajuma* sales force and this has been the cause of many of the problems faced by the large life insurers face today. The quality of the *ajuma* sales force is relatively low. *Ajumas* bombard customers with gifts until customers feel an obligation to buy a policy; in the short term this increases productivity but in the long term switching becomes a major problem as customers no longer recognise the value of the product. Another major problem with the *ajuma* sales force is the retention of the housewives. Life insurance companies are trapped in a recruitment game, where thousands of housewives are recruited each month only to have a fraction of them remaining after the first year. Recruitment and training costs are high, but most *ajumas* leave within the first few months. This further multiplies the problem of switching, since many policyholders surrender their policies once their agent leaves.

Professionalising the sales force

Although Samsung Life survived the crisis of 1998, the business was impacted by the downturn. The company was hit with major customer churn, products went to market at high price points, and the company saw little return on investment. Against this background Samsung Life found it difficult to ascertain who its customers were, what they bought, and what was the best way to reach each customer. What was more, the corporate objective was to increase its asset size from $30 billion to $150 billion by 2010. One of Samsung Life's highest corporate priorities was optimal customer benefit and convenience. Most of the South Korean life companies were adopting strategies to professionalise their sales forces. Prudential, the US insurer, and ING of the Netherlands were leading the way. Prudential's approach to recruitment was centred around hiring male college graduates. It built up a sales force of approximately 1,000 over a ten-year period, compared to Samsung Life's sales force of 60,000 agents. In contrast, Korea's oldest life insurance company, Korealife Insurance, faced a similar challenge to Samsung Life with a sales force of nearly 50,000 financial planners. Korealife's strategy was to introduce a sales force automation (SFA) system that would equip 20,000 of its sales force with a PC-based sales and marketing application that would help customise and sell insurance packages to its customers.

Samsung Life's issues and solution

Samsung Life had its own technology issues to deal with. Product and sales systems were inadequate, responses to queries were slow, and mission-critical information was simply unattainable. The company had no data on the profitability of each customer, of each product, or the ability to analyse the right channels for targeted one-to-one marketing. 'We needed to increase customer retention as well as improve the profitability of each customer through cross-selling and up-selling. To do that, we needed a data warehouse that would enable us to perform high-level sales analysis and database marketing,' says Joon Young Kim, Samsung Life's IT planning manager. Samsung also faced scalability issues with the technology.

Samsung's needs were clear. Reduce customer churn, improve individual customer and product profitability, and develop effective channel marketing programmes. Samsung Life's solution was to continue to apply technology to the problem. The company was the first in South Korea to introduce an integrated call centre linked to a 24-hour online service for its customers. During 2001, $300 million in online financial transactions went through the company's home page. A one-stop electronic authorisation and transaction system was introduced in May 2002 to offer more convenient and safer online financial services. One of the most important technology investments was the implementation of a customer relationship management (CRM) system based on a new data warehouse from the IT company NCR.

The benefits

'The results from the data warehouse were immediate', according to Kim. 'We're able to manage our customer information and use it to make effective, profitable business decisions for our company, as well as move our customers smoothly into the twenty-first century.' The data warehouse holds two years of current contract information, three years of new contract information, and a single year of agent performance history, enabling Samsung Life to perform sales and marketing analysis on its customers, agents and prospects. The data warehouse generates 22 reports in all.

'In 1997 our agents averaged 8.4 contracts each month per agent. That number jumped to 10.1 after the NCR data warehouse was installed,' Kim adds. Samsung Life is improving its profitability using the information gathered from the data warehouse. It now knows that 2 per cent of its total customer base generates 16.5 per cent of its total revenue. Armed with that information, it created 16 new targeted services and campaigns, creating a higher level of customer loyalty and retention. In addition to better customer management, Samsung Life has decreased the number of IT hours for database administration. According to Kim, 'Our analysis time by policy went from seven days down to one day. This benefit alone saves Samsung Life over a million dollars per year in data processing costs.'

He went on to say, 'Our data warehouse is an integral part of our overall strategy. In the near future, we will be able to extract additional customer-centric scoring models, enhancing our cross-selling capabilities and extending our marketing capabilities to our internet site.'

Epilogue

The South Korean life insurance industry continues to undergo phenomenal changes. Consolidation is now a significant trend, with 33 companies consolidating down to 21 between 2000 and 2002 (in 2001 two smaller companies – Hyundai and Samshin – were transferred to Korealife, while Youngpoong was acquired by Prudential).

Sources: Samsung Life website (www.samsunglife.com, 2003); NCR website (www.ncr.com, 2003); NMG Financial Services Consulting website (www.nmg.com.sg/korealeon1.html, 2003).

Case study questions

1 To what extent is Samsung Life's system a true CRM system, as opposed to a system that was introduced to increase operational efficiency in the traditional workforce?

2 Contrast Samsung Life's approach to distribution with that of Prudential.

3 'Technology is at the heart of an efficient life insurance company.' Comment.

4 Describe some of the immediate benefits of the new data warehouse system that Samsung Life implemented.

5 How do you think Samsung Life can increase their 'cross-selling capabilities'?

Questions and exercises

Questions

1 Evaluate the differences between building a relationship and conducting transactions.

2 What do you understand by the term customer relationship management (CRM)?

3 Discuss different approaches to building customer loyalty. Give examples of companies that, in your view, effectively build customer loyalty.

4 Why is it important to have a 'single view of the customer' in an organisation?

5 Why is technology so important in implementing CRM?

6 What is the relevance of ERP systems to CRM?

Online exercises

1 Visit the Broadvision site (www.broadvision.com) and discuss how its products can assist in relationship marketing.

2 Visit CRMGuru's website (www.crmguru.com) and register as a user. You will receive e-mails providing updates on aspects of CRM. Comment on how the website seeks to build a relationship with you.

3 'Technology is at the heart of an efficient life insurance company.' Comment.

4 Describe some of the immediate benefits of the new data warehouse system that Samsung Life implemented.

5 How do you think Samsung Life can increase their 'cross-selling capabilities'?

References

1 Berry, L. (1983). 'Relationship marketing, in Berry L. et al. (eds) *Emerging perspectives on services marketing*, Chicago: American Marketing Association.

2 Levitt, T. (1983). 'After the sale is over . . .' *Harvard Business Review*, September–October.

3 Gordon, I. (1998). *Relationship Marketing – New Strategies, Techniques and Technologies to Win the Customers You Want and Keep Them Forever*, Toronto: John Wiley & Sons.

4 O'Malley, L., Patterson, M. and Evans, M. (1999). *Exploring Direct Marketing*, London: Thomson Press.

5 Shultz, D., Tannenaum. S. and Lauterborn, R. (1993). *The New Marketing Paradigm*, Lincolnwood, Ill.: NTC Business Books.

6 Hunt, J. (2002). 'Bollywood in your inbox', *The Guardian*, 12 August.

7 Borch, F.J. (1957). *The Marketing Philosophy as a Way of Business Life*, New York: General Electric.

8 Alderson, W. (1958). *The Analytical Framework for Marketing*, Conference of Marketing Teachers, University of California, pp. 15–28.

9 O'Malley, L. and Tynan, C. (1999). 'The utility of the relationship metaphor in consumer markets: a critical evaluation', *Journal of Marketing Management*, Vol. 15.

10 Buchanan, R.W.T. and Gillies, C.S. (1990). 'Value managed relationships: the key to customer retention and profitability', *European Management Journal*, Vol. 8, No. 4.

11 Reichheld, F.F. and Sasser, W.E. (1990). 'Zero defections: quality comes to services', *Harvard Business Review*, September–October.

12 Reichheld, F.F. (1996). *The Loyalty Effect: The Hidden Force Behind Growth, Profits, and Lasting Value*, Boston: Harvard Business School Press.

13 O'Malley et al., *Exploring Direct Marketing*.

14 O'Connor, J. Unpublished research.

15 Edmunds, M. (2001). 'Some optimism amid the gloom', *Financial Times*, 17 October.

16 Jones, T.O. and Sasser, W.E. (1995). 'Why satisfied customers defect', *Harvard Business Review*, November–December.

17 Hart, S., Smith, A., Sparks, L. and Tzokas, N. (1999). 'Are loyalty schemes a manifestation of relationship marketing?', *Journal of Marketing Management*, Vol. 15.

18 Evans, M., O'Malley, L. Mitchell, S. and Patterson, M. (1997). 'Consumer reactions to data-based supermarket loyalty schemes'. *Journal of Database Marketing*, Vol. 4, No. 4.

19 NOP (1995). *Loyalty Card Usage Report*.

20 Mitchell, A. (1995). 'A quest for successful relations', *Marketing Week*, 4 August.

21 Reed, D. (1995). 'Jumping on the brandwagon', *Marketing Week* (Customer Loyalty supplement), 24 March.

22 McKenzie, S. (1995). 'Distinguishing marks', *Marketing Week,* 17 November.

23 Henley Centre (1995). *Dataculture Report*, London: Henley Centre.

24 Future Foundation (2001). *Changing Lives Report*, London: Future Foundation.

25 Sharp, B. and Sharp, A. (1997). 'Loyalty schemes and their impact on repeat-purchase loyalty patterns', *International Journal of Research in Marketing*, Vol. 14, No. 5.

26 Miller, R. (1998). 'Locked in by loyalty', *Marketing*, 2 April.

27 Garrahan, M. (2002). 'Battle to woo customers to loyalty cards hots up', *Financial Times*, 12 September.

28 Cook, R. (1998). 'Football clubs seize the chance to target their fans directly', *Campaign*, 31 July.

29 Conlin, R. (2001). 'Suns, Diamondbacks give Onyx a sporting chance,' CRMDaily.com, 13 April.

30 Coyles, S. and Gokey, T.C. (2002). 'Customer retention is not enough', *McKinsey Quarterly*, No. 2.

31 Coyles and Gokey, 'Customer retention is not enough'.

32 Dick, A. and Basu, K. (1994). 'Customer loyalty: toward an integrated conceptual framework', *Journal of the Academy of Marketing Science*, Vol. 22, No. 2.

33 Dick and Basu, 'Customer loyalty'.

34 Evans, M. (1999). 'Food retailing loyalty schemes and the Orwellian millennium?' *British Food Journal*, Vol. 101, No. 2.

35 Evans, M. (2002). 'The unreliable marketing route map and the road to hell', Academy of Marketing Conference, Nottingham, July.

36 Hughes, R. and Evans, M. (2001). 'Relationships are two-way: the neglected role of "inbound" contact in the financial services sector', with Rebecca Hughes, SmartFocus Ltd, Bristol Business School, World Marketing Congress, June.

37 Howard, S. (2000). 'Rewarding customer loyalty', www.howard-marketing.com/resource/images/pmm-8.pdf

38 Day, J. (2001). 'Vodafone promises to end junk mail', *The Guardian*, 19 March.

39 www.experian.com/tec/cdi_whitepaper.html

40 Bowen, D.E. and Lawler, E.E. (1992). 'The empowering of service workers: what, why, how and when?', *Sloan Management Review*, Vol. 33, No. 3.

41 Peppers, D. and Rogers, M. (1996). *The One to One Future: Building Relationships One Customer at a Time*, New York: Currency Doubleday.

42 Cap Gemini Ernst and Young (2002). 'Cracking the code: unlocking new value in customer relationships', www.cgey.com/life

43 Harvey, F. (2002). 'Making the connection', *Financial Times*, 28 May.

44 Gofton, K. (2002). 'Support for the frontline', *Financial Times*, 28 May.

45 Berry, *Relationship Marketing*.

46 Gordon, *Relationship Marketing*.

Part IV

DEVELOPING THE CUSTOMER OFFERING

Earlier sections of this book have been concerned primarily with the customer – gaining customer insight, building customer databases and using customer information to target specific groups and build relationships with individual customers. In the next four chapters we use the concept of the marketing mix. This is a well-accepted concept in marketing that is also called the 'four Ps'. It describes the four key elements of the marketing of any product or service in terms of product, price, place and promotion. Product refers to the characteristics of the product or service, price is its price positioning, place is how it will be distributed or sold and promotion refers to how it will be promoted. Part IV of this book examines the role of IT and other technologies in the different elements of the marketing mix. Part IV contains four chapters:

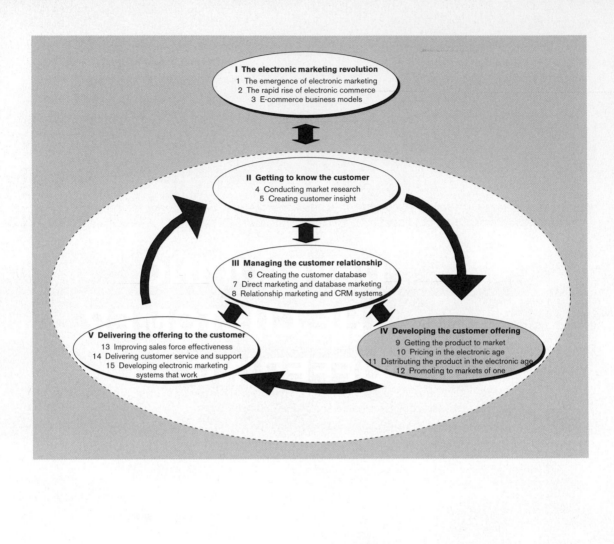

9

Getting the product to market

Learning objectives

Once you have read this chapter you will:

- understand how technology can be used to improve product/service offerings;

- appreciate how technology can increase speed to market;

- understand how technology can help in all stages of the product development life cycle, right up to the commercialisation of the product;

- appreciate how advanced manufacturing techniques can be used to speed up commercialisation.

Contents

USING ADVANCED MANUFACTURING TECHNIQUES IN PRODUCT COMMERCIALISATION

■ Reducing time-to-market through simultaneous engineering

■ Reducing costs using design-for-manufacture techniques

■ Implementing product life-cycle management (PLM) tools

■ Building to order

SUMMARY

CASE STUDY

Introduction

The ability to develop and launch new products and services rapidly is a key competitive advantage. Developing new products and services presents the marketing manager with a number of challenges. These include:

■ the failure rate for new product/service concepts is very high;

■ new product/service introductions typically require large investments, particularly if the objective is to develop a national or global brand;

■ the number of potential product/service configurations is often extremely high, making it difficult to decide on what options to pursue;

■ coordinating development across different parts of an organisation, such as research and development (R&D), production and marketing, is difficult.

However, in many industries, such as consumer electronics, new products are critical to success. We start this chapter with a discussion on how technology is changing the way companies bring new products to market. We then examine how technology is being used to increase speed to market. We finish with a look at some of the advanced manufacturing techniques that are being used to speed up the product-commercialisation process.

Using technology to improve product/service offerings

Incorporating technology into products

New technologies such as the internet, digital video disks (DVDs) and third-generation (3G) telephones create large new markets in their own right. Technology is also being incorporated into many existing products and services. For example, the addition of smart chips on everyday products like washing machines, toys and many household goods gives these products many new capabilities. Even contraceptive devices have entered the electronic age (*see* Exhibit 9.1).

Cars are increasingly using technology to control functions that were traditionally operated by mechanical means. These include ignition control, central locking, braking systems and air conditioning. Automatic braking systems (ABS) in cars employ fuzzy logic, a particular branch of information technology that is used in the control systems of many products today. One of Canon's handheld cameras uses 13 rules, controlled by fuzzy logic, to tune the auto-focus on the lens. The control system requires little memory and uses image sensors to measure picture clarity. The data from the image sensors, combined with the fuzzy logic decision rules that drive the lens settings, help the system to focus twice as well as other controllers. Other products employing similar control systems include:

EXHIBIT 9.1

WHEN GREEN MEANS GO FOR IT

Unipath, formerly the healthcare division of Unilever, launched Persona after 15 years of research and development. It is a unique method of contraception that works in harmony with a woman's body to identify the fertile days of a cycle – in effect, a computerised version of the rhythm method. On most days of the month a woman does not need to use contraceptives. By monitoring hormone levels, Persona identifies those days of the month on which a woman is free to make love without using a contraceptive.

Persona is made up of a small hand-held monitor and simple, disposable urine test sticks. The test sticks collect hormones from the user's urine and process them into information that the monitor can read. The monitor then reads, stores and uses that information to let the woman know whether she is at risk of becoming pregnant or free to make love without a contraceptive. The woman's most recent personal information (last six monthly cycles) is stored in the monitor. Using the monitor couldn't be easier: a green light means go and a red light means no. Persona is 94 per cent reliable as soon as you begin to use it.

Sources: Persona websites (www.unipath.com/persona.cfm and www.persona.org.uk, 2003).

- *Air conditioners* – to prevent temperature fluctuations and to reduce power consumption.

- *Dishwashers* – to adjust the cleaning cycle and rinse and wash strategies, based on the number of dishes.

- *Elevators* – to reduce waiting time, based on passenger traffic.

- *Toasters* – to set toasting time and heat levels for different thicknesses of bread.

- *Transmission systems* – to select gear ratios, based on engine load and other driving conditions.

- *Video camcorders* – to cancel hand-held shake and to adjust auto-focus.

Another industry that has been transformed as a result of the electronic age is the toy industry. Microchips and other computing devices have been incorporated into toys for many years. One of the leaders in the electronic toy industry is profiled in Exhibit 9.2 and Figure 9.1.

EXHIBIT 9.2

VTECH – THE MICROSOFT OF TOYLAND

The toy industry is dominated by American giants such as Hasbro, Mattel and Fisher-Price – huge marketing machines that control most of the shelf-space at Toys 'Я' Us and other retailers. But VTech is the market leader in electronic learning toys, with dominant market share in all major markets around the world such as the USA, UK and other European countries.

The VTech group was founded on the principle of applying the latest technology to design and develop innovative products. It introduced its first product in 1978 – a portable electronic game based on a single-chip microprocessor. This initiative was soon expanded into a full range of in-house designed electronic games that won many export and design awards. The group's first electronic learning product – the Lesson One, launched in 1981 – was a product of the group's vision of technology and design excellence.

More recently, Smarty's Workshop, the recipient of the 2002 National Parenting Publications (NAPPA) Gold Award and named as a top pre-school product in *Toy Wishes 2002 Holiday Guide*, lets preschoolers ages three and up hammer, saw and magically 'build' and 'fix' their own creations. Smarty's Workshop helps teach children to follow step-by-step instructions as they build simple projects, like a birdhouse or a swing set, and the LCD screen lets children see their progress in real time. Smarty, the cheerful, encouraging carpenter robot, moves, talks, dances and even gets children into the habit of cleaning up after themselves with his catchy 'Pack it up and put it away' tune.

Source: VTech website (www.vtech.com, 2003).

Figure 9.1 Electronic learning products from VTech
Source: VTech website (www.vtech.com, 2003).

Turning products into services

Because commodity products do not command a premium in the marketplace, marketing managers strive to augment the products, or even turn them into services, using information technology. In doing so, they enhance value, make the products more difficult to replicate, and allow premium prices to be charged. One example of a value-added service being bundled into product sales is the use of remote monitoring services:

▪ *Industrial equipment.* Remote monitoring sensors are routinely incorporated into machine tools, chemical processing and other industrial equipment to monitor their operations. In the event of a problem, the machinery is either repaired remotely, or an engineer dispatched before a machine component fails and causes further damage. GE provides such services for its aircraft engines and medical systems. Otis operates a similar service for lifts and elevators (*see* Exhibit 9.3).

▪ *Security services.* House alarms no longer simply let the neighbourhood know that an intruder is on the premises – many will automatically notify the police or security company as well.

EXHIBIT 9.3

I'M ABOUT TO GO DOWN ON YOU

Developed to optimise performance and minimise downtime, Remote Elevator Monitoring (REM) from Otis tracks hundreds of system functions on thousands of elevators around the world.

- *REM makes the call.* If the REM system detects a problem, it correctly diagnoses the cause and location, then automatically makes the service call – dramatically reducing the time your system is out of service.

- *Fast response.* If the REM system detects an urgent problem, it reports the condition to the OTISLINE 24-hour communications centre, and an Otis mechanic is dispatched if necessary. Elevators are often back in service before you or your tenants realise there is a problem.

- *Preventing callbacks.* The REM system identifies most problems before they occur. REM detects deteriorating components and intermittent anomalies, and notes the small nuisances that might have gone undetected until they caused service disruptions. Intermittent problems are often fixed before they annoy you or your tenants.

Source: Otis website (www.otis.com, 2003).[1]

■ *Trucks and delivery vans.* Many vehicles are now equipped with global positioning system (GPS) technology, which allows operators and fleet managers to schedule their movements more accurately.

Car manufacturers have also started to bundle value-added services into their products, through the use of advanced digital technologies. For example, if the driver of a General Motors car equipped with its On-Star system locks the key in the car by mistake, an emergency centre can transmit a digital signal via satellite to unlock the doors. On-Star also automatically calls for help if an accident triggers the airbags to open. Toyota and General Motors are among a growing list of car manufacturers to introduce in-car navigation systems as standard. BMW and Mercedes-Benz recently introduced navigation hardware that not only plots the route but also alerts the driver to traffic jams along the way. These systems have been available in the USA for some years and have more recently been deployed in other countries (*see* Exhibit 9.4).

Another example of making smart appliances is the introduction of radio frequency (RF) microchips and radio frequency identification (RFID) tags into products. Originally designed and used for improving logistics and supply chain management (*see* Chapter 11), RFID tags can also be adapted to improve the service provided by products. Exhibit 9.5 describes how one Italian company is experimenting with RF microchips as part of its drive towards creating smarter and better products and services.

EXHIBIT 9.4

BMW TAKES ON SINGAPORE

BMW has become Singapore's first car model to boast an onboard navigation system as a standard feature. The BMW Navigation System will be factory-installed into all BMW 7-series cars to offer information on all Singapore roads, and locations of more than 20 categories of places of interest such as shopping centres, hospitals and police stations. Each onboard BMW Navigation System has a global-positioning system (GPS) antenna and receiver, which can simultaneously communicate with up to six satellites. BMW's in-vehicle magnetic sensors are also able to fix the position of the car, accurate to within 10 metres.

According to company officials, the BMW Navigation System is the first in Singapore to provide voice guidance to drivers. It will not only locate the car on an in-built colour LCD monitor on the dashboard, but will also provide timely instructions to guide drivers to their destination. The audible instructions do not compromise safety, as drivers are able to keep their eyes on the road instead of looking at the LCD monitor. Other features of the system include a television screen, radio, VCD and teletext. The television and VCD features will automatically shut down once the car moves faster than 8 kilometres per hour.

The BMW Navigation System was made available in Germany five years ago, according to Felix Herrnberger, president of BMW Asia, who added that the company had already managed to get a return on its investment in Germany. The system made its Asia Pacific debut in Japan before being brought over to Singapore.

Source: *Asia internet* (4 June 2001).[2]

However, there are issues with RFID technology, which we discussed in Chapter 7 – Benetton faced a potential marketing disaster in 2003 when it sought to implement radio frequency tagging on their clothes. The RFID tags were withdrawn after consumer groups complained about the potential of such technology to invade their privacy.

Using technology to 'mass-customise' products

Another option that is enabled by technologies such as the internet is the facility that allows customers to design the product – an extension of the concept of 'mass customisation'. Here are some examples of how consumers are invited to design their own products:

- *Dell Computers*. Dell is the world's leading direct seller of PCs, and sells more that 50 per cent of its products over the internet. Corporate customers and consumers can visit Dell's website (www.dell.com) and design and assemble a PC to their

EXHIBIT 9.5

MAKING SMARTER APPLIANCES

Several consumer goods manufacturers, such as Gillette, have started to tag their products in recent months with radio frequency (RF) microchips, which contain and transmit product data, in order to increase security and enhance logistics control. Picking up on this 'smart tagging' trend, domestic appliance manufacturer Merloni Elettrodomestici said it would fit several of its Ariston brand appliances with antennas that can read the information on these tags. In the case of washing machines, smart tags on clothes will enable the appliances to select the washing programme appropriate to the items in the load. 'And if any incompatible fabrics end up in the drum, such as whites with coloured items being washed for the first time, the display will tell the consumer which items to take out', said a Merloni spokesperson in a statement. It also claimed that its fridges will be able to indicate what food they contain, the optimum preservation temperature, best-before dates, descriptions of food and its nutrition data, as well as recipes that can be prepared using the available food. Users will get messages such as 'Eat your strawberry yoghurt – it expires tomorrow', and 'Move the chicken into the meat compartment'. Similarly, its ovens will be able to automatically select the most appropriate cooking programme such as 'Aubergines gratine alla Mediterranea: defrost for 8 minutes, fan bake for 5 minutes, grill for 10 minutes'.

'By applying smart-tag technology to Ariston products we're taking another step forward in our programme of innovation', commented Vittorio Merloni. The company claims to have over 200 people in its R&D department and to have spent more than €90 million on developing new processes and products in 2002.

Source: *Electric News* (8 April 2003).[3]

own specifications. Once the order is taken, the PC is assembled to order, and shipped within days.

■ *GE*. At GE Power Systems customers can use technology to design their air conditioning systems. By answering a series of questions, they are guided towards the most appropriate system to meet their needs.

■ *Rover Group*. Multimedia point-of-sale systems are also used by UK-based Rover Group to allow prospective customers to 'configure' their own model. The kiosks have been rolled out to Rover's dealers in the UK and elsewhere across Europe.

■ *BMW*. By accessing the BMW site (www.bmw.com), customers are invited to configure their own car – by combining paint colours and internal finishes, customers can get exactly the look they are after (*see* Figure 9.2).

We will return to this concept at the end of this chapter when we discuss the manufacturing implications of mass customisation.

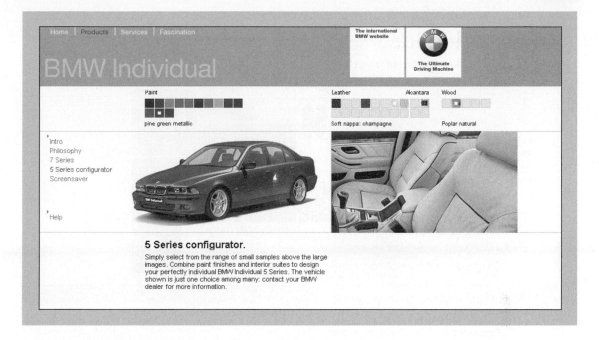

Figure 9.2 BMW's self-configuration tool
Source: BMW website (www.bmw.com, 2003).

Using technology to increase speed to market

Increasing the rate of new product introduction

Before marketing managers can define the role of IT and other forms of technology, they must set their objectives for new product/service development. For example, 3M has long had a commitment to new products – more than 30 per cent of every division's annual sales must come from products invented in the previous four years. 3M employees are encouraged to spend up to 15 per cent of company time on 'skunkworks' projects that interest them and which do not require corporate approval. The company also uses this commitment to innovation as a key marketing differentiator, as can be seen from its website (*see* Figure 9.3).

Another company that has turned product innovation into a competitive advantage is Casio, which has a reputation for bringing a regular stream of new competitive products to market. Rather than postpone profits until the later stages of the product life cycle, Casio aims to make its money on products with very short life cycles. It achieves this by integrating design and development with marketing so that those closest to the market are responsible for developing new products in line with customers' needs.

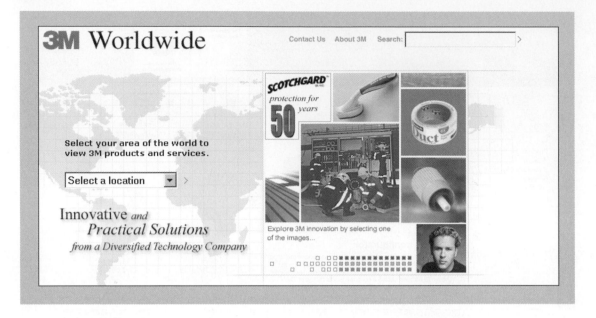

Figure 9.3 Product innovation at 3M
Source: 3M website (www.3m.com, 2003).

Accelerating the research and development (R&D) process

Each year, vast sums of money are spent by the world's largest companies on research and development (R&D). In 2001 16 companies spent in excess of $3.5 billion on R&D (*see* Table 9.1).

The largest spenders are the motor manufacturers, but the pharmaceutical companies tend to be among the most R&D-intensive, re-investing an average of 13 per cent of their revenues back into research and development of new products each year. Little wonder that these firms are attempting to squeeze more productivity out of those R&D dollars and are employing advanced IT applications to help in the process. Some years ago, a senior executive of Eli Lilly (the US drugs company with an annual R&D spend of $2 billion) described his company's business as: '50 per cent information technology, 50 per cent pharmaceuticals'.[4] His comment highlights the increasingly crucial role played by technology in a business where delays in bringing a product to market can cost millions of dollars in lost revenues (*see* Exhibit 9.6).

Companies like Eli Lilly are attempting to cut the typical clinical trial process by half, from 30 months to 15 months, by using technology to manage the process more efficiently and effectively. Traditionally, a clinical trial centred around a paper-based process that began with a general practitioner filling out a piece of paper after seeing a patient, and sending this report back to the company conducting the trial, where it would be input by a data entry clerk for analysis. More recently, doctors have started to use PCs to enter the data directly. Clinical research assistants, who normally visit the doctors every six weeks, have been provided with mobile computers and digital telephones so that they can access the latest clinical trial information remotely.

Table 9.1 Largest spenders on R&D (2001)

	Company	2001 R&D spend ($billion)	2001 R&D spend (as a % of sales)
1	Ford Motor Company (USA)	7.4	4.6
2	General Motors (USA)	6.2	3.5
3	Siemens (Germany)	6.0	7.8
4	DaimlerChrysler (Germany)	5.2	3.9
5	Pfizer (USA)	4.8	15.0
6	IBM (USA)	4.6	5.4
7	Ericsson (Sweden)	4.4	20.1
8	Microsoft (USA)	4.4	17.3
9	Motorola (USA)	4.3	14.4
10	Matsushita (Japan)	4.3	8.2
11	Cisco (USA)	3.9	17.6
12	GlaxoSmithKline (UK)	3.8	12.9
13	Intel (USA)	3.8	14.3
14	Toyota (Japan)	3.6	3.6
15	Johnson & Johnson (USA)	3.6	10.9
16	Lucent (USA)	3.5	16.5

Source: UK Department of Trade and Industry (2002).[5]

EXHIBIT 9.6

DELAYS CAUSE HEADACHES

Testing new drugs is a costly and frustrating headache for pharmaceutical companies – and the pain is about to get worse as stricter regulatory standards are compounding the problems. Delays can cost pharma companies at least $800,000 a day in lost sales for a niche medication such as Amaryl, an oral anti-diabetic treatment, and as much as $5.4 million for a blockbuster like Prilosec, a gastrointestinal medication. If some of this revenue is merely deferred, it may be recouped once a drug goes on the market, but millions of dollars can vanish if a competitor catches up, or worse, gains the advantage with an earlier debut.

Source: Cruz Rowe et al. (2002).[6]

EXHIBIT 9.7

DRUGS AND DATA

For companies in the pharmaceutical industry, the paper-intensive process of tracking experimental medications and getting approval to market them is tailor-made for web technology. Kyowa Pharmaceutical last week began implementing digital-workspace applications to facilitate the flow of information throughout clinical trials, a key capability as the company takes steps to increase its US business. Currently, Kyowa Pharmaceutical – the New Jersey arm of $3.5 billion Japanese healthcare product maker Kyowa Hakko – seeks approval in the USA for drugs developed in Japan, and then markets those products through other companies such as Bristol-Myers Squibb. But Kyowa, best known for manufacturing an oncology medication called Mutamycin, wants to retain the licenses to its own drugs. As the company moves toward those goals, Kyowa needs an efficient collaboration system that will easily accommodate its expanding head count, says Dr Yutaka Waki, VP of global clinical development. 'It will be very easy to bring people up and running on this system because it uses basic web technology that doesn't require a lot of training', he says.

IntraLinks provides the workspace for Kyowa to store documents online so employees and partners, including institutional review boards and the labs that conduct the trials, can access data any time and from any location, using a password they receive from the pharmaceutical company. On paper, some documents related to clinical trials can reach 250 pages and take up to three weeks to print, package, and distribute. IntraLinks will also provide an archive of records, which Kyowa can give to the Food and Drug Administration (FDA) as proof that the trial process met all requirements.

Source: *Information Week* (13 August 2001).[7]

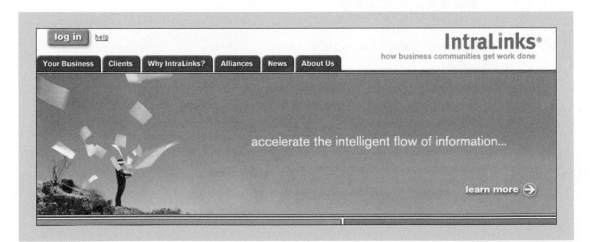

Figure 9.4 Collaborative services from IntraLinks
Source: IntraLinks website (www.intralinks.com, 2003).

Given the escalating costs and risks involved in new drugs, many pharmaceutical companies are also attempting to manage the spread of risk by forming research partnerships. In these cases, collaboration tools and videoconferencing can help geographically remote teams exchange data and work more closely together. The need to collaborate and share information has also encouraged drug companies like Kyowa Pharmaceutical (*see* Exhibit 9.7) to become early business adopters of the internet as a networking medium.

One of the biggest opportunities to improve R&D productivity is through the use of collaborative software. This is much more than e-mail and includes data repositories, version control on documentation and project management functions. IntraLinks (www.intralinks.com) is a good example of a leading technology company in this area (*see* Figure 9.4). To understand more about the role that technology plays in the pharmaceutical industry, it is worth visiting the websites of IntraLinks and Kinematik (www.kinematik.com) to see the tools that they market to the pharmaceutical and life-sciences industries.

Larson (1998)[8] outlines the likely R&D laboratory that will exist in 2008 and emphasises the use of 'technology intelligence' for managing the R&D process, outlining a model of greater networking with customers and third-party information providers:

> The future use of technology intelligence (TI) [will be] centred on developing an appropriate, effective system, with a core group of experts trained in collecting, analysing, and applying needed information. Being close to the market and one's customers will be particularly important ... Partnering with customers who have unique strengths will be essential, as will the acquisition of competing technologies ... Effective use of third-party information providers will be supplemented by automated or smart information-gathering systems. Personnel exchanges with national laboratories and universities will become more common. Warehousing of business and technical data will be necessary, but must be carefully protected from outsiders ... Finally, as in all operations, it was suggested that one hire and retain the best people for technology intelligence.

Accelerating the new product development (NPD) process

Lynn et al. (1999)[9] state that the two most important factors leading to increased success rate and increased speed to market in new product development (NPD) are:

- having a structured new product development process (such as screening, evaluation, development and testing);

- having a clear and shared vision on the new product development team.

In rapidly changing industries such as telecommunications, the difference in timing can be the difference between success and failure. The speed of development in the telecommunications industry is further illustrated by the fact that 30–40 per cent of sales come from products launched over the previous two years. Figure 9.5 provides a graphical representation of how these changes are changing the shape of the traditional product life cycle.

The analysis carried out by Lynn et al. stresses the importance of managing the period of time involved before the product is introduced – the NPD cycle. If real

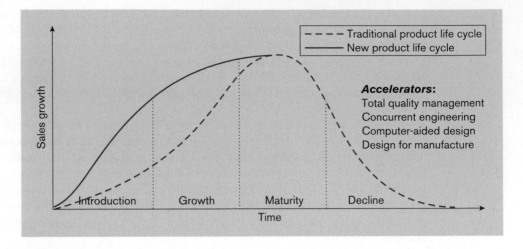

Figure 9.5 'Traditional' and 'new' product life cycles

financial benefits are to be gained in the early stages of the product life cycle, the NPD process itself must be streamlined.

Using technology to streamline the six stages of NPD

The success rate for new products is low, and managing the NPD process is a complex task. Information technology can help marketers and new product development managers throughout the development process. At the very beginning, it can help identify customers' needs. Dahan and Hauser (2001)[10] see a role for the internet even at the very earliest stages of the process:

> The internet also provides the means to identify customer needs by passively observing interactive customer behaviour on a website. By organising the website by agendas based on features or customer needs, a virtual engineer can listen in and observe how customers process attributes and, in particular, when they search for attributes, features, or needs that cannot be satisfied by any extant product.

To understand the full impact that technology and the internet can have on the NPD process, we now look at their applicability in the six different stages of the life cycle (*see* Figure 9.6).

Stage 1 New idea/concept generation and screening

At least 50 per cent of all new product ideas are developed internally. We have already seen that technology has a role to play in the sharing of ideas and obtaining feedback from remote locations. Executives from different offices or countries can be involved in the idea-generation and screening process through the use of videoconferencing and e-mail. Groupware tools and internal websites (intranets) allow team members

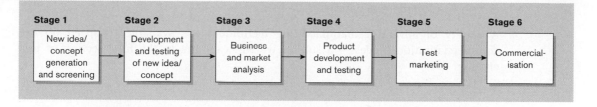

Figure 9.6 The six stages of product development

to collaborate on ideas. Expert systems can also be used to evaluate each idea by asking a series of questions on each and attaching a pre-determined weighting to each response.

Stage 2 Development and testing of new idea/concept

Software tools such as computer-aided design (CAD) programmes can be used to design the product and illustrate what it will look like. Car manufacturers such as Ford and Rover routinely build virtual models to check ergonomics and help develop a new model before it is built physically. If the members of a design team are split up and located in different countries, they can stay in touch using internet technologies, videoconferencing and e-mail. Dahan and Srinivasan (2000)[11] have even developed and tested a web-based method of parallel concept testing using visual depictions and animations for bicycle pumps. Respondents viewed 11 new product concepts and expressed their preferences by 'buying' their most preferred concepts at varying prices.

Stage 3 Business and market analysis

In Chapter 4 we examined the use of IT in the five stages of market research. Basic software applications such as spreadsheets can also be used to perform the business analysis, sensitivity and 'what if' analysis.

Stage 4 Product development and testing

Applications such as collaborative product development (CPD) and similar technologies are now used routinely by geographically-remote teams to prototype and develop products. The case study on Baldwin Filters at the end of this chapter provides a good example of collaborative software.

Stage 5 Test marketing

Geographic information systems and geo-demographic analysis tools have become commonplace in determining the most appropriate locations for test marketing particular products. Simulated test marketing (STM) is also used to speed up the test marketing process (*see* below).

Stage 6 Commercialisation

A variety of advanced manufacturing techniques are available to speed up the commercialisation process – a subject we will examine in the final section of this chapter.

Future use of technology in new product development

To sum up the current and future use of technology in the NPD process, we return to Dahan and Srinivasan (2000),[12] whose vision of the future of product development is as follows:

> Toward the end of the 1990s, the challenges of product development began to change as markets and competition became more global, as engineering and design talent became more dispersed, as internal product development efforts migrated into the extended enterprise, and as information and communication technologies changed the way people worked. The new challenges call for a product development process that is integrated, information intensive, almost instantaneous, and makes strong use of new technologies such as the internet. We call this new vision i4PD: integrated, information, instantaneous, and internet.

Accelerating the market testing process

One important development in test marketing is the use of simulated test marketing (STM) – a concept we introduced in Chapter 4 when we introduced ACNielsen's BASES product (*see* Figure 9.7) – which improves the likelihood of new product success. Clancy and Shulman (1991)[13] believe that STM is the best way of reducing risk when launching a new product or repositioning an existing product.

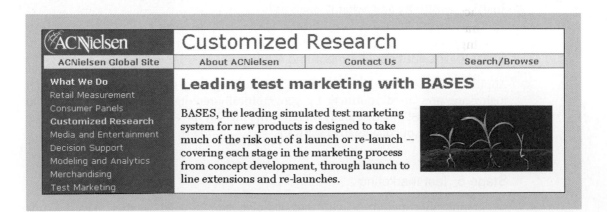

Figure 9.7 Test marketing using STM

Source: ACNielsen website (www.acnielsen.com/services/custom, 2003).

A typical STM system will use information on each element of the marketing mix and assess the effect of changes to any part of the plan. STM allows a marketing manager to test key components of the plan and conduct 'what if' analysis. Using STM has a number of advantages over traditional methods of test marketing:

■ *It reduces risk.* Typically eight out of ten new products fail. STM costing $100,000 to $150,000 can provide timely feedback, compared to several million dollars to test market and substantially more to launch nationwide.

■ *It increases efficiency.* STM can help prioritise different projects by providing feedback on which provides the greatest potential return.

■ *It maintains security.* Real test marketing alerts competitors to a company's intentions and allows them to react. STM does not.

■ *It can save company time.* As time has become a key competitive weapon, identifying and serving a customer's needs quickly is critical; STM can give results in three to six months as opposed to over a year for a real test.

Using advanced manufacturing techniques in product commercialisation

Reducing time-to-market through simultaneous engineering

Many manufacturing concepts were imported from Japanese companies to Western companies during the 1980s and 1990s. One of the more important, from a marketing perspective, is that product design should be carried out in a multi-disciplinary way where all relevant functions of the business should be brought to bear on all stages of product development, especially marketing, production and finance. In particular, the integration of product design with the production processes is of major importance in bringing products to market more quickly and at lower cost (Brown and Eisenhardt, 1995).[14] The term given to these advanced manufacturing practices is simultaneous engineering, the objectives of which are to:

■ reduce time lag between different stages in product development

■ minimise development and final production costs

■ increase product quality

■ increase market share through early entry.

Ericsson, the Swedish telephone-switching equipment firm, has cut its development time dramatically by using 'simultaneous' engineering rather than sequential development. This new development approach has allowed Ericsson to cut the time from order to delivery of a switching system from six months to ten days.[15] In the 1980s and 1990s other firms that used simultaneous engineering to achieve dramatic cuts in their time to market included:

■ *Honda* – which cut its five-year new car development cycle by 50 per cent.

■ *AT&T* – which also reduced the time taken to introduce its new cordless telephone by 50 per cent.

■ *Hewlett-Packard* – which reduced the time to develop its printers from 4.5 years to 22 months.[16]

Today, simultaneous engineering concepts and the associated use of collaborative product development (CPD) tools have become part of mainstream manufacturing practice and are applied routinely in the design and manufacture of many industrial and consumer products.

Reducing costs using design-for-manufacture techniques

Manufacturers have also incorporated design-for-manufacture principles into their development efforts. Design-for-manufacture is another concept that differs from the traditional product development process, where designs were passed from one design team to a separate production unit. In the traditional approach, difficulties often arose when the original design was found to be difficult to produce and the iterative redesign/rebuild process was found to be time consuming and expensive. The objectives of design-for-manufacture are to simplify both product and process, including:

■ *Fewer components in the product.* With fewer components, the product is not only easier and less costly to produce; it will probably have greater reliability.

■ *Fewer steps in the process flow.* With the emphasis on the elimination of unnecessary steps, more value is added to the product. This applies to any process, whether factory operations or office procedures.

■ *Fewer components in the fixtures and tooling used for machining.* The simplest fixtures and tools require the least time and cost to alter when a machine is changed from producing one item to another.

Using design-for-manufacture principles, potential problems or breakthroughs can be identified before significant costs are committed (*see* Figure 9.8).

Implementing product life-cycle management (PLM) tools

Product life-cycle management (PLM) is gaining popular acceptance as a generic term that covers the collaborative design and CAD/CAM/CAE technologies:

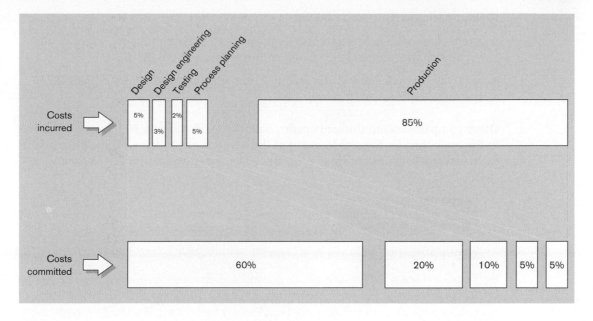

Figure 9.8 Costs committed at different stages of the product development process
Source: *Business Week* (30 April 1990), The McGraw-Hill Companies Inc.

■ *Computer-aided design (CAD)*. CAD systems can help design products because designers can view the design from any angle and obtain customer feedback on how it looks. CAD programmes can be used to test different product designs based on the characteristics of the materials used, without building the products.

■ *Computer-aided manufacturing (CAM)*. CAM is used to manufacture products and incorporates a number of components, including shop-floor control (monitoring and controlling the production process in a factory), process control (directly controlling a physical process), machine control (directly controlling machines) and robots (controlling a machine with human-like capabilities).

■ *Computer-aided engineering (CAE)*. CAE is the general term used to cover both CAD and CAM.

PLM tools are broader than any of these individual applications and encompass the collaborative tools that are used to manage the entire lifecycle from initial design through to maintenance management. PLM tools have particular application in the management of complex industrial products in the automobiles, aerospace and defence, and similar industries. O'Marah (2002)[17] cites the example of General Motors whose global PLM initiatives support 18,000 users and 1,800 suppliers, resulting in the following benefits:

■ system simplification – 1,500 product development applications in 1995 had been rationalised down to 500 in 2002;

- total systems savings of $1 billion;

- a reduction of 35 per cent in overall global product development budget, while expanding the number of development programmes from 19 to 30;

- reduction in cycle time – from styling freeze to production – from 60 months in the early 1990s to 18 months in 2002.

Other companies claim similar benefits. Bailly (2002)[18] claims a 30 per cent reduction in the cycle time for the development of the new Renault Mégane. Bailly also explains the massively complex nature of modern collaborative design and PLM systems:

EXHIBIT 9.8

DESIGNING THE ULTIMATE FORKLIFT

Toyota Industries Corporation (TICO, a world leader in the industrial vehicle market), IBM and Dassault Systemes today announced that TICO has significantly reduced development costs and cycles of its High Pick Lift forklift using IBM product life-cycle management (PLM) solutions, including CATIA developed by Dassault Systemes.

TICO began using PLM solutions from IBM and Dassault Systemes in late 2000. The solutions were implemented to develop forklifts as part of IT Propulsion, a company-wide programme designed to improve business reactivity through the use of 3D data and improved information management and sharing. CATIA technology helped TICO achieve these goals by allowing the company automatically to combine standard design definitions with customer-specific functional requirements. This presents a major advantage in forklift development, commonly dictated by the built-to-order model consisting of many variations and options. Using the collaborative functions of IBM PLM solutions, TICO has been able to integrate its 3D forklift product information with its manufacturing processes and resources and design and simulate virtual factories using Dassault Systemes' DELMIA digital manufacturing solution.

'We achieved our original targets both by shortening the High Pick Lift development period from 18 to 10 months and by reducing development costs by 53 per cent. In addition, this product won the Japan Society of Industrial Machinery Manufacturer's Award for its gentle curved design, which was achieved thanks to CATIA's 3D design functionalities,' said Kimpei Mitsuya, director and member of the board, Global IT Division, TICO.

Dassault Systemes first created CATIA, which ranks as one of the most pervasive 3D modelling software in the world. The company then expanded its product line by proposing an integrated 3D PLM solution with DELMIA, its manufacturing process definition and simulation software package. ENOVIA and SMARTEAM complete the 3D PLM offering, enabling companies to manage all product-related data and components by sharing best practices throughout the enterprise.

Sources: Dassault Systemes press release (20 November 2002)[19]; Dassault Systemes website (www.3ds.com, 2003).

- 700 connected companies

- 40,000 files exchanged every month

- 40 gigabytes of compressed data transferred every month.

One manufacturer of PLM software is Dassault Systemes (www.3ds.com), a French company that has developed an entire suite of PLM tools since its formation in 1981. Typical users of its tools are major industrial manufacturers such as Toyota (*see* Exhibit 9.8).

Other manufacturing tools that are used in conjunction with PLM software are those used in managing the 'bill of materials' associated with the actual production process. These tools tend to come in two different formats:

- *Materials requirement planning (MRP)* is used to plan the types of materials required in the production process with the aid of computers.

- *Manufacturing resource planning (MRPII)* helps integrate MRP with production scheduling and shop-floor control.

In one empirical study of the use of PLM and manufacturing systems, Brassler (2001)[20] found that car manufacturers were the most advanced users of PLM systems, while consumer goods industries were the least advanced in their use of technology throughout the supply chain. Given the levels of expenditure on R&D by the motor manufacturers that we saw in Table 9.1 earlier, this is not surprising.

Building to order

Exhibit 9.8 introduces another revolution in manufacturing in recent years – the principle of building to order. Using this system, manufacturers only begin building or assembling the product when they receive a firm customer order. This contrasts with a 'build-to-stock' system whereby products are built to a forecast of demand and stored as inventory. While building to order is a common feature in the manufacture of industrial equipment, it is only in recent years that the concept has been extended to smaller, cheaper consumer goods that have traditionally been mass-produced. Dell Computers is one of the greatest proponents of this mass customisation approach, and one of its biggest success stories. Once a customer places an order for a computer, the Dell manufacturing plant assembles the PC and ships it to the customer within days. The business and marketing benefits of building to order include:

- lower investment in inventories and work in progress through just-in-time policies, better planning and control of production and finished goods requirements;

- improved customer service by reducing out-of-stock situations and producing high-quality products that better meet customer requirements;

- faster manufacturing of new products and quicker delivery to the customer.

Figure 9.9 Overview of BMW's production processes
Source: BMW website (www.bmw.com, 2003).

BMW (www.bmw.com) is another company that works with its customers to build its products to order. Figure 9.9 and Figure 9.10 provide some insight into the manufacturing process at the company's manufacturing plants. To find more detailed coverage of the manufacturing process, BMW's website is well worth a visit.

Figure 9.10 Building to order at BMW

Source: BMW website (www.bmw.com, 2003).

Summary

Being able to develop and launch new products and services rapidly is a key competitive advantage. Technology is increasingly used to improve product and service offerings. We have seen many examples where technology has been incorporated into products – from toys to large industrial machines – and also where technology is used to 'mass-customise' products like cars. Another key application of technology is where it is used to speed up the product development process. Groupware, collaborative software and accelerated market testing are just some of the ways technology can speed up the time-to-market process. In the final section we also saw how techniques such as simultaneous engineering, design for manufacture and product life-cycle management can improve the commercialisation process.

Case study

Baldwin Filters (and MatrixOne)

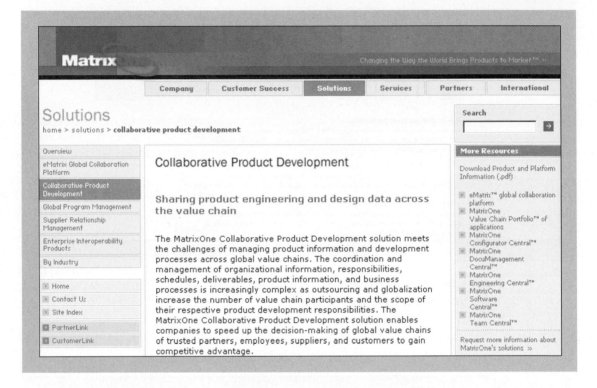

Figure 9.11

Baldwin Filters works to protect engines and engine-powered systems from dirt. Known as the heavy-duty people, Baldwin Filters builds air, oil, fuel, hydraulic, coolant and transmission filters for a wide variety of applications, including agriculture, automotive, construction, mining, industrial, marine and trucking. With 1,200 employees, sales of $200 million, and facilities in the USA, Mexico, China, UK and South Africa, the company designs and manufactures more than 4,100 different types of air, coolant, diesel/gas fuel, hydraulic, lube and transmission filters. Baldwin's strategy is to design each filtration product rather than assemble components made by other companies. This design process provides Baldwin engineers with constant opportunities to improve and to deliver the world's best filtration products.

The challenge: delayed time to market and reduced revenues

Baldwin's 20-person engineering staff and 10-person support team introduces an average of 700 new filters per year. In the past, processing up to three new products and an average of 12 engineering change orders (ECOs) per day generated an overwhelming amount of paperwork that slowed down Baldwin's engineers considerably. New products faced similar delays, averaging 10–12 months to reach the market. These delays reduced revenues and meant that an extensive portion of an engineer's time was devoted to shuffling papers rather than meeting customer needs.

Baldwin managers wanted to automate this process using a product development management system but were concerned that such a system would require hundreds of thousands of dollars' worth of customisation before users could perform even the simplest tasks. Baldwin contacted Avatech Solutions, a design automation integrator with experience in product development management solutions, to analyse the company's engineering processes and develop a formalised set of specifications. The Avatech team brainstormed with Baldwin managers to develop these specifications for a system capable of automating the company's approval process. After a thorough evaluation, Avatech recommended MatrixOne's eMatrix solution as one that could automate Baldwin's existing processes with minimum customisation and training.

MatrixOne

MatrixOne's collaborative PLM solutions, which include the eMatrix global collaboration platform, claimed to target specific business issues:

- the MatrixOne Collaborative Product Development solution enables companies to share product engineering and design data across their value chains;

- the MatrixOne Global Programme Management solution enables companies to manage product development programmes across global teams;

- the MatrixOne Supplier Relationship Management solution enables companies to accelerate strategic sourcing and supplier management business processes.

Upon Baldwin's acceptance, Avatech began the process of installing the eMatrix solution, providing initial employee training, and assisting Baldwin engineers in laying out the implementation process. The first area addressed was Baldwin's ECO process. Through eMatrix automation, Baldwin estimates that the company has saved approximately one month per ECO, a saving of $125,000 per year. Furthermore, an indeterminate amount of additional savings comes by reducing the time engineers spend on paperwork.

Next, Baldwin engineers focused on automating its five-step new product release (NPR) process – request, design, approval, implementation and release. With this process automated through the eMatrix solution, management estimates that the company will reduce the product development cycle by one month and thereby produce $50,000 in additional revenue per year. Further benefits are expected. The new NPR cycle also enables the contribution of many others in the process, a benefit that is expected to result in higher quality new product decisions and additional revenue.

The results

- *Faster time to market* – reduced product development cycle by one month, resulting in $50,000 additional revenue.

- *Increased revenue* – reduced average ECO implementation by one month, generating savings of $125,000 annually.

- *Increased engineering productivity* – reduced paperwork, freeing up engineering to develop next-generation products.

Sources: Matrix One website (www.matrixone.com, 2003); Baldwin Filters website (www.baldwinfilter.com, 2003).

Case study questions

1 Did Baldwin Filters face a marketing or a manufacturing problem?

2 What were Baldwin Filters' real marketing issues?

3 Compare Baldwin Filters' NPD process to the one outlined earlier in this chapter. What, if any, are the differences?

4 How does eMatrix compare to any of the PLM products from Dassault Systemes (*see* Exhibit 9.8)?

Questions and exercises

Questions

1 Describe how technology is driving the development of new products and services.

2 Why would companies want to turn products into services?

3 How can technology accelerate the new product development process?

4 Outline three reasons why companies want to reduce time to market.

5 What do we mean by 'design-for-manufacture'?

6 'IT and other forms of technology are critical to modern manufacturing.' Discuss.

Online exercises

1 Assume you are the manufacturing manager for a factory producing PCs. Visit Dassault Systemes' website (www.3ds.com) and write a short note on the three products you think would be most useful in your plant and why.

2 Visit the site of MatrixOne (www.matrixone.com). What are the key benefits of the kind of products it has developed?

References

1 www.otis.com/innovationdetail/0,1416,cli1_iid805_res1,00.html

2 Ee, E. (2001). 'BMW first to offer onboard navigation in Singapore', *Asia internet*, 4 June.

3 McLindon, A. (2003). 'Merloni builds smarter appliances', *Electric News*, 8 April.

4 Taylor, P. (1996). 'Increasingly crucial role', *Financial Times*, 10 June.

5 UK Department of Trade and Industry (2002). R&D 2002 Scorecard, www.innovation.gov.uk/finance

6 Cruz Rowe, J., Elling, M.E., Hazlewood, J.G. and Randa, Z. (2002). 'A cure for clinical trials', *McKinsey Quarterly*, No. 2.

7 Greenemeier, L. (2001). 'Pharmaceutical firm streamlines clinical drug trials, *Information Week*, 13 August.

8 Larson, C.F. (1998). 'Industrial R&D in 2008', Industrial Research Institute, www.iriinc.org/webiri/Publications/cfl-industrial2008.cfm

9 Lynn, G.S., Abel, K.D., Valentine, W.S. and Wright, R.C. (1999). 'Key factors in increasing speed to market and improving new product success rates', *Industrial Marketing Management*, Vol. 28.

10 Dahan, E. and Hauser, J.R. (2001). 'Product development: managing a dispersed process', MIT working paper, November.

11 Dahan, E. and Srinivasan, V. (2000). 'The predictive power of internet-based product concept testing using visual depiction and animation', *Journal of Product Innovation Management*, Vol. 17.

12 Dahan and Srinivasan, 'The predictive power of internet-based product concept testing'.

13 Clancy, K.J. and Shulman, R.S. (1991). *The Marketing Revolution*, New York: HarperBusiness.

14 Brown, S. and Eisenhardt, K. (1995). 'Product development: past research, present findings, and future directions', *Academy of Management Review*, Vol. 20, No. 2.

15 Nilson, T.H. (1995). *Chaos Marketing: How to Win in a Turbulent World*, Maidenhead: McGraw-Hill.

16 Lorenz, C. (1986). *The Design Dimension*, Oxford: Basil Blackwell.

17 O'Marah, K. (2002). 'The road to PLM starts with corporate strategy', *AMR Research*, 20 November, www.amrresearch.com/research/alerts/pdf/021120alert15346.pdf

18 Bailly, F. (2002). 'New challenges for Renault in CAD/CAM/CAE/DMU', presentation at ICE conference, Rome, 17 June, www.afmicado.com/evenement/ICE2002renault.pdf

19 www.3dplm.com/en/press/ipf.asp?object_name=tico_pr_en

20 Brassler, A. (2001). 'E-supply chain management – results of an empirical study', *Proceedings of the Twelfth Annual Conference of the Production and Operations Management Society*, 30 March–2 April, Orlando, Florida.

10

Pricing in the electronic age

Learning objectives

Once you have read this chapter you will:

- appreciate how the internet is rewriting the pricing rules;
- understand the concept of dynamic pricing;
- understand how IT can be used to identify costs accurately;
- understand how to use pricing research and IT to make pricing decisions;
- appreciate the true impact of e-commerce on pricing.

Contents

MAKING WELL-INFORMED AND RAPID PRICING DECISIONS

- The use of pricing research
- Using technology to support the six key pricing actions
- Pricing for different segments of the demand curve

PRICING SUPPORT SYSTEMS

- Using pricing support systems
- Pricing support systems: yield management
- Changing prices rapidly

THE TRUE IMPACT OF E-COMMERCE ON PRICING

- The age of 'frictionless commerce'?
- Consumer reaction to complex pricing
- The impact of electronic marketplaces on pricing

SUMMARY

CASE STUDY

Introduction

Price is a crucial element in the marketing mix for a number of reasons. Prices can usually be changed very quickly, marketing and sales managers often have a high degree of discretion over the prices they set and, perhaps most important of all, price has a direct impact on the total revenue a company generates and an even greater impact on its profitability.

When developing an appropriate pricing strategy, the marketing manager faces a number of challenges:

- setting prices requires accurate data on costs, which may be difficult to gather;

- different customers or customer groups have different sensitivities to price changes;

- competitors may be rapidly changing their prices;

- new internet-based technologies such as pricing agents can commoditise products, so customers have greater access to information;

- international companies increasingly have to develop a pricing strategy across different countries.

Figure 10.1 Search for MP3 players using mySimon shopping agent
Source: mySimon website (www.mysimon.com, 2003).

EXHIBIT 10.1

ELVIS, ASSETS AND AIRLINE SEATS – BY AUCTION

Not long ago, auctions were confined to the fringe: farmers hawking pork bellies in Chicago, say, or down-at-heel aristocrats selling family pictures at Sotheby's. Over the past decade, however, auctions have moved into the mainstream. Two things have helped to spread their use: the fashion for the sale of state assets and the rise of the internet. Today, power plants, radio spectrum and even whole companies are sold by governments at auction. On the internet, private buyers and sellers are put in touch over everything from Elvis memorabilia to airline seats. Perfectly efficient markets, you might think, have arrived at last.

Source: *The Economist* (27 June 2002).[2]

The move towards price harmonisation

In 2002 GE (www.ge.com) purchased more than $5 billion of goods a year over the internet, receiving tenders from companies all over the world in the process. Electronic sales of CDs and books are also a global business. Some internet companies do maintain an element of price discrimination. In the case of Amazon, the internet bookseller, different prices are quoted from different sites. John Grisham's thrillers are priced in US dollars on Amazon.com, in sterling on Amazon.co.uk, and in euros on Amazon.de, allowing slightly different pricing strategies to be adopted from each site.

In Europe, many companies may be forced to adopt a 'one price fits all' policy for goods and services, regardless of national boundaries, following the introduction of the euro currency in 2002 and the increasing spread of the internet as a sales channel.

Auctions and the move towards dynamic pricing

The widespread use of the internet may also have a different, possibly even an opposite, impact – moving from fixed pricing to a more dynamic flexible format. This is due to the popularity of one particular format of e-commerce – the internet auction (*see* Exhibit 10.1).

Traditional economic theory indicates that if demand exceeds supply, the price of the auctioned entity rises until an equilibrium price is found. If supply exceeds demand, the price falls. However, in the industrial (B2B) world, internet auctions have become very popular for auctioning old, obsolete stock and excess inventory, since they have often manage to create a market demand where none was previously available.

As Exhibit 10.1 shows, auctions are not just confined to obsolete stock. Computer manufacturers such as Sun Microsystems and IBM are now selling increasing numbers of computer servers via auctions, as the internet changes the balance in favour of dynamic pricing. This trend that can be examined from both the buyer's and seller's perspective. The commonly used terminology for these different business models are 'buy-side' and 'sell-side'.

B2B buy-side pricing models

Auctions have proved particularly popular in B2B e-commerce. We have already seen in Chapter 2 how B2B trading exchanges are increasing in popularity for electronic procurement (e-procurement) of many items, particularly by large companies. A number of different buy-side pricing models are available, including:

■ *Reverse auction* – a single buyer accepts bids from multiple sellers, with the lowest bid ultimately determining the winning bid. Business transactions are complex, and auction infrastructures must increasingly support multidimensional auctions, in which the offering consists of multiple products and/or services, and bidders are allowed to bid on a subset of the products.

- *Request for quotation (RFQ)* – a buyer posts an RFQ for a specific product meeting certain minimal requirements, and sellers respond with a single closed bid, with possible subsequent negotiation.

- *Direct contract negotiation* – a traditional form of procurement.[3]

B2B sell-side pricing models

From the seller's perspective, the typical sell-side models are:

- *Auction* – with similar characteristics to the reverse auction on the buy-side but with the view to accepting the highest bid.

- *Online catalogue* – a fixed price model whereby customers buy from an online catalogue and pay the 'list price' (minus any pre-agreed discounts that are not posted on the website).

- *Flexible pricing in response to RFQ* – the seller can take a number of factors into consideration when responding to the request, including inventory, payment terms, volume discounts and anticipated future revenue from the customer.

- *Direct contract negotiation* – exactly the same as on the buy-side, but in this case the seller is looking to negotiate the highest possible price.

B2C internet auctions

Internet auctions are not confined to the B2B market. On the consumer side, specialist companies have established successful internet auction businesses. Priceline (www.priceline.com – *see* Figure 10.2), which was launched at the height of the internet boom in 1998 and is a strong proponent of the reverse auction, is one of a large number of consumer offerings on the market. Since Priceline opened, it claims to have sold over 14 million airline tickets, 8 million hotel room nights and 7 million rental car days. The company says that it can save its customers up to 40 per cent on brand-name products every day. The concept is simple, with customers quoting the prices they are prepared to pay and the brand-name partners deciding whether or not to accept, based on availability.

A year before Priceline opened its doors on the internet, there were approximately 150 online auction sites, selling everything from industrial machinery to rare stamps. A year later, there were literally thousands to choose from, as both traditional and internet-based companies moved into the online auction business. Most have since closed down, but the concept of the internet auction, particularly for rare or collectors' items and last-minute deals, is today firmly established in the minds of consumers.

The internet's chief advantage for auctioneers is the size of its audience. The global reach of companies like eBay (www.ebay.com), Priceline, Lastminute (www.lastminute.com) and QXL (www.qxl.com) brings a critical mass of buyers and sellers to the most popular auction sites, avoiding the problem of insufficient trading that bedevils many of their cousins in the physical world.[4] Quick, easy, virtual auctions carry a hint of the hyper-efficient capitalism and 'frictionless commerce' that internet fans have long been promised. At the end of this chapter, we will return to the subject of 'frictionless commerce' and examine if the concept has been achieved in reality.

Figure 10.2 Airline ticket auctions at Priceline.com
Source: Priceline website (www.priceline.com, 2003).

Establishing accurate costs

The importance of understanding product costs

Perhaps unfairly, we have left the matter of production costs until last. Even if the pricing rules are being rewritten as power is concentrated in the hands of the buyer, the starting point for pricing decisions is still the cost of production. This does not mean that pricing is simply a matter of adding a given margin to the cost of production, although many companies continue to take this approach. However, production costs must be understood. Otherwise, companies will cross-subsidise one product with another and end up generating large sales (and losses) on the subsidised products, while losing out on the profitable products. Unfortunately, many firms have failed to employ accurate product costing techniques, often because of a failure to understand how indirect and overhead costs should be allocated to products. Johnson and Kaplan (1987)[5] identified this as a major management accounting issue that is still, to some extent, prevalent today.

Using activity-based costing (ABC) systems

One solution to the problems facing traditional management accounting systems is activity-based costing (ABC). ABC is a technique that allocates overhead costs to the activities that generate the cost. The costs in these 'activity pools' are then further allocated or traced to individual products, based on the level of activity associated with the product. Because ABC identifies the activities that drive cost, it is able to deal more easily with non-volume-related overheads. Using ABC information, marketing managers are better positioned to consider options such as dropping unprofitable products or raising the prices of existing products.

ABC and the associated use of ABC techniques (activity-based management) became very popular in the 1990s. However, Innes et al. (2000)[6] have cast doubts over the effectiveness of ABC systems, while a separate study of more than 300 companies by Cagwin (2000)[7] found no empirical benefits from implementing ABC systems on their own. Interestingly, Cagwin did find that companies that implemented ABC in conjunction with other management practices (specifically business process re-engineering and total quality management) did achieve quantifiable benefits. This would appear to support the views expressed in an article by Watts:

> Nor is it an exaggeration to point out that rarely in the history of corporate finance has such a promising concept turned out to be so disappointing in practice. What went wrong? And why is ABC now starting to make a comeback? At the risk of oversimplifying, the main reason that the new approach often failed to live up to expectations is that many executives forgot to change their mindsets along with their spreadsheets. It wasn't that they didn't understand the theory . . .
>
> Things broke down when it came to translating theory into action. Often . . . firms were looking for a quick fix and neglected to follow an ABC initiative through to the end.[8]

Searching an organisation for all the information about the direct and indirect costs of a product or service can be a major undertaking. Creating an IT system to track cost-contributing activities and presenting the information to management is equally challenging. In many cases, the old accounting system is replaced and new measurement and incentive systems are tied to the new ABC figures.

When an ABC system is implemented correctly, managers can use it to answer many questions, including:

- What does a given product or process cost?

- What are the non-value-adding activities that contribute to its current cost?

- If a given distribution channel or market is unprofitable, where can the company reduce costs to make it profitable?

- If the company eliminates an unprofitable product or customer, how much will it save in costs?

- If the company lowers the price of a product to increase sales volume, what will be the impact on the cost per unit?

■ What can the company do during the design and engineering stages of a product to avoid unnecessary costs in the first place?

Many companies have used ABC in one-time profitability studies to help them decide which products or customers to keep. But ABC can be much more than an accounting technique that shows how much profit individual products are really making or losing. When ABC is woven into critical management systems, it can serve as a powerful tool for continuously rethinking and improving not only products and services but also processes and marketing strategies.

Making well-informed and rapid pricing decisions

The use of pricing research

In a survey of US companies, Clancy and Krieg (2000)[9] found that many companies made pricing decisions without any serious formal research. They found that only about 8 per cent of companies were sophisticated players with a serious pricing strategy based on primary research (*see* Figure 10.3). More than four in every ten companies fell into the losers' category, with neither strategy nor research capabilities.

There are benefits in being one of the 8 per cent in the 'sophisticated players' category. Green and Savitz (1994)[10] showed how one major retailer could increase profits for a line of mixers by one third by simply changing prices.

	Serious strategy	Little or no strategy
Serious research	Sophisticated players (10%)	Radical empiricists (4%)
Little or no research	Gamblers (45%)	Losers (40%)

Figure 10.3 Strategy/research pricing matrix
Source: Clancy and Krieg (2000).[11]

Direct purchase intent model

The direct purchase intent approach is probably the most straightforward and easiest pricing approach to administer. The respondents are simply asked how likely they would be to buy the product or service at a pre-determined price, using a five-point purchase intent scale. Generally, reaction is gained to four price points, including the current or target price for the product. The prices are either presented in descending order or are randomised. Once the data has been collected and processed, it is then run through a regression analysis that produces a price–demand curve. The price–demand curve graphically presents the price elasticity of the product or service, while an accompanying table presents the demand at any price along the continuum. Using this information, financial analyses can be performed to determine the best price to maximise financial objectives. The direct purchase intent approach is generally used when the client is trying to get a 'feel' for market reactions, as opposed to making a hard pricing decision. The approach works well in new product categories where there might not be direct competitors and it can be easily administered.

Dynamic pricing model

The next approach utilises a combination of both indirect and direct pricing questions. The indirect questioning sequence is used to predict the optimal price and range where most purchases will occur. During the interview, respondents are shown a price scale which lists a broad range of prices from extremely low to very high. They are then asked to select a price from the scale to match each of the following four statements:

- price begins to get inexpensive, but would still buy;

- price gets too inexpensive, doubt quality and definitely would not buy;

- price begins to get expensive, but would still buy;

- price gets too expensive, regardless of quality, definitely would not buy.

Once interviewing has been completed, the data is cleaned for logical accuracy and then the cumulative percentage of consumers who gave a particular price for each of the four questions is plotted. The intersection of the 'too inexpensive' and 'too expensive' curves results in the identification of the optimal price point (OPP). This is the price at which the least number of respondents rejected the product or service as being either 'too inexpensive' or 'too expensive', so that they would not consider purchasing. Additional points are also determined, based on the intersection of other cumulative plots. Following the questioning sequence, the respondent is taken through the direct purchase intent questions and the results are run through a regression analysis. Then the optimal price point from the analysis is plotted on the price–demand curve.

Trade-off methods

There are several trade-off techniques that can be used in pricing research. As a group, these techniques tend to be the most sophisticated and powerful types of analyses, but are more difficult and costly to conduct than the previously discussed methods. The three main techniques of interest are:

- conjoint analysis
- discrete choice modelling
- choice-based conjoint analysis.

The results for all three trade-off methods can be best presented electronically. Here, users can enter different prices into the model for one or more of the brands being tested. The purchase intent and price elasticity are then presented for various 'what if' scenarios. The choice-based conjoint analysis approach is often preferred, because of the flexibility of the model to accept realistic usage or share information, as well as the ability to produce cross-elasticity estimates. This technique combines the best aspects of both conjoint and discrete choice.

Pricing support systems: yield management

One of the most powerful applications of the demand curve is the concept of maximising revenue across all customers. This moves away from the 'one price for all' concept to true demand-based pricing. This trend is being driven by IT that allows companies to develop and market product offerings at different prices. Marketing managers are now faced with a much more complex task of identifying a range of product or service options targeted at different customers and charging different prices. Yield (or revenue) management systems can be described as 'an economic technique to calculate the best pricing policy for optimising profits generated by the sale of a product or service, based on real-time modelling and forecasting of demand behaviour per market micro-segment'.[15]

Applicability of yield management systems

Yield management systems are typically employed in industries where 'perishability' is a major issue. Desiraju and Shugan (1999)[16] describe perishability in the following terms: 'When planes, trains or ships depart, for example, unused seats are lost forever. Similar problems occur for vacant hotel rooms, unsold concert tickets, idle tables at restaurants and many other fixed-capacity services.'

In addition to perishability, there are several other characteristics that favour the use of yield management systems:

- *Variable demand and fixed production capacity*. Here, demand fluctuates while production resources are relatively fixed and adjusting capacity carries a high price.

- *Sales via reservations*. These industries sell inventory before the effective date of production, using an order-taking (reservations) system.

- *Multiple pricing structures*. Since the demand/price elasticity varies according to the segment of clientele, these sectors generally practise differentiated pricing.

EXHIBIT 10.3

MARKETING AT NORTHWEST AIRLINES

Marketing at Northwest takes a highly quantitative and strategic approach to decision making. The complexity of marketing a perishable product in this fiercely competitive environment requires shrewd strategic discipline and analysis. Even a small innovation can significantly impact the company's financial performance. The airline industry has been an early adopter of new technology since the first computerised reservation systems emerged in the late 1950s. Using the internet as a distribution channel is the most recent example, and Northwest is on the frontline making money with this new technology. In fact, airlines are one of the few industries actually making a profit distributing via the web. And as the web becomes more and more integral to our business, e-commerce opportunities at Northwest are numerous within many areas of marketing.

MBA graduates recruited by marketing begin as senior analysts in one of five groups: pricing, yield management, sales analysis, market planning and reservations. Daily activities revolve around the analysis of long-term opportunities and short-term tactical needs of the business. Spreadsheet modelling of 'what-if' scenarios and reporting results to vice-president-level management is common to all five groups.

Source: Northwest Airlines website (www.nwa.com, 2003).[22]

that night to the stores. The next morning the store manager receives a report detailing all the prices that have been changed and the new price stickers (typically shelf-edge labels rather than individual item labels) are also printed automatically. Items are scanned at the checkout desk and the price is automatically rung up on the electronic till.

Scanners were introduced in US supermarkets in 1974 to improve efficiency and productivity. This technology has brought many benefits to both consumers and the supermarket industry as scanners can:

- reduce checkout time;
- provide consumers a receipt that details the type and price of each item purchased;
- help control costs by eliminating the labour needed to mark items individually;
- generate electronic coupons for the products that customers purchase;
- provide a means to help prevent the sale of alcohol and tobacco products to minors: some supermarkets have programmed the registers to stop whenever such items are scanned, prompting the cashier to check customer ID cards;
- provide a way to enhance and monitor price accuracy on the shelf.[23]

EXHIBIT 10.4

BARCODE BOO-BOOS

Perhaps it has happened to you. You are in a store and decide to purchase an item for the price you've seen advertised or posted on the shelf or display case. When you take it to the checkout, however, the price shown by the scanner is higher. It happened to Lisa Schwartz recently when she decided to buy a camera at a local Walgreens. The price on the store display said $39.99 but when she took the camera to the checkout, the scanner registered $79.99. The store manager told her he wasn't obliged to honour the display price but did offer her a $10 gift certificate.

Schwartz found out that was the wrong answer after she filed a complaint with the state Department of Agriculture, Trade and Consumer Protection. Under state law the consumer is entitled to the lowest advertised price, 'whether it's on the shelf, whether it's in a flyer or advertisement, or whether it's on a sign', according to Judy Cardin, chief of safety and inspection.

Source: The Capital Times (18 November 2002).[24]

Scanning is now routine in all but the smallest of grocery stores. However, it is important to synchronise the price changes on the shelf and at the checkout as the checkout scanners obtain their pricing data from the store's computer system. As Exhibit 10.4 shows, this does not always happen in a timely manner. However, if done correctly, the time and effort required to change prices is significantly reduced and this provides an important competitive advantage in the highly competitive retail industry.

Despite regular newspaper and magazine stories like that in Exhibit 10.4, all the evidence shows that the introduction of scanner technology has decreased the number of pricing errors significantly, and that any errors are as likely to benefit the customer as they are to benefit the retailer. In the days before scanning, error rates were as high as 16 per cent. With the help of scanning and tighter controls, supermarkets have reduced the error rate significantly, according to a 1998 report by the US Federal Trade Commission (FTC).[25] This FTC report was one of the most exhaustive surveys carried out, with more than 100,000 items checked. It found that:

- 2.4 per cent of items checked were mispriced – half of the errors were undercharges and half were overcharges;

- each undercharge averaged $5.28, and each overcharge averaged $3.20;

- there were wide variations in pricing accuracy from chain to chain and store to store: some stores have achieved outstanding pricing accuracy – in 43 per cent of the inspections, no price errors were found;

Kannan and Kopalle (2001)[36] provide further discussion on the impact of dynamic pricing on consumer behaviour and explore the implications of certain aspects of dynamic pricing in consumer markets from the perspective of consumer price expectations.

Summary

Price is a crucial element in the marketing mix. The internet is having a dramatic effect on the way organisations set prices, since customers now have much greater visibility on prices. It is harder for companies to charge excessive prices, while online auctions are also a way of putting downward pressure on prices. The key to making any pricing decision is to understand the organisation's true cost base. We looked at models like activity based costing (ABC) and saw that they are effective, but only if implemented fully and accompanied by a change in mindset. We also looked at pricing support systems that allow businesses to price for different price sensitivities. The best example of this is the airline business, which uses yield management to charge higher prices to passengers who are looking for more flexibility in their flights. Finally, we looked at the impact of e-commerce on pricing and concluded that while we are closer to 'frictionless commerce' we are not quite there yet. In fact, we may never get there, since many consumers will continue to rank brand and convenience ahead of price.

Case study

eBay and QXL in the UK

Figure 10.4
Source: eBay website (www.ebay.co.uk, 2003), copyright © eBay Inc., all rights reserved.

Internet auctions in the UK

In early 2002, bidding closed in an internet wife auction organised by Birmingham businesswoman Kay Hammond after a bidder called Ben Webb offered £251,000 for her hand in marriage, £1,000 more than the reserve price. The auction on QXL attracted more than 38,000 hits, but only two bids. According to QXL: 'It attracted a lot of hits. It's not an item everyone wants to be bidding for, but everyone is interested in it. This is the first auction of its kind that we've dealt with.' The first of its kind, maybe, but QXL was not the only company in the UK to have built a reputation as an auctioneer of both traditional and unusual items.

A month after Kay Hammond's auction, the UK arm of the American online auctioneer eBay (and QXL's main competitor) auctioned the skeleton of a 50,000 year-old mammoth called Max. eBay's UK managing director Douglas McCallum describes the five quirkiest items auctioned on his site:

- Lady Thatcher's handbag: £103,000
- Max the mammoth: £61,000
- Joanna Lumley's Ferrari: £35,000

- decommissioned nuclear bunker: £14,000

- to be an extra on the set of Cold Feet: £4,000.

QXL history

QXL grew steadily since its launch in 1997. Quixell, the original name for the company, hosted Europe's first online auction in January 1998. It initially offered computing equipment, and rapidly expanded its range to include electrical and household goods. Gifts and accessories were added later that year, followed by a travel department. Before the end of 1998 the company opened a German site and changed its name to QXL to reflect a European-wide focus. The following year QXL floated on the London Stock Exchange and on Nasdaq, and expanded its geographical coverage with the launch of its Dutch site. 2000 was a year that saw a series of acquisitions, concluding with a merger with Germany's ricardo, resulting in a change of company name to QXL ricardo plc.

By early 2002 QXL ricardo had announced a pan-European agreement with MSN, offering services in Germany, Denmark, Norway, Sweden, France, Spain, Finland and the UK. Shortly afterwards it also announced a change in direction with its co-branding programme, providing partners with a simple solution to create an auction channel within their sites, operated by QXL, but maintaining the partners' branding throughout the auction experience. The acquisition trail continued in 2002 with the purchase in July of Aucland.fr, the number-two online auction site in France.

The success of eBay in Europe

Despite QXL's rapid growth, it is dwarfed in Europe by its US-based competitor. eBay has become one of the true success stories of the internet, and overtook Amazon to become the top e-commerce site in the UK in 2003 with more than six million users, compared to Amazon's 5.2 million. Not only that, eBay's UK operations were also profitable. eBay's Douglas McCallum said: 'I do not think that any other UK internet business has been able to say that it is profitable (on a fully allocated basis) before. The network effect will make it difficult for any other e-commerce player to make an assault on our core market.'

One of eBay's strengths is its innovative use of technology. It continues to introduce new capabilities to improve its auctioning service. Its latest service addressed the issue of 'gazumping'. Being pipped for that prized first pressing of The Beatles' *White Album* can be galling, especially when you had a higher bid in reserve but strayed from the computer momentarily only to return with the auction closed. It's a common headache, according to eBay. 'A lot of [customers] tell us that between leaving for the office in the morning and getting home they haven't had the ability to check their bidding and get outbid.' Getting caught out no longer means being out of the running, however. A service launched in June 2002 allows eBay's 46 million US customers to keep track of auction action by mobile phone and, if their bid is trumped, up the ante with a few quick keystrokes. So-called 'wireless rebidding' uses the short message service (SMS) capability that is standard on most new mobile phones. A text message alerts customers that have signed up for the $2.99-a-month service if they have been outbid on an item. Entering a four-digit code lodges a new tender at a minimum higher value or, if they really want to try to burn off the opposition, they can key in an even higher sum. However, the Yankee Group concludes that eBay customers will not baulk at coughing up a small monthly sum if it increases their chances of landing that item of pop culture ephemera they set their heart on. 'For the eBay user trying to get their hands on that hard-to-find item, such as a 1972 Rolling Stones North American tour poster (bidding starts at $36), $2.99 is a small price to pay if it makes the difference between winning and losing,' it says.

QXL in 2003

By 2003, QXL had introduced its own new offerings including QXL Marketplace, a fixed price section of its site to compete with Amazon by selling CDs and DVDs, and a classifieds section for used goods. Its auctions continued to be very popular. Each day QXL hosted literally thousands of auctions for a variety of products. For example, on the evening of 8 January 2003 an online user could bid for items in the following categories:

- antiques and art (781 items)
- automotive (568)
- books (1,958)
- collectables and toys (7,448)
- computing and software (4,293)
- football (4,653)
- gaming (1,057)
- home and lifestyle (2,822)
- home electrical and photographic (733)
- music and movies (10,635)
- over-18s (645)
- sports and fitness (1,465)
- telecommunication (4,842)
- travel (80)
- other (162).

However, QXL's financial position was precarious by the middle of 2003. Unlike eBay, it was not profitable. The company racked up pre-tax losses of more than £18 million during its previous 12 months. Despite addressing its finances by applying stringent cost controls and introducing listing fees across most of its European services, its market capitalisation had fallen to less than the value of the cash on its balance sheet – £1.6 million. How could this happen? QXL launched before eBay in the UK and established a strong brand based on heavy advertising and free publicity during the dot-com boom. Its value briefly touched more than £2.5 billion in 2000 as it embarked on a series of acquisitions to build a presence across Europe. But since the bubble burst the shares have fallen by 99.9 per cent, as investors feared that QXL might not have enough cash to take it through to profitability. Meanwhile, Douglas McCallum remained confident about eBay's future: 'I'd predict that within five years, more than half of the UK's net users will have registered with us.'

Sources: eBay website (www.ebay.com); QXL website (www.qxl.com); *The Guardian* (1 November 2002)[37]; *The Guardian* (11 September 2003)[38]; *The Guardian* (21 August 2003)[39]; *E-commerce Times* (16 May 2000)[40]; authors' research.

Case study questions

1 What are the main challenges QXL faces as the number-two player in the UK market?

2 Comment on eBay's use of new technology to improve its service.

3 Visit eBay (www.ebay.com) and QXL (www.qxl.com). In your estimation, which site is easier to use? Why?

4 What do you think QXL must do to survive?

Questions and exercises

Questions

1 How is the internet rewriting the rules of pricing?

2 Why have online auctions grown so rapidly?

3 Evaluate the effectiveness of different pricing agents.

4 Why is it important to price for different segments of the demand curve?

5 What do you understand by yield management? Give two examples where it is used other than the airline industry.

6 Outline three reasons why a business should use a pricing support system.

7 'We have not yet reached the point of frictionless commerce, but we are close.' Comment.

8 What do we mean by customer reaction to complex pricing?

Online exercises

1 You are going buy a new widescreen television. The model you have selected is a Sony 34-inch FD Trinitron television. Visit mySimon (www.mysimon.com)

and one other pricing agent site of your choice (*see* Table 10.1). What is the percentage difference between the cheapest and most expensive price you were quoted? Visit the site of Sony (www.sony.com) and see if you can find the list price for the product in the UK, the USA and Germany. What conclusions can you draw from the results of your research?

2 You are planning a flight from London to Paris. Visit the site of Ryanair (www.ryanair.com) and British Midland (www.flybmi.com) and compare the different prices for similar flights. What differences did you find in the way the sites are organised and in the way the pricing is presented to the customer?

References

1 http://dir.yahoo.com/business_and_economy/shopping_and_services/retailers/virtual_malls/shopping_agents

2 *The Economist* (2002). 'Bidding adieu?', 27 June.

3 Bichler, M., Kalagnanam, J., Katircioglu, K., King, A.J., Lawrence, R.D., Lee, H.S., Lin, G.Y. and Lu, Y. (2002). 'Applications of flexible pricing in business-to-business electronic commerce', *IBM Systems Journal*, Vol. 41, No. 2.

4 Bajari, P. and Hortacsu, A. (2002). 'Cyberspace auctions and pricing issues: a review of empirical findings', Working Paper No. 02005, Department of Economics, Stanford: Stanford University.

5 Johnson, H.T. and Kaplan, R.S. (1987). *Relevance Lost: The Rise and Fall of Management Accounting*, Boston: Harvard Business School Press.

6 Innes, J., Mitchell, F. and Sinclair, D. (2000). 'Activity-based costing in the UK's largest companies: a comparison of 1994 and 1999 survey results', *Management Accounting Research*, Vol. 11.

7 Cagwin, D. (2000). 'The association of separate and concurrent use of activity-based costing, total quality management and business process reengineering with improvement in financial performance', working paper, University of Texas at Brownville, 27 November.

8 Watts, C. (1998). 'Not as easy as ABC', *CFO Europe,* October.

9 Clancy, K.J. and Krieg, P.C. (2000). *Counterintuitive Marketing*, New York: Free Press.

10 Green, P. and Savitz, J. (1994). 'Applying conjoint analysis to product assortment and pricing in retailing research', *MCB University Press*, 3 November.

11 Clancy, and Krieg, *Counterintuitive Marketing.*

12 Clancy and Krieg, *Counterintuitive Marketing.*

13 Bestofbiz.com. (2003). 'Pricing strategy briefing: complex pricing decisions for individual retail stores in large retail chains', www.bestofbiz.com/briefings/default.asp?p=205

14 Creative Research website (2003). www.creativeresearch.com/pages/sp_pricing.htm

15 TIMS (2003). 'Definition and history of yield management', www.tims.fr/uk/hight_profits.html

16 Desiraju, R. and Shugan, S.M. (1999). 'Strategic service pricing and yield management', *Journal of Marketing,* Vol. 63, No. 1.

17 Anderson, A. (1996). 'Yield management in small to medium sized enterprises in the tourism industry', European Commission, DGXXIII, Tourism Unit.

18 Cross, R. and Schemerhorn, R. (1989). 'Managing uncertainty', *Airline Business,* November.

19 Smith, B. (1992). *Yield Management at American Airlines,* Dallas/Fort Worth: American Airlines Decision Technologies.

20 Bender, A.R. (1999). 'Yield management: a double-edged sword', http://comm.db.erau.edu/leader/spring99/toc_sp99.html

21 Bichler, M. (2001). *The Future of eMarkets: Multi-Dimensional Market Mechanisms,* Cambridge: Cambridge University Press.

22 www.nwa.com/corpinfo/career/mba/marketing.shtml

23 FMI (2001). 'Shelf price accuracy in supermarkets that scan', Food Marketing Institute, November, www.fmi.org/media/bg/price_accuracy_2001.pdf

24 Richards, B. (2002). 'Checkout scanners still not perfect', *The Capital Times,* 18 November.

25 FTC (1998). *Price Check II. A Follow-up Report on the Accuracy of Checkout Scanners,* US Federal Trade Commission, 16 December.

26 Clodfelter, G.R. (1998). 'Pricing accuracy at grocery stores and other retail stores using scanning', *International Journal of Retail and Distribution Management,* Vol. 26, No. 11.

27 Friberg, R., Ganslandt, M. and Sandström, M. (2001). 'Pricing strategies in e-commerce: bricks vs clicks', Research Institute of Industrial Economics: Working Paper No. 550, 21 June.

28 Brynjolfsson, E. and Smith, M. (2000). 'A comparison of internet and conventional retailers', *Management Science,* Vol. 46, No. 4, http://e-commerce.mit.edu/papers/friction/friction.pdf

29 Lynch, J.G. and Ariely, D. (2000). 'Wine online: search cost and competition on price, quality, and distribution', *Marketing Science,* Vol. 19.

30 Bergman, M.K. (2000). 'The deep web: surfacing hidden value', Brightplanet white paper, www.brightplanet.com

31 Sullivan, D. (2001). 'Buying your way in to search engines', SearchEngineWatch.com, 2 May, www.searchenginewatch.com/webmasters/paid.html

32 Johnson, E.J., Moe, W., Fader, P., Bellman, S. and Lohse, J. (2000). 'On the depth and dynamics of World Wide Web shopping behaviour', working paper, Department of Marketing, New York: Columbia Business School.

33 Degeratu, A. Rangaswamy, A. and Wu, J. (2000). 'Consumer choice behaviour in online and regular stores: the effects of brand name, price, and other search attributes', *International Journal of Research in Marketing,* Vol. 17.

34 Rosencrance, L. (2000). 'Customers balk at variable DVD pricing', *Computerworld*, 11 September.

35 Hall, R.E. (2001). *Digital Dealing: How e-Markets Are Transforming the Economy*, New York: Norton.

36 Kannan, P.K. and Kopalle, P.K. (2001). 'Dynamic pricing on the internet: importance and implications for consumer behaviour', *International Journal of Electronic Commerce*, Vol. 5, No. 3.

37 Gibson, O. (2002). 'Jobs under threat at QXL', *The Guardian*, 1 November.

38 Mackintosh, H. (2003). 'Interview with Douglas McCallum', *The Guardian*, 11 September.

39 Timms, D. (2003). 'QXL profits take a hammering', *The Guardian*, 21 August.

40 Conlin, R. (2000). 'European Net auctioneers in $1B merger', *E-Commerce Times*, 16 May.

11

Distributing the product in the electronic age

Learning objectives

Once you have read this chapter you will:

- appreciate the increasing importance of direct channels;
- understand how companies are 'going direct';
- appreciate how technology is also changing indirect channels;
- understand the concept of hybrid marketing;
- appreciate the challenges involved in managing multiple distribution channels.

Contents

CHANGES IN INDIRECT CHANNEL STRUCTURES

- Electronic point-of-sale (EPOS) systems
- Managing the supply chain efficiently

MANAGING MULTIPLE DISTRIBUTION CHANNELS

- Managing distribution conflicts
- Hybrid marketing
- Managing different channel attributes
- Hybrid marketing and hybrid mail

SUMMARY

CASE STUDY

Introduction

The 'place' element of the marketing mix deals with how products get to consumers, and choices about whether companies should market directly to the customer or to go through intermediaries. Channel management decisions affect pricing, product management, brand image and promotion decisions. We start this chapter with a discussion of direct channels – their importance and how companies are 'going direct' – before examining the growth of direct channels such as the telephone, ATMs and digital television. We also look at changes in indirect channels brought about by technology, including the introduction of electronic point-of-sale (EPOS) systems. Finally, we look at the concept of hybrid marketing and how organisations manage multiple distribution channels.

The importance of direct channels

The rise of direct channels

Although it is tempting to consider direct channels of distribution as a relatively new development, driven by new electronic communications technology, they can actually be traced back several centuries. In Chapter 7 we noted that Aldus Manutius published a book catalogue in Venice in 1498 – and William Lucas published a gardening catalogue in England in 1667.

Traditionally, the firm with well-entrenched distribution channels dominated the market and created high barriers to entry for newcomers. For example, one of the biggest barriers to entry in petrol retailing is the presence of large networks of petrol forecourts, most of which are tied to one of the major oil companies. Since the 1980s the oil companies have moved from using independent garages to directly owning garages. This has allowed them to standardise forecourt layouts and service quality, and to develop very important forecourt retail businesses. It also gave them control of the distribution channel, making it very difficult for other oil companies to enter the market.

More significantly, the application of information technology has created turmoil in the area of distribution. Direct marketing and telemarketing have allowed UK organisations like the Virgin Group, Direct Line and Egg (*see* Exhibit 11.1) to bypass traditional channels and build relationships directly with their customers in a much shorter period of time than it took the petrol retailers to gain control over their distribution channels.

EXHIBIT 11.1

SUNNY SIDE UP?

I am delighted to report that Egg has achieved substantial growth once again in 2002 and has made important steps in developing an international business of scale. Our progress has been rapid and today we are ranked as the world's largest pure online bank (Nielsen Net Ratings).

Egg UK had another year of strong growth as evidenced by the 610,000 net new customers acquired during 2002, leading to a year-end total of 2.56 million. UK growth was principally through our credit card business, which has now captured over 5 per cent of total balances in the UK card market. The UK business has demonstrated it is sustainably profitable, successfully growing customer numbers and revenues each quarter in a challenging and increasingly competitive marketplace.

In France, we intend to enhance and extend our product range in line with developing a profitable business of scale in this market. Our next major product will be a new loan account. We are excited about the opportunity to continue to revolutionise the credit market in France, building on la Carte Egg. Egg's total customer base in France is approximately 90,000 following the selective migration of customers acquired when Egg purchased Zebank. We are targeting in the region of 250,000–300,000 customers in France by the end of 2003, based on current market conditions.

We remain committed to developing Egg as a global business and have been researching different territories throughout 2002. Specifically, we have been exploring potential entry strategies for the US market.

Source: Egg Annual Report 2002 (www.egg.com, 2003).

Direct channels – a lower cost of distribution?

It can certainly be argued that direct channels provide flexibility in organisation–customer interaction. Telephony and internet technology facilitate this when physical branch offices or stores are usually closed. But at the same time it is worth reflecting on whether this is the real driver of 'going direct'. In many instances there are likely to be cost-based reasons for the trend – for example, in banks:

> It can reduce costs by cutting out the face to face contact with customers traditionally enjoyed in branches, whilst at the same time can take them closer to their customers because they collect so much data about them that their requirements are better understood.[1]

Transactions conducted via the internet might cost 10 per cent of those conducted in a physical environment. So claims that the intention is to create 'relationships' with customers can sometimes reflect greater rhetoric than reality. However, we have also shown that electronic channels can create new business models, such as the C2B and C2C models discussed in Chapter 2: 'The nature of some of these media, such as the internet, means that customers can have greater control . . . they can search across different suppliers, often across national boundaries'.[2]

Direct channels may actually be more expensive than companies think. Consider any retailing organisation that introduces a new direct channel such as the internet or the telephone. Direct transaction costs may well be lower if conducted over the internet rather than face-to-face. However, most retail organisations have to make significant investments when opening up new channels, and many do so without taking costs out of their existing distribution network. The result is an increase in the company's overall cost base. For years, banks have been trying to address this by migrating routine customer service transactions (such as balance enquiries, bill payments and transfers of money from one account to another) to the internet or the telephone. The results have often been unpredictable – in some cases, customers will use the internet to check their bank balances more often than before, and go to the ATM more frequently than they did in the past, but the level of branch transactions remains stubbornly high.[3]

How companies are 'going direct'

The telephone as a distribution channel

During the 1980s and early 1990s, well before the internet became a mainstream delivery channel, many companies pioneered the use of the telephone as a key sales and service channel:

- *Direct Line* (www.directline.com) started in 1985 as a UK insurance company selling motor insurance over the telephone. The company's logo is a distinctive red telephone on wheels. The telephone continues to be the key channel for the company. In 1999 it launched its first ever credit card, which could be applied for over the telephone. By 2003 the company had over 5 million customers and had expanded to 9,000 employees servicing the German, Italian, Japanese and Spanish markets.

■ *First Direct* (www.firstdirect.com) was established in 1989 by the UK bank Midland (now HSBC). It grew rapidly as an innovative telephone bank, even though it still allowed customers to use the branches of its parent.

■ *Dell Computers* (www.dell.com), the Austin-based, high-technology company, was the original pioneer of the use of the telephone as a sales channel. Using the telephone allowed Dell to build a business model based on dealing directly with its consumers rather than having to go through middlemen or dealers. True to its roots as an innovator, Dell was very quick to see the advantages of transacting over the internet and has been quick to adopt the internet as a distribution channel.

Telemarketing

Telemarketing is a direct sales channel that uses the telephone and associated technologies for marketing purposes. The advantages are its flexibility, its interactive nature, its immediacy and the opportunity to make a high-impact personal contact. It has suffered somewhat in the past from misuse and 'cold calling', with the additional disadvantages of a high cost per call, its association with pressure selling and its lack of a visual presentation. However, as consumers have become more accustomed to telesales and telemarketing and as telecoms markets were deregulated and prices driven down, the telephone has gained acceptance as a mainstream distribution channel.

Inbound and outbound telemarketing

Telemarketing can be described as either inbound or outbound. If customers hear an advertisement on the radio for car insurance for female drivers and then phone the (freephone) telephone number mentioned at the end of the advertisement, their calls will be received by an inbound telemarketing group in the insurance company. Twelve months later, when the insurance company phones the same customers to remind them that their insurance is due for renewal, the insurance company is employing outbound telemarketing. The management of telephone call centres and the technology used to handle large volumes of calls is a major topic in its own right; it is examined in more detail in Chapter 13.

Inbound communication is very important:

Consider an in-bound call . . . if a consumer calls to update his/her address, the subsequent action by call centre operatives will be to ensure the operational system is updated with the new details. However, if the front office administrator identifies the underlying consumer trigger event driving the contact, for example it might be marriage, the subsequent marketing implications of the consumer's changing financial circumstances and life stage can be understood and acted upon.[4]

In this way, the relational principle – being 'reciprocal' – can be brought into play. In other words, relationships are two-way.

The telephone becomes mainstream

By the mid-1990s the telephone was firmly established as a mainstream channel in the eyes of consumers. The vast majority of businesses today use the telephone as an integral part of their sales and service operations and have migrated significant proportions of their business to this lower-cost channel. However, while handling a transaction at a dedicated call centre with hundreds of operators may be cheaper than dealing with a customer face to face, the telephone faced serious competition from the internet.

The internet as a distribution channel

During the 1990s the internet began to challenge the telephone as a mainstream channel for sales and service. The big advantage of the internet is that it does away with the cost of having a human operator. It is also much easier to deal with large 'spikes' in demand that call centres have always found difficult. The internet allows customers to transact whenever they want, 24 hours a day, seven days a week. Examples of companies that were early adopters of the internet include:

- *Egg* (www.egg.com). In 1998 Prudential launched an internet-only bank called Egg. Within four years Egg had amassed a customer base of 2 million customers and more than a third of the UK online banking market. It successfully floated in 2000 and became profitable at the end of 2001.

- *Amazon* (www.amazon.com). The internet bookseller launched an attack on the staid world of bookselling in 1995 and quickly gained market share against its main 'physical' rivals such as Barnes & Noble (www.barnesandnoble.com), who were forced to launch their own internet-based services in response.

- *Ryanair* (www.ryanair.com). Europe's largest budget airline has been very quick to see the advantages of the internet over the telephone and has been hugely successful at migrating reservations on to the web.

Internet banking

Some industries embraced the internet with passion. The banking industry was one, launching a variety of internet services:

- *Home banking* via the internet has been available since the 1990s. Denmark's Lån & Spar Bank (www.lsb.dk) became Scandinavia's first financial services company to offer a home banking service to its customers in 1994, and within two years 10 per cent of its customer base were using the service. By 2003 the

Table 11.1 Estimated US households receiving and/or paying bills online (2001–5)

Year	View and pay bills online (millions)	Paper bills but pay online (millions)
2001	2	8
2002	5	11
2003	15	17
2004	26	21
2005	40	25

Source: Jupiter Media Metrix (November 2001).

vast majority of European banks had launched internet banking services. Internet banking is not simply a consumer service. Most business banks now allow their corporate customers to view cheque details and statements, and make local and international payments over the internet.

■ *Electronic bill presentment and payment (EBPP)* has also become a standard feature of online banking. In the USA, where cheques are still a favourite payment mechanism, millions of people now either view or pay bills online (*see* Table 11.1).

Retailing and 'e-tailing'

A traditional shopping trip involves travelling to a store, selecting items, taking them to the checkout, queuing, paying and then taking them home. It is an experience that many consumers consider unpleasant. In comparison, shopping over the internet is rapidly gaining in popularity. In today's retail world, up to 20 per cent of the price of a product goes on covering the costs of running retail stores, which represents a very significant opportunity for internet retailing. The implications for retailers are enormous, as location no longer becomes a barrier to entry. Two major PC manufacturers that have been fighting a battle to distribute over the internet are described in Exhibit 11.2. As the Exhibit shows, the valuations of both companies have been determined to a great extent by their ability to win this battle.

Thanks to the convergence of telecommunications and computer technology and the rapid take-off of the internet, many consumer industries have moved quickly to embrace direct delivery channels. The internet is a disruptive technology that has created a new breed of retailer sometimes referred to as an 'e-tailer'. E-tailing has been adopted more quickly in some industries than others. For example, the travel industry has seen the arrival of a number of non-traditional players like Microsoft's Expedia and Sabre's Travelocity (*see* the case study at the end of this chapter).

One of the traditional barriers to the acceptance to the internet as a distribution channel is its virtual nature. That is, for some product-markets customers prefer to 'feel the fabric' and 'smell the fruit', but obviously this is impossible with online distribution. However, compromises are being forged by allowing customers to

EXHIBIT 11.2

DELL VERSUS COMPAQ

Thanks to the convergence of telecommunications and computer technology, and the rapid take-off of the internet, many consumer industries have moved quickly to embrace direct delivery channels. Or, at the very least, to increase the number and variety of delivery channels to give consumers greater buying choice. The personal computer (PC) industry is a case in point. Despite its strong growth and success, Compaq, the industry leader with annual sales of more than $30 billion, realised that survival in an increasingly cut-throat industry meant adapting its existing distribution model. Compaq had always depended upon its reseller network to provide service and support to its customers, and to expand the company's breadth and depth in the market. However, it now faced intense competitive pressure from rivals Dell Computer and Gateway 2000, both of which had been building market share by selling directly to their customers. Dell, in particular, had turned itself into one of the top five personal computer companies in the world by concentrating on sales over the internet and by telephone. By early 1999, less than two years after it began taking electronic orders from its website, Dell was generating sales of more than $6 million a day. Compaq's share price suffered dramatically in the face of the onslaught from Dell and other direct sales competitors. During the first half of 1999, Compaq's share price dropped from a high of more than $50 to around $20; it removed its chief executive and embarked on the difficult task of implementing a direct sales model that would complement, not cannibalise, its channel of resellers.

The scale of the change is impressive. For example, part of Compaq's new direct model outside North America centred on the creation of a pan-European call centre based in Dublin. With more than 1,000 agents speaking 15 different languages, the centre provides technical support for queries from Compaq's channel partners, key corporate accounts and end-consumers across Europe, the Middle East and Africa. In the Asia/ Pacific region, Compaq created a one-stop-shop internet site, called Compaq Club, to serve the needs of distribution partners and customers in the region. In addition, it has revamped its global account management programme, which provides a single point of contact for its major corporate accounts across the globe.

Source: Authors' research (2003).

upload a picture of themselves and 'try on' different garments or even to use 'virtual assistants' who guide through the virtual store, as Figure 11.1 suggests.

The emergence of the mobile internet

Today, mobile telephones and personal digital assistants (PDAs) have become multi-functional, allowing them to support a range of commercial activities. In fact the two technologies are starting to merge as mobile phones provide some of the functionality

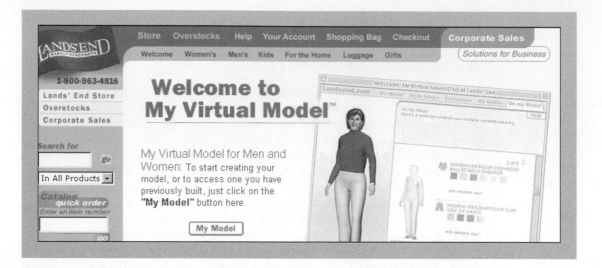

Figure 11.1 My Virtual Model from Lands' End

Source: Lands' End website (www.landsend.com, 2003), © Lands' End, Inc., 2003; © My Virtual Model, Inc., 2003.

previously associated with PDAs and vice versa. While few companies operate solely through a mobile internet, it is now becoming a recognised channel for both sales and customer service. In 2001 Starbucks launched a trial in Seattle in which customers loaded money on to a mobile phone so that they could place an order and pay by dialling the store and using short messaging service (SMS) technology.[5] In several European countries, trials are being conducted on the use of mobile telephones to pay parking meter charges for cars, and in London the congestion charge can be paid using a mobile phone and SMS text messages.

The most successful application of mobile internet technology to date has been the i-mode data service from the Japanese telecoms operator NTT DoCoMo, although opinions differ as to the likely success of i-mode outside Japan (*see* Exhibit 11.3).

The advent of multimedia messaging services (MMS) and third-generation (3G) mobile services will further increase the use of the mobile internet as a distribution channel.

The arrival of interactive digital television (iDTV or iTV)

Interactive digital television (iTV) is a relatively new phenomenon and, to a great extent, has been pioneered in the UK. British television viewing has traditionally been divided between the BBC and independent companies such as the ITV franchises, Channel 4 and Channel 5. Because the BBC stations have been financed by a national television license and not by advertising, marketing managers bought advertising time on ITV and, to a lesser extent, Channels 4 and 5. However, the television world changed

EXHIBIT 11.3

I-MODE: MOBILE INTERNET, JAPANESE-STYLE

First the good news: the i-mode mobile data service exported to Europe by NTT DoCoMo of Japan has shown how a unified content platform can greatly simplify content development and distribution. The bad news is that most of the content available is still not compelling enough to make consumers want to pay for it, and cost-sensitive operators remain weary of licensing proprietary technology that could eat into their margins. While most operators will not make i-mode their technology of choice it can be used as an interim service, which could find a niche in Europe's third-generation (3G) mobile broadband networks before they are eclipsed by new services based on open standards. 'Why should operators lock themselves into a proprietary service when they will soon have new mark-up languages and other standardised tools to create wireless internet services?' asks Martha Bennett, an analyst with the Giga Information Group.

Nevertheless, several European operators are betting on i-mode to open the door to the market for high-speed mobile data services. Leading the charge is the Dutch company KPN Mobile, which views i-mode as its primary mobile data offering for the consumer market. In March KPN Mobile introduced the service in Germany through its subsidiary E-Plus and a month later in its domestic market. Base, its Belgium subsidiary, rolled out its service in October 2002.

Source: *Financial Times* (20 November 2002).[6]

significantly in the 1990s as BSkyB captured a quarter of UK homes with satellite television. More importantly, the 1998 launch of digital television in the UK promised a new era of hundreds of channels, increasing consumer choice but correspondingly decreasing the advertising reach through any single channel. This was not necessarily bad news for advertisers: smaller television audiences are accompanied by lower advertising costs for getting a marketing message to a group of customers in a much more focused fashion than was previously possible.

To date, the success of iTV has been mixed. On the one hand, nearly 3 million people used their remote controls to vote contestants out of the *Big Brother* game show on ITV in 2001 and another 2 million interacted with the BBC's coverage of the Wimbledon tennis championship. On the other hand, Sky scaled back its own iTV plans in the same year, after less than positive feedback from both viewers and the retail partners, who had invested heavily in exclusive rights to sell through Sky's home shopping portal called Open. The executive credited with developing the interactive element in *Big Brother* left ITV in 2003 when it scaled back its interactive ambitions. Similar stories can be found in other countries, where successes have been limited but where many companies have found niche marketing opportunities through the use of iTV (*see* Exhibit 11.4).

EXHIBIT 11.4

SELLING MELISSA ETHERIDGE ON ITV

Service providers are mistakenly tying the success of iTV to direct e-commerce value. Instead, the value of iTV is more in terms of a new, stronger relationship with the viewer through interactive entertainment.

'Advertising will slowly disappear from the slots inserted into programmes as digital TV delivery becomes more non-linear, thanks to TiVo (the personal video recorder) and video-on-demand. Advertisers will choose instead to deliver their message through interactive programmes,' says Patrick Bossert, of KPMG Consulting. Assuming regulatory approval, retailers could sell food during a cookery programme or DIY equipment during a home improvements show. Viewers might eventually be able to buy a dress worn by a soap star by clicking on the screen. Television operators, content providers and retailers share the spoils. The key to successful television commerce is the ability of viewers to make impulse purchases. When KBHK, a San Francisco broadcaster, screened a rock concert by Melissa Etheridge recently, 22 per cent of the audience ordered a CD through the television during the show.

Source: Financial Times (5 September 2001).[7]

Interactive home shopping

Most people are familiar with the concept of home shopping via the internet. The interactive services that are supported by digital television may give an additional boost to television shopping. The market for such services already exists and several major retailing organisations are reorganising their entire warehousing and delivery operations to support home shopping services:

- *Caddy Home* (www.caddy-home.be), Delhaize's service, offers approximately 3,500 products and uses centralised distribution centres to service its customers in Brussels and Antwerp.

- *Albert Heijn* (www.ah.nl), the Netherlands' leading grocery retailer, uses a combination of dedicated warehouses and stores for fulfilling home shopping orders.[8]

Until iTV becomes ubiquitous, few of the television-based home shopping services will be interactive. Traditional home shopping services consist of dedicated shopping channels that display and promote a single product, and provide a telephone number for the viewers to call to place their orders. In the future, digital shopping channels will allow viewers to browse through a wide variety of items, obtain significantly more information on the product or service, and order directly through the television set.

In the USA television shopping is currently dominated by QVC and Home Shopping Network, which between them reach more than 100 million homes. However, television shopping still only accounts for 1 per cent of total retail sales in the USA. QVC (www.qvc.com) is the newcomer but has been the more aggressive in Europe,

EXHIBIT 11.5

QVC GOES DIGITAL

On the eve of its eighth birthday in the UK, and Sky Digital's third birthday, QVC, the UK's leading TV shopping channel, is proud to announce the launch of QVCActive, the latest development in the world of interactive television. QVCActive offers the first ever opportunity for viewers to use their remote control to purchase items from a live television channel. QVC has spent the last 18 months pioneering the technology to ensure that UK viewers will benefit from the convenience of home shopping via the remote control. QVCActive gives customers access to QVC's range of over 10,000 products.

'We are very excited to be the first to the global market with this technology', comments Richard Burrell, director of engineering at QVC UK. 'QVC has always been at the forefront of electronic shopping. QVCActive is the first manifestation of live interactive TV shopping where QVC customers can use the remote control to purchase items from the live TV show as it happens. Our customers are used to the quality and reassurance that QVC gives them. Shopping from live television via the remote control is another option we are giving them, ensuring more convenience and choice from the leading TV shopping retailer.'

Source: QVCUK press release (www.qvcuk.com, 1 October 2001).

launching a teleshopping channel through its joint venture with Sky called QVC The Shopping Channel. In addition to 3 million Sky satellite customers, QVC reaches another 6 million cable homes in the UK through Telewest and NTL. QVC's iTV offering, called QVCActive, was launched in 2001 (*see* Exhibit 11.5).

Video-on-demand

An interactive facility such as video-on-demand provides consumers with instantaneous access to a particular movie, simply by choosing from a menu on the television screen. Such services require broadband telecommunications, which is often either not available or too expensive. A cheaper and easier service to deliver is near-video-on-demand. This is not a true interactive service but a variation of the pay-per-view services that are already offered by many cable companies. Near video-on-demand involves showing the same movie on different channels, but starting 15 or so minutes apart.

The widespread acceptance of ATMs and self-service kiosks

The ubiquitous ATM

Automated teller machines (ATMs) are ubiquitous. There are nearly 150,000 machines already installed across Europe – one for every 3,000 people.[9] In the UK the number of ATMs rose from under 19,000 in 1991 to more than 36,000 in 2001. Over the same

for good geographical reasons, tend to dominate this business, as more and more European manufacturers start treating Europe as a single strategic unit, rather than as a series of national markets.[24]

Managing multiple distribution channels

Managing distribution conflicts

Choosing a distribution channel is a strategic decision with major investment implications. Similarly, entering another country by setting up an agency or distributor agreement will usually involve a multi-year contract that can be both expensive and difficult to break. In some businesses, such as the airline industry, it is more profitable if customers order directly from the airline rather than through travel agents. There are major drawbacks, however. If the same airline promotes its direct channel heavily, travel agents may recommend other airlines in retaliation. The prospect of 'channel conflict' has deterred many manufacturers from going direct to their end-customer. Ehrens and Zapf (1999)[25] describe how competition from the internet channel can cause a backlash from the sales force. The case of Mattel's Barbie in Exhibit 11.11 provides another good example of these channel conflict issues.

EXHIBIT 11.11

BARBIE GOES DIRECT

In late 2000, Mattel quietly began selling a wide range of toys and kid's apparel over its Barbie.com website. At the same time, it also mailed a first-ever Barbie catalogue to 4 million American homes. Although some retailers privately say the site and catalogue pose competitive problems, Mattel asserts that the initiative is designed to boost the popularity and awareness of its brands, not to compete with retailers. Mattel has been very thoughtful with its online strategy, though. Prices are deliberately set 15 per cent higher than in retail stores, and certain hot items will not be offered at all on the website.

Source: Webb (2002).[26]

Hybrid marketing

Increasingly there is a trend towards using several different channels simultaneously to target different market segments. Many banks now use call centres and online banking in conjunction with normal branch operations and ATMs. Each of these channels has its own set of advantages and disadvantages. Moriarty and Moran (1990)[27] use the term 'hybrid marketing' to describe this situation where companies use a number of different channels to go to market. They cite the example of IBM, which started to expand in the late 1970s from using only a direct sales force to new channels such as dealers, value-added resellers (VARs), catalogue operations, direct mail and telemarketing. In less than ten years IBM doubled its sales force and added 18 new channels to communicate with customers. The advantages of employing a hybrid marketing system include increased coverage, lower costs and customised approaches. When adding a new channel companies must have a clear understanding of how it will affect their overall marketing strategy. As Moriarty and Moran describe it, the coordination of multiple distribution channels can be a complex business, which relies upon technology for its successful management:

> Once a hybrid system is up and running, its smooth functioning depends not only on management of conflict but also on coordination across the channels and across each selling task within the channels. Each unit involved in bridging the gap between the company and the customer must 'hand off' all relevant information concerning the customer and the progress of the sale to the next appropriate units.

The internet did not exist as a mature distribution channel when Moriarty and Moran described hybrid marketing in 1990. Friedman and Furey (1999)[28] address this issue by adding the internet as another channel. By 2000 hybrid marketing discussions invariably centred on the 'virtual versus physical' distribution channel debate. Internet-only propositions suffered from a series of limitations, the most significant of which are described by Görsch (2001)[29] as:

- the absence of direct sensory cues
- the absence of immediate gratification (in the case of physical products)
- tendencies to commoditisation and perils of price competition
- problems in creating consumer awareness and customer loyalty
- trust and shopping-risk related issues
- lack of social shopping experience
- consumer competency requirements.

However, in conjunction with other channels, the internet is an excellent distribution channel. Figure 11.2 outlines how retail stores, catalogues and the internet can be used in conjunction with each other before the buying decision is completed.

Today, the use of the term 'hybrid marketing' has reverted to its original meaning, where the internet is typically just one of a number of direct channels to market.

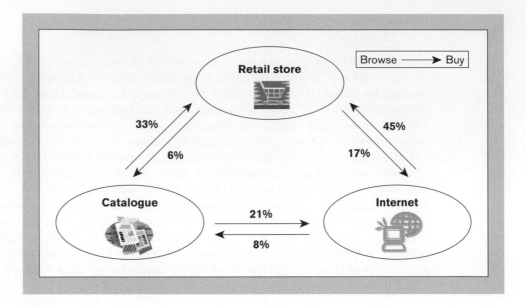

Figure 11.2 Hybrid marketing – interdependencies between channels
Source: DoubleClick website (www.doubleclick.com, 2002).[30]

Indeed, many internet-only companies have progressed down the hybrid marketing route by engaging in alliances with retailers with physical presences. Amazon is one such example in the USA, with its retailing alliances with Wal-Mart and Borders.

Managing different channel attributes

Online and offline channels have different attributes in terms of the way consumers shop. Degeratu et al. (2000)[31] analysed the importance of branding in online stores in comparison to their offline counterparts and found that internet retailing encourages consumers to pay more attention to search attributes, limiting the importance of a brand in the search process. In the twenty-first century, the pendulum may well swing back again and the importance of the brand may reassert itself. The research group GartnerG2 addresses some of these issues in Exhibit 11.12.

As well as the dramatic effects of electronic technology on the development of new distribution approaches, it must not be forgotten that existing channels are also affected by electronic developments. We have already discussed geo-demographics in earlier chapters and it is relevant to return to the topic here. Table 11.2 shows how the area around a car dealership can be analysed by geo-demographics.

If Model X is purchased by 5 per cent of the national population and the catchment area is 10,000, a sales potential of $10,000 \times 5\% = 500$ would be expected. In this case, the index is 154.4 (compared to a standard of 100), indicating a higher potential for sales, so for this catchment area the sales potential is $500 \times 1.544 = 772$.

EXHIBIT 11.12

THE WORLD MAP OF E-COMMERCE

Even with online retail on the rise in the USA, Western Europe and Asia, sales still account for just a fraction of total retail revenue. Indeed, online sales in the USA constituted just over 1 per cent of overall retail sales in 2001, according to the Department of Commerce. Similarly, European consumer e-commerce will account for just 2.3 per cent of all sales in 2002, research company GartnerG2 predicted. Therefore, it is not surprising that some analysts say business-to-business (B2B) transactions will overshadow business-to-consumer e-commerce on the world stage. In fact, B2B will account for 83 per cent of worldwide online sales in 2002 and 88 per cent in 2006, according to another research company IDC.

Despite the bullish e-commerce outlook in many regions around the world, a number of obstacles still inhibit the pace of growth. In much of Europe, for example, narrowband access discourages consumers from browsing retail sites for extended periods, GartnerG2's Cruz noted. And in Asia, e-tailers continue to struggle to serve many languages, cultures and religions with a single retail business model. Other e-commerce obstacles unique to some Asian nations include concern about secure messaging technologies and web servers, as well as widespread preference for face-to-face buying and live bargaining, Cruz added.

Coupled with developing nations' infrastructure deficiencies, some obstacles are likely to persist, inhibiting the development of a global online buying majority, analysts agreed. 'We are still very far away from [an online buying majority]', according to Mauro Guillen, an associate professor at Wharton Business School 'The internet won't develop as fast as some people thought it would.' Currently, e-commerce is growing most slowly in Japan, Latin America and Eastern Europe, IDC reported. And online transactions will remain an oddity in most of South Asia, Africa, Central America and other underdeveloped areas, according to Guillen. That said, some opportunities for growth and innovation do exist in these areas. 'E-commerce that was previously thought to be impossible – needing special contracts or administrative procedures or brokers – has become possible'.

Source: E-Commerce Times (2 April 2002).[32]

There are various ways in which such analysis could be used in building retail customer typologies. Zones and small 'grid square' areas could be produced, for example. If such classifications are considered relevant, each zone in the catchment area of each store in the analogue group can be allocated to a typology. Locations for citing new branches in a chain can similarly to profiled and those areas where the closest match of neighbourhood profile with the profile of typical customers of the product or service concerned can be selected.[33]

Table 11.2 Catchment area around a car dealership

Group	% of area	×	Model X index	=	Area sales potential
A	1.4	×	61%	=	0.85
B	–	×	108%	=	–
C	9.7	×	84%	=	8.15
D	7.9	×	39%	=	3.08
E	–	×	41%	=	–
F	11.4	×	53%	=	6.04
G	–	×	34%	=	–
H	13.9	×	124%	=	17.24
I	29.4	×	230%	=	67.62
J	22.5	×	217%	=	48.82
K	3.1	×	84%	=	2.60
Other	0.7		–		–
Total	**100%**				**154.40**

Hybrid marketing and hybrid mail

One specific application of hybrid marketing that has gained the attention of postal services companies is hybrid mail: the combination of a traditional and electronic postal service to improve the effectiveness of direct mail campaigns.

Hybrid mail began life as a means of delivering time-sensitive items, such as invoices and statements, to a geographically dispersed list of addressees more quickly and cheaply than traditional mail. Customers supply hybrid mail companies with their mailing list and transactional data on magnetic tape, diskette or compact disk. One example is China's Postal Bureau, which launched a hybrid mail service in 2001 that enabled computer users to send standard letters to an electronic address list at the click of a mouse. Using special mailing software and an electronic stamp card, the service covers 18 provinces, autonomous regions and municipalities, including Beijing, Shanghai and Nanjing. Mail sent to an online post office is automatically transferred to paper, put in an envelope and then delivered as normal. Another proposition from the Taiwan postal service is more clearly focused on direct mail campaigns:

> It's a one-stop computerised mail production and delivery service for those who routinely mail large volumes of mails. It gives you all the benefits and convenience of having your direct mail produced for you. We take away the hassles of printing, processing and delivering your mail, thus allowing you to concentrate on your core business activity.[34]

Today, hybrid mail is incorporated into more sophisticated direct marketing campaigns like those used by Toyota (*see* Exhibit 11.13).

EXHIBIT 11.13

HYBRID MARKETING CAMPAIGN FOR PRIUS LAUNCH

The much-anticipated US launch of Prius, Toyota's revolutionary gasoline/electric car, is underway with the unveiling of an innovative marketing campaign spearheaded by Toyota Motor Sales (TMS), Saatchi & Saatchi, and Oasis Advertising of New York. The teams have created a unique and fully integrated media plan. Broadcast and print advertising combined with interactive, outdoor and lifestyle marketing are fully synthesised within a campaign that strives to intrigue the buyer to make the intelligent choice, without compromising comfort, convenience or performance. The campaign theme, 'PRIUS/genius', is not only reflective of the new technology, but of the creative web-based marketing approach. The inherent challenge of marketing new technology to a new audience led TMS marketing to utilise a unique tactic. For nearly two years, the campaign has revolved around developing a dialogue with interested consumers. This resulted in a pool of over 40,000 interested consumers, or 'handraisers' in industry-speak. These prospects were given early access to the Prius microsite (http://toyota.com/prius) and its special order feature. Even before arriving in showrooms across the country, nearly 1,800 of the revolutionary Toyota Prius have been sold via online purchase requests. Toyota dealers started placing US orders for the world's first mass-produced gasoline/electric vehicle on 30 June 2000. The site officially opened to the public on 14 July. 'Prius enthusiasts have been following the development and availability of this new technology for more than two years', said Steve Sturm, vice president of marketing for TMS. 'We wanted to reward the enthusiastic reception for Prius among these early intenders by offering them the first opportunity to submit an online purchase request.'

Source: Auto Intelligence News (25 July 2000).[35]

Summary

Channel management decisions are changing rapidly with e-commerce. Many organisations are following the lead of companies like Dell and selling their products direct to the end consumer. Dell was already selling direct to consumers via the telephone, so the move to the internet was a logical extension of its existing business model. Other direct channels, such as the telephone, ATMs and more recently digital television, are also experiencing rapid growth. We also looked at changes in indirect channels brought about by technology, including the introduction of electronic point-of-sale (EPOS) systems. The use of such systems allows the sharing of information between channel partners like supermarkets and manufacturers and can ultimately lead to better supply chain efficiencies. In the electronic marketing world the concept of hybrid marketing is important, since organisations now need to manage multiple distribution channels.

Case study

Online travel (Travelocity, Expedia and Orbitz)

Figure 11.3

E-commerce is alive and well online. Those who want solid evidence need look no further than the online travel industry. As one of the few consumer industries that has established itself and shown measurable growth on the internet, online travel is no longer focused on basic survival. Instead, the industry is concentrating on its quest for the ingredients of longevity: market share, saturation and profit. Travelocity reported earnings of US$4.9 million for the fourth quarter of 2001. For the same period in 2000 – long before terrorist attacks threatened to put serious dents in the online travel industry – Travelocity reported a fourth-quarter loss of $2.4 million. Reflecting the impact of terrorism on online travel, Travelocity reported that gross travel bookings dropped by $60 million over the 12-month period. But fewer sales apparently did not affect the company's ability to boost its profits. Now, there's an equation that's easy to live with. So, what is it about the online travel industry that continues to allow it to emerge as a leading light for e-commerce? Some might say it has everything to do with convenience and cost savings for consumers – and they would be partly correct. But online travel's pull goes deeper than that, especially since the September 11 terrorist attacks. Booking travel online gives consumers a greater sense of control – especially compared with placing their trust in a travel agent or a faceless phone sales rep from an airline company.

In addition to its ability to make consumers feel like they are in control of their own destiny, online travel caters to customers' ongoing love of instant gratification – such as printing e-tickets minutes after purchasing them. Airlines apparently sense this trend and are making moves to capitalise on it. Several airlines have begun charging extra fees for some paper tickets in an aggressive move to persuade consumers to go the e-ticket route. Too much too soon? Not at all. According to Forrester Research,

70 to 80 per cent of all airline tickets were issued electronically in 2003. Another reason online travel continues to flourish is that it never gets too comfortable with its own progress. Even now, with a growth spurt in full force, the top three players – Travelocity, Expedia and Orbitz – continue to vie for position and innovate. Expedia, for example, is expanding its operations to include passport and visa services. Users will be able to research travel access requirements for most countries on the Expedia site, then download necessary document applications and send them directly to Expedia's new partner, Express Visa Service. Travellers can also check the status of their travel documents at any time.

The new economy calls for new definitions of old consumer services. The online travel industry is doing it right by giving consumers total control over their itinerary and by providing self-directed and comprehensive trip planning. For example, before a journey to London, a traveller can update or initiate travel documents, research promotional rates, book a flight, find hotel packages, buy a Eurail pass, arrange to be met at the airport by a driver and have a rental car waiting at the hotel. Isn't that what e-commerce promised us in the first place?

And which site is the best? According to the latest evaluation by ConsumerReports.org and Consumer WebWatch, Expedia and Travelocity come out on top for booking airline tickets online, with Orbitz running close behind. Six websites – Cheap Tickets, Expedia, One Travel, Orbitz, TravelNow.com and Travelocity – were judged on their privacy and security policies, customer service, and clear disclosure of advertising relationships, usability and content. The winners were praised for promising to maintain customer privacy, enabling easy navigation through the site and providing a satisfying online experience. 'Overall, we were pleased to see that the top airline-ticket booking sites provided consumers with a great deal of control when booking flights, and several sites kept their promise of having 24/7 customer service available for users,' wrote Helen Popkin, associate editor of ConsumerReports.org. The 'e-Ratings' findings included:

- While many of the sites earned solid marks for low fares and for customer service, all could be more forthcoming in disclosing their relationships with advertisers, and some could improve their privacy policies.

- None of the six sites reviewed adequately disclosed the scope of the relationship between the site and its airline partners, which made it next to impossible to judge the objectivity of flight prices.

- Some sites could better explain what they do with personal information. The evaluation reported that Expedia and Travelocity have excellent privacy policies, promising that they won't rent or sell personal information, but policies at other sites, such as Cheap Tickets, are more confusing.

The issues for corporate travellers are slightly different. The proliferation of internet offers and the rise of low-cost airlines have led to corporate travellers feeling that airlines see them as a captive market – and that the best deals have eluded them. The result is a quickening race to provide corporate travel managers, agents and individual passengers with access to an ever-more comprehensive array of software that enables them to compare more easily the plethora of fares available and avoid paying more than they need. The technology is known as website 'scraping' in industry jargon. Several factors helped to spark this current frenzy of activity. Large airlines posted special deals on their own websites that were not available through the global distribution systems (GDS), whose terminals are in the offices of business travel agents. Online agencies such as Orbitz, launched by a group of five leading US carriers, also offered new options. Most no-frills operators have shunned the GDS companies to avoid the cost of appearing on their screens. The US National Business Travel Association says travellers have been discouraged from paying higher 'flexible fares' as airlines waived restrictions on cheaper leisure fares and offered internet-only deals. When they realised business passengers were switching to leisure fares, carriers stopped offering corporate clients negotiated discounts, exacerbating the problem by weakening customer loyalty. In Europe the difference between business and leisure fares has also been blurred as carriers, including British Airways and KLM, have removed restrictions. BA is among those offering discounts to passengers booking via its website.

For business travellers and their managers, the outcome of these developments has been confusion. It has become difficult – if not impossible – for those on tight budgets to discover whether they are getting the lowest fare available. Travel managers have suffered the added headache of keeping tabs on expenditure by staff booking low-cost flights with airlines other than those preferred by their companies. Efforts to sort out the muddle are gathering pace. They involve business travel management firms, the GDS companies and even some airlines. Agency consultants have been provided with the technology to surf and book a range of airline and other online sites. All four main GDS operators – Sabre, Galileo, Amadeus and Worldspan – have either done the same or intend to. Sabre has incorporated it in its GetThere self-booking online tool for US customers and has extended the ability to search for some low-cost airline fares to European users. Worldspan and Galileo are on the point of adding it to their self-booking tools. The former plans to make it available worldwide, the latter said it would be launched first in the USA, then in Europe, the Middle East and Africa.

UK-based P&O Travel uses two different search engines: one for short-haul, the other for long-haul bookings. They throw up the fare options on any given route, scanning web-only and low-cost airline fares and highlighting the cheapest available. The firm's agency staff is able to split their screens to view GDS fares on one side and alternative offers on the other. One of its customers is Research Machines of Abingdon in Oxfordshire, a leading supplier of software, systems and services to UK education. The firm says that since signing up with P&O in August, the technology has cut its fare costs by 20 per cent – or about £100,000 in a full year.

But 'scraping' websites for deals is not yet the perfect solution. New low-cost airlines have been popping up so frequently that search tools may not yet include them. Much better, then, to have airlines abandon the idea of internet-only fares and make them openly available, in real time, on GDS screens. So Sabre and rival Galileo are offering to cut their fees by 10 per cent, and freeze them for three years, for carriers that agree to do so. As one industry commentator puts it: Airlines must realise that the traditional model of corporate travellers contributing a disproportionate amount of revenue is outdated. 'With business travellers becoming much more price sensitive, they should make all their fares available through all distribution channels.' That ideal world still appears to be a long way off.

Sources: Travelocity website (www.travelocity.com, 2003); *E-Commerce Times* (22 January 2002);[36] *Atlanta Journal-Constitution* (4 March 2003);[37] *Financial Times* (5 December 2002).[38]

Case study questions

1 Why do you think the online travel industry has been such an e-commerce success story?

2 'Online travel caters to customers' love of instant gratification.' Comment.

3 What type of additional services should online travel agents look at providing for their customers?

4 Why would customers want to know more about the relationship between online travel agents and the major airlines?

5 Why would business travellers want to switch to leisure fares and how is the industry responding?

6 Explain how the company Research Machines of Abingdon was able to reduce its fare costs by 20 per cent.

7 'With business travellers becoming more price sensitive, airlines should make all their fares available through all distribution channels.' Discuss.

Questions and exercises

Questions

1 Comment on the role of distribution channels in the marketing mix.

2 What is the impact of e-commerce and the internet on distribution?

3 Why should a manufacturer consider using an intermediary?

4 Why are EPOS systems so important in the retailing industry?

5 What do you understand by the term 'hybrid marketing'?

6 Outline three challenges associated with managing multiple distribution channels.

Online exercises

1 Both Dell and IBM product PCs. Log on to their websites (www.dell.com and www.ibm.com). What is the apparent difference in the way they go to market? Compare and contrast the two sites under the following headings: a) product range; b) capability to purchase a PC online; c) ease of use of different sites; d) prices.

2 Visit Egg (www.egg.co.uk) and Citibank (www.citibank.co.uk). Compare and contrast the two different product offers.

References

1 Evans, M. (2000). 'Database marketing: a wider social responsibility?' Academy of Marketing Conference, University of Derby, July.

2 Evans, M. (2003). 'Marketing communications changes' in Hart S. (ed.) *Marketing Changes*, London: Thomson Learning.

3 O'Connor, J. (2003). Unpublished research.

4 Hughes, R. and Evans, M. (2001). 'Relationships are two-way: the neglected role of "inbound" contact in the financial services sector,' World Marketing Congress, Cardiff, June.

5 Ody, P. (2002). 'A lingering goodbye to the checkout', *Financial Times*, 3 April.

6 Blau, J. (2002). 'Operators pin hopes on Japanese success story', *Financial Times*, 20 November.

7 Ward, A. (2001). 'Persuading viewers to pay for services could be tough', *Financial Times*, 5 September.

8 Younger, R. (1998). 'New structures will be required', *Financial Times*, 1 December.

9 *Electronic Payments International* (1996). 'Sweden heads ATM league table', April.

10 Association for Payment Clearing Services (2002). www.apacs.org.uk

11 Callender, B. (2002). 'The British Museum exhibits its kiosks', www.kioskmarketplace.com, 29 August.

12 Buxton, J. (1999). 'Cashing in on the hole-in-the-wall', *Financial Times,* 21 July.

13 *Business Week* (1999). 'Grab some cash, check out a flick', 26 April.

14 Beer, R. (2002). 'MCBD creates interactive poster in first campaign for Pretty Polly', *Campaign*, 1 November.

15 Sappal, P. (1996). 'Sampling the market', *Direct Response*, November, pp. 63–4.

16 Denny, N. (1995). 'Sampling takes the top slot for launches', *Marketing*, 4 May, p. 8.

17 Barwise, P. and Styler, A. (2002). *Marketing Expenditure Trends*, London Business School/Havas and Kudos Research.

18 *Electronic Payments International* (1995). 'Taxis to try mobile EFTPoS', March.

19 Leicester City Council (2002). 'Smart technology gets gyms fit for 21st century', www.leicester.gov.uk, 3 January.

20 Roy, M. (2002). 'Forget fantasy: move back to the data basics', *Precision Marketing*, 2 August.

21 Batchelor, C. (1998). 'Buzzword – or the way of the future?' *Financial Times*, 1 December.

22 Procter & Gamble (2003). 'Gaps on shelves are expensive! Innovation required . . .', www.eu.pg.com/news/gapsonshelves.html, 3 March.

23 Batchelor, C. (1998). 'Working with mixed pallets', *Financial Times*, 1 December.

24 Terry, M. (1998). 'Taking a continent-wide view', *Financial Times*, 1 December.

25 Ehrens, S. and Zapf, S. (1999). *The Internet Business-to-Business Report*, New York: Bear, Stearns & Co.

26 Webb, K.L. (2002). 'Managing channels of distribution in the age of electronic commerce', *Industrial Marketing Management*, Vol. 31.

27 Moriarty, R.T. and Moran, U. (1990). 'Managing hybrid marketing systems'. *Harvard Business Review*, November–December.

28 Friedman, L.G. and Furey, T.R. (1999). *The Channel Advantage*. Oxford: Butterworth-Heinemann.

29 Görsch, D. (2001). 'Internet limitations, product types, and the future of electronic retailing', Proceedings of the Nordic Workshop on Electronic Commerce, Halmstad.

30 DoubleClick (2002). *Multichannel Holiday Shopping Study*, www.doubleclick.com, January.

31 Degeratu, A.M., Rangaswamy, A., and Wu, J. (2000). 'Consumer choice behaviour in online and traditional supermarkets: the effects of brand name, price, and other search attributes', *International Journal of Research in Marketing*, Vol. 17.

32 Vigoroso, M.W. (2002). 'The world map of e-commerce', *E-Commerce Times*, 2 April.

33 Evans, M., Moutinho, L. and van Raaij, F. (1996). *Applied Consumer Behaviour*, Harlow: Addison Wesley.

34 www.post.gov.tw/ehybrid_1.htm

35 *Auto Intelligence News* (2000). 'Innovative hybrid marketing campaign launches Toyota's clean car for the future', www.autointell-news.com/news-2000/July-2000/July-25-00-p5.htm

36 Greenberg, P.A. (2002). 'And the winner is – online travel', *E-Commerce Times*, www.ecommercetimes.com/perl/story/15936.html, 22 January.

37 Thrasher, P.C. (2003), 'Expedia, Travelocity rated best sites for air booking', *Atlanta Journal-Constitution*, 4 March.

38 Bray, R. (2002). 'Online booking update: savers get into an online scrape', *Financial Times*, 5 December.

12

Promoting to markets of one

Learning objectives

Once you have read this chapter you will:

- understand why television advertising is becoming more fragmented and targeted;
- appreciate how direct response television and teletext can be used to promote products;
- understand how technology is impacting other advertising media such as radio and newspapers;
- appreciate how the internet is set to become a mainstream channel for selling and advertising;
- appreciate how digital services, both radio and television, offer tremendous potential to marketers;
- understand recent trends in sales promotions and public relations.

Contents

TRENDS IN OTHER ADVERTISING MEDIA

- Public and commercial radio advertising
- Direct response radio advertising
- Newspapers and magazine advertising
- Place-based media advertising
- Growth of direct mail

THE INTERNET AS AN ADVERTISING MEDIUM

- Websites and 'brochureware'
- Banner advertising and 'destination websites'
- Internet search advertising
- The future of internet advertising
- PR activities on the internet

THE POTENTIAL OF INTERACTIVE MEDIA

- The interactive power of digital media
- Digital television
- Videotex
- Digital radio
- Digital teletext

SALES PROMOTIONS

- Trends in sales promotions
- Loyalty programmes

SUMMARY

CASE STUDY

Introduction

The promotional mix contains several ingredients, including:

- *Advertising* – a means of broadcasting messages to a target audience through a mass medium such as television, radio, newspaper, magazine, catalogue, direct mail, public transport or outdoor display. It can be cost effective but success is often difficult to monitor.

■ *Personal selling* – informing customers and persuading them to purchase products through personal communication. There is a wide variety of personal selling roles, including direct calls by a salesperson and telephone sales.

■ *Sales promotions* – short-term incentives to distributors and sales people to stock products and for customers to buy them. Examples include coupons, bonuses, and contests used to increase the sales of a product.

■ *Public relations* – non-personal communication transmitted free of charge through mass media. Examples include newspaper, radio or TV stories about personnel changes in an organisation, the opening of new stores or the launch of new products.

In this chapter we will concentrate mainly on how electronic media has impacted advertising and sales promotions; in the next chapter we will examine its impact on sales management in more detail. We start by looking at television advertising and the changes it has undergone in recent years, primarily as a result of new electronic capabilities such as cable and digital television. We examine direct response television (DRTV) and teletext before moving on to other advertising media. We then focus on the internet as an advertising medium and look at the potential of other interactive media, before finishing with an examination of sales promotions and loyalty schemes.

Television advertising trends

Historic growth of television advertising

In most Western countries total expenditure on mass media advertising amounts to between 0.5 and 1 per cent of gross domestic product (GDP), typically through one of the following primary media:

■ newspapers and magazines

■ television

■ radio

■ outdoor

■ cinema.

Newspapers and magazines account for the majority of advertising expenditure, but the medium of choice depends on the nature of the product or services being advertised, as well as the country or region in question. Food, drink and consumer goods tend to carry a much greater proportion of their expenditure on television than other media, while advertising of property and items such as clothing and computers is

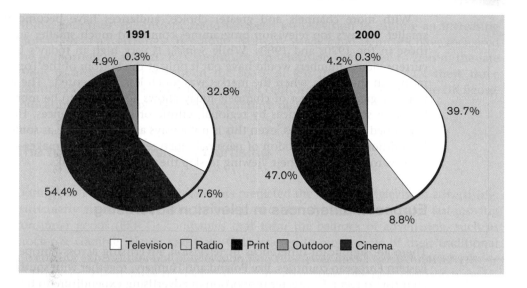

Figure 12.1 Advertising expenditure by media type (1991 versus 2000)
Source: European Group of Television Advertising website (www.egta.com, 2002).

dominated by newspapers and magazines. For example, in the UK where one third of all advertising expenditure is devoted to the medium of television, Kellogg's and Procter & Gamble spend nearly 95 per cent of their advertising budget on this medium.[1] During the 1990s advertising revenues also switched, mainly from print into television (*see* Figure 12.1).

Expenditure across all media types grew significantly during the 1990s, although this trend faltered somewhat in recent years, as noted by Barwise and Styler (2002).[2] In this research, media advertising expenditure fell by 2 per cent between 2001 and 2002, partly because of some high media card rates and the perceived lack of accountability of such mass media, and also because of fragmenting audiences, which can reduce the cost-effectiveness even further.

Fragmentation of television audiences

Most Western economies have seen a dramatic increase in the number of television channels that have been made available as television is deregulated and opened up to greater competition. In the UK the BBC was the only broadcasting company until 1965, when Independent Television (ITV) was launched. This was followed by BBC2 in 1967 and more recently by Channel 4 and Channel 5. However, the range of television services really only increased dramatically in the 1990s with the launch of the multi-channel satellite systems. The arrival of BSkyB's satellite channels has altered fundamentally the balance of power between the traditional broadcasters and the newer upstarts. More importantly, the arrival of digital television has vastly increased the number of channels available to viewers, and has allowed advertisers to target their marketing messages much more effectively than in the past.

EXHIBIT 12.3

LED SPECTACULARS

To date, LED video billboards have matured into two specific applications of use (spectaculars and roadside displays) and its third application (multiple signs as a network system) is just beginning to emerge as a viable outdoor advertising format. In its first and most expensive application, LED video billboards appeared as sign components to Times Square and Las Vegas spectaculars. In Times Square you can turn in any direction and come face-to-face with three or four LED video spectaculars all at once. Most prominent is the front (its north face) of One Times Square, which is filled up with LED video billboards. Similarly, many of its surrounding Times Square buildings have equally overwhelming LED displays, including NASDAQ (Smartvision), ABC NEWS (Multimedia, Rancho Cordova, California) or Lehman Brothers (Daktronics – Brookings, South Dakota).

The third application provides the possibility of creating a city-wide or regional display-advertising network. Here, a series of connected video screens can provide everything from a broad-based advertising presence (sign messages on continuous video loops) to very tightly controlled demographic-specific displays tailored to week-morning commutes or mid-afternoon shoppers (depending on sign locations) or special weekend sales announcements presented to a Friday evening home commute.

Source: Signindustry.com (30 July 2002).[18]

Outdoor electronic displays are also becoming more sophisticated. Recent developments have enabled light-emitting diode (LED) screens to produce a true red, green and blue, so that they can reproduce colour as faithfully as television and cinema. LED video billboards are perhaps the most spectacular formats of outdoor display advertising (*see* Exhibit 12.3).

Growth of direct mail

Direct mail's share of promotional expenditure has increased steadily over the years. For example, the average person in the Netherlands received 82 pieces of direct mail in 1996, almost double the figure five years earlier. In the UK the 1996 figure was 54 pieces, up 35 per cent from 1991. Again there are significant differences across Europe. Germany and Austria are among the greatest proponents of direct marketing markets in the world, while the markets in Portugal and Greece are almost non-existent.

Direct mail's share of advertising expenditure in the UK has steadily increased over the years. Between 1988 and 1992 its share rose from 7 per cent to 11 per cent, mainly at the expense of press advertising, which dropped from 60 per cent to 55 per cent over the same period. By 2001 direct mail had a 13 per cent share, according to Barwise and

Styler (2002). Barwise and Styler also found that direct mail expenditure continues to grow: by over 3 per cent per year since 2000.[19]

The average household in the UK now receives between six and seven pieces of direct mail every month.[20] The more highly targeted groups, typically ABs and those over 35, will clearly receive significantly more. There is evidence to suggest that particular segments of the market are already being over-targeted. For example, 84 per cent of the 'grey' market (those over 55) considers the level of targeting to be excessive.[21] Other findings from such surveys give a similar and somewhat predictable picture:

- 95 per cent consider telemarketing to be unethical;

- 76 per cent consider direct mail to be unethical;

- 71 per cent consider the sale of lists between companies to be unethical;

- 67 per cent of respondents do not consider that direct communications provide information;

- 47 per cent consider direct marketing to be an invasion of privacy.

As the amount of material dropping through the letterbox increases, the chances of it being read decreases. There is some evidence that people react well to material that is of interest or directly relevant to them and that the key to successful direct mail advertising is very close analysis of the target audience. The ability to target customers closely is dependent on building an accurate database with sufficient information to identify key customer groups. As Evans et al. (1996)[22] describe it:

> The sooner marketers move to using direct mail in response to customers' requests, rather than 'cold' prospecting, the better it will be for all concerned. Marketers will be able to target more accurately and more effectively, and consumers will see a phenomenal reduction in unsolicited direct mail. This will lead to more true 'relationships' between marketer and consumer and will probably significantly alleviate privacy concerns among consumers and legislators, and will clearly be beneficial for the industry.

Direct mail should not simply be seen as a stand-alone means of communicating with a customer. All forms of communication with a customer offer the opportunity to include a marketing message. Companies that have regular correspondence with customers, by way of monthly statements for example, can tailor marketing messages for inclusion with the correspondence. Although direct mail has received bad publicity through the proliferation of unsolicited 'junk mail', it does have a number of advantages:

- it is more targeted than traditional media advertising (*see* Figure 12.3);

- in many cases, it is also cheaper than traditional advertising;

- its effectiveness can be measured.

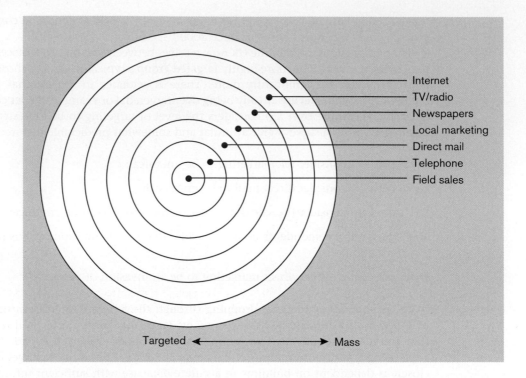

Figure 12.3 Degree of targeting of advertising messages

The internet as an advertising medium

Websites and 'brochureware'

The internet is increasingly seen as an important advertising medium. By the end of the 1990s most large organisations had migrated a proportion of their advertising expenditure to the internet and almost all had established some sort of presence on the web. The most common form of internet advertising was still the creation of 'brochureware' – using the corporate website to advertise the company's range of products and services.

While creating a quality online brochure is a important step, it is not an effective from of advertising or a way of generating traffic to a site. For example, Sony uses a whole range of advertising techniques including advertising on other websites to generate traffic to its own website, Once people have been persuaded they would like a Sony TV, the brochureware on the Sony website can then be important to help them select the exact model they require.

Banner advertising and 'destination websites'

The primary mechanism for carrying advertisements on websites is the banner: the rectangular advertising space on the website that is often animated and encourages consumers to 'click through' to the relevant page on the advertiser's own website. Not everybody is happy with these banner advertisements, which make up the majority of all internet advertising expenditure (*see* Exhibit 12.4).

EXHIBIT 12.4

STICKING YOUR NECK OUT

On the face of it, internet advertising has been established for a few years, despite the collapse of the boom. According to the Internet Advertising Bureau, £165 million was spent on online advertising in the UK in 2001, a rise of 7 per cent on the year before. The 2002 figures are expected to show a similar increase; the picture for 2003 looks even rosier. Estimates vary for this year, but growth is expected to soar into double-digit figures, with predictions spread between 20 per cent and 46 per cent.

But the advertising community feels quality is losing out to quantity. Media buyers believe the sector is being held back by a lack of imaginative, high quality ads. As a result, online advertising is dominated by bland banners and buttons. The finger is being pointed at the big creative agencies, which develop expensive TV, billboard and cinema campaigns and leave the internet by the wayside. 'It is holding our industry back. Clients place a huge amount of trust in the feedback they get from creative agencies. I can spend a lot of time working on a great media plan for online advertising but the missing link will still be the creative side, because the client does not think the right creative solution is in place. Even the creative agencies themselves would tell you that they have not engaged it in the way that media buyers have. If you reeled off great creative work in TV and billboards and then asked what their offering was like online, there would be a big difference,' says Robert Horler of media buyer Carat Interactive.

Charlie Dobres, of online media buyer i-level, thinks net advertising has proved it can work but not enough companies are listening. Double-digit growth for 2003 would be impressive, but still a drop in the ocean compared to the spending on TV, radio and outdoor campaigns. The IAB's key target is to double the web's share of UK advertising to 2 per cent by 2004. 'The main issue is making people know about it, and when they know about it, will they believe what they hear? Going from spending 2 per cent of your advertising budget on the internet to spending 5 per cent is sticking your neck out.'

Source: *The Guardian* (14 March 2003).[23]

There is also scepticism in the USA, the world's most developed internet market, about the effectiveness of banner advertising. Falling 'click-through' rates are even causing some companies to rethink the migration of advertising expenditure to the internet.

A more effective form of banner advertising recognises that internet traffic is concentrated around a relatively small number of 'destination sites'. These sites are either:

■ high-content websites (such as Amazon or eBay)

■ search engines (such as Google)

■ portals that internet users use as their starting point to surf the internet
(such as Yahoo or MSN).

These sites are particularly attractive to advertisers seeking a wide audience for their products. Yahoo (www.yahoo.com) has more than 200 million users, 60 per cent of whom are outside the USA.

Internet search advertising

Internet search advertising is a new business but was worth around $1 billion in 2002 and growing at a fast rate (according to one of its main proponents, Yahoo). It will soon be worth half as much as the entire market for more familiar forms of internet advertising, such as banners.[24] Search advertising takes two forms:

■ *Pay for placement* – a sponsored search that involves putting a small number of paid-for links in a separate section at the top of a search page. Because they are highly targeted, such commercial messages generally get click-through rates of 12–17 per cent, according to Yahoo. Conversion rates like these are highly attractive when compared with the banner advertising market, and advertisers pay 30–35 cents for each click.

■ *Paid inclusion* – advertisers pay to have their websites 'crawled' by an internet search engine and their information is included in the regular search results, rather than in a separate advertising section. Companies that provide this service, such as Look-Smart which feeds websites such as MSN, advise advertisers how to write their listings in a way that gives them the best chance of showing up prominently in a search.

Paid inclusion is more controversial because only the companies providing the service understand how the algorithms inside their search engine 'black boxes' work. The controversy surrounding paid inclusion is dividing the search business. Google, the industry's leading search company, has rejected the idea, claiming it will destroy the integrity of internet searches, but Yahoo (*see* Exhibit 12.5) is developing its own service.[25]

EXHIBIT 12.5

SEARCHING FOR INTERNET AD REVENUES

When Terry Semel, Yahoo's chief executive, arrived in May 2001, the company was in disarray: its sole source of revenue, internet advertising, was collapsing. With a strong self-assurance founded on its earlier meteoric success, it was ill-prepared for the challenge. The new boss's first moves came direct from the management textbook. A new management group was quickly assembled, particularly in the troubled advertising sales area. 'We changed the whole sales team. We started all over again,' Semel says. That involved bringing in executives with experience from other corners of the media business and repairing frayed relationships with customers to whom Yahoo had paid scant attention when times were good. 'We had relationships with advertising agencies – they were all bad', Semel says. Yahoo's success since Semel arrived has been to latch on to a handful of promising new ideas. One is known as 'sponsored search' – selling targeted advertisements that plug into users' internet searches – a big success in the USA last year. Yahoo is now bent on extending sponsored searches to Europe, where the idea is still in its infancy. Semel's second big idea revolves around classified advertising. 'We looked at what works best on the internet: simply put, it was the world of classifieds', he says. By buying HotJobs.com, the second biggest online recruitment company in the US, and building the second biggest 'personals' service from scratch, Yahoo now believes it has two services that are ripe for export.

Source: *Financial Times* (17 February 2003).[26]

The future of internet advertising

According to the consultancy eMarketer (www.emarketer.com), advertising revenues in the USA fell from a peak of $8 billion in 2000 to $6 billion in 2002. Despite this scepticism, internet advertising spend is increasing again, albeit at much lower growth rates than in the late 1990s. Leading the charge are the global motor and FMCG companies attracted by the fact that there are more than 120 million active web users in the USA alone (*see* Exhibit 12.6).

The internet will undoubtedly account for a growing proportion of advertising revenues for the foreseeable future, because even if most people who see a banner do not click it, the banner can still build up brand awareness and perception.

The internet is also seen as an important mechanism in conjunction with other advertising formats. Most companies now combine the internet with traditional forms of advertising. There is an increasing propensity for companies to include their internet addresses alongside other forms of advertising – on posters, magazine advertisements, and even on television advertising. Some companies have taken the concept one step further: Joe Boxer (www.joeboxer.com), a manufacturer of men's underwear, and EasyJet (www.easyjet.com), the low-cost airline carrier, have emblazoned their web addresses clearly and visibly across their respective products – boxer shorts and aircraft (*see* Figure 12.4).

EXHIBIT 12.6

ONLINE LAUNCHES FOR VOLVO S60 AND XC90

Advertising on the internet is a no-brainer for Scandinavian carmaker Volvo. 'It's where our customers are', explains the company's e-business manager, Phil Bienert. He represents the contemporary face of online advertising. Traditional companies are now the mainstay of internet advertising following the demise of the dot-coms. Although the web has been less favoured as an advertising vehicle in the past two years, consumers have never deserted the internet. Proven businesses such as Pepsi, Procter & Gamble, Frito-Lay and Unilever are now in the vanguard of online advertising and its fortunes look far more assured in such hands. From 2000 to 2002, Johnson & Johnson and Unilever increased their online advertising expenditure by staggering rates of nearly 18,000 and 80,000 per cent, respectively.

Leading TV advertisers such as Ford and Chrysler were initially reticent about the web because they 'didn't know how to use it', says Gartner's Garcia. 'Now they have figured out their channel strategy.' Dawn Winchester, of New York interactive advertising agency R/GA agrees. 'For most large clients, the internet is not the mystery it was two to three years ago.' This has gone two ways, she notes. Some companies have tightened their belts as they took more realistic views of the web's possibilities; others have increased their spending as they have cottoned on more to its possibilities. Moreover, there is more understanding of where the internet fits into overall corporate advertising strategies, she says. Clients are now coordinating seamless campaigns spanning different media, Winchester reports. Volvo, for one, needs no convincing about the merits of the web as a buzz-building mechanism. It was the first car manufacturer to make a web presence back in distant 1994, and in 2000 it marketed its new S60 model exclusively online. Bienert says the web-only campaign netted $100 million in clear profit from sales. The sports saloon was something of a departure for a company more associated with family-sized estates, and Volvo also chose the web to launch its latest new category entrant, the XC90 sport utility vehicle. The web is the ideal place for Volvo to break out from its 'traditional reputation for safe wagons', explains Bienert. 'Now our cars are more fun to drive, the internet allows people to encounter us in a different way.'

Source: *Financial Times* (15 January 2003).[27]

Figure 12.4 Easyjet's internet branding
Source: *Easyjet website* (www.easyjet.com, 2003).

PR activities on the internet

The internet is being used more and more for a variety of marketing and corporate public relations (PR) activities. Essentially, the approach is to target 'opinion leaders' of 'opinion formers' with the aim of initiating a two or multi-step flow of communications to those who are 'followers'. With their recognised expertise, prowess or particular knowledge or skills, opinion leaders are those who are able to guide and lead the thoughts of others in particular product areas.[28] Some influencers have a status of expertise bestowed upon them by the nature of their employment or training (for example journalists). These are referred to as opinion formers: people who are actively and deliberately involved in the process of shaping and forming the thoughts of others about specific products and services. Very often opinion formers will use mass media to communicate their reprocessed information (journalists), although they can all be regarded as active influencers, or talkers.[29]

Electronic media are providing new ways of communicating with these opinion leaders and opinion formers. E-mail targeting via the internet is becoming popular and in some cases extremely effective (if dubious). For example, in research into the use of press releases, some PR managers declared that they e-mail such documents to journalists who sometimes 'paste' these into their articles. The persuasive power can be great because readers often view such reports of, say, new product launches as being written by knowledgeable, objective and independent experts, when in fact many of the 'positive adjectives' being applied to the product have been compiled by the promoting company.

Typical public relations activities that are conducted using the internet include:

- *Investor relations*. Many companies will place the annual, half-yearly or quarterly accounts or financial statements on the internet for investors to view or download. Almost all major investors will use corporate websites as a key source of information and intelligence about target companies.

- *Product and service information*. The internet has become a key distribution channel for marketing PR material. Most corporate websites will devote most of their web pages to descriptions of their products or services. The general 'look and feel' of a corporate website can significantly enhance (or detract from) the organisation's overall public image.

- *Press releases*. Most companies who distribute press releases on the web will archive these releases so that users can access them easily again. Hewlett-Packard was one of the first companies to launch its own press releases and news information on to a news bulletin board that was shared with several hundred publications worldwide. Most corporate websites will have one or more pages devoted to recent press releases. Marketing departments will now e-mail statements to newspapers for immediate release, as opposed to using fax, courier or mail.

- *Recruitment*. A company's website can be an invaluable source of reference material for prospective employees. Many companies now solicit and receive job applications over the internet. Specialist internet recruitment companies such as the global Monster (www.monster.com) and the more locally-based IrishJobs.ie (*see* Exhibit 12.7) have emerged to address this market.

EXHIBIT 12.7

OH BROTHER, WHERE ART THOU?

The Franciscan order will become the first religious institution in the Republic of Ireland to recruit on the internet. The order is to advertise on the recruitment website Irishjobs.ie, a move that friar Caoimhin O'Laoide OFM describes as 'a new departure'. Some 200 Franciscans are members of the Irish province. They work as teachers, counsellors, hospital and school chaplains, and social and community volunteers.

Source: Irish Times (11 April 2003).[30]

The potential of interactive media

The interactive power of digital media

Analogue television and radio services made significant progress in the 1990s but they suffer from one drawback – they are broadcast media, which do not allow any form of interactivity between the broadcaster and the viewer (or listener). Even teletext is not interactive – the broadcaster decides what information to send to the television, not the viewer. Interactivity requires greater bandwidth and different technology, both of which can only be provided by digital media.

As Figure 12.5 shows, digital media do not automatically mean interactivity, only the potential for interactive services.

Digital television

Digital television (DTV) is an improved way of transmitting television pictures – improved because it can compress the digital signal and fit five digital channels into the frequency bandwidth currently used by a single conventional station. Digital signals are first scrambled or encrypted and compressed at the transmission site before they are sent to the viewer's home. In the viewer's home, an electronic device called the set-top box is tuned to the digital channels, decrypts and decompresses the signal, and sends the resulting pictures to the existing television set. The digital signal is received in one of three generic ways:

- *Satellite*. Satellite television requires a satellite dish and a set-top box but is generally available to anybody who is willing to purchase the requisite equipment and pay for the service.

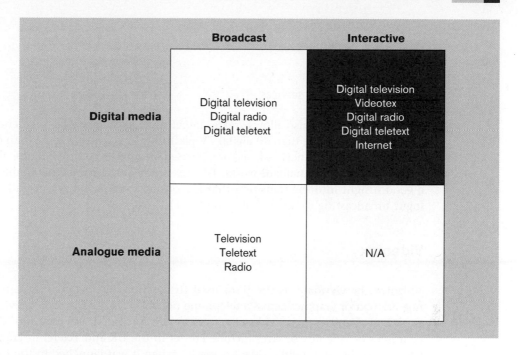

Figure 12.5 Interactive services

- *Cable.* Cable requires no new hardware for existing cable television subscribers but requires non-cable subscribers to have cable installed in addition to their existing set-top box.

- *Terrestrial.* Somewhat confusingly entitled, digital terrestrial television (DTT) refers to television signals that are received via an ordinary aerial. It requires no new wiring but does require a set-top box and is more limited in bandwidth than satellite or cable.

Satellite is the delivery channel used for most digital services. However, digital terrestrial networks can achieve positive results. At the beginning of 2001, ITV Digital (now Freeview – *see* the case study at the end of the chapter) and Quiero TV (Spain) accounted for 1 million and 210,000 subscribers respectively. The UK's first digital broadcast satellite service was Sky Digital, which went on the air in late 1998. Since the beginning of 1996, the EU digital TV market has enjoyed a relatively high growth rate both in terms of numbers of subscribers and in value.[31] The number of digital households rose to over 18 million in 2000 from only 2 million at the end of 1997. Nevertheless, although this trend is encouraging, the digital take-up remains relatively low in most EU countries: only 12.5 per cent of European TV households were digital at the end of 2000.

From a marketing perspective, some of the more interesting developments in digital television are the interactive services that are being promised to consumers. Although not yet widely available, they will eventually provide services such as:

- electronic programme guide (EPG)

- home shopping

- home banking

- games

- e-mail

- other e-commerce services.

Digital television also allows greater targeting of specific market segments. By mid-2000 there were more than 30 digital TV platforms broadcasting more than 600 digital channels. These channels can, and are, focused on smaller niches than the mass broadcast channels of the analogue world. The case study at the end of this chapter provides a good insight into the transition that all countries are making from traditional analogue broadcasting to the digital world.

Videotex

Videotex, or viewdata, is the term used to describe any two-way system for transmitting text or graphics across a telephone network, for display on a television screen or PC. Typically, these videotex services are provided by telecoms companies. Examples of videotex services include Prestel in the UK and Teletel in France. Prestel was the world's first public videotex service when it was launched in the UK in 1979. It was initially a very popular service, with more than 1 million customers in the 1980s. Teletel began service in France in 1984 and built up a customer base of 3 million by 1988.

In general, videotex has been less commercially successful as a vehicle for marketing promotion. In theory, the proposition looked attractive to potential business customers. Videotex promised to provide the business user with a wide variety of electronic services available from a single terminal. It also promised the business user access to many of the telecom company's business and residential customer base, who were expected to use the service. All these opportunities would be made available for a relatively low fee. In practice it worked out quite differently:

- videotex was beset by technical problems related to the speed at which information could be accessed and transactions could be carried out;

- despite the initial rush of subscribers, the end-consumers did not feel that they received sufficient value to continue paying for the service;

- customers also did not want to pay for separate terminals when they already had expensive personal computers on their desks;

- other technologies such as the internet were beginning to provide a faster, more reliable service than the videotex service was capable of delivering.

By 1989 there were fewer than 100,000 terminals attached to Prestel, less than one-tenth of the peak customer numbers. In 1994 the service was relaunched as New Prestel with 30,000 customers. In France, the fact that France Telecom had provided the Minitel terminals free of charge to their customers helped to sustain the market. Even now, the installed base of Minitel is formidable. For example, France's largest mail-order company, La Redoute, receives 20 per cent of its orders via Minitel.[32]

Digital radio

Digital radio brings listeners CD-quality sound, more channels, and interactivity via small screen displays. However, it does not have the same obvious benefits associated with digital television. By the year 2000, only a handful of radio stations were granted digital licences by the UK's Radio Authority. Most commentators believe that it will take 10 to 15 years before digital radio overtakes analogue.

Digital teletext

In the future, digital teletext will offer a faster, more comprehensive service than its analogue rival. In time, the graphics and 'look and feel' of digital teletext will also change, and may eventually look similar in format to the internet. The advantages of digital teletext claimed by Teletext Limited (www.digital-teletext.co.uk), the operator of the UK teletext service on ITV and Channel 4 are:

- *Greater interactivity* – viewers will be able to interact with the service rather than being limited to the narrow range of information broadcast to them by ordinary teletext. More information will be available on sport, weather, travel, education, entertainment, polls, games, listings, community news, leisure and activities.

- *Greater viewer control* – user-friendly navigation that is more intuitive to use than the existing analogue service.

- *Enhanced graphics and animation* – including photographs, video clips and much higher resolution, which cannot be supported by traditional teletext.

Sales promotions

Trends in sales promotions

Since the 1970s, sales promotions have become an increasingly important element of the marketing mix. In the USA the ratio between advertising and promotion was 60:40 in 1977. By 1987 the ratio had been reversed.[33] Not all these promotions have been successful, as we discovered in Chapter 1 and as the case of Hoover in Exhibit 12.8 illustrates.

In the past, promotions served to jump-start sales and rarely involved the use of technology. Many campaigns were aimed at a broad audience with little differentiation made on the basis of a customer's past activity or behaviour. Customer databases were rarely used because they tended to be out-of-date or inaccurate. Using information technology, marketers can now address customer behaviour. Detailed transaction databases using information on previous purchase histories can be used to generate

> ### EXHIBIT 12.8
>
> **HOOVERING UP THE FREE FLIGHTS**
>
> One of the most spectacular corporate mistakes in recent years was the UK Hoover promotion in the autumn and winter of 1992–3. The net result of the promotion was a cost to the company of over £20 million plus an effect on reputation, which is difficult to evaluate. In contrast, the effect on the executives responsible was very measurable as most of them lost their jobs. The Hoover promotion ran in two stages. Stage one, during the early autumn of 1992, offered customers two free return air tickets to continental Europe if they purchased any Hoover product worth more than £100. Stage two, which began on 1 November, was an offer of two free flights to the USA if the customers purchased a Hoover product worth more than £250. Stage one of the promotion started off fairly well with satisfied customers and little general attention. It was only months after the promotion had ended that adverse comments started to appear.
>
> Stage two was almost instantly a news story. The Hoover promotion was not the first of its kind, several companies had run free flight promotions previously but without the attention and side effects Hoover was soon to experience. The Hoover promotion caught the imagination of people, especially when alert journalists realised that the company had not made any commitments as to how they would send the participants in the promotion over the Atlantic. Then, they started to fuel doubts as to how the details of the promotion were designed. The promotion was created so that prospective participants would be discouraged to go through the whole process. One such aspect was that there were six steps to be taken, five by post, within eight weeks to obtain the free tickets. The customers were expected to tire of the process and not bother to complete the offer. In the case of Hoover that did not happen. In addition, the company also misjudged the way the customers would respond to the offer. Normally one would expect a 5–10 per cent redemption rate; the Hoover promotion went significantly over that.
>
> The end result was that a large number of appliances were sold but the costs to the company proved to be enormous. The attention to detail that is necessary in a turbulent world was missed and safeguards to allow for the unpredictability of the consumers were not installed – actually the reverse, as apparently no tickets at all were purchased prior to the promotion.
>
> *Source*: Nilson (1995).[34]

offers aimed at changing customer behaviour. Promotions can be used either to retain existing customers or acquire new ones. Using the concept of customer lifecycle profitability, companies can use promotions that lose money in the short term but generate profitable relationships over the longer term.

Modern promotions are more effective because they relate directly to the customer's likes and lifestyle. Major opportunities exist in marketing to the customer who is about to make a purchase and is most susceptible to a marketing message. This can be called 'just-in-time marketing' and examples include point-of-purchase coupons tailored to the buying preferences of the customer. Indeed, as Peattie and Peattie (2003)[35] suggest: 'It is in sales promotions that many of the most exciting marriages of technology and creativity are occurring'. These writers cite the use of virtual-reality-based promotions and Hewlett-Packard's downloadable virtual pet (fish) which:

> can act as a screensaver . . . HP will provide 'tank' furniture including a plant, rock, bubble and a thermometer. These can only be downloaded in exchange for . . . points and the chief way of accumulating these is to use your HP printer to make 'multiple original printouts'. In exchange for 3,200 points you can acquire some aphrodisiac fish food . . . which makes . . . [the pet] so affectionate that it will plant a kiss on the inside of the monitor. This is a good example of the use of technology in getting extra custom out of people by offering additional benefits.

Loyalty programmes

Another aspect of sales promotions is the use of loyalty programmes to build stronger relationships with existing customers. Having recognised the importance of a core customer group that remains loyal to a brand, many organisations are implementing loyalty programmes to identify and reward these customers. Customer loyalty programmes are not new. For years, savers could collect Green Shield Stamps and motorists were able to collect Tiger Tokens every time they filled up their car with Esso petrol. A multitude of retailers have offered stamp-based schemes to entice consumers away from the competition and to turn them into loyal customers of their own. Information technology had a very small role in these early programmes, but is increasingly becoming a vital component in developing customer loyalty.

Loyalty, however, should go beyond regular purchasing, as we have already seen from Dick and Basu's (1994) loyalty model (*see* Figure 8.3 in Chapter 8). Some consumers are loyal because they make a deliberate choice of one brand over another and they repeat, over time, to choose this brand on this basis. The loyalty scheme not only has the potential to acquire customers but also to retain them – and if this potential is realised then they can be a significant extension of traditional sales promotion discounting approaches.[36] Thus in addition to consumers benefiting from cheaper shopping (in the sense of 'customer-specific pricing' rather than scatter-gun discounts) loyalty schemes can also provide the retailer with a great deal of information about individual customers. This information can be used in targeting with relevant tempting offers via direct marketing mechanisms, at point of sale or later in-home. Tesco, for example: 'shifted the emphasis of its £30 million advertising and marketing budget from above-the-line to direct marketing. The Tesco Clubcard was put at the forefront of the new marketing drive: using Clubcard data the supermarket was able to target its customers more carefully.[37,38]

When the Clubcard initiative was first introduced, it was regarded in the industry as an extremely innovative means of winning customer loyalty (or at least, repeat patronage). Most of the other large retailers in the UK have followed Tesco's lead by introducing loyalty schemes of their own. The reason for the investment in such loyalty schemes is the belief that it will make the customers much more loyal to the store, and reduce the need for multi-million-pound advertising and discount battles to gain or retain market share. Will it work? It seems to have done for Tesco. In 1996, for the first time ever, it moved ahead of Sainsbury with nearly 23 per cent of the £2.8 billion packaged grocery market in the UK, compared to Sainsbury's 19 per cent.[39] Will it continue to work? Inevitably, the competition will retaliate, but if it gives Tesco a lead for a couple of years until the next major marketing battle, Tesco will regard it as worth the investment.

Companies need to understand that the loyalty scheme itself is no substitute for a good product or a good brand.[40] They must also understand that a successful loyalty programme will not happen overnight. In addition, investments in analysing the data to develop marketing campaigns must be made to capitalise on information gathered from customers. Other initiatives such as self-scanning in supermarkets can be linked into loyalty schemes.[41]

Summary

The internet and e-commerce have made significant changes to the elements of the promotions mix. In the coming years the changes are likely to be far more significant, as the internet, digital television, customer databases and other information-rich promotional methods become more sophisticated. In this chapter we saw some of the key trends, such as the fragmentation of the market, that are affecting television advertising. We saw how direct response television offers a much more dynamic relationship with consumers. Technology is also impacting on other media such as radio, print and place-based advertising. The internet is growing as an advertising medium and is moving past its earlier focus on banner ads. Already marketing people are getting excited about the next generation of interactive digital media, which offers new opportunities to promote their products. Technology is also shaping the way in which promotions are being conducted, as evidenced by the continuing love affair that consumers have with supermarket loyalty schemes.

Case study

Freeview (and the state of digital broadcasting in the UK)

Figure 12.6

Source: Freeview website (www.freeview.co.uk, 2003), © Freeview 2003.

Digital TV in the UK

Even the inevitable, to paraphrase Karl Marx, sometimes needs a helping hand, and British television's notoriously dilatory digital revolution is about to receive yet another much-needed shove in the back. Freeview, the fresh start following the sour end of ITV Digital (previously known as OnDigital), is charged with the task of dragging the whole sorry process back on track. When ITV Digital collapsed in early 2002 owing creditors about £1.24 billion, 10 million households in the UK had already 'gone digital'. That's 40 per cent of the total number of households in the UK. Just three years after the launch of digital television, satellite had picked up nearly 2 million new customers (and converted a further 3.7 million existing analogue customers), cable had converted over 1.5 million, and digital terrestrial television (DTT) – in the form of ITV Digital – picked up almost 1.25 million from a standing start. Now, anyone with a decent roof-top aerial and the appropriate set-top box will have unlimited access to Freeview's 30 free channels. That, at any rate, is the idea, although the still-painful memory of the ITV Digital debacle does not suggest that its long-term success is either logically or materially guaranteed. ITV Digital had hoped to become profitable by the end of 2003. However, the savage downturn in the advertising industry during 2001 put paid to those plans.

ITV and ITV Digital

The downturn in the advertising industry was bad news for ITV, the UK's biggest commercial broadcaster. ITV is in serious decline, which in turn affects the whole of British broadcasting. Some 40 per cent of UK homes now receive multichannel television, mostly in digital format. By 2006, when the BBC charter is renewed, this figure could rise to as much as 80 per cent. ITV once gave advertisers a 50-per-cent share of UK audience; now, in multichannel homes, it has less than 30 per cent – and falling – of commercial audiences. By using the channels that can be received in the 10 million homes that have multichannel TV, such as Discovery, Paramount, UK Gold, Living and Sky One, as well as Channels 4 and 5, advertisers can now reach significant numbers of viewers without paying ITV prices. When ITV woke up to the threat of multichannel television, it made its own foray into platform wars. To compete with satellite and cable, it decided to build ITV Digital, which enables subscribers to receive a limited number of additional channels through a normal aerial without a cable connection or satellite dish.

The problem with ITV Digital was that it lacked the bandwidth of cable and satellite; in other words, it couldn't carry as many channels. This led to an interesting decision: the owners packed this limited service with channels that people didn't want, such as Carlton Food Network, which has so few viewers it doesn't even register an audience share. They didn't take, say, Discovery, a well-known niche TV brand that gets a 0.5-per-cent share in multichannel homes. In retail terms, this was like filling limited shelf space with brands you have never heard of. In contrast, Sky, backed by the might of News Corporation, has spent billions on building its satellite network, giving away boxes and buying major sports rights. Along with brilliant marketing, this has made it the UK's most successful multichannel pay-TV delivery system.

The Freeview proposition

According to the consortium behind Freeview (comprising the BBC, BSkyB and the transmitter company Crown Castle), all the right lessons have now been learned. Rather than mimic its predecessor's hubristic mix of first-rate promises and second-rate fare, Freeview intends to keep the key relatively low, the brow relatively high and the hyperbole firmly in check, and aims simply to please those for whom the phrase 'There's nothing on the telly' has long been a regular lament. Besides the five established terrestrial channels, the service is set to include, among other things, four rolling news channels; all eight of the BBC's current and forthcoming digital channels; one shopping, one lifestyle, two music and two travel channels; 11 public and commercial radio stations; and various interactive options and additions. The interactive offerings (digital text and enhanced TV) include additional video streams for sports events such as Wimbledon and Open Golf. Viewers using BBC Interactive (BBCi) could choose between two additional video streams during live *Fame Academy* broadcasts. Other highlights in autumn 2002 included *Great Britons* and *The Life Of Mammals*, both of which received the interactive treatment with a number of world firsts, taking audiences beyond the linear viewing experience to reach new heights in audience engagement.

The Freeview proposition is straightforward. Watching Freeview should cost nothing apart from the price of an adapter to enable your television to receive Freeview. That's £100. If a new rooftop aerial or extra connection leads are needed, that costs extra – say another £100. According to Freeview, a new aerial may be required because some aerials are old and damaged, and in some parts of the country Freeview signals use a different frequency or transmitter to the one normally used for your analogue reception. Once the bits and pieces are paid, the viewer receives over 30 digital channels and interactive services with no further payment. News channels, for example, are probably the best – or least-worst – introduction to the multichannel universe. Viewers resentful of the increasingly patronising and parochial bulletins on their five conventional channels will probably find much to admire on the likes of the slickly efficient *Sky News* and the steadily improving *BBC News 24*, and sports addicts will certainly come to value the immediacy of *Sky Sports News*. As for the art and entertainment on offer, it is limited but mainstream. Apart from appreciating the enhanced sound and picture quality of their old familiar channels, the Freeview audience will no doubt also discover some watchable discussions and documentaries on BBC4 and UK History, as well as the odd whimsical confection on the newly extended ITV2. Without, however, a channel dedicated either to sport or movies – those two great subscription service staples – there are bound to be some, and perhaps even a worryingly large minority, to whom the Freeview menu will seem unbearably plain and spare. Negotiations are still under way to fill a spare slot with output from Turner Classic Movies, but the lucrative Sky movie packages and pay-per-view offerings will remain well out of reach.

The BBC seems to be optimistic. At the launch of Freeview, Greg Dyke, the BBC Director General, said, 'Today is an important day in the development of British television with the launch of Freeview – a new digital platform which means that three out of four homes in Britain will now be able to receive digital television completely free. It's also a big step forward for the BBC, making all of the BBC's digital television, interactive and radio services available to many more people.'

The government position

The hope is that by dipping their toes in this way into the vast digital ocean, viewers will gradually acquire both the curiosity and the confidence to jump in fully and start to swim. It had better work, because this time, one way or another, will be the last time; there can be no more backward steps. The Government remains committed to its intention to turn off the analogue signal by 2010 (when, according to its estimates, 95 per cent of Britain's households should have been converted to the new system), and yet recent surveys suggest that as much as a third of the nation remains stubbornly uninterested in the prospect of switching over to digital: something, very soon, will have to give. Chris Smith MP believes that the demise of ITV Digital has forced the government to put some thought into what public policy issues arise about the wider future of digital television. He believes that two fundamental aims should remain firmly in place.

First, we must continue to press for a wholesale transition from analogue to digital in due course. Already, some 40 per cent of households have made that change, far ahead of anywhere else in the world. The objective of achieving switchover – with all the advantages for viewers in terms of choice and quality, coupled with the potential economic advantages of being first movers – is still an eminently desirable one, even if it may now become more difficult to achieve. Second, we must secure a genuine choice for consumers between different digital platforms. The now-fragile nature of terrestrial subscription television, coupled with the huge problems of cable, could potentially threaten this objective. It may of course yet happen that financial deals are re-arranged and ITV Digital itself survives. But we need to prepare for the eventuality that it doesn't. And the overriding public interest in such circumstances, surely, must be to secure the survival of the digital terrestrial platform itself.

Smith suggests that three steps are needed in order to do so:

- The first is something the government could and should be doing anyway: turning up the power on the digital signal that's being transmitted. One of the problems that has dogged digital terrestrial television has been the limited proportion of the population that is able to receive it through their aerials. Improving the signal means that more people can be reached.

- The second is a joint task for government, broadcasters, retailers, and manufacturers. There must be a clear and simple 'explanation campaign' to lead the public through the confusing maze that is digital television. There is a need to demystify digital for ordinary consumers, who are interested at heart in programmes, not in platforms or technologies. Making sure that they have clear information about the choices that are available to them ought surely to have a high priority.

- The third step will become essential if the administrators are ultimately unsuccessful. If the main subscription option for digital terrestrial disappears, it will be necessary to ensure that the platform can still be attractively offered to consumers as a largely free-to-view environment. The BBC, ITV, Channel 4 and Channel 5 must get together to prepare precisely such an offering. We know that preliminary talks have already taken place, but they must now assume a greater urgency, and they must involve all the public service broadcasters, not just the BBC. If a 'cheap and cheerful' set-top box can be made available, providing a plug-in-and-play option at a reasonable one-off cost to viewers, it will provide a real terrestrial alternative to the satellite or cable platforms that are, by their nature, either expensive or only available in limited places. It would be even better if the box allowed the possibility that in future it could carry a small number of subscription services as an upgrade to the free-to-view content.

    I have believed for some time that there is only a certain portion of the population who want to have a choice of 200 or 300 channels, albeit focused on sport, movies and cartoons. There are many more who want a little bit more than the current free analogue range of five channels, but are still only interested in a modest selection, at no cost or modest cost. Perhaps if ITV Digital had aimed at those viewers from the start, history might have been different. With hindsight, we can see that trying to compete head to head with Sky was always in danger of ending in tears.

Will it succeed?

Freeview is certainly the industry's best bet yet to win over the sceptics. Armed with a significant marketing campaign, and boosted by the BBC's on-screen support, the service is unlikely to frighten away many of the most tradition-bound viewers, and may well intrigue more than a few. The most obvious of its attractions is the fact that it is so cheap. There is also something reassuringly tame about this exotic little addition to the techno-timid home. Freeview is digital television dressed up ready for a visit from the vicar: no smut or soft porn, no outrageous wastes of space, just solid, reasonably sober and fairly sensible stuff. However, for the digital revolution to truly succeed, people will need to be impressed by what is on show at the front of their set, not merely by what happens to be stuck in its back. As Chris Smith concludes: 'Fashioning, now, a different product, aimed at a different potential audience, may yet be possible. When all is said and done, ITV Digital has – at huge cost to its owners – kept digital terrestrial television alive. It may now need to be in a different form, but we must ensure it continues to live.'

Sources: *Financial Times* (23 October 2002);[42] *Financial Times* (2 April 2002);[43] *Financial Times* (4 September 2001);[44] Freeview website (www.freeview.co.uk, 2003).

Case study questions

1 What is the difference between multichannel television and digital television, and why does it matter to advertisers?

2 What impact will the move to a digital broadcasting environment have on marketing?

3 Why does the government care about the future of digital broadcasting?

4 Compare the approach of ITV Digital to that of Sky. Why was Sky more successful?

5 In your opinion do you think Freeview can succeed?

Questions and exercises

Questions

1 Why are television audiences becoming more fragmented?

2 Outline some of the key developments in television advertising over the last 20 years.

3 Outline three reasons why marketing managers should be interested in direct response television.

4 Why does radio advertising continue to be so important?

5 Why has direct mail continued to grow?

6 'The internet has had mixed results as an advertising medium.' Discuss.

7 Why is interactive media such an exciting area in marketing?

Online exercises

1   You are a financial journalist and have just been asked to write 200 words on the challenges facing Nokia. Use the company's website (www.nokia.com) and other sources on the web to write your short article.

2   Surf the web on a topic of your choice. Record the details from the first 20 screens that you access. How many banner ads and how many other advertising messages did you encounter? Comment on how effective they were.

References

1   *European Marketing Pocket Book 1998 Edition* (1997). Henley-on Thames: NTC Publications Ltd.

2   Barwise, P. and Styler, A. (2002). *Marketing Expenditure Trends*, London: London Business School/Havas and Kuelos Research.

3   *The Economist* (1998). 'Infinite variety', 21 November.

4   Mellor, P. (1996). 'P&G slashes advertising to cut price', *Sunday Times*, 18 February.

5   DMA (1996). *Census of the Direct Marketing Association*.

6   Fletcher, K. (1996). 'Vera goes a-wooing', *Marketing Direct*, December.

7   Blackford, A. (1997). 'Never mind the quality', *Marketing Direct*, April.

8   Darby, I. (1996). 'Calling for attention', *Marketing Direct*, September.

9   Baird, R. (1998). 'Next 25 years for commercial radio', *Marketing Week*, 8 October.

10 Littlewood, F. (1998). '25 years of commercial radio', *Marketing Week*, 8 October.

11 Douglas, T. (1998). 'Digital TV has radio to thank for the multichannel revolution', *Marketing Week*, 8 October.

12 Book, A.C. and Cary N.D. (1978). *The Radio and Television Commercial*, Chicago: Crain Books.

13 Roberts, M.L. and P.D. Berger (1989). *Direct Marketing Management*, Englewood Cliffs, NJ: Prentice Hall, p. 342.

14 Nash, E.L. (1982). *Direct Marketing: Strategy, Planning, Execution*, New York: McGraw-Hill.

15 Block, L.G. and Morwitz, V.G. (1999). 'Shopping lists as an external memory aid for grocery shopping: influences on list writing and list fulfilment', *Journal of Consumer Psychology*, Vol. 8, No. 4.

16 Inman, J. and Winer, R. (1999). 'Where the rubber meets the road: a model of in-store consumer decision making', *Marketing Science Institute*, Working Paper 98.

17 Nijs, V.R., Dekimpe, M.G., Steenkamp, J.E.M. and Hanssens, D.M. (2000), 'The category demand effects of price promotions', *Marketing Science*, Vol. 20.

18 Brill, L. (2002). 'LED billboards: outdoor advertising in the video age', www.signindustry.com/led/articles/2002-07-30-LBledBillboards.php3, 30 July.

19 Barwise and Styler, *Marketing Expenditure Trends*.

20 DMIS (1994). *Direct Mail Information Services (DMIS) Report*, London.

21 Evans, M., O'Malley, L. and Patterson, M. (1994). 'Direct marketing: rise and rise or rise and fall?', *Marketing Intelligence and Planning*, Vol. 3, No. 6.

22 Evans, M., O'Malley, L. and Patterson, M. (1996). 'Direct mail and consumer response: an empirical study of consumer experiences of direct mail', *Journal of Database Marketing*, Vol. 3, No. 3, pp. 250–62.

23 Milmo, D. (2003). 'Top 10 advertisers on the net', *The Guardian*, 14 March.

24 Waters, R. (2003). 'Lure of ad dollars drives web search deals', *Financial Times*, 11 March.

25 Waters, R. (2003). 'Search industry scours scrap heap for bargains', *Financial Times*, 12 March.

26 Waters, R. (2003). 'Putting Yahoo back in the picture', *Financial Times*, 17 February.

27 Phillips, S. (2003). 'Old economy stakes a claim on the web', *Financial Times*, 15 January.

28 Evans, M. and Fill, C. (2000). 'Extending the communications process: the significance of personal influencers in the UK motor market', *International Journal of Advertising*, Vol. 19, No. 2.

29 Kingdom, J.W. (1970). 'Opinion leaders in the electorate', *Public Opinion Quarterly*, Vol. 34.

30 *Irish Times*. (2003). Oh brother, where art thou: Franciscans recruit online, 11 April.

31 Bajon, J. and Fontaine, G. (2001). *Development of Digital Television in the European Union*, Institut de l'audiovisuel at des telecommunication en Europe (IDATE), June.

32 Salz-Trautman, P. (1996). 'French prove resistant to change', *Digital Media*, Issue 1.

33 Nilson, H.T. (1995). *Chaos Marketing: How to Win in a Turbulent World*, Berkshire: McGraw Hill.

34 Nilson, *Chaos Marketing*.

35 Peattie, K. and Peattie, S. (2003). 'Sales promotion', in Baker M. (ed.) *The Marketing Book*, Oxford: Butterworth-Heinemann.

36 Uncles, M. (1994). 'Do you or your customers need a loyalty scheme?' *Journal of Targeting, Measurement and Analysis for Marketing*, Vol. 2, No. 4.

37 Lee, J. (1995). 'Tesco switches spend to direct', *Marketing*, 2 November.

38 Johnson, B. (1995). 'Supermarkets cut back on Christmas presence', *Marketing*, 17 November.

39 Moore, L. (1996). 'City loses its taste for Sainsbury's', *Sunday Business*, 5 May.

40 Stead, J. (1996). 'Loyalty is back in fashion – at any price', *Sunday Business*, 7 July.

41 *Computing* (1996). 'Supermarket chain adopts self-scanning', 2 May.

42 McCann, G. (2002). 'Digital oasis could be just a mirage', *Financial Times*, 23 October.

43 Smith, C. (2002). 'Platform alteration: whatever happens to ITV Digital, it is essential to secure the survival of digital terrestrial television', *Financial Times*, 2 April.

44 Singer, A. (2001). 'ITV leader criticises BBC', *Financial Times*, 4 September.

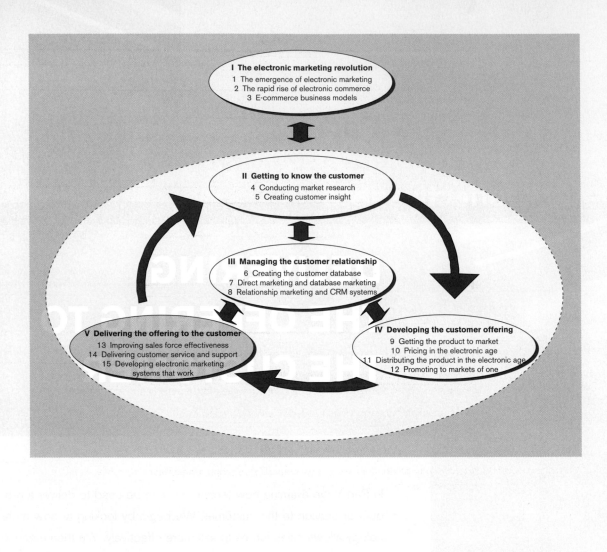

13

Improving sales force effectiveness

Learning objectives

Once you have read this chapter you will:

- understand how selling and the sales force have changed in recent years;

- appreciate that improved sales productivity has been a primary driver of early sales systems, and be able to describe the three generations of sales force automation software;

- be able to explain how the wireless revolution is affecting the way sales forces are now being supported by technology;

- understand the importance of the human side of sales force automation;

- appreciate why some sales force automation programmes have failed and how such programmes can be implemented successfully.

Contents

EMERGING TECHNOLOGY IN THE SALES FUNCTION

- The 'wireless revolution'
- The adoption of wireless sales technology
- Hosting sales force software on the web

THE HUMAN SIDE OF SALES FORCE AUTOMATION

- The importance of creating 'sales infusion'
- Addressing the human factors

IMPLEMENTING SALES FORCE SYSTEMS SUCCESSFULLY

- Why sales force automation projects fail
- Achieving benefits from sales force automation programmes
- Re-engineering sales processes
- Incorporating customer relationship management (CRM) principles

SUMMARY

CASE STUDY

Introduction

In Part IV of this book we saw that the internet and other forms of technology have pervaded many functions of the organisation, the sales force has been largely untouched. This is not to say that no attempts have been made to automate the sales function. Some companies have had success, but many attempts have proved less than successful. To understand why this is so, and what actions can be taken to improve the success rate, we begin this chapter with a perspective on how the sales force has changed in recent years and a review of the different attempts that have been made to improve the productivity of the sales force using technology. We also look at some of the emerging trends in sales force automation (SFA). Much of the chapter is then devoted to an analysis of the human side of the sales force automation – an area that is often ignored, generally at great expense in the form of failed SFA implementations. The final section brings together a number of themes, including the human factors, to examine how marketing and sales executives can improve the success rate of sales force automation programmes.

Selling in the twenty-first century

The changing nature of the sales function

Because selling has sometimes been seen as an art form, it has been more resistant to change than other functions. We have seen decades of application of IT and technology to functions such as manufacturing but it is only since the 1990s that we have seen any significant changes in the sales function. Personal selling is becoming more sophisticated with sales people requiring consulting and advisory skills in addition to their traditional sales skills. This is particularly true in industrial, or business-to-business, marketing. While companies of fast-moving consumer goods (FMCG) rely heavily on promotions and advertising to market their products, industrial goods such as raw materials, major equipment, component parts and industrial services are marketed in a different fashion. In these business-to-business situations, personal selling, using a direct sales force, is more effective than advertising and receives a correspondingly higher share of the overall marketing budget (*see* Figure 13.1).

One of the greatest changes in the sales function has been the move from a product focus to a customer or account focus, with the resulting changes in the mindset of the sales manager and salespeople. Companies like IBM traditionally organised their sales forces around their products such as PCs, mainframes and servers. IBM now has a customer account manager for key customers: the sales of all IBM products are to coordinated the customer through the account manager. There is now a much greater focus on understanding the likely buying patterns of individual customer accounts at a local level and aggregating them into an overall sales plan. With a focus on individual accounts, many companies are now spending more time trying to increase the profitability of specific accounts. This has become feasible through the use of IT, which

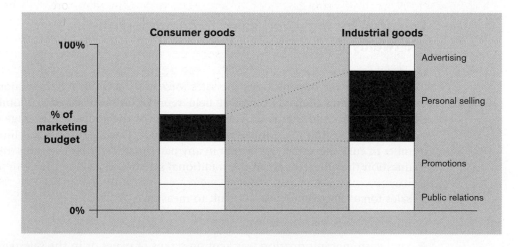

Figure 13.1 Importance of personal selling in industrial marketing

Table 13.1 The changing focus of the sales function

From: Product Focus (1990s)	To: Customer or account focus (2000s)
Product focus	Customer focus
Product marketing	Regional brand marketing
National promotional plan	Local account strategy
Volume focus	Profitability focus
'Sell to' philosophy (push)	'Sell through' philosophy (pull)
Relationship selling	Relationship and information-based selling
Single-brand focus	Category focus
Uniform sales force	Team selling:
	• account
	• category market specialists
	• merchandising

enables sales departments to track sales and profitability at an individual customer or account level.

Salespeople have always relied on relationships with their customers, but companies are now moving more towards a team approach to selling where the depth and breadth of that relationship is increased and the chances of follow-on or repeat sales are enhanced. Team selling requires greater coordination and relies heavily on good quality information being shared between different members of the sales team.

Table 13.1 provides a summary of the major changes that have taken place in the sales function in the past decade.

The drive for improved sales force productivity in the twenty-first century

In many industrial organisations the sales force costs account for the majority of the overall marketing budget. A typical field representative has a car, mobile phone, expense account and bonus scheme: by the end of the 1990s the average industrial sales call was costing US companies around $200.[1] However, there are limits to the number of customers that can be met in any particular day. Many organisations began to question the effectiveness of the traditional sales force, feeling that:

■ sales force effectiveness was difficult to measure;

■ business leads were being lost;

■ vital customer information was kept on scraps of paper or in the salesperson's head;

■ if a salesperson left the company, important customer information also left;

■ salespeople were always busy, but sales results were often mediocre.

As sales migrated to the internet and other direct channels throughout the late 1990s, the impact on the traditional sales force was dramatic. According to one US survey, the average US sales force was 26 per cent smaller at the end of 1998 than it was two years previously.[2] As pressure on the traditional sales force increased, many organisations invested in automating and modernising to improve productivity. For example, US insurance companies such as Progressive and State Farm each issued more than a thousand PCs to their employees to improve sales productivity and cut costs.[3] Companies like Progressive, State Farm and Prudential made these investments in sales force automation because they believed that the benefits of such projects would significantly outweigh the costs. Exhibit 13.1 shows the benefits that can be achieved from a successful sales force automation implementation.

EXHIBIT 13.1

THE BENEFITS OF SELLING TABASCO

G Costa & Co, importers of speciality brands including Tabasco, French's Mustard and Blue Dragon, has begun to quantify productivity improvements since implementing the m:Sales sales force automation application from ITM. The company supplies major retailers, independent stores, delis, cash and carry outlets, caterers and wholesalers with a range of speciality foods. 'The system has proved so easy to use that m:Sales was rolled out to the sales team without taking them off the road and in record time,' explains Robert Gruszka, the company's field sales manager. An initial review has identified a series of improvements:

- a dramatic reduction in time spent by sales reps entering and downloading orders each evening;

- a reduction in data entry errors;

- increased sales through better visibility of customer, product and stock information;

- the elimination of the burden on customer services staff to keep sales reps informed of order progress and other customer issues;

- improved credit control as the sales reps are more aware of customers' current credit status.

Gruszka is looking for a financial return: 'I am anticipating revenue growth through a direct increase in sales and faster product replenishment. However, I am also expecting an improvement in the individual performance of field sales staff. I believe that G Costa now has one of the best equipped sales forces in the FMCG sector.'

Source: ITM Group website (www.itm-group.co.uk, 2003).[4]

The benefits and issues of sharing sales data

Sales forces need to be able to share important information about their customers. This may seem obvious but does not always happen. For example, too much competitiveness in the sales force can lead to the 'hoarding' of important information on customers by some salespeople. Entering customer information on one database can provide more transparency on customer data (as long as others can access the relevant data).

One of the cornerstones of integrated marketing communications is for data to be available to all who might have contact with (potential) customers. The information can include 'tacit data,'[5] which is less tangible and can be more 'affectively' based on items such as:

- expertise
- 'gut feel'
- subjective insights
- intuition.

For example, tacit data includes the reaction of an individual customer during a telephone contact. This can be captured: contemporary databases allow 'fields' to capture such data. The data can then be shared across all those members of the organisation who might be in contact with the customer concerned. However, the data needs to be used with care. Perhaps experience suggests that our customer is a bit grumpy on Monday mornings. There have been examples of (surely innocent) errors occurring such as the sending of mail shots that include the tacit data field (Dear Mr Jones <pain in the neck!>). Such negligent abuse of databased knowledge is not frequent but is clearly unacceptable. It is also an example of how electronic communications vehicles can enhance or destroy relationships between salespeople and customers.

Improving sales force effectiveness

Automating the sales force

While sales representatives traditionally operated with limited technology support, in recent times technology has been used to improve productivity. The technology to improve the productivity of the sales force, typically using laptop computers, is often referred to as sales force automation (SFA). Technology can increase the overall professionalism of salespeople as they work through the sales cycle with potential customers. Some of the benefits provided by this type of laptop software applications include:

- freeing salespeople from routine office administrative tasks, enabling them to spend more time with customers;

- providing better customer service because the salesperson has immediate access to information such as stock levels or quotations;

- capturing information that allows management to measure and monitor sales performance;

- helping to create and manage sales opportunities so that a greater proportion is converted into sales.

The important caveat here is that sales force productivity issues cannot be solved completely by technology. Selecting salespeople with the right skills, training them and motivating them with good incentives are also critical to sales force productivity.

Three generations of sales force automation (SFA) software

According to the Yankee Group (www.yankeegroup.com), the current technology is actually the third generation of sales force automation software to be released on to the market. The progression is:

- *Generation 1* Personal information and contact management.

- *Generation 2* The networked sales force.

- *Generation 3* Technology-enabled selling.[6]

Generation 1 Personal information and contact management

The first generation involved equipping the sales force with laptops and other types of computing and data storage devices. At first, these machines contained the typical office productivity applications such as spreadsheets and word processors. Before long, salespeople clearly saw the value of personal information managers (PIMs) and over time these applications became tied into other personal productivity applications on the PC. Products such as ACT!, Goldmine and Maximizer were designed to help a salesperson manage contacts and time, and increase their selling effectiveness. Powerful time and contact management tools that had not existed previously were quickly developed and implemented.

Generation 2 The networked sales force

As managers realised that this technology was helpful to their field sales representatives, they began to wonder how they might also harness this information for corporate purposes. The second generation SFA tools were essentially networked versions of the first, connecting the contacts database and personal productivity tools of the sales force to the corporate network. This was usually accomplished via data replication, by plugging the laptop into a phone line, typically at night. While sales representatives retained their interest in time and contact management, these tools offered them little if any additional advantage over the first generation, although some were much smaller, portable and lighter than their predecessors.

Generation 3 Technology-enabled selling

Technology-enabled selling is the name give by the Yankee Group to the latest generation of SFA tools. Technology-enabled sales systems incorporate a much richer variety of functions to help sales people acquire and close more business, including some combination of the following:

- *Lead management* – the ability for sales to receive leads from marketing and other departments.

- *Opportunity management* – organises all information around a sales opportunity to give a complete view of the sales cycle, coordinate schedules and resources, and bring the sales process to closure.

- *Account management* – the ability to track successfully closed opportunities. This can also track business contacts through companies, subsidiaries, branch offices, departments, etc., with multiple addresses and contacts.

- *Proposal management* – the ability of the sales force to produce on-the-spot, customised, accurate product configurations and proposals. This is critically important for complex product and service sales opportunities.

- *Win/loss reporting* – the ability to evaluate wins, losses, and return on investment objectively. It allows people and companies to learn and improve their sales and customer support processes.

EXHIBIT 13.2

TECHNOLOGY TO SUPPORT SEED SALES

Headquartered in Basel in Switzerland, Syngenta is a world leader in agribusiness. Syngenta Seeds is one of its two main divisions, employing approximately 5,000 people. While the seeds division uses advanced technology to help customers select and purchase the most appropriate seeds, until recently the sales force employed less advanced technology. When it came time for a sales representative to place an order, the transaction was decidedly low-tech and labour-intensive.

'The sales reps would call a customer service person who would write the order down and then enter the order into the system. It was all a manual process,' says Tom Garite of Syngenta. In addition to their need for a more automated sales process, they needed a way to ensure a reliable and frequent update of the information to their representatives in the field.

Syngenta turned to a company called XcelleNet to automate its sales force. Sales people in the field using mobile devices now have the latest product and pricing information downloaded to them. The XcelleNet solution allows the system administrators in the home office to push pricing information so that the mobile sales representatives in the field and the office-based customer service representatives can receive the most accurate and up-to-date pricing information at the same time.

Source: XcelleNet website (www.xcellenet.com, 2002).[7]

Table 13.2 US sales force automation (SFA) software packages

SFA solutions aimed at large enterprises	SFA solutions aimed at small and medium enterprises
Amdocs/Clarify (**www.amdocs.com**)	Pivotal (**www.pivotal.com**)
E.piphany (**www.epiphany.com**)	Onyx Software (**www.onyx.com**)
Firepond (**www.firepond.com**)	Interact Commerce (**www.saleslogix.com**)
J.D. Edwards (**www.jdedwards.com**)	
Oracle (**www.oracle.com**)	
PeopleSoft (**www.peoplesoft.com**)	
SAP (**www.sap.com**)	
Siebel Systems (**www.siebel.com**)	

Source: Gartner (2002).[8]

Many organisations still operate first-generation systems. Other companies like Syngenta (*see* Exhibit 13.2) are leapfrogging directly to the third generation of SFA technology.

There are literally hundreds of different software solutions aimed at the sales force automation market. Some well-known US packages are shown in Table 13.2.

Using technology to optimise sales territories

Another area of opportunity is the allocation of sales territories to particular sales-people. This can be an inefficient manual process that can be automated using statist-ical techniques to optimise the ratio of time spent with clients to time spent on the road. Zoltners and Lorimer (2000)[9] believe that many sales forces are losing millions of dollars each year because of sales territory imbalances. They cite a study of 4,800 sales territories from 18 companies in four different industries where more than half of the territories were imbalanced because they were either too large or too small. They also note that there are significant obstacles that prevent companies from optimising their sales territories:

- sales forces may resist change;
- sales force incentives and compensation plans can work against achieving the best alignment;
- realignment is a cumbersome task;
- data that is required for alignment is often not readily available.

These are the internal difficulties associated with any changes to existing sales terri-tories. The realignment or optimisation of sales territories can also be problematic and

EXHIBIT 13.4

CUTTING THE WIRES TO THE WORKPLACE IN SWEDEN

Once, the mobile workforce was made up of a small elite of 'road warriors'. These frequent travellers only needed occasional access to the corporate network, and so their needs could be met with laptop computers and dial-in modem connections. Nowadays, companies are trying to wean their mobile professionals off expensive notebook computers and on to PDAs and smartphones, for reasons of cost.

The high cost of laptops was one of the reasons why SAS, the Scandinavian airline, recently started a project to provide its staff with wireless connections and handheld Pocket PC devices. 'We wanted to get rid of our laptops as they are the most expensive device in the company', says Arvid Elias, senior IT consultant at the airline. But the initiative also has a broader aim. SAS has 25,000 employees and many use their desktop computers for a few basic functions, such as reading e-mail or updating their calendar. SAS wanted employees to use the Pocket PC for these common functions instead of their desktop PCs.

Like many large organisations, SAS already had some employees using their own handheld computers. But these users had to master complicated rules to keep the data synchronised with that on their desktop PC. 'Before, everyone had to be their own technician', says Elias. Now, the process is more user-friendly, he claims. Synchronisation is done automatically via infrared synchronising stations located throughout SAS's premises. The Pocket PC is synchronised to the network, rather than a specific desktop PC, so users no longer feel so attached to their office PCs. The network also downloads the frequently changing schedules of SAS flights to each Pocket PC. Employees who are travelling can connect to the SAS network via a wireless connection that plugs into the Pocket PC and lets them send e-mails, synchronise information or surf the internet. SAS believes the benefits of a mobile workplace are worth the investment. 'Using the Pocket PC, our employees can keep doing business on the move', says Elias.

Source: Financial Times (16 October 2002).[12]

Table 13.3 Advantages and disadvantages of wireless sales applications

Advantages of wireless sales applications	Disadvantages of wireless sales applications
• Provides sales force with instant access to corporate information (as opposed to access to yesterday's or last week's information using a dial-up connection)	• Limited coverage in certain parts of the country
	• Poor data transfer rates
• Allows sales force to transmit sales data and sales orders immediately (as opposed to nightly dial-up)	• Increased expense for handheld devices
	• Higher technology support costs for mobile devices
• Allows time-sensitive messages to be delivered	• Potentially less secure than more traditional dial-up technologies
• Strengthens internal collaboration among teams	

EXHIBIT 13.5

HANDHOLDING THE ALCATEL SALES FORCE

As a leader in the high-speed access and transmission market, Alcatel Carrier Inter-networking Division (CID) is a major player in the area of telecommunications and the internet. The Alcatel CID e-business team needed a simple and cost-effective way to deliver consistent messages and tools directly into the hands of its sales people.

AvantGo makes it easier for employees with mobile devices to access information. 'It takes less than a second to turn on a handheld device', comments Neli Madeira, Alcatel CID e-business specialist. 'It takes three to five minutes to boot up a computer. Our busy salespeople prefer the former, especially if they are on their way to a meeting or in front of a customer. They also tell us that they use the handheld device when they just want to check on the latest news and have been very complimentary about the new online services.'

The Alcatel CID 'handheld portal' is available to employees throughout the world and new users are added every day. Using the portal, Alcatel CID gains the following benefits:

- *Real-time information*. With AvantGo and handheld devices, employees are able to access essential information via wireless or offline mode – on their handheld devices.

- *Cross-platform device support*. Employees have flexibility and choice when purchasing a handheld device – AvantGo supports both Microsoft Pocket PC and Palm Computing platform handheld devices, as well as internet-enabled handsets including WAP phones.

- *Rapid development and deployment*. The time from proof of concept to application deployment is less than two weeks.

- *No training required*. Alcatel CID does not have to spend time or money training end-users.

Source: AvantGo website (www.avantgo.com, 2003).

Hosting sales force software on the web

Another recent development is where companies buy licences to use sales force software that is hosted on the web. The business model can be compelling, since many smaller companies do not have the resources to host their own sales force applications. By using third party software, they avoid the need to develop and maintain their own software and sales systems. Their salespeople can gain access to the software using a standard internet browser and the data is then transferred to the company's database. One of the best examples of this is salesforce.com (www.salesforce.com), the subject of the case study at the end of this chapter.

The human side of sales force automation

The importance of creating 'sales infusion'

As we mentioned earlier in the chapter, technology is not the only driver of increased sales force productivity. Because it is a relatively new area, there is still little research devoted to investigating the impact of technology on individual salesperson effectiveness.[13] Ahearne and Schillewaert (2001)[14] point out the conundrum of making heavy investments in equipping the sales force with modern technology:

> Although the relationship between information technology and sales performance remains primarily unsubstantiated, many organisations spend considerable human and financial resources in equipping their sales force with information technology. Yet, organisations need justification for these substantial investments and cannot afford to continue to invest in sales technology as a matter of blind faith alone.

Ahearne and Schillewaert introduce the concept of 'sales infusion' – the ability to integrate different information technology tools into a salesperson's activities. They conclude that sales infusion can have a positive impact on sales performance. However, they also admit that the impact of technology alone is small and that there are other more important variables that explain the enhancement of a salesperson's performance. These variables include:

- targeting skills
- market knowledge
- technical/product knowledge
- sales presentation skills.

Technology and sales force automation tools can help the sales person in each of these areas but ultimately they are just enablers to support the salesperson's own skills. Companies like GE approach the problem with a strong measurement focus. They look to measure the amount of time that their salespeople spend with customers. They measure the effectiveness of technology by the amount of additional 'face time' it will give salespeople with customers. The key message is that experience, training and overall motivation of the salesperson are as, or more, important than the SFA tools that they use.

Addressing the human factors

As we see in the next section when we look at how to implement successful sales force systems, addressing the human factor is key. Rasmussen (1999)[15] suggests five steps for the successful implementation of technology-enabled selling, all of which relate to human factors:

■ *Know what you want to accomplish.* One way of establishing this is to ask the sales force questions such as: What part of the sales process can be improved? What information is not available now? What administrative tasks are the most time consuming? What ideas are our competitors using? What are we overlooking?

■ *Involve the sales force in vendor selection.* Software must be easy to use and have the minimum amount of administrative overhead if salespeople are to spend the maximum amount of time with customers. The performance and ease-of-use of the system must be such that salespeople will want to use it rather than being forced to use it. The best way to achieve this is to involve them in designing and selecting the system.

■ *Get executive buy-in.* Given the high rate of failure of SFA initiatives, it is important that the initiatives have the strongest sponsorship from within the organisation. These initiatives must be seen by all employees as critical to the organisation's future success.

■ *Take time to implement.* Rushing a sales force automation often results in poor user acceptance and ultimate failure. Software should be tested on a small pilot group initially, before the entire sales force is converted to the new system. The pilot group should consist of people with a positive attitude towards the new system, who will act as 'product champions' during its rollout.

■ *Train and support like crazy.* Not all salespeople are computer literate and some will be apprehensive about technology-based selling. After all, these people have carried out their duties for years (often decades) without any support other than pen and paper and, more recently, a mobile phone. A training programme must be designed that will cater for those salespeople who are already familiar with PCs, as well as those who are computer illiterate.

This comprehensive list can also be applied to other sales and marketing projects.

Implementing sales force systems successfully

Why sales force automation projects fail

Sales and marketing is littered with examples of failed implementations of sales force automation projects. Some commentators estimate that 50–60 per cent of such projects fail. In one study of 454 sales people across two firms (Speier and Venkatesh, 2002),[16] most of those surveyed had very positive perceptions about the sales force automation tools immediately after training. However, six months later, the technology had been widely rejected and salesperson absenteeism and voluntary turnover had increased significantly. There were also significant decreases in perceptions of organisational commitment and job satisfaction across both firms. Finally, salespeople with stronger professional commitment indicated more negative job-related perceptions as experience with the technology increased. In an interview in 2002, Roger Siboni, the CEO of E.piphany (a leading sales force automation software companies) had this to say about the failure of many implementations:

> The promise of sales-force automation is that by giving salespeople these tools, productivity will go up and the cost of sales will go down. The truth is, that hasn't really happened. Because if you really look at what sales-force automation has been so far, it's been about achieving contact management, sales-lead tracking and pipeline reporting. If you look at these three pieces of functionality, what you find is the technology is very hard to work with. Once you surpass 100 or so salespeople, it's very hard to synchronise data when the salesperson has to use it on the road. The disconnected use has been very, very spotty.[17]

Other commentators cite a variety of reasons for failed SFA implementations, including:

- salespeople are reluctant to share information unless they receive something in return – as a result, updates to the central database are infrequent;

- connecting to an SFA system on the road is often cumbersome: salespeople must boot up a laptop and find a dial-up line – as a result, road access is sporadic and limited to after-hours;

- SFA systems are designed primarily to meet the needs of sales managers and not field sales persons – sales managers expect better forecasting, yet salespeople desire real-time access to relevant customer information;

- most SFA systems do not help a sales professional react to customer events while on the road – many deliver irrelevant or unimportant alerts to the sales force.[18]

Achieving benefits from sales force automation programmes

While strong functionality is important, the introduction of technology-enabled sales systems is often part of a much wider transformation of the sales function. The two characteristics that distinguish successful projects (successful in the sense of achieving the claimed benefits) from the rest are:

- they are often accompanied by a radical re-engineering of processes, from pre-sales through to delivery (re-engineering involves the detailed analysis of existing processes and the redesign of these processes to improve efficiency);

- they are also accompanied by the introduction of customer relationship management (CRM) initiatives.

Exhibit 13.6 provides an example of how one company combined both approaches for its SFA implementation.

EXHIBIT 13.6

PAPER-BASED SALES REPS

New sales representatives for Toshiba America Medical Systems, the world's leading manufacturer of ultrasound equipment, used to have one option for learning about their territory: rooting through a cardboard box full of paper files. That was before director of sales support Tommy Stewart set about to find a better way to manage sales for the division of $6.4 billion Toshiba America. His efforts culminated in a rollout of Clarify's customer-relationship management products, including its ClearSales sales force automation tool. Today, to become familiar with a new territory, all a salesperson has to do is open a notebook computer to check the account's history and view current information.

Stewart believes that there's more to successful sales than simply installing a sales force automation tool. Companies must revamp sales processes as part of the SFA implementation process; otherwise, the tool merely automates inefficient processes. 'The tool was an enabler of process changes', says Stewart of his combined sales process redesign-SFA tool implementation. 'It was important that we did both at the same time.'

Source: Information Week (21 August 2000).[19]

Re-engineering sales processes

The business case for automating the sales force does not have to stop with the sales representative. The re-engineering of business processes and the use of CRM principles has helped companies like AlliedSignal Aerospace to improve sales significantly (*see* Exhibit 13.7).

Other processes can also, and usually must, be re-engineered, including:

- sales forecasting

- product administration

- customer support

- order control

- finance (accounting and settlement).

In particular, getting the sales forecasting process right is critical for manufacturing productivity and for maintaining customer service levels and preventing out-of-stocks.

Improving sales forecasting

Until the 1960s, senior level executives did most of the sales forecasting in US organisations simply by using their own executive judgement. These managers relied on past industry experience and knowledge to determine what they thought the company's sales

EXHIBIT 13.7

FLYING HIGH

AlliedSignal Aerospace had a problem. The engineering company (a Honeywell International division) had four business units with no way to share information about sales opportunities, the status of maintenance requests or the products customers had on their aircraft. Large customers sometimes had as many as 50 points of contact with the company. To stop antagonising customers, the company implemented Atlas, a sales force automation (SFA) tool from Siebel. But few salespeople wanted to use it, having seen two past SFA efforts fail and feeling loyal to their own databases. To handle resistance, Honeywell created the manager of CRM business processes position to work with each sales unit to fashion a new, single sales process tied into Atlas. Today, AlliedSignal has account teams to serve customers, rather than a dozen different sales-people in different businesses. In addition, response centre agents are empowered to resolve customers' issues.

The team overcame legacy loyalty by transferring data from existing databases into Atlas and then shutting down salespeople's old databases. The payoff: with the same number of salespeople, after-market revenues increased from $45 million to more than $100 million. Although some of that jump can be attributed to offering new, more expensive products, the after-markets special programmes group attributes 20 per cent of the growth to efficiencies brought about by Atlas.

Source: *CIO Magazine* (1 April 2002).[20]

could or should be (Mentzer and Bienstock, 1998).[21] Indeed, this executive judgement method was seen as appropriate and worked well in the stable post-war economy of the USA.[22]

As world markets have become more competitive and volatile, reliance on executive judgement or plain 'gut feeling' was seen as too simplistic. Yet this traditional form of sales forecasting is still very prevalent today, even if it has been supplemented in some organisations with more modern approaches. An investigation of the wholesale industry by Peterson and Minjoon (1999)[23] identified managerial judgement as the primary basis for sales forecasting in almost 100 per cent of the firms in this study.

The main application of technology to achieve improved sales forecasting comes from improving the 'visibility' of sales and stock through the entire supply chain. For example:

- *EDI and extranet links* between manufacturers and retailers allow all parties to see where the inventory is in the supply chain.

- *Electronic point-of-sale (EPOS)* systems provide instant feedback on how well different products and product lines are selling.

- *Mobile sales applications* allow direct sales forces to share sales orders and inventory information with their head offices.

Two primary benefits ensue from good sales forecasting capabilities:

■ *Higher sales*. If a company knows what sales are likely to be in any particular day, week or month, it can reduce or eliminate stock-out situations. Cuisine de France is an Irish-based company that delivers part-baked food products to retail outlets in the UK and Ireland. Its bread and confectionery products are baked in-store and must be sold within hours. If a store does not receive an accurate delivery every few days, products will be out of stock in the store and each stock-out is a lost sale that can never be recovered. Cuisine de France places a lot of emphasis on gaining accurate sales forecasts and orders from each of its retail customers in order to reduce stock-outs.

■ *Reduced costs*. One of the main drivers for improved sales forecasting is the desire to reduce costs in an organisation. The effect of accurate sales forecasts on inventory levels can be profound. Raw materials and component parts can be purchased much more cost-effectively when last-minute, spot-market purchases are avoided. Such expenses can be eliminated by accurately forecasting demand. Perhaps most important of all, accurate forecasting can have an impact on a company's inventory levels. In many firms, inventory exists to provide a buffer for inaccurate forecasts. Thus, the more accurate the forecasts, the less inventory that needs to be carried.[24]

The application of technology alone is not the answer. In one survey of nearly 500 US companies, Kahn and Mentzer (1997)[25] discovered that most companies used only personal computers and had very little access to mainframe systems where the really useful information to support accurate sales forecasting is often held. One answer is to create an integrated forecasting function, allowing both customers and suppliers into the process. Another is to combine the use of technology with managerial experience.

Incorporating customer relationship management (CRM) principles

We examined customer relationship management (CRM) in Chapter 8. Many of the major sales force automation vendors such as Siebel (www.siebel.com) and Clarify (www.clarify.com) market the CRM capabilities of their products. Others combine the CRM messages with a more commercial message about improving sales force productivity. For example, Vantive, a sales force automation product from PeopleSoft (www.peoplesoft.com), claims that:

Vantive supports the entire sales and marketing process, giving you tools that not only make your sales reps more efficient but actually help them sell more effectively. Vantive's unique approach delivers full functionality in all areas that are critical to your sales organisation:

■ makes your sales reps more effective with tools to improve win rates, increase deal sizes, shorten sales cycles, and increase margins;

■ gives your sales reps more time to sell with tools for reducing administrative tasks, decreasing preparation time, using down-time effectively, and condensing training;

■ increases sales management precision with tools for accurate forecasting, territory and rep reporting, cost control and planning.

The software alone will not achieve this. Implicit in Vantive's claims is the need to restructure sales and marketing organisations to gain full benefits of the software tools. More important is the need to carry out such restructuring using customer relationship management principles so that the customer is guaranteed the same experience and

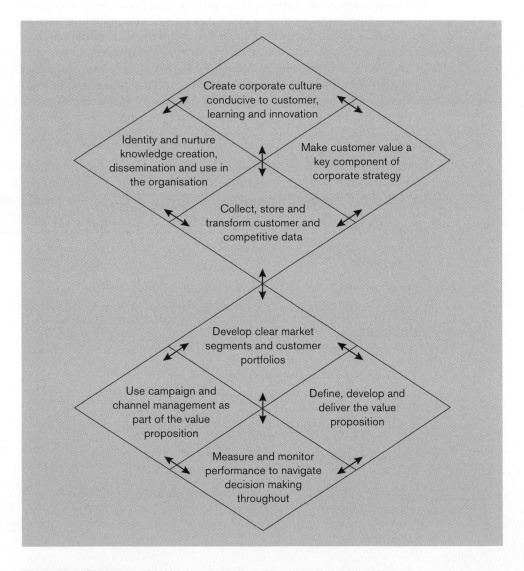

Figure 13.2 CRM elements
Source: Plakoyiannaki and Tzokas (2002).[26]

quality of response, regardless of the channel through which contact with the company is made.

As Plakoyiannaki and Tzokas (2002)[27] declare, a key problem with CRM programmes is the relatively narrow focus, especially on software. They propose a more holistic approach that is more market-orientated and leads to much greater integration of wider issues, as summarised in Figure 13.2.

The point addressed by Figure 13.2 is that the selling function needs to be integrated with other CRM elements and across functions – and perhaps even with partners in the supply chain. An example of this last point is category management. Here, the old scenario of a salesperson 'selling in' a specific brand to a retailer is increasingly being replaced by a more inclusive approach. Instead, retailers and suppliers are collaborating to a much greater extent and salespeople are helping with in-store merchandising across brands within a product category with a view to growing that category. The entire product category – for example washing powder – might be jointly developed by the manufacturer and retailer. Rather than salespeople trying to sell their brand into a retail operation, there is an alliance that tries to grow the entire product category.[28]

The same principle can be applied to data sharing, which we have discussed elsewhere. For example the communications company TANK! (www.tankgroup.com) provides its financial services partners with pooled data from sales and other campaigns to evaluate response rates to different sorts of direct and interactive campaigns.

Summary

During the 1990s the global economy went through a very strong growth cycle, with significant investments being made in technology. Strangely, the sales force was one of the areas of the corporation given the least investment in technology. In companies where technology was employed to improve the effectiveness of the sales force, the results were patchy. This was due partly to the immaturity of the earlier generations of sales force automation (SFA) software that were deployed. In many cases, it was also because the human side of SFA implementations were ignored and there was insufficient buy-in from the sales force. Thus salespeople had new sales tools foisted upon them without the required training to use them properly. With the benefit of better designed software systems (some of it deployed through handheld devices), an improved partnership approach with the users, and the incorporation of CRM and re-engineering principles, today's salespeople are likely to adapt more readily to the latest generation of sales force automation tools. The following case study shows how relatively small organisations can deploy professional sales technology in a cost-effective and efficient manner.

Case study

Products of Technology Limited (PTL) and salesforce.com

Figure 13.3

From an idyllic setting in Killearn in the heart of Scotland, Graham Sinclair effectively manages a global business using new internet technology. From his office Sinclair can look across the Blane Valley and view the water rolling from Dumgoyne Hill, which feeds into the local Glengoyne Distillery. Graham Sinclair is managing director of Products of Technology Ltd (ptl). The company provides gas generators of all sizes, and exports to Sweden, Finland, Denmark, Germany, France, Spain, Ireland, India and the USA, as well as the rest of the UK. Founded in 1998, ptl's product range contains nitrogen, hydrogen, oxygen and zero air generators, along with a new range of dryers and extractors. Oil-free compressors, piping and a variety of services, which provide customers with a complete gas generating solution, complement this extensive product portfolio. The company has a wide range of industry sectors and customers to track, since applications range from food processing and cosmetics to pharmaceuticals and semi-conductors. This is very much an enterprise of the new business age. Manufacturing of the generators is outsourced to subcontractors in Dundee, Scotland and Milton Keynes, England.

The sales challenge

The sales function is organised through a rapidly expanding network of currently 12 global distributors. Using this business model, Sinclair manages a team of 12 people, four of whom are involved in managing the international sales distribution channel. He describes how ptl has grown rapidly since it was formed in 1998: 'As we grew globally we realised we needed some form of customer relationship and sales management system', says Sinclair. 'We had nothing. Literally, sales contacts might be written on the back of a cigarette packet and placed in a filing cabinet somewhere'.

The solution

Graham Sinclair evaluated a number of sales force automation systems before he was introduced to salesforce.com. As easy to use as a website, salesforce.com provides all the power of enterprise-class customer relationship management software for £45 per user per month. By offering the application as an internet service, salesforce.com eliminates the need to buy, install or maintain hardware, software or networks and can be implemented at a significantly lower cost than traditional enterprise software. 'I'm a great believer in making full use of the internet rather than storing information on expensive-to-maintain servers in-house', says Sinclair. Also used by ptl is the 'Case' element of the salesforce.com service. This is a feature that records frequent customer questions and solutions, which are stored on the salesforce.com server, thereby boosting customer service.

Sinclair spends a lot of time travelling, visiting customers, distributors and potential distributors. 'The beauty of salesforce.com is that I can log on from anywhere in the world and get the same information as if I'm sitting back in my office in Killearn.' Senior managers in ptl who are responsible for new business sales are themselves dispersed. The sales manager is located in Newton Mare, two hours away from Killearn, while the business development manager is based in Dalgety Bay, Fife on the other side of Scotland. 'Distance is no barrier to business when you use salesforce.com', says Sinclair. 'We all have access to the same customer information in real time and it doesn't matter whether we are in Scotland or North America.'

When searching for a CRM system, Sinclair was anxious to find something that the sales team would find easy to use. 'Salespeople as a rule tend not to be systems people. They have taken very easily to salesforce.com. It is now their daily work platform for e-mail, contacts and leads. We could not have grown so rapidly without salesforce.com,' says Sinclair.

The results

Salesforce.com is now integrated with ptl's distribution channel. 'Distributors' eyes light up when I demonstrate the salesforce.com service', says Sinclair. 'It has actually helped us attract new distributors.' Sinclair adds that in terms of productivity, 'I have little doubt that it has boosted productivity by 100 per cent. It is central now to the running of our business on a global scale.' One of the key features is the web-to-leads functions: ptl's website generates a significant number of sales leads, which are automatically directed to the relevant global distributor via salesforce.com. Because the system is integrated, Sinclair and his sales team can keep track of how the leads are developing.

Sources: salesforce.com website (www.salesforce.com, 2003); ptl website (www.gasgen.com, 2003).

Case study questions

1 What are the advantages to Products of Technology Ltd (ptl) of using the salesforce.com software product?

2 'Salespeople as a rule tend not to be systems people.' Discuss.

3 Why would a company like ptl find the web-leads functionality so useful?

4 How could this system increase productivity by 100 per cent?

5 'Distance is no barrier using sales force automation tools.' Discuss.

Questions and exercises

Questions

1 'In industrial marketing, the productivity of the sales force is a key driver of profitability.' Discuss.

2 What have been the major changes in the focus of the sales function over the last decade?

3 'The sales force has been slower to adopt new technology than other functions such as manufacturing.' Discuss.

4 Discuss three benefits of automating a sales force.

5 Why is the human factor so important when implementing technology for the sales force?

6 Why is new wireless technology likely to play such an important part in the development of sales force systems?

7 When implementing a sales force solution, why is it so important to look at re-engineering the supporting processes?

Online exercises

1 You are the sales director for the UK division of a large car manufacturing company. You have over 100 salespeople working for you and they service over 500 distributors across the UK. Visit the website of Siebel (www.siebel.com). Prepare a short note to your CEO outlining some of the advantages of migrating your sales force to this software.

2 Now visit Salesforce.com's website (www.salesforce.com). Prepare a short note to your CEO outlining the benefits of this system.

References

1 Heide, C. (1999). *Dartnell's 30th Sales Force Compensation Survey*, Chicago: Dartnell Corporation.

2 Ligos, M. (1998). 'The incredible shrinking sales force', *Sales and Marketing Management*, December.

3 Lykins, D. (2002). 'The insurance industry goes mobile', www.e-businessadvisor.com/doc/11170

4 www.itm-group.co.uk/solutions/web-services/transactionweb/articles/gcosta.jsp

5 Kreiner, K. (2002). 'Tacit knowledge management: the role of artifacts', *Journal of Knowledge Management*, Vol. 6, No. 2.

6 Yankee Group (1997). 'Power to the field: technology-enabled selling', *Yankee Watch Enterprise Applications*, Vol. 2, Issue 12.

7 Syngenta (2002). 'Syngenta germinates efficient IT systems with Xcellenet', www.xcellenet.com

8 Close, W. and Eisenfeld, B. (2002). 'CRM sales suites: 1H02 magic quadrant', *Gartner Research Note M-14-7938*, 1 March.

9 Zoltners, A. and Lorimer, S. (2000). 'Sales territory alignment: an overlooked productivity tool', *Journal of Personal Selling and Sales Management*, Summer.

10 Signorini, E. (2001). *The Enterprise Wireless Data Application Opportunity: a Segmentation Analysis*, Yankee Group, December.

11 Yankee Group (2001). *Wireless Connectivity to the Enterprise: 2001 Survey Analysis*, Yankee Group, March.

12 Nairn, G. (2002). 'Cutting the wires of the workplace', *Financial Times*, 16 October.

13 Marshall, G.W., Moncrief, W.C. and Lassk, F.G. (1999). 'The current state of sales force activities', *Industrial Marketing Management*, Vol. 28.

14 Ahearne, M. and Schillewaert, N. (2001). 'The effect of information technology on salesperson performance', eBusiness Research Centre Working Paper, Penn State.

15 Rasmussen, E. (1999). 'The five steps to successful sales force automation', *Sales and Marketing Management*, March.

16 Speier, C. and Venkatesh, V. (2002). 'The hidden minefields in the adoption of sales force automation technologies', *Journal of Marketing*, Vol. 66.

17 Gilbert, A. (2002). 'Rethinking the case for CRM', *ZDNet*, 9 May.

18 Unwired Express (2002). 'Bridging the gap between sales force automation and truly effective selling', executive briefing, www.unwiredexpress.com

19 Agnew, M. (2000). 'CRM tools offer sales-force solutions', *Information Week*, 21 August.

PRINCIPLES OF GOOD CALL CENTRE MANAGEMENT

- Characteristics of well-managed call centres
- Monitoring call centre performance
- Managing the fulfilment process
- Potential issues with call centre technology

MOBILE FIELD SERVICE

- Supporting service engineers in the field
- Advantages of mobile technology in field service

SUMMARY

CASE STUDY

Introduction

Customer service is a critical component in the delivery of any product or service to the customer. In this chapter we start by examining the application of a relatively old technology to the customer service function – the telephone. The technology may be old, but the way it has been deployed in recent years has become increasingly sophisticated. We examine the main technology components of call centres and plot the migration of the call centre to the newer breed of customer contact centres that allow the customer to interact with the organisation using telephone, internet and fax. Given the increasing sophistication of these centres, we then look at the principles that underpin good call centre and contact centre management, and the role that technology plays in managing the centres. We conclude the chapter by examining the application of technology, and in particular wireless technologies, in supporting field engineers and service personnel who need access to customer and product data when they are 'on the road'.

Growth in telephone-based customer service

The increasing use of the telephone for customer service

While businesses have always used the telephone to communicate with customers, a recent trend has been the consolidation of telephone operations into call centres. These are large centres often with hundreds of staff that provide centralised telephone support to an organisation. Much like the consolidation of manufacturing into large factories, the call centre provided a way of streamlining the provision of customer service. The case of banks is a good example where, prior to call centres, customers called their local branch. People liked this personal touch, but as the volume of queries grew it became increasingly expensive to handle queries on an essentially ad hoc basis. Often there might not be enough staff in a branch to handle the volume of calls or the quality of service could vary significantly. As we will see, the call centre became the most cost-effective solution for many organisations.

Historically, large companies have been faster to use IT and call centre technology in customer service than small to medium-sized enterprises (SMEs). However, the call centre has become a key component of most companies nowadays. The most common functions supported by these centres are the provision of customer services and the handling of customer complaints. However, successful resolution of a customer's query presupposes the availability of accurate information to deal with the query. It also assumes that the caller can get through to the right person in the organisation with the minimum inconvenience. Quite often the experience from the customer's perspective can be as follows:

- 'The phone rings 20 times before somebody answers.'

- 'They keep passing me around.'

- 'I keep having to repeat information.'

- 'They never return my calls.'

In-bound communications can also provide an opportunity to engage in dialogue:[1] the consumer calls in to advise the company of an event that has occurred, and the company makes the subsequent action (*see* Figure 14.1).

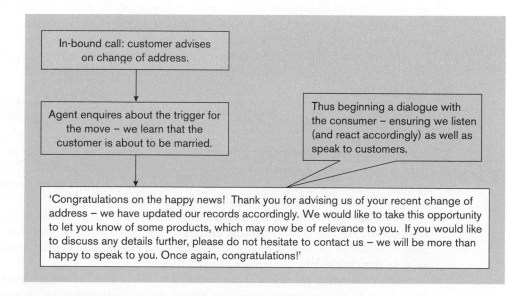

Figure 14.1 Customer dialogue using call centres
Source: Hughes and Evans (2001).[2]

Table 14.1 Major international call centres in Ireland (1999)

Call centre	Year established	Number of agents
Gateway 2000	1994	850
IBM	1996	800
Dell	1993	720
AOL/Bertelsmann	1995	650
Hertz	1996	500
Citibank	1997	450
UPS	1995	300
Xerox	1998	300
Lufthansa	1998	270
Oracle	1996	250
Compaq	1996	200
Merchants Group	1998	145

Source: Industrial Development Authority of Ireland website (www.ida.ie, 1999).

Growth in call centres

Call centres became big business when customer service migrated to telephone-based service channels. Call centre services were either set up in-house or were bought in as a third-party service from specialist providers. Many organisations used third parties when they realised that they did not have the skills or the resources to manage a telephone-based customer service operation. Increasingly companies are now making the decision to outsource their call centre operations to third parties with the required scale and expertise.

The USA traditionally led the world in call centre implementation with more than half a million customer service representatives (CSRs), or agents, employed in 25,000 call centres. Europe soon caught up with 685,000 call centre seats by 1999.[3] Countries started to see the opportunity of focusing on this growing market. One of the more notable successes in Europe was Ireland: with more than 100 Irish-based call centres serving the pan-European market,[4] it had claimed more than its share of major international call centres by the end of the 1990s (*see* Table 14.1).

The Netherlands and the other Benelux countries were also seen as good locations for multilingual call centres because citizens typically have more than one language. Some companies are also setting up call centres in Finland to serve the Russian market because they prefer the investment climate there.[5]

Within countries, particular regions started to target this call centre market: in the UK market areas like Scotland and the Bristol area have higher than average concentrations. Interestingly, research has indicated that there were also some very human

EXHIBIT 14.1

UK CALLS CENTRES MOVE TO INDIA

If you phone British Telecom's directory enquiries later this year, the chances are someone will answer the call in New Delhi or Bangalore, rather than Glasgow or Milton Keynes. The UK telecommunications operator announced on Friday that it is opening two call centres in India with the creation of 2,200 jobs. The move confirms a growing trend as more companies look to outsource jobs in their search for cost cuts. BT joins a string of companies such as British Airways, banking group HSBC and Powergen, a utility company, that are considering or have already announced similar moves.

Source: *Financial Times* (5 February 2003).[6]

reasons for the success of call centres in places like Scotland, because people found the Scots trustworthy and the accent pleasant to deal with.

The rise of global call centres in the twenty-first century

The success of countries like Ireland at attracting call centre investment was often based on a combination of factors that included tax incentives and a lower-wage environment. As wage costs increased, companies found that the costs of running call centre operations in relatively high-cost locations made it difficult to maintain a grip on the call centre market. Today, outsourcing of call centres has taken on a global dimension as lower-cost countries such as India have begun to emerge and outsourcing to these lower-cost locations has increased (*see* Exhibit 14.1).

The rise of India as a global player is causing a major restructuring of the existing call centre industry. Countries like Ireland are losing competitiveness while, according to one report, the closure of a third of Britain's larger call centres between 2003 and 2005 involves about 90,000 job losses.[7]

The benefits of moving to offshore locations like India can be significant. In 2003, Indian call centre operators earned the equivalent of about £2,200, compared with about £15,000 in the UK. This translates directly into hard cost savings for companies. Online travel provider ebookers claimed that it is saving £1 million every three months by moving back-office operations to Delhi, where 350 employees provide telesales, billing and customer services.[8] Indeed, many young Indian graduates, who cannot get other well-paying jobs, are opting for a stint in call centres. An estimated 5,000–7,000 fresh graduates are hired each year.[9] Leading players agree that third-party business-process outsourcing providers such as Daksh (*see* Figure 14.2), Spectramind, eFunds, Brigade, EXL, eServe, Transworks, Firstring, Tracmail, iSeva, Global eCMS, Tata, Sitel and Convergys, and the captive units of a number of multinational companies such as American Express and GE, are all poised for major growth in India.

times is reduced dramatically. This factor makes automated systems ideal for large campaigns.

- *Access*. Automated services provide access to the organisation 24 hours a day. Customers value such services, which go a long way towards building and maintaining relationships.

- *Consistency*. The message given to the customer is consistent because there is no chance of live operators deviating from the script. Thus the organisation can feel secure in the knowledge that its brands are being properly and consistently represented.

- *Cost*. Automated systems can be more cost effective than using live operators who have to be trained and equipped.[11]

Computer telephony integration (CTI)

The key to success in a call centre is having the right information at hand to deal with the customer query. Typically this information is held on computers and databases. The convergence of telephone and computer technology is known as computer telephony integration, or CTI. It provides the ability to retrieve customer data and deliver it to the agent together with the incoming phone call. Automatic retrieval of customer data, based on information given to the IVR system, reduces both the amount of time an agent has to spend before addressing the customer's needs and the amount of information the customer has to repeat. Using CTI, the caller's files can be accessed on screen in a matter of seconds and the caller's query answered. If the agent cannot deal with the call, it can be diverted to a supervisor. When the call is transferred, the supervisor's screen is automatically filled with that customer's details by using CTI. This 'screen-popping' reduces the frustration of the customer because the same questions that the agent asked need not be repeated.

Additional call centre productivity systems

Other applications of information technology that improve productivity in the call centre include:

- *Predictive dialling* – an outbound IT application whereby customers or prospective customers are automatically dialled using a list of telephone numbers from a customer database. Predictive dialling also employs statistical techniques in the form of a 'pacing algorithm' to reduce the risk that there will be no free customer service agents available to deal with a successfully connected call. The pacing algorithm monitors and controls a number of key variables in the call centre, such as the connect rate, average call length and customer wait time, and can predict when the next outbound call should be made.

- *Tracking software* – records and tracks customer interaction with the company, so every employee has the necessary information to deal with the customer. It also tracks customer problems from initiation to resolution, so if the problem happens again it can be resolved more quickly.

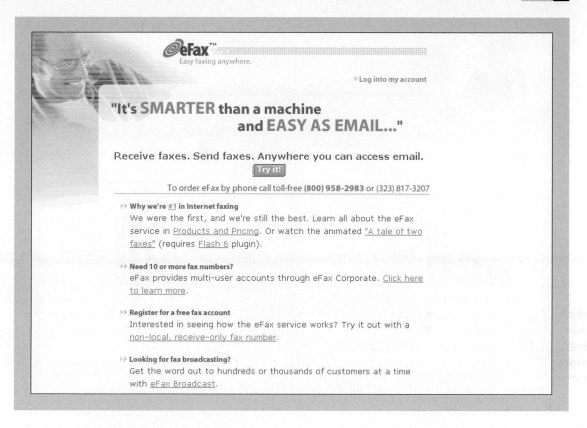

Figure 14.3 Electronic faxes from eFax

Source: eFax website (www.efax.com, 2003), eFax is a registered trademark of J2 Global Communications, Inc.

- *Imaging software* – allows agents to view documents such as product catalogues, diagrams and customer correspondence. Viewing the actual documents online allows the agent to provide an accurate and up-to-date service.

- *Fax-on-demand* – allows information to be faxed automatically to the customer without any human intervention. Many third parties such as eFax (*see* Figure 14.3) provide these services.

The migration from call centre to contact centre

By 2000 there was much speculation that the call centre was becoming an out-dated concept. As companies moved into the electronic age, would customer service functions not simply migrate to the internet? There is clear evidence that some companies are trying to persuade their customers to use the internet for customer service. One clear trend, as evidenced by the case study at the end of this chapter, is the integration of call centres with the internet. If properly implemented, web-enabled call centres will improve the levels of service and support that can be provided to customers.

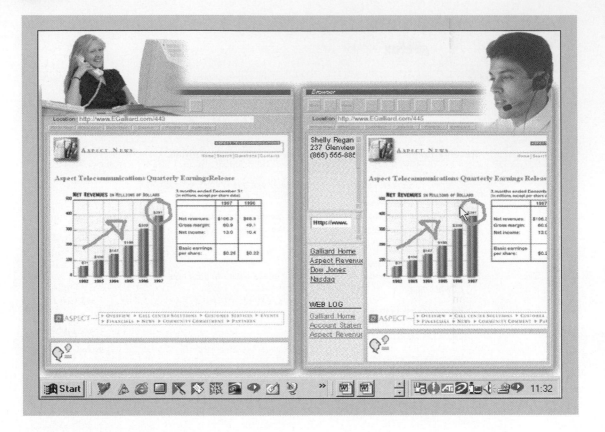

Figure 14.4 Web agent with contact centre integration
Source: Aspect Communications (1998).[12]

Many companies are now referring to their call centres as 'customer contact centres'. Whereas sometimes this might mean little in practice, there is evidence that it is a real shift in the nature of contact management, at least in terms of the vision of the future. In a survey of 200 senior managers of call centres in UK, the main finding was that the future contact centre will be multimedia-enabled and will be able to handle not only telephone contact but also fax, e-mail, interactive TV and web communications as well.[13] Contact centre agents will be more empowered to deal with issues and will not be as confined to the old call centre 'script' as used to be the case. An example of integrating technology is shown in Figure 14.4, which depicts a customer–agent interaction about investment decisions. Customers contacting the centre can speak to a customer service representative at the same time as having an interactive session via the internet. This allows forms, for example, to be shown on screen; the agent can even highlight sections of the form on their screen and this appears on the caller's screen as well, thus aiding correct completion.

Customer contact centres are also embracing 'call-back' concepts such as that depicted in Exhibit 14.2.

EXHIBIT 14.2

DON'T CALL US, WE'LL CALL YOU BACK

'Your call will be connected in 15 minutes . . . you are fifth in the queue.' Some customers hang up when they get a message like this, but queue-busting software could be the answer to slow call centre service. Queue-busters take the customer's place in the queue, promising to call them back as soon as a call centre agent is available. Products include Queue Optimizer and Queuebuster. Aspect Communications has just added a feature to its call centre software that enables the customer to leave a voice mail with more details when requesting a call back.

There are two main ways for a customer to initiate a call back. The first is when the customer contacts the call centre during a busy period and is asked to set up a call back or remain on hold. 'This is done by interactive voice response (IVR)', according to Steven Cooper, business support director at call centre company Kingston incontact. The second method is available on some websites. If the customer needs more information, he or she may be given the option of clicking on a call-back button and recording the time and date when they want to receive a call or an e-mail from the website provider. 'A web call back can be as simple as dumping text into an e-mail', says Cooper, 'or it could involve complex integration with databases.'

Queue Optimizer gives customers three options: they can be called back when their place in the queue is reached, they can be called at a different time or number, or they can stay on the line.

Source: Financial Times (18 September 2002).[14]

Principles of good call centre management

Characteristics of well-managed call centres

Good customer contact centre experiences are not likely to happen by accident. Companies invest millions of dollars to ensure the customer's experience is not only good but also consistent. Cleveland and Mayben (1997)[15] describe a number of characteristics of well-managed call centres. Several relate to the interplay between people management and advanced technology in these call centres:

■ *They view the incoming call centre as a total process.* The days of the call centre as an island unto itself is fast fading. A call centre is an important part of a much bigger process, and has to be integrated into the manufacturing, sales, delivery, fulfilment and after-sale support processes. It also has to be managed as an integral part of several delivery channels including the internet.

■ *They have an effective mix of people and technology.* In the emerging call centre environment, personal contact with callers will need to be managed. It is more effective for technologies such as IVR and the internet to handle routine calls. This frees up the time of the human operators to deal with more complex calls that require human intervention.

■ *They have a practical balance between specialisation and pooling.* Although pooling of resources is at the heart of incoming call management, a balance must be struck that both avoids unnecessary complexity in agent group structures and expands the responsibilities of call centre representatives.

■ *They leverage the key statistics.* Good call centres ensure that the right statistics (*see* below) are generated accurately and used in an unbiased manner. Gathering the statistics is not enough: they must also be acted upon.

■ *They effectively bridge distance and time.* While new technologies have provided new capabilities, they have not eliminated the natural barriers that exist between people who work in distributed environments. The best call centres work hard at getting results from people who work in different locations, have different reporting lines or who work at different times.

Monitoring call centre performance

Regardless of whether an operation is outsourced or in-house, organisations using the telephone as a customer service tool need to answer the following questions if they are to monitor the level of service they provide:

■ How many calls do not get through?

■ How long do customers have to wait?

■ How many calls do not get through to the right person?

■ How many queries are answered correctly first time, and how many require one or more follow-up calls to resolve the issue?

Other metrics should also be carefully monitored. Call centre revenues and costs must be measured accurately. Key ratios include:

■ average call revenue (for revenue-producing call centres)

■ forecasted call load versus actual load

■ scheduled staff to actual staff

■ average call time.

Most of these figures and ratios can be gathered through the combination of computer and telephone technology. Typically, the ACD system will provide many of the basic performance statistics. In many cases, specialist software from companies like Performix Technologies is required (*see* Figure 14.5).

Figure 14.5 Contact centre software from Performix Technologies
Source: Performix Technologies website (www.performix.com, 2003).

Managing the fulfilment process

Fulfilment is another crucial element of effective customer service. It is concerned with receiving orders or enquiries via the mail, telephone, internet, or interactive TV and delivering those orders. A process in its own right, fulfilment offers an opportunity to capture data on potential customers. Systems must be set up to deal with receipt of customer mail/calls, capture their details, produce personalised response output, enclose and mail information or products (which in turn involves order picking, packing and dispatch), analyse the statistics on enquiry nature, level, timing profiles, bank monies for orders and update stock control systems. Figure 14.6 summarises some of the stages and components of this system.

Other fulfilment issues are concerned with planning for levels and timing of response.[16] For example:

■ Once a direct response TV (DRTV) advertisement is broadcast, how many calls might we expect within half an hour of the broadcast? In reality, the burst of inbound calls is almost instantaneous and, if customers cannot get through, their business will be lost.

■ How long should we plan the time lag to be for responses to a poster campaign?

■ What level of mailing response might we expect, and have we discussed it with the local postal service?

■ How many catalogues should we print?

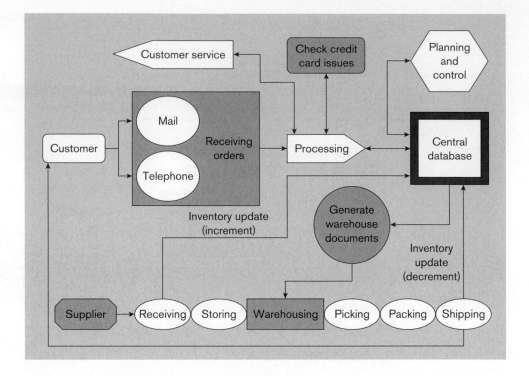

Figure 14.6 The fulfilment process

Source: Roberts and Berger (1989), reprinted by permission of Pearson Education, Inc., Upper Saddle River, NJ.[17]

■ What stock holdings should be considered for product orders?[18] (Remember the case of Hoover in Chapter 12, when they could not meet demand for their sales promotion offer of free flights!)

■ How do we handle complaints? (In this area of contact management 'carelines' are becoming more prevalent.)[19]

Potential issues with call centre technology

Call centre technology is not without its issues. Customer service on a '24 × 7' (24 hours a day, seven days a week) basis can be great but would not be economically feasible for most companies without the use of voice response systems. However, there are some disadvantages with voice response systems:

■ *They may appear artificial.* IVR can be cold and impersonal, whereas human operators provide greater warmth and give a better impression of the product or service. Given the choice, most consumers would probably prefer to deal with a live operator and some simply refuse to talk to machines. Furthermore, there are some situations in which there is no substitute for a well-trained operator and where automated systems would be of little use. In certain sectors, such as financial services and charities, live operators are more beneficial. Many people feel uneasy about discussing financial details with a machine and donations are often acknowledged more effectively by another person.

■ *They limit data collection.* Automated systems provide limited utility in terms of collecting customer data. Live operators are able to improvise and to get more information out of people. They can deal with ad hoc queries and can ask the caller to clarify information where there is any doubt.

In addition, comprehensive CTI systems can be complex and expensive to implement, as they require the call centre equipment to be linked to a variety of customer and other databases. Indeed, one of the biggest obstacles that call centres face is the lack of integration with other company systems.[20]

Mobile field service

Supporting service engineers in the field

In the previous chapter we discussed the use of wireless technology in sales and mentioned that field sales was the single largest application of wireless technology in large enterprises. In addition, field service staff and field engineers account for more than two in every five US users of enterprise wireless data applications (*see* Figure 14.7).

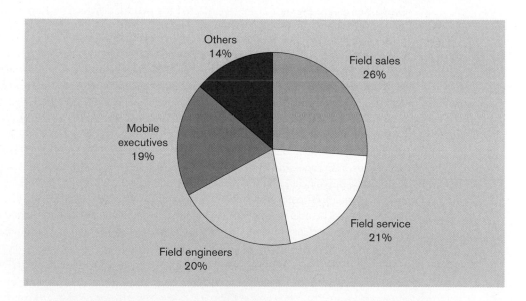

Figure 14.7 Distribution of US mobile workforce
Source: Yankee Group (2001).[21]

Advantages of mobile technology in field service

The advantage of mobile field service technology is that technicians can arrive on-site with full, up-to-date details of the work they need to perform and all the information they need at their fingertips. Full, up-to-date information means access to customer records and service history, service manuals, diagnostic and testing procedures, and so on. Field engineers can also gain access to parts information (price, part numbers, available for shipping, delivery times etc.) and can dynamically reserve specific parts, generate requisitions and confirm delivery schedules. While many field service engineers and technicians have laptop PCs today, mobile solutions such as PDAs can be even more effective in the field – as long as they are:

- portable and light enough to fit into a pocket or bag;
- 'always on' or can be booted up in seconds;
- robust and in some cases 'ruggedised' to allow them to withstand extreme working environments;
- rechargeable, or have multiple back-up power sources or battery packs;
- easy-to-use, often with touch screens.

Exhibit 14.3 provides one example of an organisation deploying such devices to support its service technicians.

EXHIBIT 14.3

SAVINGS IN THE FIELD

BT, as a member of Toyota Industries Corporation of Japan, is a leading supplier of warehouse trucks with 8,000 employees, of which 3,000 are in service functions. BT's service technicians in Europe carry out some 5,000 assignments each day and have been equipped with PDAs, which can communicate with the company's main financial systems using mobile technology. During the spring of 2002, BT carried out pilot tests in Sweden, Belgium and the UK using the Compaq iPAQ Pocket PC and PDAs of other leading suppliers. If these tests produce the expected results, the solution will be put into full-scale operation during the year so that it can be used by 1,200 of BT's service technicians in Europe. The system will replace the current routines where 1.2 million work orders are annually sent on paper to the administrative office to be fed into BT's business system. BT estimates that a fully developed system will save €2.5m each year. Technicians will be able to use PDAs to plan their work days, create, receive and report service orders and assignments, order spare parts, review service contracts, and access extensive data about service objects and customers. Other features will include advanced online billing, where customers can approve invoices directly from the PDA using electronic signatures.

Source: Cap Gemini Ernst & Young website (www.cgey.com, 2003).

Another example is PepsiAmericas (www.pepsiamericas.com), the second largest bottler of Pepsi-Cola in the USA, which delivers many popular beverage brands to retailers in the USA and European countries including Poland, Hungary, the Czech Republic and Slovakia. PepsiAmericas' sales delivery system was based on 'route agents' having a set number of accounts, often going out with a full truckload, with a limited view of actual customer demand until arriving at their location. PepsiAmericas' problem was that the trucks would come back still 30–35 per cent filled. This resulted in additional fuel and labour costs to offload the trucks, while also having to worry about damaged goods. The company is now equipping its mobile workforce with more than 5,000 rugged PDAs.[22] In Sweden the utility company Sydkraft (www.sydkraft.se) has reduced costs for its resource planners and work schedulers by 25 per cent after giving mobile technology to its field service personnel. [23]

Summary

In the search for a greater competitive edge, marketers are increasingly looking to the customer service function to provide that critical element of differentiation. Given two products with a broadly similar price proposition and features, customer service can make the difference. In areas like banking, where the customer has many interactions with bank staff, the level of customer service is critical. In the 1980s and 1990s customer service moved into the age of the telephone. Large specialist telephone call centres for customer service became commonplace, often with the operations outsourced to third-party organisations with the skills and the resources to handle thousands of customer calls every day. More recently we have seen the internet become increasingly important as a customer service channel, as the call centre migrates to a customer contact centre capable of supporting dialogue with the customer through a number of different channels including telephone, internet and fax. Wireless technologies are also becoming increasingly popular in support of field service workers. The full potential of telephone and internet-based customer service is only starting to be realised, and companies using these electronic channels are stealing a march on their competitors.

Case study

Call centres at Compaq and HP

hp services | global service desk management

global service desk management

» Services

HP Services portfolio
» Business Applications
» Continuity & Availability
» Industry Services
» Infrastructure Services
» Managed Services
» Packaged Services
» Support Services

enhance end-user service while reducing IT costs

Managing IT support for your global workforce can be a challenge. While IT budgets are shrinking, technology is growing more complex and end-users are demanding better service to help them stay productive. It can be difficult to find and train staff to deliver first-rate technical support on the latest products.

🖨 **printable version**

contact hp support UK

» contact hp

» contact hp in other countries/regions

call hp

We offer telephone support for most Hewlett-Packard products. Depending on your product's warranty, there may be a fee charged.

before you call
For faster service and to ensure that we use your time wisely, please make sure that you can access your hp product and have the following information available when you call:
• Product number and serial number.
• Operating system; for example Windows 98.
• Messages displayed when the problem occurred.
• Any recent changes to hardware or software.
• What you've already done to try to solve the problem.

self-help

» download software & driver updates
» support for your product

Figure 14.8

Compaq

Compaq, the world's largest maker of personal computers, now owned by Hewlett-Packard, manages to keep a healthy distance from one current technology vogue – interactive voice response (IVR). Iain Murray, information management manager at Compaq's new £25-million UK call centre in Glasgow, shares the popular distaste for IVR systems that demand too much time from the caller before a real human voice is found. 'As a company, we have a policy of minimum use of IVR systems. Some people hang up straightaway when they get an IVR system at the end of the line.'

The Compaq call centre does employ some IVR technology, but Murray stresses it has a limited use, primarily for late-hour calls. 'The whole point of having a call centre is that it allows you to talk to the customer.' One new method of getting in contact with those customers is a cheap and practical piece of software from a small UK company called PhoneMe. The service that PhoneMe offers to call centres consists of an internet-related freephone number that callers access by clicking a button on the screen of the company website. So a customer making an enquiry about Compaq hits the PhoneMe button and is directed to type in their phone number, which is then linked via the PhoneMe switch to the Glasgow call centre. The PhoneMe switch reconciles the two numbers, automatically routing a call from a Compaq call centre agent through to the prospective customer. Damon Oldcorn, founder and managing director of PhoneMe, explains that simplicity and speed of service are key to his product. 'For customers such as Compaq, the important objective is to capture the interest of someone who has come across the website while browsing on the internet before that person wanders off to another site.' The temptation to click on the freephone button is considerable, and as the phone rings almost instantly, there is none of the frustration of working through the disembodied voice and numerous prompts of an IVR system.

But members of the public are slow to exploit the simple internet-response option. According to the latest figures from Compaq, only 17 per cent of the visitors to its website who decide to speak to the company use the PhoneMe option, while the remaining 83 per cent pick up their phone and dial the number manually.

Hewlett-Packard

Not every transaction suits conventional phone contact. Trevor Crooks, UK senior manager for call centre solutions at Nortel, the Canadian telecoms giant, notes that some potential customers for credit card purchases prefer to enter their credit card details in a box on a website rather than divulge them to an anonymous telephone operator. Nortel's switching equipment sits at the heart of many call centres and company phone exchanges. For example, Hewlett-Packard has installed a Nortel ACD system and associated call centre software at its computer products support centre in the Netherlands. According to Crooks, the 450 agents there handle 18,000 calls a day from across Europe, the Middle East and Africa. 'HP has identified 650 types of call that might arrive there. So they have to be able to distinguish between types of call and route them to the right agent.' The ACD system contains software that picks up the point of origin of each call, routing it to an agent with the appropriate language. This is what is known as 'granularity': the ability to filter each call through the structure of a massive call centre to the right human voice.

Voice or electronic?

The move to integrate call centres has led to them being renamed contact centres. The role of the contact centre is to manage all dealings with a customer, be it by phone call, e-mail, web chat or fax. The overall aim should be to allow customers to make contact however they choose, and get the same level of service in every case, says Tim Stone, marketing manager for contact centres at Cisco, the telecoms equipment manufacturer. 'If I was to ring your call centre about an e-mail I sent you on Monday, regarding an order I placed on your website on Friday, would your agent be able to handle that interaction?' However, Ad Nederlof, chief executive of Genesys, the Alcatel subsidiary that provides customer relationship management (CRM) solutions for contact centres, says that at present only about 10–15 per cent of consumer interactions are through non-telephone channels, leaving clients questioning why they need to invest in integrating channels. 'So this is not a revolution, but companies cannot afford not to accommodate customer interactions through other channels. Beside that, these channels are growing much faster than voice,' he says. Furthermore, the theory is that integration between websites and call centres will increase the amount of business done on the web, because people will be less likely to abandon a transaction if they run into a problem. Customers who get half way through filling in a form can talk to an agent who will be able to see exactly the same screen and help the caller complete it, without having to start all over again.

Despite the slow take-up of the PhoneMe buttons, both Compaq and Hewlett-Packard are keen to promote the non-voice options and so drive down the cost of call handling. Today, customers with technical queries can opt for a self-service option where they search the website for solutions to their technical problems. All common problems and questions have solutions posted on the internet. Customers who are online can have an internet chat with a service operator as well as the traditional call. Customers may prefer the human touch, but contact centre operators have a good reason to persuade them to go electronic.

Sources: Compaq website (www.compaq.com, 2003); Hewlett-Packard website (www.hp.com, 2003); *Financial Times* (18 September 2002);[24] *Financial Times* (3 February 1999).[25]

Case study questions

1 Search the internet for other companies that provide similar software or service to PhoneMe. Which websites provide such call-back functionality?

2 'Not every transaction suits conventional phone contact.' Discuss.

3 Search the HP and Compaq websites to find how they provide customer service and technical support. Which service mechanism do they promote more heavily – human operator or electronic self-service?

Questions and exercises

Questions

1 Why have call centres grown in popularity for the provision of customer service?

2 Select a mid-sized company that you know well (such as your own bank). Find out how many different points of telephone contact there are for that organisation, and discuss how service and support might be improved.

3 Why have call centres grown so quickly in countries like Ireland?

4 How is the internet impacting the way customer service is delivered? Give examples.

5 Describe a typical day in the life of a field service engineer who has been equipped with the latest mobile technology.

Online exercises

1 You are the customer services director for a European hotel chain responsible for 400 customer services representatives located across Europe. Your people provide telephone booking services to customers. Go online to the IDA website (www.ida.ie) and find out what the Irish government has to offer if you consolidate all your call centre activities in Ireland.

2 As above, but this time visit Daksh's website (www.daksh.com). Prepare a note to your CEO comparing the advantages of setting up the call centre in India.

References

1 Evans, M. (2001). 'Contact management', *Future Marketing*, Milton Keynes: Open University.

2 Hughes, R. and Evans, M. (2001). 'Relationships are two-way: the reglected role of "inbound" contact', Financial Services Sector World Marketing Congress, Cardiff, June.

3 Shillingford, J. (1999). 'It's not just a question of knowing the language', *Financial Times*, 3 February.

4 Price, C. (1999). 'Suppliers woo the next generation of PC users', *Financial Times*, 3 February.

5 Shillingford, J. (1999). 'It's not just a question of knowing the language', *Financial Times*, 3 February.

6 Guthrie, J. (2003). 'Message may soon be: don't call us, we'll call you', *Financial Times*, 5 February.

7 Singh, S. (2003). 'The revolution hots up', *Financial Times*, 9 March.

8 Glick, B. (2003). 'The pros and cons of offshore outsourcing', *IT Week*, 13 February.

9 Saxena, N. (2002). 'Employment blues: call C for a career', *Times News Network*, 19 February.

10 Darby, I. (1996). 'The right staff', *Marketing Direct*, November.

11 Evans, M. (2001). Course material.

12 Aspect Communications (1998). *WebAgent*, demonstration CD.

13 Future Foundation (2000). 'Customer management in the 21st century', commissioned by London First Centre.

14 Shillingford, J. (2002). 'Queue busting', *Financial Times*, 18 September.

THE ROAD AHEAD

■ A bleak future?

■ Six steps to success

SUMMARY

CASE STUDY

Introduction

If you have followed each chapter of this book to this point, you may now be convinced, like us, that technology has a critical role to play in marketing. However, we should also highlight some of the problems and difficulties that marketing and business executives have encountered when attempting to design and implement marketing systems. We begin this final chapter with a discussion of why marketing and technology have not always worked comfortably together. We then examine some of the wider trends in IT and systems management – the increasing use of packaged software, the rise in outsourcing, and the concept of the 'extended enterprise'. We conclude with some practical lessons for the successful deployment of electronic marketing systems.

The IT productivity paradox

The nature of IT systems implementation

Designing, developing and managing marketing and IT systems is a complex business. The research company IDC states that the average company with $3 billion in annual revenues and 9,000 employees needs 500 IT professionals to look after the 4,300 desktops and 470 servers, spread over the 40 sites in the company.[1] The design and implementation of any computer system is often characterised by the following:

■ *Complexity*. In a major systems development project several hundred thousand lines of computer code must be written and tested. Different hardware, software and telecommunications standards have to be integrated.

■ *Long elapsed time*. A typical systems development effort can last anywhere from several months to a number of years. It is rarely possible to design, develop, test, install and roll out a new computer system in less than six months.

■ *Project management difficulties*. Many computer systems do not deliver the required results. The reasons for failure are numerous, but often include inadequate management of the multitude of strategic, technical, design, operational and change management issues.

The IT productivity paradox

One of the more intriguing debates since the 1980s has been the so-called 'IT product-ivity paradox' in which some commentators have discussed – often in scathing terms – the lack of benefits associated with IT investments. Macdonald et al. (1999)[2] sum-marises this discussion neatly:

> The information technology (IT) productivity paradox is the perceived discrepancy between IT investment and IT performance, between input and output. The particular perception which launched public discussion of the issue can be dated, with some precision, to a book review by Robert Solow published in the *New York Times* in July 1987 which included the line, 'we see the computer age everywhere except in the productivity statistics'. From mighty aphorisms little aphorisms grow and other sages readily declared on the issue; Lester Thorow, for example, announcing that 'the American factory works, the American office doesn't' and Paul Strassmann that 'there is no relation between spending for computers, profits and productivity'.

The Paul Strassmann in question is a well-known author who has studied the issue for many years: he claims in his 1997 book *The Squandered Computer* that tens of billions of dollars have been wasted on computer systems in the USA alone.[3] Other studies analysing the impact of internet usage (for example, Andersen's 2001 study of 185 US companies)[4] arrive at similar conclusions. On the other hand, Oliner and Lichel (2000)[5] suggest that the impact of IT on the productivity figures was really only evid-ent from 1995 onwards, when significant investments in IT started to be made. They believe that IT accounted for about two-thirds of the increase in labour productivity between the first and second halves of the 1990s.

Davenport and Prusak (1997)[6] take a slightly different view. They examine the rela-tionship between technology and the other organisational, behavioural and cultural elements of an organisation, and find that information technology, in and of itself, will not provide solutions to company's marketing needs. These same themes come through in many other studies. Bensaou and Earl (1998)[7] also talk about companies spending millions of dollars on consulting fees trying to resolve IT problems, with little to show for their money.

The human dimension

Bresnahan et al. (1999)[8] examine the human dimension of the paradox. They argue that too much attention has been paid to investments in IT and not enough attention has been paid to the human capital structure in the firms investing in IT. They find that the balance between the IT and human capital elements is crucial. Firms with high levels of both IT and human capital are most productive. Furthermore, firms with low levels of both IT and human capital are more productive than firms that are high on IT and low on human capital, or vice versa.

From our own practical experience of implementing IT and marketing systems, this is the nub of the issue. It has been a recurring theme throughout this book. At the end of the day, it is the marketing and sales staff that will make the CRM system – or the marketing database, or the contact management system – a success. The key question is whether they are capable of doing this.

The IT paradox and electronic marketing

The IT skills gap in the marketing function

Until recently IT was rarely viewed as a fundamental component of marketing – an indispensable tool that most marketers need to understand. Few traditional marketing professionals could really claim to be fully technology-literate or to state that they could:

- appreciate fully the potential of internet and wireless technologies for marketing;

- discuss the pros and cons of data warehousing;

- have strong views on wider technology issues such as enterprise resource planning (ERP) systems or whether outsourcing is a good idea.

In research conducted for the Chartered Institute of Marketing,[9] such a major skills gap was uncovered. The purpose of that research was to explore how technological change is affecting marketing, how marketers should respond and indeed how they should be skilled. The research involved extensive executive interviews with senior marketing managers with the emerging themes validated via Delphi groups of experts drawn from interviews. The research found that the new marketer needs to utilise quant-itative analysis techniques and measurement/accountability metrics. In the research, respondents felt that there was a real need for marketers to know, at least something, about IT and how it can be used to generate measurement metrics. They felt that unless marketers can talk the same language with IT managers and data mining people, they have little chance of influencing the IT department or even the segmenta-tion and targeting decisions within companies. One internet company consultant commented:

> How many times have marketers actually got outside their comfort zone and really got their hands dirty with this new technology? Unless you know how difficult it actually is, it's easy to under-estimate the time and effort in getting these things off the ground. I know because I've been a one-man band for the last ten years, but most marketers just hand over a brief to IT. And then when IT turn round and say no, marketers don't know enough to challenge it.

Conversely, as one respondent to the CIM research argued, IT people often exaggerate their business awareness and, especially in a big meeting, tend to deny any gaps in their knowledge. Does this represent ignorance on both sides? Perhaps, it indicates that IT people are starting to educate themselves more about marketing. Several respondents, unprompted, pointed out a 'new breed' doing mixed marketing/IT Masters courses. There is, therefore, a significant skills gap in this respect and it has been suggested that the marketing curriculum needs to be revised in order for this to be addressed.[10]

Unrealistic internet expectations

The internet age spawned a number of companies wanting to buy market share. Amazon (www.amazon.com) was valued at more than $30 billion in early 1999, even though it had never generated a single cent in profit. In the UK the insurance company Prudential bet that its £200 million investment in a direct and internet bank called Egg (www.egg.com) would also be viewed in retrospect as a wise investment. In both of these cases, the companies in question managed to weather the post-dot-com period relatively well. However, most of the internet and electronic marketing models that emerged from the internet age failed to stand the test of time. In fact, as we discovered in the opening chapters of this book, they failed to grasp the principles of commerce (not to mention e-commerce) by ignoring whether there was a real market out there and whether any money could be made from their product or service. The cost of providing services such as home shopping is a case in question. Supermarket delivery costs cannot always be covered fully, even though they can provide a marketing advantage over the competition. Home shopping was introduced by supermarkets such as Peapod in the USA, Sainsbury in the UK and Albert Heijn in the Netherlands, but even as the services were being introduced, people were questioning whether the typical charge of £5 was enough to cover the cost of selecting the goods from the shelves.[11]

As long as marketing and business managers understand the underlying economics, then the business decisions to provide such services can be assessed realistically. Often, the economics are not understood fully and proper business cases are not produced for such internet-enabled (or any technology-enabled) ventures.

Subsequent under-delivery against expectations

The consequence is often a failure of marketing systems, sales systems and technology-enabled services to live up to expectations. Exhibit 15.1 provides an example of the expectations that were made for in-flight entertainment systems in aircraft. While the proposition was solid, the practical difficulties and teething problems of implementing complex systems are nearly always under-estimated. The views expressed by Virgin here are interesting and informative. Although there may be a temptation for systems providers to over-sell their products, there is a major obligation on the part of the buyers to understand what it is they are buying. Under-delivery against expectations is as much a function of over-enthusiasm of buyers as it is of over-selling on the part of the systems providers.

As discussed in Exhibit 15.1, both British Airways and Virgin had three years of unsatisfactory trials, and spent many millions of pounds without either airline

EXHIBIT 15.1

DISAPPOINTMENT IN THE MILE-HIGH CLUB

As the aviation industry gathers at the Farnborough air show in England, a sober realism surrounds the in-flight entertainment industry. It has been a difficult infancy for new in-flight entertainment systems, which were introduced with circus-like hoopla in 1992 and 1993. The initial difficulties resulted in supplier–client friction, a lawsuit and at least two companies pulling back from the market. Carriers including British Airways, Northwest Airlines, United Airlines and Virgin Atlantic Airways have had early expectations dashed by the failure of new equipment. Reliability proved poor in the brutal environment of an airline cabin, and airlines, which had entered complex revenue-sharing deals with device makers, discovered that gambling and pay-per-view movies weren't the revenue-spinners expected. British Airways, after three years of 'unsatisfactory' trials, decided in 1997 not to proceed with an interactive entertainment system. Virgin installed a Hughes-Avicom system in 1993 at a cost of £1 million per aircraft. After finding that some of the gaming functions didn't deliver as expected, it decided in 1996 to install a Matsushita system on its newest aircraft at a cost of £1.7 million per plane. 'It's certainly more reliable', says Lysette Guana, in-flight entertainment manager at Virgin.

So, with systems costs that can exceed £2 million per plane, the makers need to prove to airlines that the painful part is over. Indeed, the in-flight entertainment industry is in a critical transition period and must demonstrate that the new systems have been fine-tuned to deliver the sort of reliability that carriers insist upon.

Source: Goldsmith (1998).[12]

achieving its business objectives. The same problems are routinely encountered by other organisations during the implementation of customer databases, direct marketing systems, sales force automation systems and, more recently, electronic commerce and internet operations. Managers now commonly expect that these systems development efforts will fail to be delivered on time and within the original budget. The impact of such failures is to increase the level of scepticism within the marketing and business community for information systems.

Information technology trends

Increasing use of packaged software

In the past, companies tended to design and develop their own marketing systems. Today, there are many off-the-shelf software packages available to support all aspects of sales and marketing. We have mentioned many of them in earlier chapters of this book:

■ in Chapters 4 and 5, we saw how systems from CACI, Smartfocus and Claritas were used for customer segmentation and insight;

■ in Chapter 13, we examined customer relationship management (CRM) and sales force automation (SFA) software from vendors like Siebel, Vantive and salesforce.com;

■ in Chapter 14, we saw how there were literally hundreds of software solutions for managing telephone call centres.

In the age of electronic marketing, managers will need to gain a better understanding of the software packages that are available to support their marketing objectives.

The rise of outsourcing

The outsourcing of IT and related functions has undergone phenomenal growth in North America, the UK and Australia throughout the 1990s. Now the market is taking off in Western Europe, South America and parts of South-East Asia, including Japan, which have previously resisted the trend.[13] Exhibit 15.2 shows the scale of some of these outsourcing deals in the UK.

EXHIBIT 15.2

OUTSOURCING WINS FOR BIG BLUE

IBM (or Big Blue, as it is known in the industry) has overtaken EDS as the biggest provider of software and services in the UK, according to analyst Ovum Holway. EDS held the top spot for many years, and last year the two suppliers were neck and neck, but a recent series of major deals has put IBM in the lead. 'IBM now has the culture right for selling services rather than products', said Anthony Miller, analyst at Ovum Holway. Big Blue has announced two huge deals in the past week: a ten-year $7 billion outsourcing deal with Fiat; and a $2 billion contract to run all of NTL's IT operations in the UK and Ireland. Savings to NTL under the 11-year deal are estimated at about £320 million. The cable operator is holding on to elements of IT, which it considers 'fundamental to its competitive advantage'. Nearly 500 IT staff will transfer from NTL to IBM. 'It frees us from the day-to-day IT demands so that we can focus on delivering great service and innovative communications solutions for our customers', said NTL's UK managing director Stephen Carter. Big Blue is enjoying a growing reputation for winning fresh customers, according to Miller. 'EDS is doing well in established accounts, as is Computer Sciences. But IBM is doing well in new business. It is going up against EDS with great confidence,' he said. According to researcher IDC, IBM won 22 of the world's largest outsourcing deals in the last year, followed by Computer Sciences with 17 and EDS with 14. The number of $1 billion-plus deals rose from 12 in 1999 to 17 last year, with these deals mainly having a ten-year term.

Source: Computing (30 May 2001).[14]

One interesting development in recent years has been the increasing use of outsourcing partners to help develop internet-based marketing solutions. Since the right blend of technology, marketing and web design skills are unlikely to be present in abundance in most companies, the outsourcing route is seen by many as the natural choice. For example, when the Danish toy company Lego launched its first interactive products on the web in 1999, it chose IBM as its outsourcing partner for the creation of the company's World Shop (www.legoworldshop.com) internet site. According to World Shop's marketing manager:

> We are manufacturers, not [internet] retailers. With all the internal and technical challenges inherent in launching the site, it became apparent that having a single partner was the best decision we could have made. Had we to deal with multiple vendors, we would probably not have the site up and running by now.[15]

We saw in the previous chapter how India has become an outsourcing powerhouse for many call centre functions. In fact, India is also a provider of outsourcing solutions for most technology-enabled functions (*see* Exhibit 15.3).

The trend towards outsourcing to India and other low-cost locations may be complicated by the possibility of US legislation post-September 11, making the export of data difficult, if not illegal. Job protection may also be a factor in such legislation (*see* Exhibit 15.4).

EXHIBIT 15.3

PRUDENTIAL OUTSOURCES TO INDIA

ICICI, India's biggest financial services group, processes 91 million customer transactions a year involving products such as loans and share brokering. Armed with these back-office skills, it decided to buy a call centre and leverage its 'domain expertise' – the most valued skill in business process outsourcing – in rich foreign markets. The pay-off came quickly. Prudential, a large UK insurer and ICICI's partner in an Indian asset management joint venture, said it would outsource a big chunk of its back-office work to ICICI's new call centre division at Bangalore in south India.

This was Prudential's first foray into offshore outsourcing. It entered a market crowded with Western companies, such as GE, whose pioneering initiatives practically created India's outsourcing market, and Citigroup, the biggest financial services group in the world. They are among scores of foreign companies outsourcing not just 'safe' back-office jobs, but increasingly high margin tasks such as actuarial analysis. The consequence is that India's IT-enabled services sector is set to continue its recent annual growth rate of 60 per cent plus this year, and emerge as a powerful source of job creation. Nasscom, the industry group, says 1 million jobs will be created by 2008.

Source: Financial Times (5 February 2003).[16]

EXHIBIT 15.4

BUY NY

Senator Hillary Rodham Clinton led a welcoming ceremony in Buffalo, New York for the new local office of Tata Consultancy Services, an IT services firm based in India that competes with US companies. Meanwhile, 400 miles across the state in New York City, council member Gale Brewer introduced Resolution 2126 calling for businesses and government agencies to 'Buy NY' – that is, strongly consider local technology vendors and developers for IT work. The juxtaposition exemplifies the growing divide over offshore outsourcing. While the US IT workforce is shrinking – joblessness among IT workers was 5.6 per cent in December according to the Bureau of Labor Statistics – the offshore IT services business has never been stronger, as companies flock to foreign firms that offer high-quality work at substantially lower costs than in the USA. For private business, the equation is just too compelling to pass up. Now offshore outsourcing is poised to grow in the public sector, as foreign services firms target what they see as a growth market of cash-strapped state and local governments looking to cut costs.

There has also been pushback in other states. New Jersey's state senate recently approved a bill that forbids state agencies from sending services work – IT work included – offshore. An Assembly version of the bill is pending. It's a dilemma-in-the-making for government agencies: save taxpayers' money or protect US jobs.

Source: Information Week (17 March 2003).[17]

One final message about outsourcing – the outsourcing of marketing or IT operations should not be seen as a quick way to solve existing technology problems. Most outsourcing companies will advise their clients to get their systems into shape before they outsource.

The 'extended enterprise'

As companies outsource more and more activities, management of the links between the company and its partners become more important. Deise et al. (2000)[18] describes network management as: 'The process of effectively deciding what to outsource in a constraint-based, real-time environment based on fluctuation'.

Electronic communications is becoming more important to outsourcing as it enables the transfer of the information that is necessary to create, manage and monitor partnerships. The danger of course is that with data being at the hub of relational strategies it is not always prudent to let it slip away to an outside organisation.[19] The compromise, as alluded to earlier, is for less formal outsourcing and more alliance and partnership relationships to emerge.[20] The communication links are not necessarily mediated directly through the company but may also be through intermediaries (known as value chain integrators) or directly between partners.

The road ahead

A bleak future?

All this may sound like depressing news for electronic marketing. To a certain extent, the news is sobering. Recall the discussions in earlier chapters about the difficulties of achieving the desired benefits from investments in CRM systems and sales force automation tools – the majority of these marketing systems have failed to achieve the benefits expected of them. However, there is some evidence that the functions that have benefited most from the implementation of IT systems have been marketing and sales. The study by Ravarini et al. (2001)[27] of 2,000 small to medium-sized Italian companies finds some, but limited, correlation between technology investment and overall company performance. The functions that show the greatest correlation are marketing and sales, R&D and customer care. There is also strong evidence that the marketing/IT gap is closing. Today, more marketing courses contain modules on information technology. Marketing managers have greater exposure to online services for research and are familiar with the capabilities of the internet. They are beginning to understand the issues associated with using and maintaining customer databases. Future generations of marketing managers should have the required IT skills to operate more effectively than the previous generation.

Marketing professionals are also embracing new business models. One such model is illustrated in Figure 15.2. It can show how to improve marketing systems in an integrated manner and also move interaction into an expanded relational paradigm that includes suppliers and partners as well as customers.

The vectors in Venkatraman and Henderson's model are:

- *Customers*. Customer data was a focus of Chapter 6 and our discussion of CRM emphasised the importance of integrating data within the organisation, and integration (for example via EDI) with . . .

- *Suppliers*. Strategic sourcing relates to suppliers, and it is the combination of customer and supplier data that provides . . .

- *Knowledge*. In these new business models, knowledge equates to power.

As each company has a number of supply chains for different products, the use of the term 'chain' seems limiting: a supply chain network is a more accurate reflection of the links between an organisation and its partners. Indeed Kalakota and Robinson (2001)[28] describe the structure of a supply chain as a complex network of relationships that organisations maintain with trading partners to source, manufacture and deliver products. The existence of such a network increases the need for electronic communications technology to manage and optimise all the links. Communication technology is vital since managing relationships with customers, suppliers and intermediaries is based on the flow of information and the transactions between these parties.

According to Rayport and Sviokla (1995),[29] the internet enables value to be created by gathering, organising, selecting, synthesising and distributing information. They

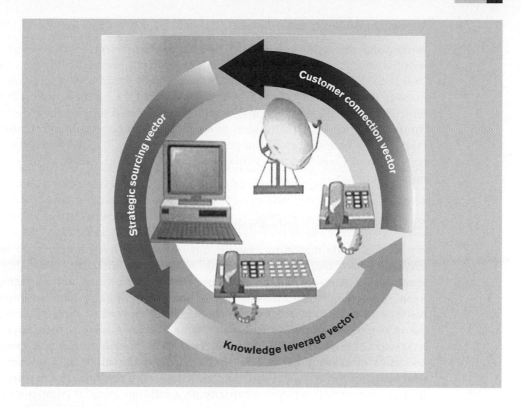

Figure 15.2 Relational vectors
Source: Venkatraman and Henderson (2000).[30]

refer to this as a 'virtual value chain' that is mirroring the physical value chain. This description of the virtual value chain indicates the importance of information flow in relational value chain models of today. Deise et al. (2000)[31] suggested a revised model that emphasises the importance of real-time environmental scanning, which has been made possible by the electronic communications links with distributors and customers.

Six steps to success

All is not lost, however. If the following six steps are taken, most organisations and marketing departments will stand more than a reasonable chance of gaining value for their investments in IT. These steps are:

- a clearly defined business case;
- senior management sponsorship and support;
- winning hearts and minds: involvement of marketing and sales users;
- a rigorous systems development methodology;
- good project management;
- a new attitude and mindset.

A clearly defined business case

While some marketing systems and infrastructural investments may seem intuitively sensible, the discipline of preparing a good, clearly defined business case is vital. Unless costs and benefits have been defined up-front, it can be difficult to monitor and manage the success of the investment. Without such a business case, it is also often difficult to convince senior management to sponsor and support the investment with the required degree of enthusiasm to see it through successfully to completion. The creation of a business case in support of any marketing system will ensure that costs, revenues and timescales are estimated at the outset, and tracked closely throughout implementation.

Senior management sponsorship and support

While small-scale marketing systems can often be delivered with little senior-level involvement or sponsorship, large-scale systems are different because they typically involve re-engineering internal sales and marketing processes and changing the way people go about their day-to-day work. Often, they will also have an impact on the way the company interacts with its suppliers and customers. Without active involvement and support from senior levels within the organisation, such large-scale projects will fail to achieve their full objectives. Many organisations will appoint a senior executive or director as the official sponsor of major marketing projects, with full responsibility for the successful implementation of the project. In some cases the project sponsor will act in this capacity on a full-time basis. If companies are serious about creating the new customer contact centre or implementing that sales force automation system, who better to lead the charge that the sales director or marketing director?

Winning hearts and minds: involvement of marketing and sales users

For any computer system it is important to involve the eventual users in its development – and this is particularly true of sales and marketing systems. User involvement in all stages of the development will ensure that the system will meet the needs of the users. All too often, computer systems are developed and 'handed over' to the users without their full involvement or 'buy-in' (*see* Exhibit 15.5). It is also important that users are involved very early in the process, particularly in the design phase, which has a major impact on the rest of the project.

A rigorons systems development methodology

The design and development of any computer system are major undertakings and require a considerable investment in management time and resources. Successful implementation requires a framework to be adopted and clear stages of development to be addressed in sequence. Such methodologies are built around the concept of a systems development life cycle. Understanding the life cycle and the particular challenges to be faced at each stage is a critical first step in developing successful computer applications. Typically, there are five major phases in this systems development life cycle (*see* Figure 15.3).

EXHIBIT 15.5

FAILING TO SELL TO THE SALES FORCE

British Columbia Telecom (BC Tel) is one of Canada's largest telephone companies and for many decades held a virtual monopoly on the vast majority of long-distance traffic in Canada's most western province. According to Drew McArthur, BC Tel's business transformation manager, the company recognised that in such a competitive environment it is the level of relationship with a customer that determines whether or not BC Tel retains the business. To help with the task, McArthur introduced customer relationship management (CRM) software to the BC Tel sales force. 'To increase our advantage in the marketplace, we required the ability to capture and share more customer information', he adds. But he admits it has not been completely plain sailing – he had not anticipated the initial 'underwhelming' response of the sales force to having such a solution introduced. 'We had expectations that the sales people would have had more of a propensity to learn how to use it', he adds. 'The challenge is to help sales reps to understand the advantage to themselves if the system is used well.'

Source: *Financial Times* (2 September 1998).[32]

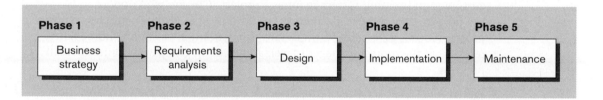

Figure 15.3 Major phases in systems development

Within these major phases, there are many lower-level steps and tasks. Indeed, a variety of systems development methodologies exist that show how to develop a system in great detail. However, the typical activities in each phase are:

- *Business strategy*. The starting point for any marketing system is a clear understanding of what that system is attempting to achieve or support.

- *Requirements analysis*. Analysis of business requirements involves a number of steps from analysing existing systems through to interviewing business and marketing managers to identify their issues and objectives.

- *Design*. In this phase the business requirements are turned into a set of programming specifications for the implementation phase. Today, good systems design will often incorporate prototypes for eliciting feedback and response from marketing managers.

- *Implementation*. Implementation covers programming of new software, configuration of packaged software, testing, training and conversion of existing marketing data to the right format for the new system. Testing and data conversion typically account for the majority of the effort involved in any marketing system, while training is often the area that receives less attention that it deserves.

- *Maintenance*. Once the marketing system is converted, or commissioned, there is still much development work to do, ranging from fixing the inevitable 'bugs' in the new system through to the enhancements or new features that marketing managers soon want.

Good project management

On an ongoing basis throughout the project, the following management activities will increase its overall chances of success:

- *Tracking and resolving issues*. During a project, a multitude of different issues will arise. These issues may be technical or may relate to aspects of the business that need to be resolved by marketing managers or general business managers. The technical issues are often the easiest to resolve; issues that require the cooperation of different functions can be more intractable.

- *Monitoring project progress and risk*. Any project to develop a marketing or customer information system requires a project manager who understands the project management mechanisms of deadlines, milestones, progress reports, progress meetings, escalation procedures for issues that cannot be immediately resolved at the project manager's level, and steering groups to monitor overall progress.

- *Establishing a project office*. A project office contains all the project plans, files, notes, deliverables and any other relevant material relating to the project. On smaller projects, a formal project office may not be required.

A new attitude and mindset

However, all these steps will come to nought if marketers themselves do not make a fundamental change in their own perception of what technology can and cannot do for them. On the positive side, there are signs that the gap between marketing and IT is narrowing. Many marketing courses now include either a module on IT or a practical course on the application of technology in the field of marketing. Marketing managers also have greater exposure to online services for research and are familiar with the capabilities of the internet. They are beginning to understand the issues associated with the use and maintenance of customer databases. Future generations of marketers will have the required IT skills to operate more effectively than the previous generation.

Summary

Marketing and technology have had an uneasy relationship over the years. Indeed, some 'traditional' marketers are sceptical about the very concept of electronic marketing. To some extent, their scepticism is well-founded. Electronic marketing has promised more than it has delivered in the past. However, future marketers will be unable to escape the electronic marketing concepts and trends that are outlined in this book.

We firmly believe in the marriage of the traditional marketing approaches and the newer technology trends. Our premise is that the successful marketers of the future will combine the marketing flair of the traditional brand managers with a hard-nosed understanding of how to translate a dream into a practical reality. Hopefully, this book can contribute in some way towards this goal. If you feel that it doesn't, e-mail us at the following addresses with suggestions for improvement:

- john.oconnor@hotorigin.com

- camonng@indigo.ie

- evansm7@cardiff.ac.uk

In fact, please e-mail us with any comments you may have – good, bad or indifferent. In the meantime, happy electronic marketing!

- Pantene s/poo&cond norn/grsy 200/2

- Pantene shampoo 250m/cond.200m nm/gy ba

- Pantene twin pk sham/cond.nrm/greas 450m

- Shampoo Pantene shampoo 250ml normal//+cond

- Pantene shampoo 250m/cond.200m.

Some of these descriptions are inaccurate and lack details that would be of value to marketing departments, such as the type of hair for which the product is designed. Only two itemise both elements of the twin-pack: the quantity and the hair type. Does it matter? The store that uses the first definition is probably happy after all. Yet it is losing the opportunity to analyse its sales by missing out essential information. It will be unable to figure out whether twin-pack promotions are popular with its customers, for example, or what sort of hair type they have. If it has a loyalty card scheme, it will know less than it could about what each customer buys.

These inadequacies in information may have a knock-on effect all along the supply chain if sales data are shared between manufacturers, wholesalers and retailers. All across the industry, comparable data are essential for the marketing information companies such as ACNielsen, which produce the sectoral sales reports that all consumer companies need to run their businesses. The difficulty is increased by growth in cross-border trading in Europe, with companies supplying several countries with products manufactured in one. Over the years, some large groups have allowed product item barcodes to be assigned to different products in different countries.

Sources: *Financial Times* (1 September 1998);[33] *The Grocer* (2 August 1998);[34] Global Exchange Services website (www.gxs.com, 2003).

Case study questions

1 How do the retailers in this case study exemplify the concept of the 'extended enterprise'?

2 What are the benefits of sharing sales, forecast and promotional information between retailers and their key suppliers?

3 Why has it not been easy for the three retailers to set up their respective collaboration efforts?

4 Use the internet to research how a company like Tesco can implement electronic links with its suppliers.

Questions and exercises

Questions

1 Choose a company that, in your opinion, employs information technology systems effectively in its marketing function. What distinguishes this company from its competitors?

2 'Unrealistic expectations of what technology can achieve has led to many systems disappointments.' Discuss.

3 What do you understand by the 'IT skills gap' in the marketing function?

4 Why are companies increasingly using packaged software?

5 What is contributing to the rise in outsourcing?

6 Why is engaging the marketing and sales staff in systems so important for final success?

Online exercises

1 Visit Third Age's website (www.thirdage.com) and comment on the range of products and services that Third Age has created as part of its extended enterprise.

2 How is the same concept developed at Home Advisor (www.homeadvisor.com)?

References

1 Taylor, P. (1997). 'Management software comes to the rescue', *Financial Times*, 1 October.

2 Macdonald, S., Andersen, P. and Kimbel, D. (1999). *Government Policy and the Productivity Paradox. Economic Study to Support the ISI Evaluation.* UK Government, Department of Trade and Industry.

3 Strassmann, P.A. (1997). *The Squandered Computer: Evaluating the Business Alignment of Information Technologies*, New Canaan, Connecticut: The Information Economic Press.

4 Andersen, T.J. (2001). 'Information technology, strategic decision making approaches and organisational performance in different industrial settings', *Journal of Strategic Information Systems*, Vol. 10.

5 Oliner, S. and Sichel, D. (2000). 'The resurgence of growth in the late 1990s: is information technology the story?', *Journal of Economic Perspectives*, Vol. 14.

Index

Beers, M.C. 132
Belgium 98
Bender, A.R. 277
Benetton 149, 198–201
Benjamin, R. 416
Bennett, M. 301
Bensaou, M. 409
Berger, P.D. 332, 398
Bergman, M.K. 281
Berners-Lee, T. 6
Berry, L. 206, 225
Bezos, J. 40
Bienert, P. 340
Bienstock, C. 376
Big Brother 188–9
Bigg, A. 154
biographics 122
Block, L.G. 333
BMW 172, 241, 242, 257
Bollywood 208
Book, A.C. 331
Borch, F.J. 208
Borden, N. 171
Borna, S. 189
Bossert, P. 302
brand
    extensions 12–15
    importance 64–5
    loyalty 181
    management 11–15
branding response television advertising
        329–30
Brassler, A. 255
Bresnahan, T. 409
Brewer, G. 415
Briggs, A. 101
Bristol-Myers Squibb 129
British Museum 304
British Nuclear Fuels 130
British Rate and Data 82
British Telecom 329, 400
Broadband 329
Brobst, S. 193
brochureware 336–8
brokerage 56
Brown, S. 251, 329
Brynjolfsson, E. 280–1
Buckley, P. 41–2
building to order 255–7
Burrell, R. 303
business analysis 249
business case 420
business models 55–72
    air travel 70–2
    assessment framework 58–60
    brand importance 64–5
    business-to-business 65
    buyer-driven world 66
    categorisation 55–7

e-commerce myths and realities 61–5
framework in twenty-first century 68–9
internet as a channel 63–4
profit importance 58
technology-enabled marketing 66–7
Business Monitor 81
business-to-business 31–9, 65
    buy-side pricing models 267–8
business-to-consumer 39–42
    internet auctions 268–9
'Buy NY' 415
buyer behaviour 87
buyer-driven world 66
buying online content 60
Byron, M. 130

cable TV 343
Caddy Home 302
Cagwin, D. 270
call centres 388–90, 391–3, 395–9
Canada 45
Cardin, J. 279
Carlson, J. 221
Carson, C.D. 129
Carter, S. 413
Cary, N.D. 331
CASPIAN campaign 200–1
category management 124
census data 187–8
chambers of commerce 80
change 9
Chauvel, D. 133–4
Chenet, P. 92
China 45, 222
Chisnall, P. 96
Christensen, C.M. 15
Chu, V. 199
claims analysis 124
Clancy, K.J. 250, 271–2
Clark, H. 44
Cleveland, B. 395
Clinton, H.R. 415
Clodfelter, G.R. 280
coffee bars 14
commercialisation 250
communication 177
community 57
Compaq 299, 402–3
competition 174–5, 286–7
complaints 173
computer telephony integration 392
computer-aided design 253
computer-aided engineering 253
computer-aided manufacturing 253
computer-assisted personal interviewing
        (CAPI) 90
computer-assisted telephone interviewing
        (CATI) 90–2
computerisation, three ages of 5